Liberty, Property, and Government

SUNY Series in the Constitution and Economic Rights

Ellen Frankel Paul, Editor

Liberty, Property, and Government: Constitutional Interpretation Before The New Deal

edited by
Ellen Frankel Paul and
Howard Dickman

State University of New York Press

Published by
State University of New York Press, Albany

© 1989 State University of New York

For information, address State University of New York
Press, State University Plaza, Albany, N.Y., 12246

Library of Congress Cataloging-in-Publication Data

Liberty, property, and government : constitutional interpretation before the
    new deal / edited by Ellen Frankel Paul and Howard Dickman.
        p. cm. — (SUNY series in the constitution and economic
    rights)
    Includes index.
    ISBN 0-7914-0086-7. — ISBN 0-7914-0087-5 (pbk.)
    1. Right of property—United States—History. 2. United States—
Constitutional history. I. Paul, Ellen Frankel. II. Dickman,
Howard. III. Series.
KF562.L53 1989
323.4'6—dc19   88-38771
                                                                          CIP

10   9   8   7   6   5   4   3   2   1

Contents

Acknowledgments

The editors wish to acknowledge the generous support of the National Endowment for the Humanities (Ref: GB-20081-86), and especially the encouragement of the Bicentennial Division and the Division of Public Programs. Additional support was received from the Bowling Green State University Office of University Relations, the College of Arts and Sciences, and the Graduate College. Many individuals at the Social Philosophy and Policy Center, Bowling Green State University provided invaluable assistance in the preparation of this volume; they include: Assistant Project Director Kory Tilgner, Jeffrey Paul, Fred D. Miller, Jr., Dan Greenberg, Terrie Weaver, and Tamara Sharp.

Introduction

The political and economic philosophies that animated the Founding Fathers and the citizens of the Revolutionary Era placed a high value on protecting individual property rights and economic freedoms from arbitrary governmental interference. Generally speaking, the view then was that the individual's opportunity to engage freely in a business, trade, occupation, or profession was among the most important liberties society could protect. Several important clauses of the Federal Constitution (including the Bill of Rights) reflected these values and commitments; and for the greater part of American history the Supreme Court was not loath to entertain challenges to the constitutionality of legislatures' alleged incursions on property and contractual rights.

Americans cannot fully understand the meaning and significance of the Federal Constitution—and of the kind of society this Constitution presupposed and was established to support and maintain—without understanding the changing role and significance of constitutional protections of private property and contractual freedom throughout our history.

The essays that comprise this volume represent the thought of leading constitutional experts from diverse disciplines—including history, political science, and the law—who examine aspects of the changing role the Constitution has played in protecting economic rights. The authors range over a wide span of history, from the mid-nineteenth century to the first third of the twentieth, often with extended references to what preceded this period and to what would follow. The central focus of many of the essays, not surprisingly, is the United States Supreme Court and its seminal functions, as both the guardian of individual rights enshrined in the Constitution and their leading interpreter.

While the constitutional protection of economic liberty is an important aspect of the American heritage, it is also among the more controversial ones. Inevitably, there is a constant tension between our desire to preserve individual liberty and society's need to restrict individual behavior to protect the social order. On the one hand, the very reason for constitutional provisions which restrict governments' power to impair the obligation of contracts, or to take property without just compensation, is to reserve a sphere of private right

1

free of government interference. On the other hand, from the inception of the United States Constitution, no one denied that state governments (at least) had an inherent, if not well-defined, "police power" to regulate economic and social activity in the interest of the community as a whole. Attaining a "balance" between vested rights and the police power—between individual liberty and a stable social order—has been an enduring problem of constitutional theory and practice, as well as a source of dramatic social and political conflict, particularly in the twentieth century.

Since the constitutional crisis of the New Deal era, the Supreme Court has emphasized certain "personal" or "civil" liberties such as free speech, religious freedom, the right to vote, and procedural fairness in the criminal law. Governmental actions that are claimed to trench on these "preferred" freedoms are subjected to a standard of strict scrutiny. On most property rights and economic issues, however, the Court has consistently deferred to legislative policy judgments, applying a much looser standard of review. This state of affairs has been called a "double standard."

Nevertheless, the constitutional issues surrounding the protection of individual economic rights are still the subject of much ongoing scholarly research. Indeed, despite the Court's modern reticence to "sit as a superlegislature to determine the wisdom, need and propriety of laws that touch economic problems, business affairs, or social conditions,"[1] the very *complexity* of modern economic problems, business affairs, and social conditions has rendered the judicial separation between property and other personal rights more and more questionable.[2]

Constitutional Clauses and Judicial Interpretation

The Constitution affords protection to property rights in several of its key clauses, among which are: Article I, Section 10, which bars states from impairing the obligation of contracts; the Fifth Amendment, which stipulates "nor shall private property be taken for public use, without just compensation"; both the Fifth and the Fourteenth Amendments, which bar governments from depriving persons of "life, liberty, or property, without due process of law"; Article IV, Section 2, which provides that the "citizens of each State shall be entitled to all privileges and immunities of citizens in the several States"; and the Fourteenth Amendment, which prohibits states from abridging the "privileges and immunities of citizens of the United States" and from denying to any person "equal protection of the laws."

If we briefly examine the shift in interpretation of the due process clause which occurred in the 1930s, it should be apparent just how vast is the Supreme Court's discretionary power in interpreting the often cryptic phrases of the Constitution. The due process clause was the pivotal constitutional linchpin of the much-reviled laissez-faire era in constitutional interpretation. The "due process" clause is one of the most controversial in American history. When the Fourteenth Amendment's due process clause first underwent judicial interpretation in the *Slaughterhouse Cases,* 16 Wallace 36 (1873), the Supreme Court refused to use it as a vehicle for examining economic regulation. But within a few years the Court changed its collective mind. From the 1890s through the mid-1930s, the so-called "Old Court" (the laissez-faire Court) used the due process clause as a wedge against regulations which it deemed to be overzealous and, hence, unconstitutional. This trend in interpretation was, again, reversed in the mid-1930s. The due process clause as a device for invalidating statutes regulating property has fallen into such disfavor that one has to search back to 1936 to find a case where the Court invalidated a state regulation on substantive due process grounds. To this day, the Old Court's habit of supplanting legislative judgments with its own has received nearly unanimous condemnation by commentators and judges alike.

When the Court was still employing the due process clause as a vehicle for protecting property rights, it invoked a strict standard of review. The Court most often employed a tripartite rule, according to which the challenged legislation was examined by (1) balancing the restriction placed on the property owner against the public benefit of the statute, (2) evaluating the legitimacy of the objectives sought by the legislation and the means used, and, finally, (3) applying a means-end test to determine whether the statute would tend to achieve its purpose.

While the test was often phrased a bit differently from case to case, it is captured quite well in this quotation from one of the Old Court's most notorious decisions, *Lochner v. New York,* 198 U.S. 45 (1905):

> The act must have a...direct relation, as a means to an end, and the end itself must be appropriate and legitimate, before an act can be held to be valid which interferes with the general right of an individual to be free in his person and in his power to contract in relation to his own labor. (at 57-58)

Thus, in *Lochner* the Court invalidated a provision in a New York State law that limited the working hours of bakers to no more than sixty a week and ten a day. Basing its decision on the right to contract protected by the due process clause of the Fourteenth Amendment, the Court found no circumstance in the state's defense of the statute which was compelling enough to override this right.

In another leading case of that era (the one that first declared liberty of contract to be a property right of the citizen protected by the due process clause), *Allgeyer v. Louisiana,* 165 U.S. 578 (1897), the Court invalidated a Louisiana statute which prohibited companies from obtaining marine insurance from out-of-state corporations.

The right to contract was likewise at issue in two subsequent cases of great notoriety, *Adair v. United States,* 208 U.S. 161 (1908), and *Coppage v. Kansas,* 236 U.S. 1 (1915). In both cases the Court declared that a statute making it a criminal offense to fire an employee because of membership in a labor union was an unconstitutional deprivation of the employer's personal liberty and property rights. The latter decision was particularly controversial insofar as the Court dismissed as false and irrelevant the state's defense that inequality of wealth, power, or position (of "bargaining power") between employers and employees made "freedom of contract" unfair in practice without special protections for workers.

Yet the Court's decisions during this era of "substantive due process" were not monolithic. Many times the Court departed from strict "laissez-faire" principles.[3] It upheld zoning regulations in *Euclid v. Ambler Realty,* 272 U.S. 365 (1926), for instance, and it sustained wartime rent control in *Block v. Hirsh,* 256 U.S. 135 (1921). Moreover, the Court sustained a regulation of the working hours of women in *Muller v. Oregon,* 208 U.S. 412 (1908), by unanimous vote.

The other exceptions are too numerous to cite here, but they represent part of a fascinating puzzle. What philosophical justifications do members of the Court employ to reach such varied decisions on cases that appear factually similar? How are these decisions related to larger currents of thought and social developments in American society? Perhaps the most puzzling decision is that delivered by Justice Sutherland in *Euclid.* Here, one of the staunchest defenders of substantive due process found that zoning regulations could pass constitutional muster. He reached this conclusion by employing a much weaker test than the one he and the Old Court usually endorsed. The *Euclid* test—that if the matter were fairly debatable the Court should defer to the government and uphold the legislation—would become the *dominant* view of the Court as it struck off in a new direction in the 1930s.

The beginning of the end for substantive due process was prefigured in 1934, in *Nebbia v. New York,* 291 U.S. 502. The Court upheld the conviction of a man who sold two bottles of milk and a loaf of bread for eighteen cents, thus falling afoul of a milk control board's regulation that milk be sold at no less than nine cents a quart. The Court seemingly rejected its old test of constitutionality, and it proffered a much less onerous one for the government to meet: that the law be not unreasonable or arbitrary, and that it have a substantial relation to the objective sought.

Three years later the Court finally buried the due process clause as a vehicle for protecting property rights. Reversing a decision of 1923 (*Adkins v. Children's Hospital,* 261 U.S. 525), the Court upheld a Washington State law that established minimum wages for women and minors (*West Coast Hotel v. Parrish,* 300 U.S. 379 (1937)).

Since 1937, the Court has supplanted its old due process test with a new one that is often referred to as the "rational relation" test. Under this new standard, economic legislation which does not infringe on explicitly-mentioned constitutional rights will be upheld, if it can be maintained that such regulation bears a rational relationship to a legitimate public purpose. Under this minimal standard of scrutiny the Supreme Court—in the cases it has chosen to hear—has found every piece of economic legislation challenged on due process grounds to be constitutionally acceptable. On the other hand, the strict scrutiny standard of the old "substantive due process" era remains very much alive in First Amendment adjudication, as well as in other areas of modern constitutional law, such as the "equal protection" clause of the Fourteenth Amendment.

Due process in the economic realm, however, is not completely dormant. There are still a number of state courts that have struck down economic regulation on substantive due process grounds; and the Supreme Court has scrutinized closely the claims of individual citizens who feel they have been denied their procedural due process rights to government benefits, services, etc. (such as Social Security, civil service job rights, disability benefits), without due process of law. However, the fate of the due process clause since the New Deal sets our era apart from the turn-of-the-century laissez-faire jurisprudence as dramatically as anything in constitutional history could.

Liberty and Property: The Essays

More than fifty years have elapsed since *Lochner v. New York* (1905) and all it represented passed from the scene. And to this day the specter of *Lochner* is raised as a deterrent to activism, or is dismissed as irrelevant to the case at hand. However, a revisionist scholarship, the "new" substantive due process and equal protection rulings of the 1960s, and the widely differing agenda and advocacy of legal conservatives and liberals have raised doubts about *Lochner's* purported regressiveness, inappropriateness as a model of constitutional adjudication, and illegitimacy. Mary Cornelia Porter, in Lochner *and Company: Revisionism Revisited,* argues that *Lochner* and the jurisprudence that it personifies may serve more than one master and that while the *Lochner* holding may have been misguided, "Lochnerizing," as a means of informing constitutional choices, may transcend its source.

Paul L. Murphy's *Holmes, Brandeis, and Pound: Sociological Jurisprudence as a Response to Economic Laissez-Faire* analyzes the thought of three leading constitutional theorists who shared an abhorrence to "Lochnerizing" in any form. Murphy examines the way these leaders of American law reacted to the political and economic realities of life in the United States at the turn of the twentieth century. In this period, many thinkers became disaffected with the fact that property rights were the central legal value in American culture. Holmes, Brandeis, and Pound were united in their desire to save the economic structure of the country from itself: from its own abuses; from the mounting public criticism of its social irresponsibility; and from economic consequences which included greatly widening class distinctions, militant labor radicalism, and a growing socialist movement. Murphy contends that the sociological jurisprudence which these men advocated was a weak reed on which to base a major shift of public economic policy. While no doubt each was well-meaning, their often differing assumptions regarding the proper role of law and lawyers limited the immediate impact of the movement. Yet, as the first systematic assault on laissez faire, it stimulated the first faltering step down the road to the modern regulatory state.

Glen O. Robinson's *Evolving Conceptions of 'Property' and 'Liberty' in Due Process Jurisprudence* is an essay in constitutional interpretation, history, and principle. He begins with a brief discussion of modes of constitutional interpretation, specifically the debate between those who seek to restrict constitutional adjudication to principles and values derived from text and the "original understanding" of the Framers, and those who argue for constitutional adjudication not bound to text or historic meaning. Arguing for the first method of constitutional interpretation, he nevertheless acknowledges that even this method is dependent on historical norms, at least on our contemporary perception of them. The historical portion of the essay explores the evolution of due process, specifically the concepts of property and liberty that form the constitutional predicate of due process protection. Particular emphasis is given to the transformation of early natural law conceptions of property and liberty into modern positivist conceptions. Finally, Robinson addresses principle, i.e., the contemporary problems that have been created by this "positivist turn" in interpreting property/liberty, the effect of which has been to make constitutional norms confusingly dependent on the creation of non-constitutional entitlements by government. It is urged that this confusion can be avoided by treating property and liberty wholly as matters of constitutional interpretation or by eliminating the requirements of property and liberty as foundations for due process protection.

The Proper Scope of the Commerce Power, Richard A. Epstein's contribution to this volume, offers a detailed analysis of Congress's power to regulate under the commerce clause. It begins with a textual and structural analysis of the clause itself, and then follows the case law from *Gibbons v. Ogden* in 1824 through the New Deal. It concludes that Congress's proper power extends only so far as the instrumentalities of interstate commerce and those commercial transactions involving more than a single state. It, therefore, rejects the modern understanding that the commerce clause allows Congress to regulate all economic affairs, including manufacture and agriculture. This narrower reading of the clause is also warranted on functional grounds. It preserves federalism and helps limit the monopoly power of government generally by setting states in competition with each other. Nonetheless, it is doubtful that the original structure can be reclaimed given the extensive network of institutions and entitlements that rest on the New Deal cases.

The Framers of the Constitution fervently believed that the preservation of "republican liberty" depended upon the "security of private rights." In *Economic Liberty, Antitrust, and the Constitution, 1880-1925,* Tony Freyer examines antitrust, a body of law which has grown up since the late nineteenth century. Although not mentioned in the Constitution, few fields of law better reflected the lawmakers' attempts to grapple with the private right to enter contracts. Businessmen in this era exercised this right by creating a new form of heavily-capitalized, centrally-managed, large-scale corporate property. Bigness became identified in the public mind with corporate greed and unfair competitive advantage, and the legislative response was the enactment of the Sherman Antitrust Act. Freyer traces how the act embodied implicit moral presumptions regarding "good" versus "bad" anticompetitive arrangements and their impact upon "fair competition." Chief Justice Edward D. White's decision in the famous *Standard Oil Case* (1911) established the rule of reason as the leading legal doctrine governing the interpretation of the Sherman Antitrust Act. It was this element of the rule of reason and the enforcement of the Sherman Act which was influenced by the republican values inherited from the Founding Fathers.

Harry N. Scheiber, in *The Jurisprudence—and Mythology—of Eminent Domain in American Legal History,* illuminates how the historical development of eminent domain law in American history departed significantly on many counts from the rhetoric of "takings" jurisprudence and theory. Although private rights in property have held a place of high respect in American legal culture and constitutional law, in practice the taking of property by eminent domain has often severely abridged private rights. There has been a powerful tension in our legal history between economic individualism and community values as expressed in constitutional jurisprudence. Moreover, state constitutional law and administrative practices varied widely. Thus, Scheiber concludes, the realities of takings law conformed to no single doctrine or orthodoxy.

The assumptions of Alan Jones's *Republicanism, Railroads, and Nineteenth-Century Midwestern Constitutionalism* are "Neo-Progressive," in the sense that economic interpretations are altered by attention to ideology and to the continuity of republican ideals of the state and the "public good." The question of the connection of the Constitution to economic growth Jones narrows to a discussion of mid-nineteenth-century midwestern constitution making and to an account of the Burlington Railroad as an illustration of the role of transportation in economic growth. Mid-century constitution making reveals republican fears of the collusion of legislative and corporate power. These fears are modified in the 1870 Constitution of Illinois where republican anxiety about legislative power is diminished by greater concern over the power of railroad corporations. The outcome is a new concept of "public interest" and a new republican concept of a positive state. Both concepts are challenged by the self-interested ideology of anticommunism.

Created to enforce the Thirteenth Amendment and anticipating the Fourteenth, the Civil Rights Act of 1866 was a global pioneer. For the first time, Harold M. Hyman contends in *Up from* Dred Scott; *Down to* Slaughterhouse: *Inventive Interim Judicial Protections for Property in Reconstruction America,* a government imposed on itself a duty to secure positively the bedrock rights of free Americans, and now all were formally free. But in America, unlike societies abroad, in the enduring federal system the states, not the nation, retained intimate, primary, workaday impact on individuals, and by law and custom actually defined the limits of freedom. These diverse limits varied greatly from place to place, time to time, race to race, and gender to gender, in the multitudes of both civil and criminal relationships constituting daily life. The diversities obtained both within states and between them, involving civil and criminal law, contract, suffrage, and access to semi-public accommodations (trains, taverns, hotels, etc.). The Civil Rights Act of 1866 did not aim to end the diversities that were central facts of American federalism. Instead that law aspired to have all officials and private persons, on every level of government and community—federal, state, local—accept as a new federal standard equality of individuals before their state's laws and customs, so far as race was concerned, but not only race. *Slaughterhouse* helped greatly (and tragically) to frustrate this aspiration, especially by limiting the outreach of the 1866 law and its surrounding amendments to official state action and to ex-slaves. Coming coincidentally with the new Langdellian law schools and with such standardized finding-aids as West Publishing Company provided, *Slaughterhouse* reopened possibilities for bigots to regain respectability by means of a revived state-rights constitutionalism, by ignoring or distorting the contextual history of the 1860s and '70s in favor of a new formalism. In this "twistery" the Supreme Court played a leading role that helped it to regain influence it had forfeited because of the 1857 *Dred Scott* decision.

The essays in this volume, each lively and provocative, should assist us in understanding the historical controversies which underpin our current constitutional debate over such unresolved issues as: the proper manner of constitutional interpretation, rent control, zoning and land use regulation, antitrust, and more generally, the continuing viability or lack of same of the New Deal's regulatory state.

Notes

1. Justice William O. Douglas, in *Griswold v. Connecticut,* 381 U.S. 479, 480-481 (1965).

2. The Supreme Court is not entirely comfortable with the distinction between economic and other rights, either. In *Lynch v. Household Finance*, 405 U.S. 538 (1971), the Court said that the

> dichotomy between personal liberties and property rights is a false one. People have rights. The right to enjoy property without unlawful deprivation, no less than the right to speak or the right to travel, is in truth a 'personal' right.... In fact, a fundamental interdependence exists between the personal right to liberty and the personal right in property. Neither could have meaning without the other. That rights in property are basic civil rights has long been recognized.

3. Nor, indeed did it ever enunciate such a principle. In *Allgeyer v. Louisiana*, for instance, the Court explained that "[i]ndividual liberty of action must give way to the greater right of the collective people in the assertion of well-defined policy, designed and intended for the general welfare." (at 585) And in *Adair*, the Court claimed that "no contract, whatever its subject-matter, can be sustained which the law, upon reasonable grounds, forbids as inconsistent with the public interests, or as hurtful to the public order, or as detrimental to the common good." (at 172)

Lochner *and Company: Revisionism Revisited*

MARY CORNELIA PORTER

"Revitalization," "renaissance," and "recrudescence" are words used to describe the United States Supreme Court's renewed interest in traditional property rights.[1] Some developments have been startling. The contracts clause, for example, long after having been relegated to the constitutional trash heap, has been—in Justice Brennan's words and according to his lights—"dusted off," and is now "threatening to undermine the jurisprudence of property rights developed over the last 40 years."[2] The takings clause, never considered a reliable weapon in the property rights arsenal, is now viewed as showing some promise of holding the regulators at bay.[3] And today an antitrust opinion is said to "look as much like a 1910-style constitutional substantive due process opinion as it is possible to look at this late date. The economics is the same and so is the discretionary policymaking power that courts assign themselves."[4] There is evidence that the Court is climbing on the deregulation bandwagon.[5] The rights of free speech and property have, it is claimed, become so closely intertwined that it may be asked which has priority.[6] Cost-benefit analysis, devised as a standard for agency review, purportedly provides manageable and evenhanded criteria for civil liberties adjudication.[7] The state action doctrine and standing-to-sue policies are allegedly employed in order to protect the rights of the more affluent against the claims of the less fortunately situated.[8] Heartened by the possibility that courts may once again champion economic liberty, conservatives favoring deregulation and "right to work" laws lobby for favorable outcomes in courts as well as in legislatures.[9] The developing judicial trends (and they are just that: the Court is still far from fulfilling best and worst expectations)[10] evoke memories of the Old Court era.[11]

During the brief existence of the "New Property"[12] jurisprudence of the late 1960s and early 1970s, many commentators felt compelled to explain why it was acceptable for courts to protect the rights of "have-lesses" while maintaining a deferential stance toward governmental interference with the rights of "have-mores."[13] Similarly, those who now welcome the Court's protection for property rights the old-fashioned way, must somehow come to terms with the discredited judicial activism in behalf of economic interests of the Old

11

Court era. While the Court is sometimes commended for patiently and pru-
dently developing a methodology that provides coherent principles for the
judiciary's essential role of regulating the regulators, it is urged to proceed
with caution as well. For example, one commentator wrote of the Burger
Court:

> While government regulation of business has proliferated, contemporary
> public opinion has questioned the ability of such regulation to promote the
> general welfare. The Supreme Court has the constitutional discretion to
> check, balance and prevent this increase in regulation. Constitutional his-
> tory, however, contains many examples of the abuse of judicial discretion to
> declare unconstitutional legislative and executive determinations of regula-
> tory power. Thus, the expansion of judicial authority itself raises issues of
> political concern. As the Burger Court revitalizes its discretion and extends
> the reach of its authority, the risk increases that the Court will ignore the
> mistakes of its predecessors, succumb to the allure of power, and overreach its
> institutional limitations.[14]

Taking the experiences of the Old Court as preamble, this essay considers the
options that the new/old economic activism presents to both its friends and
foes.

I. *Lochner's* Ghost

The Old Court's protection of property rights is subsumed under the label
"substantive due process." But whether a modern ruling resembles rulings of
that type often lies in the eye of the beholder. But for both critics and
enthusiasts alike, the case that epitomizes the era is *Lochner v. New York.*[15]

For example, as if searching for the most scathing criticism of *Roe v.
Wade,* dissenting Justices Rehnquist and White accused the majority of engaging in the "exercise of raw judicial power" reminiscent of the *Lochner* era[16]—
an assessment with which some commentators have emphatically agreed.[17]
Justice Blackmun and those joining him, of course, believed that the ruling
comported with longstanding constitutional principles.[18]

Three years earlier, in one of a series of welfare-rights cases, *Lochner* had
likewise given pause—but for the majority. The ruling in *Dandridge v. Williams* sustained a state ceiling on benefits regardless of family size against a
claim of discrimination among AFDC recipients. With Justice Stewart point-
edly commenting that "we deal with a state regulation in the social and
economic field that does not affect freedoms guaranteed by the Bill of Rights
and the Fourteenth Amendment," the "classical liturgy" against Lochnerizing
was intoned.

For this Court to approve the invalidation of a state economic or social regulation would be far too reminiscent of an era when the Court thought the 14th amendment gave it power to strike down state laws because they may be unwise, improvident, or out of harmony with a particular school of thought. That era has long since passed into history.

Dissenting, Justice Marshall sought to distinguish between rulings that validated regulations of economic activities and occupations and those which would have the effect of denying the very essentials of life. It would not suffice, he vainly argued, "merely to invoke the spectre of the past and to recite [from past decisions] to decide the case. Appellees are not a gas company or an optical dispenser. They are needy dependent children."[19]

Remembrance of *Lochner* has been intimidating and sobering. Justice Powell's majority opinion in *San Antonio Independent School District v. Rodriguez* provides an instance of a majority so anxious to avoid even the appearance of Lochnerizing that it was willing to gloss over what it conceded was a deprivation and a form of discrimination. The ruling sustained a state school finance system that in essence created "rich" and "poor" districts, thereby providing children, depending on where they lived, with greater or fewer educational resources. Powell was, however, clearly troubled by the inequities under review:

> This Court's action today is not to be viewed as placing its imprimatur on the status quo. The need is apparent for reform in tax systems which may well have relied too heavily and too long on the local property tax. And certainly innovative new thinking as to public education, its methods and its funding is necessary to assure both a higher level of quality and greater uniformity of opportunity.

He went on to sound the old refrain that "reforms must come from the lawmakers and from the democratic pressures of those who elect them." And as with Stewart's *Dandridge* opinion, Powell's was rich in the language of judicial self-restraint. He warned against the dangers of judicial legislation, against "intruding" into and "interfering" with "difficult" state and local fiscal and educational policy matters—areas in which the Court lacked the "expertise" to make informed judgments. He spoke of "rights reserved to the states under the Constitution," and of the "traditional limits on the Court's function."[20]

Of course, the Court's more deferential members were, however uncomfortably, aware of the dissimilarities between the pleadings of "old" and "new" property claimants. As Justice Stewart acknowledged in *Dandridge:*

> In the area of economics and social welfare, a state does not validate the equal protection clause merely because the classification made by its laws are

imperfect. If the classification has some reasonable basis it does not offend the Constitution.... To be sure, the cases enunciating this fundamental standard have in the main involved state regulation of business or industry. The administration of public welfare assistance, by contrast, involves the most basic needs of impoverished human beings. We recognize the dramatically real factual difference between those cases and this one....

Nonetheless, however regretfully, the Court could "find no basis for applying a different constitutional standard," for "the Fourteenth Amendment gives federal courts no power to impose upon the states their views of what constitutes wise economic or social policy."[21]

The Court's willingness to again take the contracts clause seriously has aroused fears, at least for some members of the Court, that *Lochner* has been rehabilitated. *United Trust Co. v. New Jersey,* which invalidated a statutory covenant providing that revenues of the Port Authority of New York and New Jersey would not be used to subsidize mass transportation, provides an illustration. Dissenting Justice Brennan reminded the majority that the Court had forgotten errors of the past and the consequences of those errors. While Old Courts "treated 'the liberty of contract' under the due process clause as virtually indistinguishable from the contract clause," the modern Court has "wisely" assumed a more deferential stance. But now, alarmingly, the Court "signals a return to substantive review of state's policies, and a new resolve to protect property owners whose interests or circumstances may happen to appeal to members of this Court." Disregarding accepted precedent, the Court has reshaped the contracts clause "into a potent instrument for overseeing important policy determinations" made by state legislatures. Further, "this Court should have learned long ago that the Constitution—be it through the contract clause or the due process clause—can actively intrude into economic and policy matters only if my Brethren are prepared to bear enormous institutional and social costs."[22]

Justice Marshall's concurrence in *Cleburne v. Cleburne Living Center* provides the final example of the cautionary uses to which *Lochner* has been put. Here the Court invalidated a zoning ordinance requiring that all group homes for the retarded obtain a special use permit. Ordinarily, and following longstanding precedent, the Court would have sustained the regulation as a valid exercise of the police power. However, because of the issue of discrimination against the mentally retarded, it held that the use permit violated equal protection guarantees. Marshall, who would have preferred that the Court invalidate the ordinance squarely on the ground that the mentally retarded were, at the least, a "semi-suspect" class, was disturbed by the implications of the ruling for zoning regulations in general. As far as he was concerned, since only "minimal scrutiny" had been employed, the decision represented a "small and regrettable step backward to *Lochner v. New York.*"[23]

At least one commentator would agree with the analysis, if not the assessment.

> The Court says it is not using strict scrutiny but only the "rational means to serve a legitimate ends test" that it has used since 1937 to uphold economic regulations of old-style property. It then proceeds to declare a municipal zoning ordinance unconstitutional as applied to a privately owned piece of land because it unreasonably regulates a profit-seeking entrepreneur's business. Has the Reagan revolution come? Is the New Deal Court finally gone? Not quite. The private entrepreneur had been denied a special use permit to operate [the home] in an area zoned for apartment buildings. The Court's finding of unreasonableness rested on its conclusion that the denial stemmed from an irrational prejudice against the mentally retarded. This case may be regarded as part of the new equal protection, new property, "underdog" and "stereotyping" line. Nevertheless, the Court has again invalidated a classic regulation of traditional property.[24]

Lochner's ghost—but only one justice, Marshall, in a case involving doctrines and issues about which he so passionately cares, recognized it.

Anxiety about Lochnerizing is not new. Many a justice has sought to match, if not surpass, Justice Holmes's famous *Lochner* dissent; compare, if you will:

> A constitution is not intended to embody a particular economic theory, whether of paternalism and the organic relation of the citizen to the state or *laissez-faire*. I strongly believe that my agreement or disagreement with the wisdom of [the challenged legislation] has nothing to do with the right of the majority to embody their opinions in law. It is settled by various decisions of this Court that state constitutions and state laws may regulate life in many ways which, as legislators, we might think as injudicious or as tyrannical as this.[25]

with the deferential declarations of subsequent decades:

"We are not concerned here with the wisdom, need or appropriateness of the legislation. There is no necessity for the state to demonstrate before us that evils persist."[26] "We do not sit as a superlegislature to weigh the wisdom of legislation or to decide whether policy which it expresses offends the public welfare."[27] "The law may exact a needless, wasteful requirement in many cases. But it is for the legislature, not the courts, to balance the advantages and disadvantages."[28] "Whether the legislature takes for its textbook Adam Smith, Herbert Spencer, Lord Keynes, or some other is no concern of ours."[29] "It is immaterial that state action may run counter to the economic wisdom of either Adam Smith or J. Maynard Keynes, or may be ultimately mischievous even from the point of view of avowed state policy."[30] "It may commend itself to a state to encourage a pastoral instead of an industrial society. That is its concern and its privilege."[31]

As these and similar pronunciamentos renouncing earlier activism in commerce, contract, and Fourteenth Amendment due process "liberty of contract" cases suggest, substantive due process and the entire bag and baggage of laissez-faire jurisprudence had been unceremoniously dumped. Indeed, as all but announced in *United States v. Carolene Products* (1938), the Court would henceforth adhere to a double standard of judicial scrutiny. A presumption of constitutionality would attach to economic and social legislation. More exacting standards would apply to cases concerning the Bill of Rights, and "more searching judicial inquiry" would be directed to the question of "whether prejudice against discrete and insular minorities may be a special condition which tends seriously to curtail the operation of those political processes ordinarily relied upon to protect minorities."[32] A new chapter in the Court's history was apparently in the making.

However, neither substantive due process nor substantive equal protection was abandoned. Beginning in the 1950s and accelerating through the 1960s and early 1970s, the Court protected or was urged to protect what is referred to as "the New Property"—namely the right to public employment, to welfare entitlements, to occupational freedom, to equal educational opportunity, to consumer-debtor relief, to access to governmental services despite inability to pay, and to housing. But after five or so years of trying to decide what "property" if any it was being asked to protect and how, the *Rodriguez* Court brought what has been disparagingly referred to as the Warren Court's "egalitarian revolution" to a "screeching halt."[33]

There are a number of explanations for the abandonment of "New Property" jurisprudence. In the first place, justices uneasy about the possibility of wealth (or lack of it) entering the ranks of suspect classifications were joined by Nixon appointees holding similar views. Second, the "new" or "newer" equal protection and "fundamental rights" analysis, urged upon the Court by commentators and most forcefully from the bench by Justice Marshall, remained not only an amorphous concept but one that opened endless and exceedingly difficult possibilities. How were "the poor" and the nature of the "discrimination" against them to be identified? Were these tasks accomplished, what would be the range of practical judicial remedies? Where would the list of suspect classifications and fundamental rights (not firmly anchored in the Constitution) end?[34] Third, despite Justice Marshall's most trenchant observations and explanations, both his brethren and even commentators sympathetic to the new substantive due process and equal protection were uneasy about doctrinal sloppiness.[35] Fourth, some state judiciaries, raising the banner of the Warren Court, began employing equal protection guarantees (or their equivalents) in state constitutions to take a close look at wealth-based classifications.[36] As far as the *Rodriguez* majority was concerned, this had the salutary effect of firmly leaving local problems in local hands. Finally, a nation apparently weary of civil protest, of "coddling" defendants, and of wars on poverty took a conservative turn—and the Supreme Court, as may be its wont, more or less "followed the election returns."

Underlying the failure of the entire "New Property" enterprise was the Court's skittishness about reopening doors that earlier Courts had so firmly shut. On the other hand, and particularly from the perspective of over fifty years of experience with the welfare state ushered in by the New Deal, this concern may not be as worrisome as formerly imagined; it has been suggested that the Old Court may not have served the public or the institution of judicial review as badly as portrayed by commentators and judges past and present. In the first place, there is nothing inherently wrong with judicial protection of property rights, particularly since it is often impossible to draw bright lines between the rights of property and individual rights.[37] Secondly, a revisionist scholarship has made the point that the Old Court, despite the excesses most characterized by the Taft Court and the Nine Old Men of early New Deal days, made a positive contribution to American jurisprudence in particular and the public weal in general.

The revisionists have taken various approaches. Some have reviewed the *overall* thrust of the Court's work—as contrasted with a focus on a handful of "leading cases"[38]—while others have discerned something of a grand design in clusters of cases.[39] And there are those who have examined judicial output in the context of an existing or preferred political and/or theoretical framework.[40] One group of revisionists are persuaded that laissez faire embodies the system of limited government intended by the Framers of the Constitution; they exhort the judiciary to assume the task of actively enforcing constitutional provisions that protect the rights of property, and thereby of the individual, against the encroachments of the welfare state. In contrast to other revisionists, they do not illuminate or justify *Lochner* within its historical context and let the matter rest there—but promote the cause of *Lochner's* return to constitutional respectability. Unless we are to lose our ancient liberties, the (beneficent) spirit of *Lochner* must be summoned forth, not only to guard against the propensities of the positive state to transfer income, but to dismantle the positive state itself.[41]

II. The Old Court Reconsidered

With few exceptions, most histories and accounts of the United States Supreme Court between the 1880s and the early 1940s assume a pro-business, anti-labor bias on the part of the majority. There have been challenges to this presentation. Early on, many years before the laissez-faire jurisprudence had run its full cycle, Charles Warren credited the Court with being, at least between 1889 and 1918, a progressive force in the nation, "adjusting" "individual rights" "to existing social and economic conditions." By sustaining the exercise of the police power with but "few exceptions," the Court "performed one of its greatest services." Providing detailed figures to support his argument, Warren maintained that "a litigant who hopes to overturn the deliberate judgment of a state legislature...has very scanty hope of assistance from the Court."[42] In other words, although Warren did not put it this way, the Court performed the useful task of legitimating decisions made in national and state legislatures.

From a somewhat different perspective, Loren Beth has put the Old Court in its historical context, and to a degree has defended long-term judicial outcomes. First, Beth maintains, the Court reacted to the legislative reaction to industrialism. All branches of government were confronted, almost overnight, with rapid changes in the economy and the demands of a variety of interest groups. Within its institutional context, the Court attempted to reconcile experimentation, novelty, and legal formalism.

Second, public opinion had not crystallized. Trust-busting and an income tax represented a federal response to a constituency or cluster of constituencies; but "we may easily overestimate the degree to which a nineteenth century public expected or wanted legislation in the manner of the 1930s."

> [T]he results of the elections would seem to show no such pronounced desire: the Democratic majority of 1892 was dramatically converted into a Republican one in 1894 in a vote which looked like a landslide and which was confirmed by McKinley's rout of Bryan in the presidential race of 1896, just after the Supreme Court's "free enterprise decisions."

Third, Beth attributes the modern Court's "position in the governing process," one "not previously held," to the so-called laissez-faire jurisprudence. While the Court could "in no simple sense be called liberal or conservative," since "cases could always be found to illustrate either side," the Court was in the position of being able to "exercise a collective veto" over laws of any great significance. Although Beth does not so claim, his argument suggests that we may owe the modern Court's authority to protect civil rights to institutional strengths developed during earlier periods.

And finally, Beth credits the Court with finding, however haphazardly, the middle ground of American politics.

> What emerges is what might be expected of any human institution: a fumbling and vacillating response which was in the long run astonishingly but accidentally successful in allowing both for governmental regulation of the worst aspects of the Industrial Revolution and for the maintenance of the system (sometimes called "free enterprise") which was creating the revolution. We tend to read back into the events of the day a sense of purposefulness

which does not really seem to have been there. Judicial response was not all of one piece; and what emerges, finally, is a sort of pragmatism which comports very well with the ad hoc nature of the case system used by American courts. Judges were forced by the nature of the case system to decide issues which arose fortuitously or haphazardly. It is true that many judges almost instinctively supported the free use of private property—a tendency frequently overcome by the arguments for regulation or for the constitutionality of legislative actions under [state and federal constitutions]. Certainly there was no conspiracy with big business.[43]

Along somewhat similar lines, I have argued that the Old Court was not as single-mindedly determined to protect business interests at the expense of labor and consumer interests as has been commonly depicted. Far more exercises of the police power (some very stringent and costly to business and industry) were sustained than invalidated. When confronted with an idea whose time had come, such as municipal ownership of public utilities, the Court shrugged off contracts clause claims with the unsympathetic observation that investors in privately-owned plants should have been more prescient. Rates charged by public utilities, including railroads, could not be set so high as to cover waste, inefficiency, fraud, and the unrealistic expectations of investors. On occasion, with nary a nod to its own precedent, the Court supported the kind of legislative acts it had so roundly condemned but a few years back. A retreat from *Allgeyer v. Louisiana,* which created and furnished *Lochner* with the notorious "liberty of contract" doctrine, provides one example.[44] The only consistent pattern that I could discern during the period between the 1880s and 1912 was reflected in rulings that protected capital invested in well-managed public utilities that provided good service at reasonable cost. In this sense, the Court anticipated Justice Brandeis's "prudent investment" method of valuation as a means of giving "capital embarked in public utilities the protection guaranteed by the Constitution."[45]

> It is reasonable to assume that [the major premise] of the rate regulation cases was that public utility investment was the lifeblood of an expanding national economy. The Court, by supervising state supervision of the utilities, established minimal and uniform guarantees for investors. Moreover...the Justices also strongly endorsed state efforts to protect the public. The Court, by balancing the interests of investors and consumers, turned itself into something of a federal regulatory agency.[46]

While finding little to admire in laissez-faire jurisprudence, Frank Strong nonetheless also holds to the view that the *Lochner* cluster of cases had less to do with the Court's solicitude with the rights of contract and more to do with the majority's interest in preserving competitive capitalism. In other words, the justices were motivated more by their faith in the free play of market forces and less by their devotion to the principles embodied in one or another constitutional clause or doctrine.

> There is basis...for the view that liberty of contract is not the ultimate constitutional predicate of *Lochner* but one of several means to a common end. That end is the enshrining of competitive capitalism as *the* one type of economic organization compatible with the Constitution. The theory fits the facts: the bakery business is highly competitive, and, therefore, market forces rather than government edict must be permitted to set hours, wages and conditions of work.[47]

Walton Hamilton made the point even more forcefully.

> [F]ree competition is invoked to keep business going, absorb the shock of novelty, do justice between the parties. It was not privilege which Peckham, Brewer, Harlan, JJ., sought to enthrone. It was not property upon which they sought to confer the legal privilege of shaping the terms of the bargain. They professed, with little qualification, an economic creed; and the empty receptacle of "due process" and the age-old vitality of "the common right" enabled them to read "free competition" into the constitution.[48]

Yet another revisionist analysis of *Lochner* jurisprudence has been combined with an active political defense of the Court's activism. Albert Mavrinac maintains that *Lochner* performed the useful, indeed essential, task of fortifying what Mavrinac quixotically argues was labor's preference for government neutrality in labor-management relations. By so doing, continues Mavrinac, the Court not only made it possible for employers and employees to work out their differences in a manner far more beneficial to labor than government interference could have fostered, but also by "encouraging the technique of self-government by agreement,"

> prevented the transformation of American government into something positive, something making decisions for the good of the community. Government was kept a place where agreements are facilitated and not an independent source of value judgments about the proper conduct of social arrangements.

Thus, by the time the federal government, in the late 1930s and early 1940s, enacted statutes governing labor-management relations, labor and management had many years to work out the mutual accommodations that provided a basis for legislation. And "the Court had fulfilled its function of insuring the validity of the legislative process and of insuring therefore that the legislative act represented the consensus of the community. It had insisted on private agreement as the basis for social movement; and it had prevailed."[49]

Mavrinac's arguments were informed by preferences for particular political processes rather than by preference for particular economic outcomes. Nonetheless, his views on *Lochner* to some extent presage those later articulated by academic lawyers intellectually associated with the Chicago School, some of whom would have the federal judiciary (all else failing) guide the nation back to the Lockean principles upon which they believe the Republic is founded. To this end, they urge the courts to impose restrictions on a wide variety of legislative and administrative regulatory enactments.[50]

In particular, Bernard Siegan focuses on *Lochner* and its works in order that present and future courts may draw inspiration from its principles. It is Siegan's contention that economic liberties, like political freedoms and individual rights, are in peril if left to the "seriously flawed" and "infirm" legislative processes that inevitably result from voter ignorance and apathy, the shortcomings of legislators, the lack of accountability of powerful bureaucrats to the electorate, interest group domination, and the need for political and administrative compromise and expedience. Their survival depends on safe delivery via the judiciary into the haven of the Constitution. Siegan's proposal that the Court regulate the regulators relies heavily on his interpretation of constitutional history and is impelled by his faith in classical liberalism. The Framers linked their preference for "substantial freedom to engage in material pursuits"[51] to the concept of limited government, and expected the judiciary would, by guarding the one, assure the viability of the other.

Arguing that the Old Court's fall from grace was undeserved, Siegan attempts to turn the criticism on its head. Extrapolating from current as well as turn-of-the-century data, he speculates that *Lochner* must have had the effect of assuring continued employment opportunities for newly arrived immigrants, and further conjectures that the maximum hours law, if permitted to stand, would have put small establishments out of business, diminished competition, and driven up prices—harming the very groups that regulation was meant to protect. The reactions of *Lochner's* wrong-headed critics "might have been less harsh had they realized that the law probably would have reduced considerably the wages of many low-paid workers and have caused them to lose their jobs." Further, somewhat in the Mavrinac mode, Siegan holds that workers were by no means united in a desire for the regulation of work hours, and, equally important, that a willingness to engage in risky occupations is by no means unusual.

> Some critics of the *Lochner* decision assume that limitation of hours reflected the will of the workers. They note that unions strongly supported the law, and contend that the elimination of "such drudgery could only be a blessing." This conclusion is questionable. Contemporary experience discloses that people at various stages of life willingly accept what to others might be

unpleasant, difficult, dangerous or unhealthful work because it provides more pay and/or personal satisfaction than less hazardous employment.[52]

And somewhat in the Beth mode, Siegan, defending those "yellow-dog" contract twins, *Adair v. United States* (1908) and *Coppage v. Kansas* (1915), points out that since well under 10 percent "of the employee class belonged to a union," the rulings reflected labor's antipathy to the union movement, and therefore the Court's contention "that government had no legitimate interest in encouraging unions was far less controversial than contemporary generations might suppose." In other words, the Court, rather than thwarting, as is the received wisdom, reinforced majority will. Indeed, the Court majority, as contrasted with legislative majorities, had the more accurate grasp of economic realities.

> The Court believed that the labor market would operate to support the welfare of both workers and employers.... Because relatively few welfare laws and unions existed in those decades, the betterment of life must [in terms of the rise in real wages, per capita income, purchasing power and the decline in working hours, especially as compared with Europe] be attributed to the success of the economic system. It was not difficult to conclude that this success could be undermined by limiting entrepreneurial freedom: that which harms business also injures the livelihood of people. The Supreme Court's concept of liberty enabled the economy to continue providing a great measure of material benefits.[53]

As Siegan praised *Lochner,* he condemned *Nebbia v. New York* (1934), which sustained regulation of the milk industry.

> The milk control law was inspired by unusual public passions, and in its final form was dictated by lobbyists for farmers and large milk dealers. The situation is precisely the type that warrants the kind of judicial oversight that the Supreme Court repudiated in this case.... *Nebbia* had all the trappings of radical drama: powerful interests, depression, exploitation, excessive milk prices and criminal sanctions. McReynolds's opinion speaks eloquently to these issues: "A superabundance: but no child can purchase from a willing storekeeper below the figure appointed by three men at headquarters!" ... this prose is scarcely in keeping with the image of old-guard reactionaries and those who tread on the rights of the masses.[54]

The celebrated dissents of Holmes in *Lochner* and Brandeis in *New State Ice Co. v. Liebmann* do not, as may be well imagined, meet with Siegan's approval. In particular, he faults Brandeis for failing to understand that "natural monopolies such as was claimed existed in the ice industry do not occur frequently," that "almost no industry is immune from competition," and that regulation does not "necessarily provide greater service at lower rates." Indeed, Brandeis, in his long list of cited authorities, failed to mention Adam Smith's teachings on the virtues of competition and the beneficent outcomes of the free play of market forces.[55]

Those who would tinker with markets, Siegan warns, present no problems for large corporations (for which much regulation is convenient), but work against the interest of small entrepreneurs. The modern Court's insouciance in the face of regulations that clearly reflect interest group pressures, and the concomitant failure to probe legislative motives, have resulted in hardships for individuals who would pursue a variety of occupations and operations such as street vending and "debt adjusting."[56]

In exhorting today's Court to reconsider *Lochner* and its progeny, Siegan suggests that civil liberties jurisprudence provides workable guidelines for the exercise of a revived old substantive due process. The discrete and insular minorities doctrine is tailor-made for those whom the law, responding to organized pressure, bars from market entry. Tests and devices—such as clear-and-present-danger, heightened means-and-ends equal protection scrutiny, less-restrictive-alternatives, and irrebuttable presumptions—are offered as yardsticks for determining if regulations "benefit society."[57] Government should bear the burden of demonstrating a compelling need for laws that restrict economic activity. Siegan draws parallels between a free press and a free economy.

To the extent that Siegan says that courts should ask about the reasons for and necessity of economic regulation, he echoes much of what Robert McCloskey wrote almost twenty years earlier. But where McCloskey concluded that the Court simply lacked the capacity to take up the cause of the economic rights of those who have difficulty fending for themselves,[58] Siegan maintains that by focusing on the rights of those who would engage in commerce and by ignoring the "New Property" claims of welfare recipients, residents of underfinanced school districts, and indigents denied publicly-funded abortions (all of whom request that governmental expenditures be directed or increased in their behalf), judicial dockets would diminish rather than grow. Rather than engaging in the business of "income redistribution," the Court would attend to the tasks envisioned by the Framers and which it performed so well for so many years.

However, it is Siegan's larger purpose to have the courts counteract the "political shenanigans" that have taken place since the inception of the New Deal. These include, *inter alia,* the regulation of industry, welfare assistance, and the protection of the rights of workers.[59] To that end, he has sought to provide principles that will enable the judiciary to reverse the jurisprudence of over half a century.

III. The New/Old Property: Friend and Foe

While the Court's return from the wilderness has provided some cheer for the Chicago School,[60] the justices have, according to the School's lights, much farther to go. Richard Epstein, one of the most prolific and articulate exponents of the School's economic and political theories, would have the Court employ the contracts and takings clauses, particularly the latter, in order to restore the limited, night-watchman theory of the state envisioned by the Framers to its rightful place in constitutional interpretation. Accordingly, as Epstein admits, much twentieth-century legislation, both state and federal, will not pass constitutional muster. Laws that transfer property from A to B, which is mostly what the welfare state is all about, must run a judicial gauntlet so formidable that they will in most instances fall. The imperative is simple. Income transfers that are the outcome of the "rent-seeking" behavior of groups seeking to use legislative grants in order to "expropriate the wealth" of their "rivals" amount to unconstitutional takings of private property.

> The Framers were concerned that legislative deals would often be tainted by interest-group politics, and occasionally by outright bribery, and that preoccupation with redistributive matters would divert individuals from productive activities.

> The task of limited government, then, is to forge those institutions that will control the abuse of trust without depriving government of the powers needed to maintain social order.[61]

Providing a concrete example of what he has in mind, Epstein asserts that the welfare system must—there is no constitutional choice—be abolished.

> The basic rules of private property are inconsistent with any form of welfare benefits. One way to avoid failure is to throw the baby out with the bath water, to get out of the welfare business entirely. That judgment is not based upon some narrow sense of egoism or a belief that private greed is the highest form of social virtue. Nor does it rest on the hidden pleasure of watching small children starve or derelicts freeze in the streets. To the contrary, it rests on the belief that once the state runs a transfer system, it can never extricate itself from the intolerable complications that follow. The higher level of benefits, the greater the demand, until the political dynamic—rent-seeking again—produces an aggregate demand that the system itself can only meet with great cost to its productive capacities. Rather than become mired in the quicksand, do not start down the path at all.[62]

Epstein, as does Siegan, lays an awesome burden on the judiciary. It is asked to eradicate legislative enactments informed by nineteenth- and twentieth-century social, economic, and political thought, and thus restrict government to activities that comport with the social contract and higher law theories of the seventeenth and eighteenth centuries. *Lochner,* for Epstein (despite what he regards as its overly expansive view of the police power) represents one small, however faltering, step toward the ultimate objective.

> What is needed is an intermediate standard of review that says, as did the court in *Lochner,* "The mere assertion that the subject relates though but in remote degree to the public health does not necessarily render the enactment valid. The act must have a more direct relation, as a means to an end, and the end itself must be appropriate and legitimate."[63]

Epstein has read, much as did the Court in *Lochner* and in *Roe,* a substantive right into the constitution. For Epstein, of course, *Lochner's* right to "liberty of contract" is compatible with the Framers' understanding of the right to property—that is, the inalienable right to possession, use, and disposition, unless the exercise of the right causes harm. The (bare) *Lochner* majority had been faithful to original intent. By contrast, the "right to privacy" protected in *Roe* bears no relationship to the liberty that the Framers had in mind. The substantive due process of *Lochner* was legitimate; the substantive due process of *Roe* was not. It comes down to a matter of divining original intent.[64]

The revitalized judicial interest in property rights is, for Epstein and Siegan, a sign that the Court is at least headed in the right direction (although Epstein has no illusions about judicial adoption of his teachings). For other commentators, the new/old property jurisprudence appears to have presented the possibility that the constitutional right to property may be put to liberal (as contrasted with libertarian) and, for want of a better term, humanistic purposes. The "New Property" advocacy has undergone a change of course. Concern now focuses less on rights to specific goods (welfare, housing, education) and more on the basic question of what property rights, within the totality of our democratic/political/constitutional system, the Constitution protects. The possibilities that this enterprise presents for Lochnerizing are as great as those presented by the Chicago Schoolmen.

Frank Michelman, in what might be described as his post-Rawlsian phase, holds that the right to property is inextricably linked to political rights—the widely discussed *Poletown* case provides the preeminent example of his thesis. Here, Detroit exercised its eminent domain powers for the purpose of enabling General Motors to obtain a plant site. The proposal was fought by those who lived and worked in the neighborhood affected—no monetary settlement could compensate for disrupted lives. The Michigan high court sustained the taking, erring, Michelman argues, not because it was insufficiently concerned with property as ownership, but because it disregarded property as a right. Property for the Poletown neighbors represented "things that money itself can't buy—place, position, relationship, roots, community solidarity and 'security.' "

Just consider how the obliteration of Poletown and the rupture of its society, with or without payments of money to former inhabitants, may bear upon their identity and efficiency as participants in the politics of Detroit, of Michigan, or the United States, in which are constantly being forged the conditions in which their, and our, future identity and efficacy will be determined.[65]

Sounding a somewhat similar theme, Margaret Radin argues from an Hegelian perspective that property provides the means by which an individual achieves self-development and becomes a self-actualizing person.

A person cannot be fully a person without a sense of continuity of self over time. To maintain that sense of continuity over time and to exercise one's liberty or autonomy, one must have an ongoing relationship with the external environment, consisting of both "things" and other people.

In eminent domain cases, then, courts must make moral or value judgments. Rights to fungible property, unless closely connected with personhood, may be "overridden." Property bound up with a person's sense of self must be accorded a greater degree of protection. The Constitution, as it has evolved, creates a "hierarchy of entitlements." "We may simply take it for granted that government will not take homesteads when parking lots will do."

If an object you now control is bound up in your future plans or in anticipation of your future self, and it is partly these plans for your own continuity that make you a person, then your personhood depends on the realization of these expectations.[66]

While Radin does not anticipate that the Court will fully adopt the Epsteinian model, she believes that two recent cases may "herald a return to a more rigid constitutional protection of the liberal indicia of property." To circumvent the possibility, all the while apparently resigned to the property-rights revival, she proposes a takings jurisprudence that would "recharacterize" the liberal ideology so that emphasis would shift from protecting the property of individuals as such, to protecting "personal property," that is,

that which is normatively important to the freedom, identity and the contextuality of people. It would invite the Court to decide, pragmatically in the real world, in which cases property appropriately fosters individual freedom and development and in which cases it doesn't. The ideology of the protection of the individual—if appropriately reconceived to avoid the traditional stress on negative liberty—would result in two important changes in our jurisprudence of property: it would engender different constitutional statuses for personal and fungible property, and it would undergird limits on the eminent domain power for personal property.[67]

What may be necessary to accomplish this task, Radin suggests, is a post-*Lochnerian* higher law rationale that would impose some sort of substantive due process limits on the eminent domain power.

The new/old property rights jurisprudence plays to mixed reviews. But however received, *Lochner* and company remain in the wings—as is always the case when the Court interjects itself into the realm of social and economic policy. What is novel is the connection between *Lochner* and takings jurisprudence. Economic conservatives—libertarians—such as Siegan[68] and Epstein would constitutionalize the exclusive rights to possession, use, and disposition of property on the grounds that such was the intent of the Framers. Political liberals would constitionalize the right to property that forms the basis for the exercise of political rights and for the development of personhood, not because they *know* what the Framers had in mind concerning property rights, but because they are confident that the constitutional schema and the Constitution's adaptability sanction such an approach. Siegan and Epstein in one camp, however, and Michelman and Radin in another, would probably all agree that *Poletown,* because of the nature of the property that the Constitution protects, was wrongly decided.[69] And the nature of the property is fathomed, as it was in *Lochner,* by the individual scholar's interpretation of the Constitution and understanding of our institutions and our political heritage. Revisionism has come full circle; and *Lochner* serves more than one master.

IV. Conclusion

More than fifty years have elapsed since *Lochner* and all it stood for passed from the scene. Yet the more its memory is castigated, the more the Court disavows Lochnerizing, the more *Lochner* dominates the judicial decision-making processes. *Lochner,* over the protests of Justice Marshall, stood in the way of his carefully devised equal protection jurisprudence. And the very same justice discerned, where others did not, *Lochner's* influence in a zoning ruling. However, it has been claimed by others that Lochner and Company were not, after all, the villains they were portrayed to be, and that the Court need not be fearful of reinstating an economic activism that contained much that was useful in form if not in kind. For example, Robert McCloskey's objection to a modest revival of the old substantive due process is based on institutional factors solely.

Whether the Court's current interest in property rights will lead to a revival of the old substantive due process is a matter of conjecture. Bernard Schwartz believes that "the historical tendency of the contract clause and the due process clause to coalesce may be repeated in our own day."[70] And what the outcome would be, should the Chicago School be influential, is likewise a subject for speculation. Should the Court be perceived as being overly concerned with business at the expense of the public and workers, Judge Oakes has suggested that severe social dislocations might occur.

> There is a concern that goes to the very security of the system of government—or at least to the trust of people in it—and that cuts entirely away from protection under the economic argument. Property rights do come to be held disproportionately; if too many people are socially and economically disadvantaged by too much protection of property rights, then the very state may be endangered, or life in it may become very fearsome. The Watts riots of the 1960s, the Brooklyn and Bronx of the mid-1970s blackout, and the Miami of 1979 riot fame are reminders of the ultimate limitation on property rights protection.[71]

Further, should the Court be perceived as overstepping its bounds by reading a specifically defined right to property into the Constitution—be it Epstein's, Michelman's, or Radin's—the institutional and "activist" questions again rear their heads. Whatever the infirmities of the legislative processes, is it not best to simply leave economic matters to the judgments, however flawed, of the people's representatives?

Perhaps Laurence Tribe's observations about *Lochner* provide guidance: the error of that decision lay not in the Court's substitution of its judgment for that of the legislature in the economic area and not in the Court's creation of institutional problems for itself (problems which it took years to overcome). The problem lay in the Court's

> overconfidence both in its own factual knowledge about working conditions and perhaps also in its own normative convictions about the meaning of liberty; at least by 1920, if not yet in 1905, the Court should probably have paid more heed to the mounting agreement, if not the consensus, that the economic "freedom" it was protecting was more myth than reality. But it would be wrong to make too much of the point: surely there can be no general duty on the part of deliberately countermajoritarian body like a court simply to follow the election returns. At most, there is a duty not to be too pigheaded, *too* certain of all of one's premises, and a duty to connect one's decisions to an intelligible view of the Constitution. Beyond that, one can offer no advice calculated to take judges off the hook; nor should one try—for that is where, sometimes for better and sometimes for worse, our constitutional system has put them.

If Tribe has provided us with the ultimate revisionist view of *Lochner,* perhaps we should let it rest there. The ghost will remain with us—for *"There is no escape* from painting a better—a morally and economically truer—picture; to leave the canvas blank from time to time just hands the brushes over to other artists."[72] *Lochner* may have been dead wrong; Lochnerizing, as a means of informing constitutional choices, may transcend its source.

Notes

1. Epstein, *Toward a Revitalization of the Contract Clause,* 51 U. CHI. L. REV. 703 (1984); Reznick, *The Constitutionality of Business Regulation in the Burger Court: Revival and Restraint,* 33 HASTINGS L. J. 1 (1981); Schwartz, *Old Wine in Old Bottles?: The Renaissance of the Contract Clause,* 1979 SUP. CT. REV. 95 (1979). The "recrudescence" took place under the Burger Court in the mid-1970s: United States Trust Co. v. New Jersey, 431 U.S. 1 (1977); Penn Central v. New York, 438 U.S. 104 (1978).

The Burger Court has been described as "dedicated to the promotion of a libertarian political philosophy," that is, a "philosophy which places freedom of the individual above values of egalitarianism or fairness. In such a philosophic system no governmental interference with the liberty of any individual, group of individuals, or economic entity can be justified except by the necessity to ensure the respect for human life or property rights." Nowak, *Evaluating the Work of the New Libertarian Supreme Court,* 7 HASTINGS CONST. L.Q. 263 (1980). Presumably, Nowak would see the Rehnquist Court this way as well. In a survey of judicial protection of property rights from the early days of the Republic to the present, Judge James L. Oakes (United States Court of Appeals, 2d Circuit) describes the rise and fall of three stages of property rights analysis. The fourth stage, which he believes we are now entering, is a combination of the "justification of property rights on moral as well as utilitarian or economic grounds." The moral and utilitarian grounds are philosophical. "The economic grounds remain Adam Smith's, as modified by the Chicago School: through aggregation of resources, efficiency can be achieved, and production and distribution of goods improved." Oakes *infra* note 3, at 624.

2. Dissenting in United States Trust v. New Jersey, 431 U.S. 1, 45 (1977) and Allied Structural Steel v. Spannaus, 438 U.S. 234, 259 (1978).

3. Coyle, *The Reluctant Revival of Landowner's Rights,* unpublished, presented to the American Political Science Association (September 3-6, 1987); R. EPSTEIN, TAKINGS: PRIVATE PROPERTY AND THE POWER OF EMINENT DOMAIN (1985); Oakes, *"Property Rights" in Constitutional Analysis Today,* 56 WASH. L. REV. 583, 602-21 (1981).

4. Shapiro, *The Supreme Court's "Return" to Economic Regulation,* 1 AM. POL. DEV. 91, 133 (1986); *see* Gerhart, *The Supreme Court and Antitrust Analysis: The (Near) Triumph of the Chicago School,* 1982 SUP. CT. REV. 319 (1982).

5. Garland, *Deregulation and Judicial Review,* 98 HARV. L. REV. 505 (1985).

6. Dorsen & Gora, *Free Speech, Property and the Burger Court: Old Values, New Balances,* 1982 SUP. CT. REV. 195 (1982); *Cases That Shock the Conscience: Reflections on Criticism of the Burger Court,* 15 HARV. C.R.—C.L. L. REV. 713 (1980).

7. Schwartz, *The Court and Cost-Benefit Analysis: An Administrative Law Idea Whose Time Has Come — or Gone?,* 1981 SUP. CT. REV. 291 (1981); Posner, *Rethinking the Fourth Amendment,* 1981 SUP. CT. REV. 49 (1981); Easterbrook, *Method, Result and Authority: A Reply,* 98 HARV. L. REV. 622 (1985); *contra* Tribe, *Seven Deadly Sins of Straining the Constitution Through a Pseudo-Scientific Sieve,* 36 HASTINGS L. J. 155 (1984); Tribe, *Constitutional Calculus: Equal Justice and Economic Efficiency,* 98 HARV. L. REV. 592 (1985).

8. Brest, *State Action and Liberal Theory: A Casenote on Flagg Brothers v. Brooks* 130 U. PA. L. REV. 1296 (1982); Glennon & Nowak, *A Functional Analysis of the 14th Amendment 'State Action' Requirements,* 1976 SUP. CT. REV. 221 (1976); 15 HARV. C.R.—C.L.L. REV. *supra* note 6.

9. L. EPSTEIN, CONSERVATIVES IN COURT (1985).

10. EPSTEIN, *supra* note 3; Radin, *The Constitution and the Liberal Conception of Property,* unpublished, presented to the American Political Science Association (Sept. 3-6, 1987), revised version in JUDGING THE CONSTITUTION (McCann & Hauseman eds. 1989).

11. The Court has, since the late 1880s, been through three phases in which property rights were emphasized. The first phase modified earlier propensities when the Court, impressed by the Brandeis brief, accepted the principle of economic and social regulation. Muller v. Oregon, 208 U.S. 412 (1908). The second encompassed the activism of the Taft Court (1921-1930), and the third, the Court's initial resistance to New Deal legislation. For histories, *see* W. SWINDLER, COURT AND CONSTITUTION IN THE 20TH CENTURY: THE OLD LEGALITY 1889-1932 (1969), and P. MURPHY, THE CONSTITUTION IN CRISIS TIMES 1918-1969 (1972). For accounts of the advocacy that persuaded the Court to accept the task of protecting the interests of business and industry, *see* A. PAUL, THE CONSERVATIVE CRISIS AND THE ROLE OF LAW (1960), and B. TWISS, LAWYERS AND THE CONSTITUTION (1942).

12. *See infra* note 33.

13. Gunther, *In Search of Evolving Doctrine on a Changing Court: A Model for a Newer Equal Protection,* 86 HARV. L. REV. 1 (1972); Michelman, *On Protecting the Poor Through the Fourteenth Amendment,* 83 HARV. L. REV. 1 (1969); Michelman, *In Pursuit of Constitutional Welfare Rights: One View of Rawls's Theory of Justice,* 92 U. PA. L. REV. 962 (1973); Tribe, *Toward a Model of Roles in the Due Process of Life and Law,* 87 HARV. L. REV. 1 (1973).

"Substantive equal protection," wrote a commentator who took a dim view of the doctrine, "suffers from quite the same defects and has itself created some uneasiness even among its proponents. For that reason, we witness the tragicomic phenomenon for both Justices and commentators nervously seeking to distinguish between what they are doing and the rejected and reviled substantive due process of another era." Winter, *Poverty, Economic Equality, and the Equal Protection Clause,* 1972 SUP. CT. REV. 41, 100 (1972). Kenneth L. Karst, sympathetic to the idea of a poverty jurisprudence, nonetheless warned that "the doctrine of invidious discrimination [as used in the new equal protection cases] does not permit an escape from the problems associated with substantive due process." *Invidious Discrimination; Justice Douglas and the Return to The "Natural-Law-Due-Process Formula,"* 16 UCLA L. REV. 716 (1969).

14. Reznick, *supra* note 1, at 2.

15. Lochner v. New York, 198 U.S. 45 (1905), narrowly struck down a maximum ten-hour day for bakers. The Court ruled that the prohibition was not (as claimed) a valid health measure, so the Fourteenth Amendment's guarantee of "liberty of contract" had been violated. Dissenting, Justice Harlan, joined by Justices White and Day, stated that because of the hazards of the bakers' trade, governmental interference with their right to contract freely for the terms of their labor was justified. Separating himself

from what he regarded as the irrelevance of both positions, Justice Holmes maintained that the law, as an enactment of reasonable men, stood on its own. Facts and figures concerning the particular hazards of the trade need not be presented in order to excuse governmental interference with what Holmes scornfully regarded as that figment of the judicial imagination, Liberty of Contract.

While *Lochner* still remains the symbol of a now discredited judicial activism, it should be recalled that the Court sustained, with a few exceptions, a large number of labor laws as legitimate exercises of the police power. Nonetheless, the Court reserved for itself the ultimate authority to determine the necessity for the statutes, subjecting them to what now would be described as "strict scrutiny." Adair v. United States, 208 U.S. 161 (1908); Coppage v. Kansas, 236 U.S. 1 (1915); and Adkins v. Children's Hospital, 261 U.S. 525 (1923) provide prime examples of *Lochner's* influence. Justice Holmes, by contrast, applied the reasonableness test enunciated in his *Lochner* dissent. Put differently, as long as the liberty of contract and the judicial value system it embodied remained viable, any labor law and/or economic regulation ran the risk of being held unconstitutional, depending on the majority's assessment of an enactment's necessity. Under Holmesian precepts, such laws were presumed to be constitutional. Nebbia v. New York, 291 U.S. 502 (1934), sustaining a minimum price for milk, negated *Lochner's* underlying premise. While claiming to hold fast to its power to "determine in each case whether circumstances vindicate the challenged regulation as a reasonable exertion of governmental authority, or condemn it as arbitrary and discriminatory," the Court's virtual indifference to the relationship between the statute's ends and the means chosen to serve those ends all but constituted judicial deference to legislative judgment.

16. While the Court's opinion quotes from the dissent of Mr. Justice Holmes in *Lochner,* the result it reaches is more closely attuned to the majority opinion of Mr. Justice Peckham in that case. As in *Lochner* and similar cases applying substantive due process standards to economic and social welfare legislation, the adoption of the compelling state interest standard will inevitably require this Court to examine the legislative policies and pass on the wisdom of these policies in the very process of deciding whether a particular state interest put forward may or may not be compelling. Roe v. Wade, 410 U.S. 113 (1973) (White dissenting at 222, Rehnquist dissenting at 174).

17. Ely, *The Wages of Crying Wolf: A Comment on Roe v. Wade,* 87 YALE L. J. 920 (1973); Epstein, *Substantive Due Process By Any Other Name,* 1973 SUP. CT. REV. 159 (1973).

18. *Roe* established that the constitutional right to privacy guarantees a woman's right to obtain an abortion. *Lochner* gratuitously assured New York bakers their "liberty of contract" against legislative restriction of their hours of labor. Each ruling read a substantive, as contrasted with a procedural, right into the due process clause of the Fourteenth Amendment.

19. Dandridge v. Williams, 397 U.S. 471, 486-87, 522 (1970). Friedelbaum, *Reprise or Denouement: Deference and the New Dissonance in the Burger Court,* 26 EMORY L.J. 337 (1977).

20. 411 U.S. 1, 58, 40-44 (1973). The traditional approach to equal protection review has been marked by extreme self-restraint and a marked concern for limiting the judicial role vis-à-vis the legislature. While the Court occasionally frames the traditional equal protection standard in terms of whether a classification is based upon some difference having a fair and substantial relation to the legislative approach, the standard most frequently used imposes on the challenging party of burden of proving that the classification is not rationally related to furthering a legitimate government interest. The judicial deference embodied in this test has almost invariably resulted in economic laws being upheld against equal protection challenges.

While the traditional rationality test is generally used for equal protection review, the courts will employ strict scrutiny when government employs a suspect or quasi-suspect classification. For example, when the government intentionally acts on the basis of race or national origin (and sometimes alienage), strict scrutiny will be used. And when intentional gender or illegitimacy classifications are employed, the law will be tested using intermediate review.

Whether it is a law or its enforcement that is the subject of the litigation, the challenger must establish that the classification is intentional before a stricter standard of judicial review will be used. While the discriminatory effect of a law or administrative action may be evidence of discriminatory intent, that intent must be proved. Substantive equal protection refers to equality in the distribution of public services, such as welfare benefits, housing, and education. For further discussion of substantive equal protection, *see* note 33.

21. Dandridge v. Williams, 397 U.S. at 486-87.

22. 431 U.S. 1, 62 (1977). Despite the narrowness of the Court's holding, Brennan was concerned with the implications surrounding the resurrection of the contract clause.

23. 105 S. Ct. 3249, 3265 (1985); Euclid v. Ambler Realty Co., 272 U.S. 365 (1926).

24. Shapiro, *supra* note 4, at 100.

25. Lochner, 198 U.S. at 75-76.

26. Olsen v. Nebraska, 313 U.S. 236, 246-27 (1941).

27. Day-Brite Lighting Co. v. Missouri, 342 U.S. 421, 423 (1952).

28. Williamson v. Lee Optical Co. of Oklahoma, 348 U.S. 483, 487, *reh'g denied* (1955).

29. Ferguson v. Skrupa, 372 U.S. 726, 732 (1963).

30. Osborn v. Ozlin, 310 U.S. 53, 62 (1939).

31. Freeman v. Hewitt, 329 U.S. 249, 252 (1946).

32. United States v. Carolene Products, 304 U.S. 144, 151-52 n.4 (1938).

33. Reich, *The New Property*, 73 YALE L.J. 733 (1964), made the case for guaranteeing the rights of those dependent upon government largesse, be it in the form of jobs, entitlements, subsidies, or licenses necessary to enter and engage in certain occupa-

tions. In particular, he was concerned about those with the fewest resources and the "New Property" quickly became associated with the rights of the poor. *See* Michelman *supra* note 13. Successful claims of a right to public employment may have provided the basis for subsequent claims of a right to welfare benefits. For links between the categories, see Friedelbaum, *supra* note 19. Kurland, *Equal in Origin and Equal in Title to the Legislative and Executive Branches of Government,* 78 HARV. L. REV. 143 (1964); Shapiro, *supra* note 4, at 47.

34. A large literature described, analyzed, criticized, and praised the Court's new directions. For a compendium of cases and commentary, *see* G. GUNTHER, CONSTITUTIONAL LAW: CASES AND MATERIALS, 908-71 (1980). Justices such as Harlan and Black, who did not see eye to eye on a variety of questions, had serious reservations about "New Property" rights. Justice Harlan preferred a due process rather than an equal protection approach to guarantee rights he deemed fundamental, and deplored propensities to create new rights out of whole cloth. See, for example, his opinion in Boddie v. Connecticut, 401 U.S. 371 (1970), and his dissent in Shapiro v. Thompson, 394 U.S. 618, 662-77 (1969). Along somewhat similar lines, Justice Black rejected the proposition that a "lawmaking procedure" which "disadvantages...any of the diverse shifting groups that make up the American people" denies equal protection. James v. Valtierra, 402 U.S. 137, 142 (1971).

35. Justice Marshall urged the employment of an intermediate equal protection scrutiny test which fell somewhere between the minimal or rational basis "anything goes" equal protection tests employed by post-1937 Courts and the strict scrutiny applied to racial classifications. Known as "sliding scale" equal protection analysis, Justice Marshall explained that:

> The task in every case should be to determine the extent to which constitutionally guaranteed rights are dependent on rights not mentioned in the Constitution. As the nexus between the specified constitutional guarantee and the nonconstitutional interest draws closer, the nonconstitutional interest becomes more fundamental and the degree of judicial scrutiny applied when the interest is infringed in a discriminatory basis must be adjusted accordingly.

(dissenting in San Antonio Independent School District v. Rodriguez, 411 U.S. 1, 70 (1979), on the basis that education is a fundamental right and denial of equal educational opportunity thereby violates the equal protection clause). Somewhat disapproving of the reasoning, but approving of the results, two commentators noted with some resignation that "the public has come to expect the Court to intervene against gross abuses. And so the Court must intervene. Given that fact, we shall be lucky to get good explanation in substantive equal protection cases." Karst & Horowitz, *Reitman v. Mulkey: A Telophase of Substantive Equal Protection,* 1967 SUP. CT. REV. 39, 70 (1967). For a discussion of the Court's problems with substantive equal protection from the perspective of school finance reform, *see* Porter, *Rodriguez, "The Poor" and the Burger Court: A Prudent Prognosis,* 29 BAYLOR L. REV. 199 (1977).

36. State court reliance on state constitutions, often but not always for the purpose of providing more generous guarantees of individual rights than those accorded by

United States Supreme Court interpretation of the Federal Constitution, is referred to as the "new judicial federalism." Following *Rodriguez,* the California Supreme Court, which had invalidated the state's school finance system on federal equal protection grounds, rested its second ruling on a similar state constitutional provision; *see* Serrano v. Priest, 487 P.2d 1241 (Cal. 1971), 557 P.2d 929 (Cal. 1973). The New Jersey Supreme Court bypassed the United States Supreme Court by relying on the state constitutional guarantee of a "thorough and efficient education" when it took a similar action; *see* Robinson v. Cahill, 303 A.2d 273 (N.J. 1973). The New Jersey high court, as well as those of other states, has invalidated exclusionary zoning laws that have had the effect of "fencing out" minorities and the poor; *see* Southern Burlington County v. Mt. Laurel, 336 A.2d 713, 728-34 (N.J. 1971). For a discussion of *Mt. Laurel,* its implications and limitation, *see Symposium—Mount Laurel II and Developments in New Jersey,* 15 RUTGERS L.J. No. 3 (1984). The Massachusetts high court has held that the state must provide families on welfare with enough benefits to live in their own homes. New York Times, August 16, 1987, at 11, col. 3. Hayes, *Litigating on Behalf of Shelter for the Poor,* 22 HARV. C.R.—C.L.L. REV. 79 (1987) has met with some success in New York state courts. In developing the common law and engaging in statutory interpretation, especially of workers' compensation laws, state courts have shown increasing concern "with the individual, the down-trodden" and "with deliberate social change." Kagan *et al. The Business of State Supreme Courts: 1879-1970,* 30 STAN L. REV. 121, 155 (1977). It might be added that long after substantive due process disappeared from the U.S. Supreme Court's agenda, state courts continued to employ the doctrine in the traditional sense. Kirby, *Expansive Judicial Review of Economic Regulations Under State Constitutions: The Case for Realism,* 48 TENN. L. REV. 241 (1981).

37. Learned Hand wondered why nobody "took time to explain" why "property itself was not a personal right." L. HAND, THE SPIRIT OF LIBERTY, 206 (1952). Felix Frankfurter wrote: "Yesterday the active area...was concerned with 'property'. Tomorrow it may again be 'property'. Who can say that in a society with a mixed economy, like ours, these two areas are sharply separated, and that certain freedoms in relation to property may not again be deemed, as they were in the past, aspects of individual freedom?" F. FRANKFURTER, OF LAW AND MEN, 19 (1956). In Lynch v. Household Finance, 405 U.S. 538, 552 (1972), the Court, invalidating a state wage-garnishment law, observed that property rights are as worthy of judicial protection as civil rights.

> The right to enjoy property without lawful deprivation, no less than the right to speak or the right to travel, is in truth a 'personal' right....In fact, a fundamental interdependence exists between the personal right to liberty and the personal right in property. Neither could have meaning without the other.

38. 3 C. WARREN, THE SUPREME COURT IN UNITED STATES HISTORY (1923); L. BETH, THE DEVELOPMENT OF THE AMERICAN CONSTITUTION: 1877-1917 (1971); Porter, *That Commerce Shall Be Free: A New Look at the Old Laissez-Faire Court,* 1976 SUP. CT. REV. 135 (1976).

39. Strong, *The Economic Philosophy of Lochner: Emergence, Embrasure and Emasculation,* 15 ARIZ. L. REV. 419 (1973); Porter *supra* note 38.

40. L. BETH, *supra* note 38; Mavrinac, *From Lochner to Brown v. Topeka: The Court and Conflicting Concepts of the Political Process,* 52 AM. POL. SCI. REV. 641 (1958).

41. B. SIEGAN, ECONOMIC LIBERTIES AND THE CONSTITUTION (1980).

42. WARREN, *supra* note 38, at 463-67.

43. BETH, *supra* note 38, at 141-45.

44. Allgeyer v. Louisiana, 165 U.S. 578 (1897), invalidated a statute that regulated the sale of marine and fire insurance policies. Nutting v. Massachusetts, 183 U.S. 553 (1902), sustained a somewhat similar insurance regulation statute.

45. Southwestern Bell Telephone Co. V. Public Service Commission, 262 U.S. 276, 292 (1923) (Brandeis concurring).

46. Porter, *supra* note 38, at 157.

47. Strong, *supra* note 39, at 427-28.

48. Hamilton, *Common Right, Due Process and Antitrust,* 24 LAW & CONTEMP. PROBS. 24, 31-32 (1940). Quoted in Strong, *id.*

49. Mavrinac, *supra* note 40, at 642, 651-52.

50. EPSTEIN *supra* note 3; SIEGAN *supra* note 41.

51. Discussion is based in part on the author's book review. 75 AM. POL. SCI. REV. 1058 (1981). SIEGAN, *supra* note 41, at 266, 282, 325.

52. SIEGAN, *id.* at 119.

53. SIEGAN, *id.* at Chapter 5, *passim.*

54. SIEGAN, *id.* at 143. (The Milk Control Board set milk prices at levels which required storekeepers to pay prices high enough to protect dairy farmers from distributors' price-cutting practices.) Nebbia v. New York, 291 U.S. 502 (1934) (Justice McReynolds dessenting at 558).

55. New State Ice Co. v. Liebmann, 285 U.S. 262 (1932), invalidated an Oklahoma statute that, in effect, restricted competition in the manufacture, sale, and distribution of ice. In his dissent, Justice Brandeis argued that the business in question was affected with a public interest and thereby subject to regulation, and that the state was justified in providing remedies against the sort of destructive competition that was detrimental to the public interest. SIEGAN, *supra* note 41, at 132-38.

56. New Orleans v. Dukes, 427 U.S. 297 (1976); Ferguson v. Skrupa, 372 U.S. 726 (1963).

57. *Discrete and Insular Minorities Doctrine: See supra* note 38 and accompanying text.

Clear and Present Danger: The clear and present danger test, initially formulated by Justice Holmes in Schenk v. United States, 249 U.S. 47 (1919), and later elaborated by Holmes and Justice Brandeis in a series of cases, provides that governmental restrictions on freedoms of speech and press will be sustained only to prevent grave and immediate danger to interests that government may lawfully protect.

Irrebuttable Presumption: In evidence, a conclusive preemption which requires a finding of the presumed fact once the underlying evidence is introduced (*e.g.,* incapacity of a child five years old to commit a crime: evidence tending to rebut it is not admissible).

Heightened Means-and-Ends Equal Protection: At the close of the 1960s, Supreme Court equal protection rulings could be analyzed in terms of the "two-tiered" model, employing either the rational basis or compelling interest standards. More recently, however, the Court has adopted a standard of review that falls somewhere in between, holding that the classification employed by a state must be "substantially related to an important governmental interest." Cases involving discrimination based on gender and illegitimacy are illustrative. Craig v. Boren, 429 U.S. 190 (1976); Weber v. Aetna Casualty Co., 406 U.S. 164 (1972).

The Supreme Court has also altered the standard of review for laws regulating the exercise of fundamental rights. In many cases, the Court still maintains that it will employ the compelling interest test when the government allocates the ability to exercise fundamental rights differently among various classifications of persons. Although some majority opinions continue to invoke strict scrutiny-compelling interest language in fundamental rights cases, it has been more common in the late 1970s and early 1980s for the Court to review the legitimacy of such laws without stating a clear standard of review. Zablocki v. Redhail, 434 U.S. 374 (1978); Zobel v. Williams, 457 U.S. 55 (1982).

For example, the Court has found the right to vote to be fundamental, but has in some cases upheld regulation of voting rights without requiring that the government formally demonstrate a compelling interest. Ball v. James, 451 U.S. 355 (1981); Clements v. Fashing, 457 U.S. 957 (1982). SIEGAN, *supra* note 41, at 322.

58. McCloskey, *Economic Due Process and the Supreme Court: An Exhumation and Rebuttal,* 1962 SUP. CT. REV. 34, 50 (1962). ("[N]o tears need be shed for helpless General Electric, but the scattered individuals who are denied access to an occupation by state-enforced barriers are about as impotent a minority as can be imagined.") The author, noting the Court's recent tendency to re-establish review of laws which impinged on economic rights, made the point that the Court had at hand the doctrinal means for deciding economic cases. However, the Court was no longer, in McCloskey's opinion, in a position to decide economic cases and controversies, for societal pressures mandated the Court's attention in other areas, such as civil and personal rights and their "subcategories."

McCloskey relied on "old property" to support his article; however, he argued, without making predictions, that there were indeed many personal economic rights beyond the new "opportunity to work" issue of the early 1960's to be determined and litigated. Yet he expressed concern about the Court's capacity to assume such additional responsibilities.

59. SIEGAN, *supra* note 41, at 265, 316, 199. In Chapter 13 he provides nine case studies to illustrate the "failure of regulation."

The American system is replete with social programs that do not work. Income redistribution is utter folly if the outcome is that fewer people are better off. There is a difference between welfare rights and material rights. If judges affirm the former, they do so at the expense of the latter.

By providing that miners no longer employed could sue former employers for the contraction of black lung disease, Congress "in effect seized one group's property and gave it to another."

60. *See* Oakes, *supra* note 3, at n.1.

61. Epstein, *supra* note 1, at 713-15.

62. EPSTEIN *supra* note 3, at 322.

63. Epstein, *supra* note 1, at 734; EPSTEIN *supra* note 3, at 128; *Lochner,* 291 U.S. at 57.

64. Siegan, however, is an original intent true believer, while Epstein appears to employ original intent more for the purpose of supporting his arguments. *See* SIEGAN, THE SUPREME COURT'S CONSTITUTION 149-162 (1987), particularly his vehement critique of the first abortion cases. *Id.* at chapter 6.

65. Michelman, *Property as a Constitutional Right,* 38 WASH. & LEE L. REV. 1097, 1112-14 (1981). Michelman, *supra* note 13, at 1016. Michelman hoped that Rawls's theory of "just wants" would provide grounds for developing a "moral theory" that would comport with "principled constitutional adjudication" in welfare rights cases; *see* J. RAWLS, A THEORY OF JUSTICE (1971). Michelman expanded and clarified his argument that political rights and property/private rights are necessary elements of social beings in this and other republics. For an elaboration *see generally* Michelman, *Foreword: Traces of Self-Government,* 100 HARV. L. REV. 4 (1986). Poletown Neighborhood Council v. Detroit, 304 N.W.2d 455 (Mich. 1981).

66. Radin, *Property and Personhood,* 34 STAN. L. REV. 957, 1004-6, 986, 968 (1982).

67. Kaiser Aetna v. United States, 444 U.S. 164 (1979), involved a dispute as to whether Kaiser Aetna was required to obtain authorization from the Corps of Engineers before making future improvements in the marina it had developed and whether owners could deny public access to the marina because, as a result of improvements, the marina had become a navigable water of the United States. The Court held that although the marina fell within the definition of "navigable waters of the United States," when owners dredged it and connected it to a bay in the Pacific Ocean, so as to be subject to regulation by the Corps of Engineers, the Government could not require owners to make the marina open to the public without compensating the owners. In First English Evangelical Lutheran Church of Glendale v. County of Los Angeles, 107 S. Ct. 2378 (1987), the landowner filed a complaint in a California court against the county and county flood control district, alleging that the regulatory ordinance prohibiting construction on landowner's property denied landowner all use of its property. The church

sought to recover in inverse condemnation and in tort. The Supreme Court held that under the just compensation clause, when government has taken property by land-use regulation, the landowner may recover damages for the taking before it is finally determined that regulation constitutes taking of his property. Radin, *supra* note 10, at 16-19.

68. PLANNING WITHOUT PRICES (B. Siegan ed. 1977).

69. Epstein specifically objected to *Poletown* on the ground that the holding violated the public use constraint of the takings clause. R. EPSTEIN, *supra* note 3, at 83.

70. Schwartz, *supra* note 1, at 121.

71. Kaiser Aetna v. United States, 444 U.S. 164 (1979); Allied Structural Steel v. Spannaus, 438 U.S. 234 (1978); Oakes, *supra* note 3, at 625.

72. L. TRIBE, THE CONSTITUTIONAL PROTECTION OF INDIVIDUAL RIGHTS 454-55 n. 37 (1978).

Holmes, Brandeis, and Pound: Sociological Jurisprudence as a Response to Economic Laissez-Faire

PAUL L. MURPHY

Sociological jurisprudence arose as a major legal movement following the turn of the twentieth century. While its principal architect was Roscoe Pound, the jurisprudence of Oliver Wendell Holmes, Jr. and Louis D. Brandeis also came to be linked with it. The purpose of this essay is to assess the way three leaders of American law reacted to the political and economic realities of life in the United States at the time, especially the public's call for regulatory commissions and governmental intervention to create what Woodrow Wilson was subsequently to call a "New Freedom" for the American people. While sociological jurisprudence was more legal than economic, its thrust involved using the law in ways, including economic ways, that departed from the pattern of the last twenty-five years of the nineteenth century. During those years, an economic dogmatism—laissez faire—under the the mask of natural or divine law had permeated both bench and bar.

Adam Smith's (1723-90) thought had long been a central aspect of American economic thinking. But in the years of the early industrial revolution and the rise of the corporation, the judiciary got into the habit of treating Adam Smith as though his generalizations had been imparted to him on Sinai, and not as a thinker who addressed himself to the eliminations of restrictions which had become fetters upon the initiative and enterprise of his day. Basic human rights, expressed by the constitutional concept of liberty, were equated by the judiciary with theories of laissez faire, especially freedom of property from any legislatively enacted regulation. Such economic views of limited validity were treated by lawyers and judges as though the Framers had enshrined them in the Constitution. This misapplication of the notions of the classical economists, and what Felix Frankfurter was ultimately to call a "resulting disregard of the perduring reach of the Constitution,"[1] led aggressive entrepreneurs to aggregate wealth, power, and control (both economic and political), to eliminate competitors, and to restrain trade. Such frequent abuses of private economic power were impeding the free market, to say nothing of frustrating the processes of democracy.

This development was in some ways ironic. In origin, laissez faire was a reaction to mercantilism. It counseled a termination of governmental hand-outs to business. The economy was to stand on its own two feet independent of tariffs, monopolistic grants, special trading privileges, and other public boun-ties. It was this manner of economic thinking that led Jefferson and Jackson—radicals to many in their time—to embrace the philosophy of laissez faire.

By the last quarter of the nineteenth century, business leaders and their spokesmen had taken over laissez faire for their own ends, turning it into a defense against democratic efforts to regulate business for the protection of the public. Indeed, as the British political leader, Lord Bryce, observed in 1888, "one half of the capitalists are occupied in preaching laissez faire, as regards railroad control. The other half in resisting it in tariff matters. Yet they manage to hold well together."[2] Further, the influence of the Social Darwinists cannot be ignored. The popular philosopher, Herbert Spencer, was saying what busi-nessmen wanted to hear. Checks on their accumulation of wealth and eco-nomic power were unwarranted. Governmental interference for the protection of the public was a violation of nature. Or, as Spencer argued: "the poverty of the incapable, the distresses that come upon the improvident, the starvation of the idle, and the shouldering aside of the weak by the strong, which leaves so many in shadows and misery, are the decrees of a large, far-seeing benevo-lence."[3] Everyone for himself, said the elephant as he danced among the chickens.

In many ways the issue was far more subtle. Generally, I have found that philosophers make bad historians, generalizing more from their selectively evolved perceptions of reality than from reality itself. The United States has always been engaged in the delicate process of balancing individual freedom and the public interest, nowhere more so than in the performance of its economy. The general desire for prosperity, goods, and services created some body of mutual interest between businessmen and laborers, producers and consumers. Indeed, the American tradition of economic freedom has always insisted that the individual, pursuing economic interests in a free environ-ment, would simultaneously serve some basic need for society. Clearly, while the benefits of a free market economy would not be shared equally, such an economy would still serve the interest of society better than any competing system. Private enterprise would create new jobs, new products, generate profits for reinvestment in plant expansion and new industries. The public would establish the limits of acceptable business behavior through its power to express disapproval in the marketplace and elsewhere. If business went too far, an aroused public would demand political restraints to terminate dishonest, selfish, or illegitimate behavior. Thus, the free market and free elections, together, seemed enough to ensure an economic system that would be largely self-regulating, although not without some need for moderate governmental direction.

That governmental direction existed at the state level through most of nineteenth-century America. The concept of police power was ancient and well expressed by the seventeenth-century natural law theorists. In American law police power had been considered a state function. The articulation of its uses and limitations was particularly associated with the jurisprudence of Roger B. Taney, who served as chief justice of the Supreme Court from 1836 to 1863. Under it, the states were responsible for the health, safety and morals of their citizens. As Taney wrote in one of his first opinions:

> The object and end of all government is to promote the happiness and prosperity of the community by which it is established. It can never be assumed that the government intended to diminish its power of accomplishing the end for which it was created... while the rights of private property are sacredly guarded, we must not forget that the community also have rights and that the happiness and well-being of every citizen depends upon their faithful preservation.[4]

This view, expressed in 1837, was reiterated forty years later when the Supreme Court, speaking through Chief Justice Morrison Waite, upheld the state Granger laws.[5] The Court agreed that business "affected with a public interest" was certainly a legitimate object of public control. In the process, Waite underwrote the concept that the establishment of laws requiring each citizen to "so use his own property as not unnecessarily to injure another" was at the cornerstone of the social contract by which people governed and were governed.

However, business leaders during this period wanted to be freed from state police power, and they resorted to two remedies against restrictive state legislation. Business went into politics to protect its interests. It put forward its own attorneys as candidates for office, donated funds to political parties, backed this or that faction in the state legislatures, and some less scrupulous industrial leaders resorted to bribery. The 1880s and 1890s saw a new low in the moral level of the American state legislature. For this new group of legislators, state interference with industry was dangerous and, therefore, state government must be kept out of hands hostile to business enterprise. They saw their state's future and the nation's future flowing from uninhibited business enterprise.

As an additional strategy, business carried the fight against restrictive laws into the courts. There, after a long fight, it won a major victory in the general acceptance of the due process clauses of the Fifth and Fourteenth Amendments as substantive limitations upon the power of government to regulate private property.[6] To this substantive due process was subsequently added the legal doctrine of "liberty of contract,"[7] again based largely upon the due process clause of the Fourteenth Amendment. This novel doctrine allegedly provided a tool to protect individual freedom and serve the public interest, but, in practice, it served only to enhance the power of the contracting employer in a clearly unequal bargaining relationship with individual employees. Thus, as the courts came increasingly to be populated by corporation lawyers, or those within the legal profession generally sympathetic to the business community, state laws which would have been clearly condoned as late as the 1870s now began to fall under an increasingly heavily-wielded judicial axe. In fact, between 1890 and 1920, the Supreme Court ruled 172 state laws unconstitutional, most having a strong regulatory purpose.[8]

The *Munn* ruling of 1877, upholding the Granger laws, was repudiated in 1886[9] on the interesting grounds that regulation of commercial activities— interstate commerce—was a federal, not a state, function, and that the prior authority of the federal government should be recognized. But, when Congress, one year later, picked up the cue and passed the Interstate Commerce Act, some railroad tycoons were clearly taken aback. The measure prohibited rate discrimination, rebates, and the charging of higher rates for short than for long hauls over the same line, and required the publication of all rate schedules. The act lacked teeth, however, and was written in such a way as to virtually require judicial monitoring of the orders of its enforcement agency, the Interstate Commerce Commission. The result was that within ten years the chairman of the Interstate Commerce Commission wrote in that body's Annual Report: "by virtue of judicial decisions, we have ceased to be a body for the regulation of interstate carriers... the people should no longer look to this commission for a protection which it is powerless to extend."[10] Thus, as Attorney General Richard Olney had predicted five years earlier, the act to regulate railroads was tranformed judicially into "a sort of barrier between the railroad corporations and the people."[11] Only with congressional enactment of the Hepburn Act of 1906, in the new era of sociological jurisprudence, did the measure gain the power to enable the I.C.C. to operate effectively.

A somewhat similar fate befell the Sherman Antitrust Act of 1890. That measure—"An Act to Protect Trade and Commerce against Unlawful Restraint and Monopoly"—outlawed conspiracies in restraint of trade or commerce, and action designed to monopolize any part of trade and commerce. The Court defined the scope of the measure very narrowly, ruling in the famous *E.C. Knight* case of 1895[12] that manufacturing and production were not commerce and did not come under the measure. Only if such local activity had a "direct effect" on commerce did it come under the act's provisions. This undercut the act's potential clout as an instrument against monopoly and restraint of trade, all in the name of the importance of laissez faire to a free-market economic system.

Contemporaries could not fail to observe that there were internal contradictions in this development. During the last five years of the nineteenth century, an activist Supreme Court had emasculated legislative attempts to control monopoly, prevent unfair railroad rates,[13] tax income,[14] and regulate utilities and insurance companies.[15] While laissez faire on the bench meant exemption of business from the processes of democratic government, it left working people unprotected from economic exploitation and from the use of the labor injunction to curtail a variety of labor and union activities. In the two famous contempt cases, growing out of the Pullman Strike of the 1890s, a circuit court enjoined the American Railway Union for refusing to call off a boycott of Pullman cars.[16] (Union members refused to move trains with Pullman cars on them.) This interpretation was challenged by the Union's president, Eugene V. Debs, who sued out a writ of habeas corpus in the Supreme Court. But Attorney General Olney argued, and the Supreme Court responded, that the government's strike-breaking action was defensible on the broad grounds that governmental interference of this kind to protect business and keep it operating is justifiable.[17]

Critics were quick to charge a double standard. The only consistency here, they argued, was that the law worked uniformly for the benefit of those who by popular standards already had too many advantages and too much power. To make laissez faire the arbiter between democracy and property meant that the latter would win all engagements. The observations of Oliver Wendell Holmes, Jr., are revealing. Holmes, as a member of the Supreme Judicial Court of Massachusetts, had written an eloquent opinion in *Vegelahn v. Gunther* (1896) protesting against the issuance of an injunction which prohibited even peaceful picketing by strikers. "A legal system is unjust," he contended, "which allows combinations of businessmen for competitive purposes, but denies the privilege of effective action by combinations of labor."[18] In the following year, in lectures at the Boston University Law School, he went on to observe:

> I suspect that fear (of socialism) on the part of the comfortable classes has influenced judicial action both here and in England.... I think that something similar has led people who no longer hope to control the legislatures, to look to the courts as expounders of the Constitution, and that in some courts new principles have been discovered outside of the bodies of those instruments which may be generalized into acceptance of the economic doctrines which prevailed about fifty years ago and a wholesale prohibition of what a tribunal of lawyers does not think about, right.[19]

And, indeed, law and lawyers were a pertinent part of all these developments. To understand better what was occurring in the law, it is essential to understand the knowledge revolution of the late nineteenth century. After the

Civil War, the process through which Americans sought to acquire and convey knowledge was altered so pervasively and so quickly as to constitute a revolution. Post-Civil War America was attracted to an ideology that imposed upon its universe a sense of order, derived not from religious, metaphysical, or transcendent dogmas, but from organized control of the new features of the American industrial environment. Science provided that ideology, and with it came a keen interest in specialized training for the professions. Professionalization was viewed as the means by which educated Americans might master the insights of science. Legal education was affected as well. Law became increasingly focused. The proper method of accumulating knowledge regarding the law became far more scientific, consisting particularly of an increasingly specialized and intensive exposure to a limited area of knowledge.

By the late 1870s and early 1880s, this trend was also linked with "rites of entry" into the profession. Specifically this meant, in the case of the law, elimination of previous apprenticeship training and the development of a new, more formalized legal science, wherein practitioners were trained at the university or college law school. These schools of law trained their students in a legal method which focused upon the mastery of certain principles and doctrines that could in turn be applied with constant facility and certainty to the "ever-tangled skein of human affairs." Harvard was the leader in this area, under the deanship of Christopher Columbus Langdell.[20] The case method became the standard approach of legal education. Such education had two objectives—developing the student's power of legal analysis and his knowledge of what the law actually was. In time this came to represent the study of judicial opinions and all the available materials of law. This material was contained in casebooks which lawyers would study in order to see the logic of the law and begin an understanding of the law as science. It meant further division of the law into discreet departments, such as contracts, torts, property, and taxation. These were divided into courses. Charles Eliot, President of Harvard, clearly supported the system, describing full-time teachers of law as "expounders, systematizers and historians" who had brought about at Harvard one of the most far-reaching changes in the organization of the legal profession that has ever been made in this country.[21]

With this development came the establishment of the American Bar Association. Law reviews began emerging from law schools. The results of this case, inductive, or scientific method of legal study were the extension and classification of governing principles in each area of the law. Lawyers, now truly taught to think like lawyers, could apply these principles to a great variety of human problems and situations.

But by the 1890s a great many Americans, seeing the law used in a highly partisan and class-oriented fashion, were skeptical of this new legal formalism. Its use as a justification for Supreme Court rulings which seemed to be clearly biased produced cynicism and mounting public hostility. As the depression-ridden years of the 1890s wore on, the Supreme Court became a central issue in public politics. A classic example was the public response to two rulings in 1895 which struck down a federal income tax. While the two cases were in some respects contradictory[22] they did in the final analysis still reflect the Court's reliance upon the "logic" or "will" of the law to expunge a policy distasteful to those of wealth and economic power. The comments of the Democratic Governor of Illinois, John Peter Altgeld, were not uncommon:

> The Justices wear long black robes to impress the people with their infallibil-ity. Now, as these robes are not very thick and as some people might be able to see through them and be unpatriotic enough to question the justice of having to bear the burdens of government while some of the rich escape, and as there is danger that some... may doubt the infallibility of the court, would it not be well to have each judge wear two robes for a while, until the storm blows over.[23]

The Court's class bias toward economic wealth and power also became a political issue in the 1890s, with both the Populist Party and the Democratic Party in election campaigns castigating the Court for flouting the interests of the people. Indeed, the excessive judicial activism of the justices brought down such public denunciation that the mid-1890s has been seen by Constitu-tional historians as one of the three or four most serious crises of credibility in the Court's history.[24]

Still, the concept that legal reform was a primary avenue toward correct-ing what an increasing number of Americans saw as the social irresponsibility of economic power was slow to take form and draw adherents into a coordi-nated movement. The law was a body of immutable, sacred, formal rules which if applied uniformly and equitably would produce proper social outcomes. Law was the "master" of the people and should be looked to for its wisdom and for preserving a workable system. Law was not an instrument for social change, a device by which to bring about economic reorganization, redistribution of wealth, or a new approach to the solution of public problems. In fact, as a matter of policy, bar associations generally advised lawyers against profes-sional involvement in or advocacy of economic and social policy issues—state ownership of industry, the single tax, the redistribution of property—which one prominent New York bar leader observed "agitate the thinkers or econo-mists or the social philosophers."[25] Concern for social welfare or protection of the poor among the profession's leaders usually centered exclusively on legal aid. This turned out to mean principally a concern with procedure, rather than with substantive efforts to improve the economic position of the poor. "It is not of chief importance whether the legal organizations win or lose their appeals," declared Reginald Heber Smith, a prime mover in the movement. What matters is that "our common law system should have a fair chance to work itself out... by having those issues fairly argued from both points of view."[26] Clearly, legal aid societies were neither geared to nor inclined to engage in activities that would result in fundamental changes in social conditions.

I. Oliver Wendell Holmes, Jr.

But there were those in the legal profession who were disturbed by what they saw. One such was Oliver Wendell Holmes, Jr., who had sounded a widely heard call for a reassessment of the law in his lectures on "The Common Law," delivered at the Harvard Law School in 1882.[27] In these lectures, with young Louis Brandeis in the audience, Holmes tried to show how judicial creativity, responding to social change, made the law the primary institution for the rational coordination and facilitation of that change. In the process, Holmes talked about law generally, and his words were quoted widely over the subsequent years:

> The life of the law has not been logic. It has been experience. The felt necessities of the time, the prevalent moral and political theories, intuitions of public policy, avowed and unconscious, even the prejudices which judges share with their fellow man, have had a great deal more to do than syllogism in determining rules by which men should be governed.[28]

The statement was to a degree prescient, foreseeing the evils of unregulated laissez faire, and proclaiming the judicial necessity of "weighing considerations of social advantage." However, there were more subtle overtones to Holmes's position, which was itself a cultural statement growing out of the times in which he lived. Law had been good law, he contended, when it had accurately reflected human needs. Law had not been good law simply because of its impressive formal structure.

The idea of law based upon experience has frequently been misunderstood. Holmes was not saying that prior law had not been based on experience. What he was arguing was that it had all too frequently been solely the product of the experience of the powerful and the wealthy—the patriarchy. Thus, when he said that "the first requirement of a sound body of law is that it should correspond with the actual feelings and demands of the community—it must found itself on actual forces"—he was referring to the whole community, not simply those who would manipulate the law to serve their own special interests.

To some degree what Holmes was doing was proposing a new methodology. His argument was more an instrument for reform or a rallying point of liberalization of the law than an accurate description of the way the law had been before. The problem of prior law was that people had refused to admit that it was a reflection of certain narrow values within the dominant class—the values of the leaders of a deferential society. This is not to say that Holmes was advocating a system of law based totally on the immediate whim of the majority, but one based on a more stable, long-range consensus of the popular will. What this translated into was his feeling that the growth of the law should be based on legislative action, with judges exercising a bit more humility and restraint in striking down legislation carefully designed to serve a public purpose.[29] The judge's responsibility was to temper arbitrary legislation while applying reasonable legislation sensitively to changing circumstances.

As it turned out, however, Holmes spent the remaining years of the nineteenth century on the Supreme Judicial Court of Massachusetts, where few cases occurred which enabled him to work his doctrines into his opinions. This seems to have taken some of the edge of optimism off of his view of the law as organically derived from society, so that by the time he delivered his famous lecture on "The Path of the Law" at the Boston University Law School in 1897,[30] he viewed the law much more as a positive phenomenon of articulated human choice. Each case, he now argued, called for a choice between competing claims, where earlier he had hoped that "policy" meant something more abstract than the resolution of those claims supported through the mechanisms of the law. He did say in "The Path of the Law" that there are those who express the view that the law represents an inherent reality of human affairs, but more and more his concern was that law emerged from conflict, in which fair process should be assured. Holmes, in the nineteenth century at least, never finally settled on a single, internally consistent theory of law, and his judicial experience contributed importantly to changes in his essential structure of thought. Thus, in 1897 he was less prepared to move in an idealistic direction toward what ultimately came to be called "sociological jurisprudence" than he might have been in 1882. He stated at Boston University that:

> judges themselves have failed adequately to recognize their duty of weighing considerations of social advantage. I cannot but believe that if the training lawyers led them habitually to consider more definitely and explicitly the social advantage on which the rules they lay down must be justified, they would sometimes hesitate where now they are confident and see that really they are taking sides on debatable and often burning questions.[31]

Holmes's own position seems at times troublingly ambivalent. He was not totally convinced that the law should be geared to the service of ideal societal goals, i.e., that the law should be treated as normative. "The law," he wrote, "was not some brooding omnipresence in the sky." But Holmes, although he advocated using evidence drawn from a wide range of materials and references and from diverse periods, was not a pure empiricist. He was prepared to say that the study of the future would fall to the disciplines of economics and sociology, rather than to the black-letter books of the law, and to argue further that the first requirement of a sound body of law was that it should correspond with the actual feelings and demands of the community. The real justification for a rule of law, he thought, is that it helps to bring about a social end which we desire. But Holmes was certainly not interested in studying economics and sociology. And in fact his critics have contended, with considerable justification, that his perspective on economic questions was "uninformed." Francis Biddle, Holmes's former law clerk, contended that his thinking in the field of economics stopped at age twenty-five.[32]

Holmes, the common law lawyer, charged with breathing reasonableness into the law, acknowledged that one had to look at circumstances and facts to determine whether laws were working reasonably, and whether the standards they were seeking to impose were desirable. However, when empirical developments threatened to undermine operational societal standards and objectives in such a way as to create disrespect for them and generally destroy their viability, Holmes worried that this type of legal procedure held within it the potential for injustice. In other words, a lack of norms left society floating fairly freely, and to a degree subject to a kind of situational ethics. At many points, Holmes clearly manifested an allegiance to law as a force for social order, placing that value above a sense of moral commitment to proper human relationships or proper social outcomes. Brandeis, by contrast, far more often reversed that order.[33]

On the question of how much freedom the people, through their elected representatives, should have to experiment with ways of controlling economic power, or assaulting excessive laissez faire, Holmes was, as Robert Summers has argued, a pragmatic instrumentalist. The people could, through their state legislatures, create a more just and equitable society by conducting social experiments.[34] But the Court had the role of seeing that such social experiments were reasonable and not arbitrary, particularly since Holmes, in his private correspondence, viewed most of the legislation and social experimentation as misguided humbug.[35] Even so, he was prepared to say publicly that law should not be a negative instrument for telling people what they could not do to improve their society and their lives. He was generally supportive also of federal police power—the use of the commerce, taxing and postal powers—to support social legislation in the public interest, and was critical of judicial efforts to quash it. In his dissent in *Hammer v. Dagenhart* (1917), in which the Court had thrown out a federal child labor law as improper federal legislation, he forcefully stated:

> if there is any matter on which civilized countries have agreed, it is the evil of premature and excessive child labor. I should have thought that if we were to introduce our own moral conceptions, where in my opinion, they do not belong, this was preeminently a case for upholding the exercising of all of its power by the United States.[36]

Holmes, then, was more inclined to support public regulation than to question it on grounds of its threat to traditional laissez-faire economic policy. This is not to say that he had an elaborate theory of the positive use of law. He was in many ways a skeptic. "If the people want to do something and there is nothing in the Constitution to prevent them, hell, let 'em do it." "There is nothing in the Constitution that prevents people from making damn fools of themselves, nor does that duty fall to this Court."[37]

Holmes's position on the Sherman Antitrust Act is revealing. He viewed the measure with great misgivings. It was, in his mind, normative, geared toward establishing patterns of ideal behavior, not empirical, and not well-designed to accommodate current behavior. In setting forth his "rule of reason" by which the act could be applied—a rule which assumed that bigness was not necessarily badness until it was demonstrated empirically that the bigness was producing bad results[38]—he was behaving very much as a common law lawyer. He tried to see that the act was applied in reasonable ways to the immediate circumstances demanding action. There was some irony in his position. What he did, in requiring a "reasonable" test, was to give the Supreme Court a license for judicial activism, determining on a case by case basis how and when the law should be applied, based on the justices' evaluation of whether the company involved was engaging in "reasonable" activities.

Thus, it is generally fair to say that Holmes, in the abstract, was comfortable with certain dimensions of the movement for a new sociological jurisprudence. His sense of restraint, his nod in the direction of letting people and their legislators have their say, his own skepticism regarding human nature, and above all his own Darwinistic views were elements shared by the new movement. His evolutionist convictions, emanating as they did from an acknowledgement of struggle and change, were no conduit for espousing a one-sided survival-of-the-fittest philosophy. But Holmes did demonstrate a multifaceted appreciation and application of Darwinian principles to American law, reflecting a view of Darwinism in the marketplace, in politics ("the free marketplace of ideas"), and in the intellectual arena. Evolutionism taught him that growth and change are inevitable in a complex society. Needless to say, such views tended to condition heavily the degree to which he could actively operate as a sociological jurisprude for the remainder of his career.

Holmes contributes, in some ways, to the kind of thinking that produced the sociological jurisprudence movement. In many regards he was far less important in that movement than his judicial colleague of a later day, Louis D. Brandeis, and the future Dean of the Harvard Law School, Roscoe Pound. Part of this stems from Holmes's position as judge, and after 1902 as a Supreme Court justice. In the latter capacity he was under restraints not confining attorney and presidential adviser Brandeis, or law school dean Pound. Just as in Massachusetts, this limited Holmes's ability to work his doctrines into law in any way other than through his opinions, and frequently those had to be dissenting opinions.

II. Louis Brandeis

Thomas McCraw, in his recent Pulitzer Prize-winning book *Prophets of Regulation,* speaks of sociological jurisprudence as the legal methodology of the early twentieth century, contending that it had been foreshadowed by Oliver Wendell Holmes's lectures on *The Common Law,* highlighted by Brandeis's 1908 brief in *Muller v. Oregon*[39] on working hours for women, and institutionalized by the reform of the Harvard curriculum undertaken during Roscoe Pound's deanship, which began in 1916. McCraw goes on to say that "a powerful tool, sociological jurisprudence set experience, facts, and industrial conditions against the rigid formalism of an older jurisprudence that relied exclusively on legal precedent."[40] McCraw is correct. Brandeis and Pound were sociological jurisprudence's water carriers, especially Brandeis in his role as an attorney and Wilsonian planner and promoter of economic legislation leading to new social policy.

The literature of Louis Brandeis is exhaustive, and curiously, it is also growing, with new assessments adding perceptive and fresh insights.[41] The Brandeis record, particularly his economic record, grows increasingly complex and steadily more ambivalent. Clearly, his general societal views reflected concern for the people and especially for victims of economic exploitation, but his economic perceptions did not always work out consistently in practice.

Brandeis, like Holmes, was troubled by the formality and rigidity of late nineteenth-century law. But where Holmes was general, Brandeis was more specific. He saw how independent and small businessmen had fallen before the trusts and monopolies; how entrepreneurs had been forced to become workers for someone else; how the workers themselves had become mere cogs in the industrial machine, which depended upon sharp division of labor for mass production, and upon mass production for its profits; and how opportunities to become an independent businessman were declining. More specifically, he was especially concerned with how dependent the workers had become upon big companies for jobs, with the result that the responsibility for their welfare shifted from themselves to big employers, and ultimately, to the state. From this, he concluded that law had not been altered to fit new conditions of American life. Government, he argued in an address entitled "The Living Law," delivered before the Chicago Bar Association,[42] must keep order not only physically, but socially. "It must protect a man from the things that rob him of his freedom, whether the oppressive force be physical or of a subtler kind." As a lawyer, Brandeis further deplored this situation, since it produced public disrespect for law, lawyers, and judges. Lawyers' failure to keep up with social and economic progress—the divorce of the law from life—was particularly dangerous in America, where constitutional limitations were invoked by the courts to stop the natural course of legislation. Dissatisfaction with the law was clear evidence that it had not kept pace with the rapid development of our political, economic, and social ideals.

Brandeis also saw, as Holmes had, that in the constitutional area, the late nineteenth century had seen a departure from previous patterns. Whereas in previous constitutional cases the traditional policy of the Court had been to presume the validity of legislation, until its violation of the Constitution was proved beyond reasonable doubt, the Court by the 1880s had shifted the burden of proof. Anyone attacking a state law did not have to prove it unconstitutional; rather, the state itself had to prove the law constitutional. This, he argued, was practically impossible where judges and legislators did not see eye to eye on the social needs of the nation. One approach to a solution was to equip the judges with a requisite knowledge of economics and social science: "a lawyer who has not studied economics and sociology is very apt to become a public enemy."[43]

Regarding laissez faire, Brandeis saw more subtle problems and developments. He was unpersuaded by arguments from the chorus of voices in late nineteenth-century America which decried government regulation of economic enterprise as destructive of freedom. Such freedom was of one type—freedom from governmental interference—but said little about other components of freedom. It was too narrow a conception of freedom to encompass practices and policies necessary to assure that common and public interests would be well represented. In truth, it addressed only the freedom of the economically powerful, although it failed to say explicitly whose freedom it did address, and for what purpose, and with what consequences. The assumption was that such an economic policy would augment general wealth and well-being. But the theory overlooked two important factors. First, not all Americans at that time were equally "free." A competitive marketplace, Brandeis felt, was inherently unfair unless its contenders were on equal footing and unless the state stood ready to reduce, and eventually to eliminate prior, unequal opportunities.

Second, Brandeis viewed laissez-faire sloganeering as hypocritical—business wanted no governmental interference, but very much wanted to dominate the affairs of government. The noninterference principle ought not be an implicit license to promote monopoly, for monopolists could easily corner political as well as economic power in ways inimical to the public interest. What would result then is what Brandeis called the "curse of bigness": a genuine social plague. A footnote, but a vitally important one, for Brandeis was the element of social justice. Justice and social policy ought ultimately to be tested primarily by the ways in which they allocated losses, disadvantages, and other burdens, including especially those associated with decreases in socio-economic freedom and opportunity. The allocation of reward within a democratic society should ideally be tied to work done. In the meantime, he was committed to a kind of justice in which benefits should be distributed equally whether or not the burdens, the losses, and the disadvantages they entailed were apportioned equally. Further, it was time to move toward some measure of industrial democracy in which those who labored would have some input into policies that affected them.

What all this meant in practice was a much more precise, empirical approach to the law than Holmes had espoused. The brief that Brandeis introduced in *Muller v. Oregon* (1908)[44]—a case challenging a maximum-hour law for women working in laundries—was based upon a plethora of empirical data drawn from a wide range of sources. He explored the conditions of working women in industrial America and even abroad and the impact those conditions had upon their victims—economically, socially, physically, and even psychologically. Having set forth the size and shape of the socio-economic factors involved, Brandeis then closely analyzed the data. The methodology could be applied equally well to other sorts of cases. In business cases, for example, it would entail an assessment of the financial status of the business or corporation, and of the structure and charge of the governmental agency involved in carrying out a regulation. A second aspect of the Brandeis method involved collateral or comparative research of comparable situations, again looking at socio-economic factors and the implications of the policy which was being applied or was otherwise under consideration. But Brandeis, since he was a man of action, and a master tactician and strategist, was interested in developing ways to enhance his chances of creating social good through victories in court. Thus, his technique further entailed a careful assessment of the social forces aligned on either side of a public issue, with the hope that he would secure that victory that would serve the general welfare of the many.

What this translated to for Brandeis the attorney is complex and controversial. McCraw argues that Brandeis "almost perfectly embodied some of the best and the worst elements in the American regulatory tradition. On the one hand, he epitomized the dogged militance which has given that tradition its distinctive sense of righteousness and moral passion. On the other, Brandeis offered regulatory solutions, grounded on a set of economic assumptions that were fundamentally wrong."[45] Questions arise also regarding Brandeis's techniques. His emphasis upon facts became a minor legend in itself and an important part of the sociological jurisprudence he advocated later in his career. Clearly, he used facts to bolster his legal arguments. As he wrote in a memorandum to himself on the practice of law: "far more likely to impress clients by a knowledge of facts than by knowledge of law." He repeatedly won cases, often against heavy odds, by his dazzling knowledge of detail, which impressed many with his personal unassailability and infallibility. He also had a genius for publicity and for going to the public for support for his positions in a kind of holy crusade of good against evil.[46] His role in the famous Ballinger-Pinchot affair[47] was a good case in point. He managed the publicity involved in a highly controversial set of charges of impropriety made by his client against natural resources officials of the Taft administration. He vanquished his opponents. In the so-called *Advanced Rate Case,*[48] he maneuvered so skillfully that ultimately his own fascination with and commitment to managerial efficiency became a vehicle for the case's solution. The case involved a petition by American railroads to the Interstate Commerce Commission for an across-the-board increase in freight rates. Shipping interests hired Brandeis to oppose the railroad's petition. Seizing the opportunity to address the broad situation, Brandeis first conceded that the railroad companies needed much more money, but then proceeded to show how the proper source was not higher rates for shippers but lower internal operating costs for the companies themselves. He demonstrated how this could be brought about through careful and scientific management.

On another occasion, Brandeis again did his homework carefully, this time on the issue of the trusts. In an extended analysis, he described four different varieties of trusts and set forth the problems and the potential approach to those problems which each presented. In this perceptive analysis of the trust movement, however, he failed to take into consideration the nature of different types of industries. Thus, his prior commitments and sloganeering regarding the "curse of bigness" prevented him from doing the kind of detailed study of particular industries and business practices that his own methodology seemingly required before a judgment of efficiency could be reached.

As to competition under the Sherman Act, Brandeis saw legalized price fixing as a vehicle for protecting small businesses from the unfair competition of the large. The fact that price fixing did not always serve the American consumer was less important to Brandeis than the fact that it, in his mind at least, protected the small competitor from being driven out of business. Here his contempt for the consumer emerged, frequently reflecting his own frugality and hostility to what he saw as an acquisitive and materialistic society. This anti-consumption sensibility led him to a hatred of advertising, and the consumer who was influenced by it. At one point he described consumers as "servile, self-indulgent, indolent, and ignorant." The consumer, needless to say, was not Brandeis's ideal American.[49]

In his views toward business, then, Brandeis's obsession that big business could become big only through illegitimate means tended to structure much of his action. So while his arguments against big business were on their face essentially economic arguments, the bottom line was that there was a clear dominance of political over economic considerations in his thinking. When he asked the question, how could government control bigness without interfering with personal liberty, let alone with economic efficiency, the answer was to a degree implied from the question.

As he moved into an advisory capacity with Wilson's ascension to the Presidency, he came gradually to gain the informal role of "chief architect of the New Freedom."[50] One basic component of the New Freedom involved regulated competition. Here, Brandeis's influence was apparent, particularly his rejection of traditional laissez faire. Regulation was essential to the preservation and development of competition, just as it was necessary to the highest development of liberty. True liberty was freedom for the citizen or the small entrepreneur from industrial absolutism. This necessitated creation of structures within government to regulate in the public interest and see that freedom was, indeed, preserved.

Yet action did not always correspond with rhetoric. Brandeis's role in the creation of the Federal Trade Commission is pertinent and is among his most controversial actions. Charged by President Wilson with designing a program of strengthened antitrust laws that would enumerate illegal practices and create an interstate trade commission with both advisory and investigatory powers, the F.T.C. that emerged was, despite much sloganeering and public show, a minor and weak accomplishment. Brandeis conceived of it as a strong "sunshine agency," hoping, however, that it would accumulate neutral facts—in good sociological-jurisprudential fashion—that would help peripheral firms, especially in their associational activities. Yet the agency proved to be disappointment in a variety of ways. Its subsequent, erratic career derived from faulty enabling legislation and from the related absence of any coherent organizational strategy. Brandeis's hope for a commission that would function as a clearing house of information for the benefit of small business did not come to fruition. It might have succeeded as a consumer protection agency, but Brandeis's contempt for the mindless consumer precluded its playing that role. Thus, his attainment of a trade commission proved of limited impact and the agency failed to achieve much of what it was designed to accomplish.

With his nomination by Wilson to a seat on the Supreme Court, Brandeis's sociological jurisprudence had to be applied in new ways. Once on the Court, Brandeis ceased being the advocate. Possibly because of the bitter criticism of his appointment on the grounds of his alleged partisanship, once confirmed he surprised his critics with his impartiality, wisdom, and judicial depth. The central theme of his judicial career followed many of the interests of his earlier life—a preoccupation with actual social conditions, an insistence on individual rights and autonomy, and most important for his decisions on economic issues, a powerful commitment to judicial restraint. Because of this approach it is often difficult to separate law from economics in his judicial opinions, but clearly a number of themes stand out. He continued to oppose monopoly, although this did not imply an equally strong commitment to competition, and consistently favored results which would protect the small, independent, and perhaps also inefficient, producer, regardless of the effect on the consumer.

Several Supreme Court opinions are revealing in this regard. When the Court, in the 1921 *American Column & Lumber* case,[51] ruled that trade associations, in attempting to standardize prices, wages, and production quotas within an industry, eliminated competition and amounted to an illegal cartel, Brandeis dissented. He contended that unless companies were permitted to cooperate in order to rationalize competition, they might be tempted to enter the inviting field of consolidation. If they were forced into this latter course, another huge trust with highly centralized control and power enough to dominate competitors, wholesalers, retailers, consumers, employees, and in large measure the whole community, would result. Holmes agreed. If business wanted to experiment with less drastic alternatives, Brandeis favored letting them. The fittest ones would survive and "surely Congress did not intend by the Sherman Act to prohibit self-restraint."[52] In a case from Florida that involved a discriminatory tax by the legislature against chain stores—a tax the Court ruled unconstitutional[53]—Brandeis again dissented. Florida citizens, he claimed, "may have believed that the chain store, by furthering the concentration of wealth and/or power and by promoting absentee ownership, was thwarting American ideals... it is sapping the resources, the vigor and the hope of the smaller cities and towns." Again, bigness was suspect and legislative action should be given the benefit of the doubt.

His famous dissent in *Truax v. Corrigan*[54] demonstrates that his sociological-jurisprudential approach was alive and well. Arizona had passed a state law prohibiting the use of injunctions against unions following largely similar provisions in the federal Clayton Act. The owner of an Arizona restaurant which was being picketed sought an injunction against the pickets. State courts would not issue it. The owner claimed that the state law preventing the issuance of such injunctions denied him protection against injury and, therefore, the state took his property without due process of law. The Supreme Court, speaking through Chief Justice William Howard Taft, threw out the law on a narrow interpretation of the Fourteenth Amendment's due process clause, applying the conception of property as an absolute which the owner had embraced. Holmes and Brandeis dissented. Holmes stressed two themes. First, that the Fourteenth Amendment should not be used to prevent the states from making social experiments which an important part of the community desires. And second, he attacked the mechanical jurisprudence of the majority. Taft, he said, was applying the term "property" clumsily and inflexibly. To call owning a business "property" was to miss many subtleties. Although an established business might have pecuniary value which was protected by law, it was more. It was a course of conduct, and like other conduct was subject to substantial modification. In other words, the owner was under an obligation to use his property fairly and lawfully. Holmes further deplored the Court's reversion to legal formalism and the refusal of the majority to go behind the legalism and examine the way the law was working.

Brandeis's dissent was less concerned with condoning experimentation than with examining the social situation as well as the power relationships so clearly present. For Brandeis, the law corrected a social evil, and, thus, was passed to accomplish a definite and legitimate social end. Further, the validity of laws should not be measured by the effect they have on property, but by the effect they have upon people. The law of property, he contended, was not appropriate for dealing with the forces underlying social unrest. It was unwise to throw the power of the state on one side or the other according to principles deduced from law. It was particularly improper for the Court to take this action when the people's representatives had only sought to create a responsible balance between management and labor which would serve the public interest.

But here, as in so many other examples, Brandeis's application of sociological jurisprudence to the economic/political issues of his day was generally unsuccessful. While he was attempting to utilize law as an instrument for social, or in this case economic reform, here, and frequently in other judicial situations, he did not have the complete facts, or if he did, he viewed them through lenses ground by his own value system. Hence, his alternative to legal formalism was often a not very refined empiricism, based, as it was, upon certain elite assumptions and upon his own perceptions of desirable results. What he did, then, was not to let the facts drive him, but to selectively marshal the facts in order to back up his preconceived positions. The result was often a failure to come to terms with economic reality. This shallowness often led him to embrace solutions the outcomes of which proved to be largely fruitless.

III. Roscoe Pound

Roscoe Pound, a Nebraskan, attended the Harvard Law School in the 1890s but left without a degree, returning to Nebraska to begin the practice of law. Pound was also a botanist with a Ph.D., and he spent his time between 1892 and 1903 not only in legal practice, but as director of a state survey of Nebraska's plant life. In 1901, the Nebraska legislature provided for the appointment of nine commissioners of the supreme court, selected by the court, to conduct hearings and perform other duties at the court's direction. Pound, now thirty, was appointed a commissioner and in that capacity wrote well over two hundred reported opinions dealing with a wide range of subjects of local significance. In 1903, he published his *Outlines of Lectures on Jurisprudence.* Its methodology was reminiscent of his doctoral dissertation in botany, "The Phytogeography of Nebraska," a work of scientific classification explaining taxonomy and nomenclature. In the case of the *Outlines,* though, it was the nomenclature of justice. Its publication led to his deanship at the University of Nebraska College of Law. His tenure there was devoted to developing a curriculum of richer offerings of electives which would broaden the students' view of the jurisprudential process.[55]

Pound's Nebraska years were enriching in still other ways. Ideas which would eventually bloom into sociological jurisprudence were beginning to enter his thoughts. This maturing was largely due to the influence of two Nebraska social science colleagues. Edward A. Ross was a social reformer who believed in social interaction and social change rather than simply teaching and researching academic sociology. His pragmatic criticism of the system of law, where the tendency was to subordinate experience to logic, was an encouragement to Pound, who had been advocating similar ideas for some time. A second colleague, George E. Howard, influenced Pound in much the same way. His call for a "new humanism," defined in terms of social utility rather than aesthetic appeal, closely resembled the views of Pound and added encouragement to an already reform-minded dean. The influence and support of these two men provided increased legitimacy to the fundamental ideas that Pound had been advancing. The time had come for Pound to introduce this theory to a greater audience and receive its reaction.[56]

In 1907, in an address to the American Bar Association entitled "The Need for a Sociological Jurisprudence,"[57] Pound presented a concise argument for his sociological theory, with a suggestion that it provided a potential means of curing the disrespect for law that plagued the American system. In diagnosing the problem, Pound felt that the law did not have the real "hold" on the American people that it should. This disrespect was not for justice itself, he argued, but rather a result of the law as practiced, and the manner in which law was taught and expounded. Legal science, he charged, had failed to keep up with the growth of other sciences, and so had lost the respect of the public. The answer, for Pound, was a new sociological approach that would bring the law to the level of the people, and would consider less its formal structure than its relation to society and the needs and opinions of the people that it should be serving. A law tied narrowly to "natural law" was automatic, mechanical, and impersonal and left to jurists only the duty of discovery—in theory at least— while historical law was determinate and derivative and afforded jurists merely the satisfaction of exercises in erudition. Neither had any logical place for the imagination or for creative activity. By a resort to the principles of natural and historical law, judges could, and did, evade responsibility; when they voided legislative acts of which they disapproved, they generally accompanied the nullification with the confession that they had no choice in the matter.

Pound found the then influential natural rights dogma similarly distasteful. Like the corporate form of business, the natural rights doctrine was a perfect vehicle for concentrating power and dissipating responsibility. "More than anything else," Pound wrote, some years later, "the theory of natural rights and its consequence, the nineteenth century theory of legal rights, served to cover up what the legal order really was and what court and lawmaker and judge really were doing."[58] But it was an increasingly transparent cover.

Law could not permanently lag behind the other social sciences, nor could it be allowed indefinitely to short-circuit public demands for legislative protection against the abuses of power inherent in the laissez-faire system of the time. Admittedly, Pound did not so much assail laissez faire directly as he assailed the faulty and unconvincing formal structures used to defend it. Nonetheless, his assault on prior legal method and procedure carried a heavy overtone of criticism of a power structure which twisted the law into a tool for its own self-interest. A high-minded regard for an unregulated economy, free from legislative restraints, merely marked the hand of powerful private interests.

Concretely, the promises of Pound's new law were enticing. The law schools would train practitioners and jurists who would take more account, and more intelligent account, of the social facts upon which law must proceed and to which it is to be applied. Where the nineteenth century studied law in the abstract, students would now study the actual effects of legal institutions and legal doctrines. Where the last century had prepared for legislation by the analytic study of prior legislation, sociological study in conjunction with legal study now would be the appropriate preparation for legislation. Where the last century held comparative law the best foundation for wise law making, it would not be enough in the future to compare the laws themselves. In addition, their social operation and their effects must be studied. Thus, where the last century studied only the making of law, a new generation would study the means of making legal rules more effective. In Pound's vision, law was a social science, dependent upon, rather than independent of, society. It should be required to conform to social needs and judged by the degree to which it filled those needs.

But Pound was, after all, a taxonomist with precise visions for different areas of the law. In criminal law, attention should be shifted from the criminal to the crime and ultimately to the social precursors of the crime. In the field of administration, emphasis should be directed to the enforcement rather than the making of law. And in the area of public law—constitutional law and public policy—antiquated, irrelevant legal doctrines should be jettisoned to make way for a pragmatic approach which should treat law as a social process, susceptible to continuous improvement and a proper subject for social engineering.

Pound's thought was often too diffuse and speculative to have much direct influence on his time. Few of Pound's own thoughts about the law make ultimately important contributions in these early twentieth-century years. His creativity was increasingly spent on particulars.[59] Principally a legal theorist, his interest was in preserving conceptual thinking among lawyers and judges while at the same time criticizing legal doctrines that did not respond to the facts of a case. What, in restrospect, he was really about was constructing a new legal method which would save the profession from the bitter assaults it was suffering for its insensitivity and lack of social consciousness, while preserving its arcane mystery and the power of the bar. He was, as G. Edward White has written, an incarnation of the common law system: versatile, flexible and opportunistic. He admired that system and was thereby an opponent of the service state, hostile toward reforms which smacked of egalitarianism, and later a bitter critic of the New Deal. This was particularly true when he felt legislation challenged the status of the bar. Thus, he rallied the profession against New Deal administrative agencies which threatened to bypass the courts, expressing further his strong theoretical concern that the rule-making and policy-making activities of such agencies were too often extralegal and not limited by constitutional considerations. Nonetheless, he directed the trans-mission of new learning to an intellectually rigid profession, and candidly attacked mechanical jurisprudence not only because it produced morally offensive results, but because it substituted a formal logic for good sense. In the final analysis, he helped to engineer the legal profession's shift from a model of legal method as an exact, quasi-natural science to one which emphasized eclecticism and the social sciences.[60]

One is left with the rather modest conclusion that Pound's sociological jurisprudence was disappointing in the results that it achieved. Pound was, after all, a theoretician, to whom the most crucial aspect of problem solving was the development of a sound diagnosis from which proper treatment would naturally develop. Similarly, his heavy emphasis upon sociological considera-tions, rather than concrete, procedural-based reforms, made his influence and success, though just as important as his theorizing, much more difficult to evaluate.

His overall contribution, however, is not to be dismissed. He played an important role as a cohesive force between various interests and the legal profession. While his commitment to professionalism may have narrowed his intellectual range, his professional connections provided institutional chan-nels for the ideas of sociological jurisprudence, and his traditionalism made him appear safe to fellow lawyers. As a result of this, Pound made a limited but important impact on American law, and incidentally upon the use of law as an instrument for social change, that would be felt throughout his lifetime. Indeed, as Henry Steele Commager has argued:

> Anticipated by Holmes, championed unceasingly by Brandeis, supported by the muscular Harlan Stone and the eloquent Benjamin Cardozo and the learned Felix Frankfurter, sociological jurisprudence became after the great struggle of 1937, the all but official doctrine of the Court. Responsibility for what may, fairly enough, be called a constitutional revolution is widespread, but only those blind to the realization that ideas are weapons would deny that Roscoe Pound shares with such men as Holmes, Brandeis, and Franklin Roosevelt responsibility for that revolution.[61]

One need only add the obvious: that the constitutional revolution of 1937 saw the final end of laissez faire and the consolidation of the regulatory state in the positive governmental structures with which we all live.

Notes

1. A.F. of L. v. American Sash & Door Co., 335 U.S. 538, 542 (1949).

2. A. MASON & G. BAKER, FREE GOVERNMENT IN THE MAKING 506 (4th ed. 1985).

3. *Id.* at 503.

4. Charles River Bridge v. Warren Bridge, 11 Peters 420, 436 (1837).

5. Munn v. Illinois, 94 U.S. 113 (1877). The Granger laws regulated rates and charges on railroads and grain elevator facilities.

6. H. HYMAN & W. WIECEK, EQUAL JUSTICE UNDER LAW: CONSTITUTIONAL DEVELOPMENT, 1835-1875 481ff (1982).

7. Allgeyer v. Louisiana, 165 U.S. 578 (1897), marked the first judicial validation of this concept which formed a part of constitutional law until 1937, when the Hughes Court rejected it in West Coast Hotel v. Parrish, 300 U.S. 379 (1937).

8. M. JAYSON et al. THE CONSTITUTION OF THE UNITED STATES: REVISED AND ANNOTATED 1643-73 (1972).

9. Wabash, St. Louis and Pacific Railway Co. v. Illinois, 118 U.S. 557 (1886).

10. Quoted in J. SMITH & P. MURPHY, LIBERTY AND JUSTICE 285 (1968).

11. Richard S. Olney to Charles C. Perkins, Dec. 28, 1892, Letterbook IV 353-54, Olney Papers (Library of Congress).

12. U.S. v. E.C. Knight Co., 156 U.S. 1 (1895).

13. I.C.C. v. Cincinnati, New Orleans, and Texas Pacific Railway Co., 167 U.S. 479 (1897).

14. Pollock v. Farmers Loan and Trust Co., 157 U.S. 428 (1895); Pollock v. Farmers Loan and Trust Co., 158 U.S. 601 (1895).

15. Chicago, Milwaukee, and St. Paul Ry Co. v. Minnesota, 134 U.S. 418 (1890).

16. U.S. v. Debs et al., 64 Fed. 724 (1894).

17. In re Debs, 158 U.S. 564 (1895).

18. Vegelahn v. Guntner, 167 Mass. 92, 104 (1896).

19. O.W. Holmes, *The Path of the Law,* in COLLECTED LEGAL PAPERS 184 (1920).

20. On the Langdell years at Harvard *see* A. SUTHERLAND, THE LAW AT HARVARD: A HISTORY OF IDEAS AND MEN, 1817-1967 31 (1967).

21. CENTENNIAL HISTORY OF THE HARVARD LAW SCHOOL, 1817-1917 31 (1918).

22. *Id.* at 31 n.14.

23. H. BARNARD, EAGLE FORGOTTEN: THE LIFE OF JOHN PETER ALTGELD 338 (1938).

24. A. PAUL, CONSERVATIVE CRISIS AND THE RULE OF LAW: ATTITUDES OF BAR AND BENCH, 1887-1895 (1960).

25. C. Boston, *The Lawyer's Opportunity,* in ADDRESSES AND WRITINGS, BOOK II: 1912-1916 97 (1917).

26. R.H. SMITH, JUSTICE AND THE POOR 207 (1924). On the legal aid societies, *see* G. FETNER, ORDERED LIBERTY: LAW REFORM IN THE TWENTIETH CENTURY 19 (1983).

27. O.W. HOLMES, THE COMMON LAW (1885).

28. *Id.* at 1.

29. As Saul Touster has pointed out (*Holmes A Hundred Years Ago: The Common Law and Legal Theory,* 10 HOFSTRA L. REV. 677 (1982)), Holmes upheld eloquently the right of the majority, acting through their legislature to have their say and way on social legislation free of judicial interpretation or veto, although personally he saw most of the legislation and social experiment as misguided humbug.

30. Holmes, *supra* note 19, at 186.

31. On the contrasting views in the two lectures see Tushnet, *The Logic of Experience: Oliver Wendell Holmes on the Supreme Judicial Court,* 63 VA. L. REV. 975 (1977).

32. F. BIDDLE, MR. JUSTICE HOLMES 86-87 (1942). On changing views and perspectives of Holmes's career see White, *Looking at Holmes in the Mirror,* 4 LAW & HIST. REV. 439 (1986). For an interesting perspective on Holmes's controversial ruling in Buck v. Bell, upholding compulsory sterilization, see Gould, *Carrie Buck's Daughter,* 2 CONSTITUTIONAL COMMENTARY 331 (1985).

33. Smurl, *Allocating Public Burdens: The Social Ethics Implied in Brandeis of Boston,* 1 J.L. & RELIGION 59 (1983).

34. R. SUMMERS, INSTRUMENTALISM AND AMERICAN LEGAL THEORY (1982). *See also* P. MURPHY, THE CONSTITUTION IN CRISIS TIMES, 1918-1969 76 (1972).

35. 2 HOLMES-LASKI LETTERS 941-42 (M. Howe ed.) (1953).

36. 247 U.S. 251, 280 (1918).

37. M. LERNER, THE MIND AND FAITH OF JUSTICE HOLMES 147, 174 (1943).

38. Here Holmes's Darwinism clearly shows through, since he based his dissent on the Darwinian principle that great size was a natural and necessary consequence of evolutionary growth with which the state would be ill-advised to interfere. Northern Securities Co. v. U.S., 193 U.S. 197 (1904). For Holmes's view on state antitrust law, see May, *Antitrust Practice and Procedure in the Formative Era: The Constitutional and Conceptual Reach of State Antitrust Law, 1880-1918,* 135 U. PA. L. REV. 495, 545 (1987).

39. 208, U.S. 412 (1908).

40. T. MCCRAW, PROPHETS OF REGULATION 158-59 (1984).

41. On Brandeis literature see Murphy, *The Recent Fascination with Louis D. Brandeis,* 1984 WIS. L. REV. 1391 (1984).

42. The address is analyzed in A. MASON, A FREE MAN'S LIFE 245 (1946).

43. Brandeis, *The Living Law,* 10 ILL. L. REV. 461, 468 (1916).

44. 208 U.S. 412 (1908). For a careful assessment of the questionables of the brief's data and its use, Bryden, *Brandeis's Facts,* 1 CONST. COMMENTARY 281 (1984).

45. MCCRAW, *supra,* note 40, at 84.

46. *Id.,* 89.

47. On the episode see J. PENNICK, PROGRESSIVE POLITICS AND CONSERVATION; THE BALLINGER-PINCHOT AFFAIR (1968).

48. MCCRAW, *supra,* note 40, at 329-30.

49. *Id.* at 107.

50. A. LINK, WILSON: THE ROAD TO THE WHITE HOUSE (1947).

51. American Column and Lumber Co. v. U.S., 257 U.S. 377 (1921).

52. *Id.* at 412. For a perceptive analysis of a case (Pennsylvania Coal Co. v. Mahon, 260 U.S. 393 (1922)), in which Holmes threw out a piece of state social legislation over Brandeis's dissent, see *But cf.,* 1 CONST. COMMENTARY 183 (1984).

53. Liggett v. Lee, 288 U.S. 517 (1933).

54. 257 U.S. 312 (1920).

55. On Pound's early career see SUTHERLAND, *supra,* note 20, at 236.

56. Pound's career in legal education took him from Nebraska (as professor and dean, 1901) to Northwestern (1907-1909), to the University of Chicago (1909-1911), to Harvard (professor, 1911-1947; dean, 1915-1936).

57. Pound had also been impressed with Holmes's dissent in Lochner v. New York, 198 U.S. 45 (1905), hailing it as the "best exposition of... sociological jurisprudence" extant in America. Pound, *Liberty of Contract,* 18 YALE L. J. 454, 464 (1909). On Pound's overall career see D. WIGDOR, ROSCOE POUND: PHILOSOPHER OF LAW (1974).

58. Pound, *The Theory of Judicial Decision,* 36 HARV. L. REV. 641 (1923).

59. Pound was not a curricular innovator. The Harvard Law School curriculum remained traditional during his deanship. Further, he deplored the iconoclasm of the legal realists who staged a curricular revolution at law schools like Yale, Columbia, and Johns Hopkins in the late 1920s and early 1930s.

60. G. WHITE, PATTERNS OF AMERICAN LEGAL THOUGHT 107 (1978).

61. H. COMMAGER, THE AMERICAN MIND 381 (1950).

Evolving Conceptions of 'Property' And 'Liberty' in Due Process Jurisprudence

GLEN O. ROBINSON*

I. Preface: History and Interpretation

Justice Holmes, echoing Jefferson, once observed that "the present has a right to govern itself so far as it can; and it ought always to be remembered that historic continuity with the past is not a duty, it is only a necessity."[1] Holmes's observation, at least the first part of it, is quintessential American modernism. American legal culture in particular has resisted the kind of respect for historic tradition that has characterized its English antecedent. Possibly it has something to do with the character of American politics, which is predisposed towards a pragmatic governance hostile to the constraints imposed by history and tradition. Too, Americans need to assimilate, and assimilating and accommodating divergent cultural traditions undermines the authority of historical tradition.

Taking Holmes's edict seriously, one might wonder how much room it leaves for constitutionalism, insofar as it restrains contemporary choice based on historic commitments. However, a constitution is more than an artifact of history. If that were all there were to it, we should be content to allow our state and Federal Constitutions to repose in quiet archives and museums, undisturbed but for the occasional scrutiny of academic historians. It is because a constitution, especially the United States Constitution, speaks importantly to our *contemporary* needs that we accept constitutional limitations on public choice.

*For helpful comments I am indebted to Lynn Baker, Hal Bruff, Ron Cass, Ed Kitch, David Martin, Ellen Frankel Paul, Ed Rubin, George Rutherglen, Steve Saltzburg, Bill Stuntz, and other colleagues who participated in a Virginia Legal Studies Workshop presentation of an earlier draft of this paper.

63

Mindful of the fact that the ultimate authority of the Constitution (hereafter for convenience I shall refer specifically to the United States Constitution, though most of the points have application to state constitutions as well) derives from the *contemporary* relevance of its basic principles, some modern constitutional scholars—political liberals for the most part—are disposed to ignore the historical character of the Constitution and to free constitutional adjudication from the historic intent of the Framers embedded in the text. They appeal directly to "fundamental values" derived from shared social norms. The norms are associated with the principles set forth by the Framers two centuries ago. However, they are not identical to such principles; they have a life of their own.[2]

This fluid constitutionalism, 'noninterpretivism' as it is sometimes styled in constitutional law discourse, is the despair of 'interpretivists'—conservatives in the main—who insist on anchoring constitutional principles in interpretations of the text, and in meanings that may be reasonably ascribed to its creators or discerned in the *zeitgeist* of the period in which the text was written, explained, and ratified.[3] On this interpretivist view the search for fundamental constitutional values, if it is meaningful at all, must be bounded by those values that were captured in *the* Constitution at a fixed point in time; all else is the invention of judges.

It is hard to know precisely what Holmes himself would have made of the contemporary debates between noninterpretivists and interpretivists. As his comment about the past suggests, Holmes basically subscribed to a constitutional philosophy of judicial restraint in reviewing social legislation. At the same time, he also thought the Constitution represented fundamental values that bounded legislative choice, and like modern noninterpretivists he regarded these fundamental values as fluid, not fixed in the constitutional text or the original values of the Framers. The authority of the Constitution is not embedded in some forever-fixed text; it takes on new meaning over time. At the same time it is not the instant invention of contemporary judges. Fundamental values presuppose a history. To say that historical continuity is "*only* a necessity" is obviously not to deny its importance.

No doubt it is true, as modern theorists tell us, that history itself is partly a product of our present circumstances and, *pace* Thomas Kuhn, interpretive "paradigms."[4] But then it is equally valid to say that all "reality" is observer dependent. Fact is, we the observers are creatures of a past; that the past may be an artifact of our own interpretation does not change the "reality" that we are not entirely free at any moment to cast it aside. As Holmes said, "the past fixes our vocabulary and fixes the limits of our imagination"[5]—particularly, we may add, in regard to those social and cultural beliefs that underlie our constitutional norms.

By that token historical continuity is also, in a sense Holmes didn't recognize, a "duty" of sorts insofar as historical interpretation becomes an important means of establishing and authenticating authority in regard to those aspects of social life and organization that are grounded in historical continuity. The use of history as legal precedent is deeply ingrained in law, and particularly but not exclusively in the common law. Precedent has several functional purposes that are somewhat independent of historical continuity.[6] It helps to assure equal treatment of like groups, for example, and this function presupposes only minimal continuity with the past. Too, precedent promotes certainty in the law, and again this objective requires only minimal, short-term, historical continuity. However, quite apart from these functional purposes that only marginally implicate the historical sense, law does appeal to historical continuity as a means of reinforcing authority.

Legal positivists, like John Austin,[7] may insist that ultimately law is the force of sovereign authority, but every legal system depends on more than force in the crude sense of physical coercion and threat. As H. L. A. Hart put it, there is a difference between legal obligation and the gunman's threat, "give me your money or your life."[8] Intrinsic to the concept of the "force of law" is a collective sense on the part of those subject to it that the laws have some claim of legitimacy that transcends raw power.[9] This legitimacy is importantly bound to history. An appeal to the utilitarian value of particular rules of law, or an appeal to basic or fundamental rights and obligations, is almost never sufficient without some further appeal to a tradition in which utility, rights, and duties have withstood the "test of time"—what Max Weber called "the authority of the 'eternal yesterday'."[10]

Of course, laws are created every day that appear to have no important past. Traffic laws, regulatory laws, laws collecting and spending taxes for the general welfare—the routine stuff of legislation—do not draw immediately on authority, at least in their particulars. However, even here there is typically some appeal to history in identifying the general subject as one appropriate for public choice. That appeal becomes more important when constitutional questions surface. American constitutional law is perforce historically oriented. Those who want corroboration of the practical importance of appeals to history as authority have only to scan Supreme Court opinions which constantly appeal to history, even when they have to revise it to make it come out right.[11]

I mentioned that some modern scholars have sought to ground constitutional law in fundamental moral principles or shared social values in order to free constitutional interpretation from pure historical interpretation. In large measure I agree with their views, though I concede to the critics that it is maddeningly difficult to divine what values are truly shared or are truly fundamental in a pluralistic society.[12] However, part of the difficulty for a fundamental values jurisprudence may lie in the attempt by some exponents to derive it from purely contemporary political or moral argument more or less independent of precedent and historic attitudes. Such attempts are bound to be frustrated, as ephiphenomenal political controversy obscures more enduring concepts. Particularly in a heterogeneous society, historic continuity, by providing a common social identity with the past, provides the essential glue of contemporary consensus.

The importance of historic continuity should not be confused with "original intent," that rhetorical beacon of conservative politicians and (some) conservative constitutional scholars. Given that we have a written Constitution, it is natural for historical interpretation to take the form of looking for authorial intent, in order to derive our authority from the text as it was originally intended or generally understood. It is a misguided strategy, for reasons rehearsed so often they probably don't bear recounting. I will recount them anyway, but briefly.

To begin with the matter of authorial intent, in addition to significant problems of historical documentation,[13] there is the familiar problem of deriving a singular "intent" from a collective body of authors. We have it from Madison himself that drafting the Constitution was "the work of many heads and many hands,"[14] and, manifestly, the compromises that were worked out among them provide occasion for ambiguity of "intent." And presumably the understanding of the ratifiers must be consulted as well, compounding the problem of reconstructing a coherent intent. All of this is plain as a pikestaff to anyone who has thought about problems of "legislative" intent, but it is a problem typically finessed rather than resolved. The finesse commonly takes the form of adverting to evidence of agreement on general principles without the close scrutiny of possibly divergent understandings as to what the agreement meant on matters of detail. The fact that the Framers were able to reach agreement on constitutional fundamentals has tended to obscure the very different interests and ideological conceptions lying beneath the consensus[15]—interests and conceptions that inevitably produced different views of what the "agreement" meant.[16]

Even if one sets aside these problems, interpretation presents formidable difficulties. A *strict* adherence to the Framers' intent would imply not merely fidelity to the constitutional values they embraced but also their own principles of constitutional interpretation. (This may not be a logical necessity; however, one must at least offer a plausible theory justifying adherence to the Framers' substantive but not their hermeneutic principles; I am unaware of any attempt to construct such a theory.) However, fidelity to the Framers' principles of legal interpretation proves awkward if not simply embarrassing, for the historical evidence indicates that the Framers thought of constitutional interpretation as essentially an exercise in textual exegesis on the model of formalist contract construction, not a search for authorial intent in the style of modern legislative-purpose analysis.[17]

It requires no argument to demonstrate the unrealism of such a formalist approach today, for I think no serious constitutionalist would assert that we could derive meaningful contemporary guidance from the text by means of simple textual exegesis alone. Sensible interpretivists themselves allow not only for the use of extrinsic evidence of intent, but also contemplate constructions of intent that allow contemporary adaptations—providing those adaptations preserve the original basic values. No one denies application of the First Amendment to, say, radio and television simply because the Framers could not have had any notion of "speech" by these media. Similarly, it would be considered frivolous to gainsay that the Fourth Amendment applies to wiretaps and other modern surveillance technology, even though the Framers would have been entirely innocent of such devices. And so on. It is enough, the interpretivist argument goes, that we maintain fidelity to the relevant social values as the Framers conceived them. A similar approach underlies the view that the source of constitutional meaning is not strict authorial intent, but the general understanding of the time.[18]

But the quest for original values can be highly misleading. Even if one could retrieve an accurate original understanding in general or a specific authorial intent, there is still a problem of relevance. The inquiry into "intent," for example, cannot be confined to what the Framers thought about two hundred years ago. After all, we know that they did not think about the lawfulness of television regulation or of aerial surveillance of industrial sites or... The list of contemporary constitutional disputes that they did not think about is endless. Plainly, we must be a little "creative" in how we think about original intent. It cannot be simply a matter of what, say, Madison thought, but what Madison would think today, for it is only in the latter context that his values can make any sense to us. The same is true for the collective Framers, ratifiers, or even general public whose views are supposed to be the basis for an "original understanding."

The problem of reconstruction is not solved simply by extracting the core values from the Framers' thought and transporting them to the present, as some originalists appear to suppose. Values are not Platonic ideals or Kantian *noumena* lying outside the realm of phenomenal existence; they are the contingent product of our environment and our experience. Consider, for example, the recent emphasis, in historical and constitutional scholarship, on the influence of "civic republican" thought on the Framers.[19] The discovery of civic republicanism provides an important perspective on historical understandings, and thence on "original" constitutional values. However, quite aside from controversy about the importance of republican thought to the Framers,[20] one has to be cautious in interpreting republicanism both in the context of their time and ours. The Framers' admiration for the civic virtues of ancient republics was as much the product of eighteenth-century Whiggish politics as it was of anything to be found in classical Rome, Athens, or Sparta. Indeed, in some instances it is apparent that the conception of traditional republicanism was more the product of romantic imagination than reflective political theory. Samuel Adams's dream of reconstructing a "Christian Sparta" in Boston[21] cannot have been based on an informed understanding of *historic* Spartan or Christian values.

So too with contemporary constitutionalism: while the appeal of a republican vision of public life is considerable, one ought not to imagine that its revivification today is a simple matter of translating eighteenth-century letters and pamphlets into modern prose and plugging them into contemporary controversies.[22] Even applying an originalist perspective, how can we be sure that the core principles we discern in the Framers' world would still be so regarded (by them) if they lived in ours? Would Samuel Adams believe in a Christian Sparta for modern Boston? Even if the *general* principles would survive the transferal, can we determine the scope of their application? Would the Framers have the same view of the value of "freedom of speech and of the press" if they had television? I am not asking whether Madison would think "Friday the 13th, Part 10," or "The Dating Game" worthy of protection; I am asking how his view of the press's function generally might be influenced by exposure to such a radically new sociocultural phenomenon as television.

Some modern philosophers of interpretation have suggested the idea of a dialogue with authors, be they literary or legal, as a means of recovering the contemporary essence of the author's intent. Stanley Cavell, for example, has suggested such an approach to literary interpretation, and Ronald Dworkin has extended it to legal interpretation.[23] Something similar has been suggested by Richard Rorty in the context of the history of philosophical thought.[24] The argument for "dialogic reconstruction," if we can call it that, seems especially strong in the case of constitutional interpretation of a text written two hundred years ago. If we wish to recapture the values Madison sought to embody in the Constitution, Madison must be given a voice we can understand. We cannot be put back into his world; he must be brought into ours, through the heuristic of transhistorical conversation.

Needless to say, at this point we have come so far from what is conventionally regarded as "originalism" that the usefulness of that perspective is brought into doubt. Strict interpretivists will undoubtedly agree that we have ventured too far, though they will derive a different conclusion from the point: an updated Madison is a fiction that only obscures the fact that we are no longer "interpreting" the Constitution; therefore the historical conversation must be rejected. However, rejecting the historical conversation is not logically compelled, for it is equally sensible to reject the idea of interpretivism itself, in every form. After all, if we cannot adhere to literal rendering of text or a precisely historical account of the original understanding, what is gained by interpretivism? It really comes down to a choice of fictions.

Interpretivists, of course, want to fix on original intent out of fear that anything but a fixed reference point will open up constitutional interpretation to free-form judicial lawmaking in accordance with contemporary convenience. The fear of an unconstrained judiciary is reasonable, though much exaggerated in my view. One must keep an eye on social purpose. Curbing judicial discretion in matters of social choice is not an end in itself; the rationale for constraining judges is to give greater rein to democratic public choice—to "we the people," through our political representatives. However, that preference necessarily assumes the preeminent legitimacy of the political process whatever outcomes it produces; the argument from democracy turns out to be an argument against constitutional judicial review generally. Constitutionalism without judicial review is not unthinkable of course, as the English experience demonstrates, but it is not the system we have accepted since *Marbury v. Madison* in 1803.[25]

I do not propose here to review the case for constitutional restraint on political choice. It is enough to observe that the virtues of democratic political choice are not enhanced by being attached to original intent as a lodestar of constitutional review. If judges are not reliable representatives of contemporary public preferences, they are surely more so than the small, elite group of delegates to the Constitutional Convention who, by modern democratic standards, could not be thought representatives of the general public even then.[26] Again, *mutatis mutandis*, the same point is valid even if one refers not to the Framers but to the entire American society at the time of the Constitution. We are back to Holmes's dictum (and Jefferson's). In short, if what we want is democracy, it is hard to see the relevance of value choices made by our forebears two hundred years ago.

As an argument for originalism, the appeal to democratic political choice simply cannot be taken seriously. A more substantial argument is that originalism at least preserves the special status of constitutional values against the erosion of everyday political convenience. In a sense, this is just the reverse of the argument from democracy, and it appeals precisely to the nature of constitutionalism as a means of anchoring basic institutional arrangements and basic public values against the ebb and flow of ordinary political controversy.

The argument for stable political arrangements and social norms is intrinsic to any meaningful conception of what constitutionalism is all about. But, once more, it is not an argument for originalism. A lot of history has passed since the United States Constitution was adopted; its constitutional meaning has changed in light of contemporary circumstances. We could not recover the constitutional world of the eighteenth century if we wanted to, and we should not want to.

Suppose tomorrow we were to discover a manuscript in Madison's handwriting in which he records that it was the unanimous and *explicit* view of everyone present in the First Congress that enacted the Bill of Rights that the due process clause of the Fifth Amendment applied only to judicial proceedings and had no application to administrative proceedings. Is it conceivable that we would reverse over one hundred years of contrary judicial interpretation[27] in order to restore fidelity to Madison's world?[28] It is not credible that Madison himself or his colleagues would have wished us to do so.[29] Imagine a conversation with Madison in which it is explained how contemporary administrative proceedings have assumed roles unanticipated in the eighteenth century—including many adjudicatory tasks then performed by the courts for which the due process clause was centrally designed. If we take as a constant the animating purpose of due process to protect life, liberty, and property against arbitrary government action, one can construct a sensible—if fictional—dialogue in which Madison would come easily to the conclusion that this modern extension of due process is in the spirit of original intent even though the need for such an extension could not have been entertained at the time. Notwithstanding the desire of some modern "strict" constructionists to return us to the original understanding regardless of intermediate glosses, such a move would be disruptive to the very conservative political values that the strict constructionists profess to honor. Leaping over intervening history in order to recapture some original intent, even supposing we could recover that intent, would not promote historical continuity so much as it would historical archaeology.

I do not say that original meanings, original understandings, are of no consequence either to historians or to constitutional lawyers; I mean to argue only that the appeal to history is not a mere appeal to permanently fixed reference points scattered over time. It is rather an appeal to historic evolution, to an evolving understanding of intent and meaning.

It is on this account that this paper is concerned with the *evolving* conceptions of due process jurisprudence, particularly the evolving conceptions of 'property' and 'liberty'. I shall not be indifferent to the Framers' original conceptions; indeed I hope to show that those conceptions were rather broader than have sometimes been supposed by contemporary interpreters. Nevertheless, I am more interested in the evolution of due process jurisprudence and particularly conceptions of 'property' and 'liberty' within the meaning of the Fifth and Fourteenth Amendments.

I start with some general, and brief, comments on the reach of due process, its substantive and its procedural applications. The primary focus of this paper is procedural due process. I thereby hope to finesse most of the interpretive and philosophical controversies over whether and how far due process should constrain substantive legislation, controversies that must be considered independently of the meaning of property and liberty. But, of course, procedural and substantive due process protection for property and liberty are derived from the same text. For this reason some brief observations on the realms of both substantive and procedural due process will be appropriate. Whether or not the Framers ever intended the due process clause to have substantive application (about which more later), we have no reason to think they would have thought the words 'property' and 'liberty' meant one thing in the context of substantive constitutional protection and another in the context of procedural protection. (Again notice the need for "creative" interpretation, for it does not appear that the Framers thought of due process in terms of a substantive/procedural dichotomy.)

Next I turn to a closer examination of the conceptions of property and liberty. It is a little odd that after two hundred years of constitutional history the basic meaning of these concepts continues to be a matter of vexing uncertainty. Inasmuch as the due process clauses of the Fifth and Fourteenth Amendments apply only to deprivation of "life, liberty and property," one might expect that defining these terms—at least the latter two ('life' being essentially unproblematic in the due process context)—would be an important judicial ambition from the outset of due process adjudication. In fact it was not. The Court did give some attention to the concept of 'liberty' in the context of substantive due process cases after the Civil War (specifically on the question of whether liberty embraced occupational freedom), but it gave no comparable attention to "property."

In both substantive and procedural contexts the Court has historically regarded property and liberty more as broad, "atmospheric" concepts than as terms of legal precision. In earlier times, the Court gave little attention to how the underlying rights were defined, to what were the precise bases for 'property' or 'liberty'. The Court appears to have regarded these questions as unimportant; the emphasis was on the process, not the precise characterization of the interests protected. Only in recent times has the Court, in the context of procedural due process, focused on these terms as artful words of limitation on the application of due process. In doing so the Court has sparked a controversy that is the principal reason for this inquiry into the historical evolution of these concepts. In my view of the history, the Court's earlier treatment of property and liberty is more congruent with the Framers' understanding and purpose.

It is also, I argue, a more sensible rule of construction for contemporary constitutional judgments. However, this argument is perhaps made most boldly by my further conclusion that, as a practical matter, the debate over the definition of property and liberty probably does not have very large importance in contemporary due process jurisprudence, for the simple reason that these terms have become so protean as to be essentially formless. Too, I shall argue that the question of what constitutes property and liberty is generally overwhelmed by the question, what is the scope of protection afforded them by the procedural or substantive standards of due process? Where substantive due process retains any vitality, the Court's concerns tend to focus on the effects of and the justification for government action; seldom is there any occasion for considering the origin or nature of the property or liberty right. In procedural due process the nature of the threshold right has recently been given more importance by the Court, but the question is still but a prelude to the dominant issue of what process is required—a question that turns only slightly on the definition of the underlying right.

II. The Reach Of Due Process:
Substantive and Procedural Applications

Interpreting the scope of the due process clauses of the Fifth and Fourteenth Amendments is one of the most vexing problems in constitutional law, and one of the most important. At its most fundamental philosophical level it involves nothing less than a determination of the limits of governmental power. On a more instrumental (practical) level it involves a determination of the allocation of government power among the judiciary, the legislature, and the executive.

The Uses of Due Process

There have always been misgivings about the use of due process as a substantive constraint on legislative power. As I said earlier, doubts have been expressed as to whether the Framers ever intended the Fifth Amendment to have substantive application, and the same doubts have been extended to the Fourteenth Amendment, which applied due process to the states. Both the literal text and its origins in English constitutional history support a limited construction.[30] On the other hand a broader conception of due process is suggested by the fact that the Framers were deeply suspicious of government power, particularly (though not solely) legislative power. As inheritors of the Whiggish tradition, the Framers embraced the Constitution as an expression of the social contract, an instrument of fundamental law, the essence of which was to protect man's natural rights—life, liberty and property—against government power, however exercised.[31] In contrast to English constitutionalism, moreover, the Framers considered and explicitly rejected the English concept of parliamentary supremacy. Indeed, it was the foremost innovation of American constitutional theory that it not only rejected legislative supremacy in principle but did so by making legislatures accountable in ordinary law courts, in effect incorporating natural law into positive law.[32]

It does not follow, of course, that the Framers intended the *due process clause* to shoulder the burden of substantive protection of life, liberty and property, and obviously the due process clause was not intended to carry the *full* burden, as the text demonstrates throughout by its array of constitutional constraints on government action, for example: the contracts clause (Article I, Section 10), the privileges and immunities clause (Article IV), the takings clause (Fifth Amendment). Nevertheless, giving substantive content to due process is at least faithful to the animating spirit of the Framers. The very essence of their commitment to a higher law embedded in the Constitution is the notion of a substantive limit on government interference with basic individual rights.

In any event, however the historical record is interpreted, it has long been accepted that the due process clause does impose some substantive restraints on government action. Just how long it has been accepted is a matter of some dispute, a dispute that turns on one's interpretation of pre-Civil War precedent, mainly state decisions construing state constitutional text and "natural law" doctrine. We shall have occasion to review some of those precedents later (see pp. 82–86) insofar as they illuminate early conceptions of 'property' and 'liberty'.

The history of the United States Supreme Court's treatment of this question begins essentially with post-Civil War interpretation of Fourteenth Amendment due process. Prior to the Fourteenth Amendment there was scarcely any occasion to address it, since the Fifth Amendment applied only to the federal government, the activities of which at that time did not involve important confrontation with liberty or property rights. After refusing to give substantive content to due process in the 1873 *Slaughterhouse Cases*[33] the Court eventually followed the lead of several important state court precedents (and the insistent arguments of Justice Field who had dissented on this point in the *Slaughterhouse Cases*). In *Allgeyer v. Louisiana*[34] in 1897, the Court formally embraced substantive due process, providing the foundation for the "infamous" *Lochner* case[35] in 1905 and the "era" named after it. We need not pause to review the history of that era; it has been adequately chronicled by others.[36] A few general comments suffice to provide the foundation necessary for further reference.

Allgeyer, Lochner and their progeny are commonly associated with judicial review of economic regulatory legislation, but, of course, the underlying principle swept across other legislation with equal if not greater force. *Meyer v. Nebraska* (1923)[37] described the ambitious scope of the principle. Meyer had been convicted of violating a state law prohibiting the teaching of foreign languages to school children until after they had passed the eighth grade. He challenged the law as an infringement of his liberty under the Fourteenth Amendment. Upholding his challenge, the Court, through Justice McReynolds, offered a breathtakingly expansive definition of the liberty that was protected against "arbitrary" legislation. Liberty includes:

> the right of the individual to contract, to engage in any of the common occupations of life, to acquire useful knowledge, to marry, establish a home and bring up children, to worship God according to the dictates of his own conscience, and generally to enjoy those privileges long recognized at common law as essential to the orderly pursuit of happiness by free men.[38]

Justice Holmes dissented, in an opinion that carries neither the clear conviction nor rhetorical power of his celebrated *Lochner* dissent.[39] Two years later, when the Court in *Pierce v. Society of Sisters*[40] invoked *Meyer* to invalidate a state statute compelling attendance at public schools, no dissent was registered by Holmes or any other member of the Court.

As is well-known, some of the rights catalogued by Justice McReynolds have proved to be more robust than others. *Meyer's* right to pursue an occupation and Lochner's right to contract—"economic liberties" generally— became essentially subordinate interests when the Court virtually abandoned substantive review of economic and social legislation after *West Coast v. Parrish* in 1937.[41] *Lochner,* though never overruled, was discredited; "Lochnerism" became an epithet, a one-word slander of a dishonored era of judicial arrogance. But active judicial review did not die; nor did substantive due process. Among *Meyer's* expansive list of liberties the Court perceived certain so-called "personal liberties," for which legislative judgment would not be given the same broad latitude as in the case of economic interests.

In 1965, *Griswold v. Connecticut,*[42] invalidating a state law criminalizing the use of contraceptives, became the new model for substantive due process, by recognizing a personal right of privacy. Despite an effort by Justice Douglas, writing for the Court, to eschew due process doctrine, the case was generally acknowledged as an application of due process, as was its celebrated offspring in 1973, *Roe v. Wade,*[43] striking down a state law criminalizing abortion. In *Roe* and *Griswold* significant reliance was placed on *Meyer* and *Pierce;* their authority was untouched by the decline of *Lochner.* Four years later, in *Moore v. East Cleveland,*[44] the Court provided what is probably the clearest exemplar of modern substantive due process in the course of invalidating a city ordinance that interfered with family living arrangements. The evil of *Lochnerian* interference with legislative judgments was acknowledged but set aside, because of the personal liberty interest in family living choices. The Court has been chary about extending the *Griswold-Roe-Moore* line. Indeed, the Court's 1986 decision in *Bowers v. Hardwick,*[45] rejecting a constitutional challenge to a state law criminalizing sodomy, could be taken as signaling a retreat from this line of cases.

The evolution of substantive due process doctrine has proceeded more or less separately from the evolution of procedural due process. Substantive and procedural due process share a common text and little more. In political theory it has long been conventional to see process constraints as a substitute for substantive limitations on the power of government. This is a consequence of the triumph of interest group political theory. Interest group theory, which became mainstream political theory *circa* the 1950s,[46] taught us that there was no "public interest," that is, no fixed set of substantive criteria by which legitimate public interests could be identified. Legitimacy was wholly defined by fair and "responsible" process. This pluralistic political theory has been influential in modern constitutional theory, as John Hart Ely's work attests.[47]

For Ely, judicial review is legitimate only to correct or compensate for structural failure in the political process whereby certain groups are denied fair representation.

It is important to notice that Ely's theory of review is process-*based* ("representation reinforcing"), but it does not prescribe or define particular political processes, except in the sense of guaranteeing electoral representation and forbidding Congress from delegating broad power to unelected bureaucrats.[48] Subject only to these minimal conditions, the internal dynamics of the legislative process are of no concern to Ely, just as they are of no concern to constitutional doctrine, which imposes no procedural constraints on the legislative process apart from requirements prescribed for enactment of laws and related institutional constraints.[49] However, when legislative power is transferred to the executive, and thence to administrative agencies, the exercise of that power is subject to procedural due process. As the role of executive officers and administrative bureaucrats has expanded, it is natural that process theorists should come to think of procedural due process as *the* guarantee of individual rights.[50]

One might perhaps explain the Court's retreat from *Allgeyer-Lochner* as opting for procedural over substantive due process. Unfortunately, that explanation presumes more coherence to the Court's procedural due process jurisprudence than exists in fact. As with substantive due process, the Supreme Court's development of constitutional doctrine has been uneven. Actually to call it "uneven" is a bit misleading to the extent it might imply minor surface bumps, when in fact it is often difficult to define the surface.

It is now conventional to identify two separate questions in procedural due process analysis: first, what interests are protected—the definition of "liberty" and "property" ("life," as I noted earlier, is nonproblematical in this context); second, what process is "due" when those interests are threatened.[51] My main interest is in the first question; it is, I think, the more theoretically interesting of the two, and it has been the more deeply controversial throughout the history of due process, even though for most of that history it was the second that received primary attention.

Protected Interests

The origins and general content of the due process clause were identified fairly early. The Supreme Court, in *Murray's Lessee*[52] (1855), authoritatively traced the origins of due process to Magna Charta and interpreted the general procedural content to embrace the elements of traditional judicial procedure as applied by the common law. The Court there did not have to ask what interests were protected by due process. The underlying interest in *Murray's Lessee* was unambiguously "property"; the only question was whether seizure of the property pursuant to a distress warrant was *due* process. The Court, relying on long historic usage, held that it was.

For over one hundred years after *Murray's Lessee,* the focus of due process adjudication was on the content of due process. The interests protected by it received little, if any, attention. In most instances, as in *Murray's Lessee,* the existence of the requisite interest—"right"—was plain. However, even where it was not plain, courts tended to avoid a close examination of the issue by resort to summary labels: protected interests were declared to be "rights," unprotected interests were mere "privileges." Their defining characteristics were left unidentified.[53]

To make matters worse, the right-privilege dichotomy was intertwined with another notion that tended to obscure inquiry into the nature of protected and unprotected interests; this was the idea that individual rights could be limited or even terminated as a condition of receiving benefits dispensed at the discretion of the government.[54] Both the right-privilege notion and that of conditioned rights (or, as it has been more commonly but misleadingly labeled, "unconstitutional conditions") have had a checkered history. The notion that "rights" could be limited or terminated as a condition of receiving benefits or "privileges" such as public employment was never unambiguously embraced by the Court. By the same token its supposed repudiation in modern times has been equivocal. The modern doctrine is invariably phrased as a simple absolute principle: the grant of privileges (benefits) may not be conditioned on the relinquishment of "constitutional rights." Its application, however, is rather more complex and subtle. The government may not require individuals to forfeit their rights as a condition of receiving government benefits or employment or other "privileges." But such "privileges" are nevertheless routinely accepted as an occasion and a reason for restricting the exercise of rights.[55]

The right-privilege distinction, which draws inspiration from much the same spirit as the conditioned rights idea, enjoyed more recent currency, though it too was eventually discredited. Again, however, the formal rhetoric is somewhat misleading. It is a widely shared perception that the distinction lives on in fact if not in name, as we shall see.

In its heyday, the right-privilege distinction was frequently invoked in the context of occupational licensure cases to decide whether persons whose licenses were revoked or suspended were entitled to some kind of notice and hearing. The cases are not uniform and it is difficult to find the traces of a coherent theory or policy. About the most one can say is that the courts regarded some occupational pursuits as being wholly at the sufferance of government, hence unprotected, while others were intrinsic rights of the individual, hence entitled to due process.[56] Even this generalization is problematic, however, because the question of whether due process was applicable is frequently obscured in these cases by the finding that its requirements were satisfied by, say, opportunity to seek subsequent judicial review of the action.[57]

Bailey v. Richardson[58] (1950) is commonly regarded as a leading example of the right-privilege approach. The court of appeals there upheld the summary discharge of a government employee pursuant to a loyalty-security program (which provided for dismissal of employees where there were "reasonable grounds" to believe that the employee was disloyal). Bailey was given notice that "informants believed to be reliable had made general statements purporting to connect her with the Communist Party." She was allowed to respond to the allegations in writing, but was given no further specifics as to who made the allegations or the factual basis for them. The court purported not to reach the question whether the process was sufficient, though it suggested it was. It held that, in any case, due process was inapplicable inasmuch as she had no right to government employment—neither "property" nor "liberty," within the meaning of the Fifth Amendment, was implicated.

Bailey was affirmed by an equally divided Supreme Court, but it was soon marked as an endangered precedent. In the 1950s and 1960s, in a variety of substantive constitutional cases, the Court rejected the notion that public employment or receipt of other government benefits could be terminated without constitutional constraint because they were mere privileges.[59] The Court was reluctant to acknowledge procedural due process rights in such cases, but the drift of its decisions was headed in that direction.[60] It was only a matter of time before the results coincided with the rhetoric.

That time came in 1970 in *Goldberg v. Kelly*.[61] *Goldberg* involved a due process challenge to state and city regulations establishing procedures for terminating financial aid payments (AFDC payments) to ineligible recipients. Under the regulations, local officials proposing to discontinue or suspend aid on grounds of ineligibility were required to give notice to recipient of the reasons for the determination of ineligibility and an opportunity to seek review of the determination by a welfare officer superior to the one making the initial decision. While no provision was made for personal appearance or oral hearing prior to termination, a full hearing after termination of aid was specified. The Court, with but a single dissent (Justice Black), held that these procedures were inadequate. Considering welfare recipients' dire need for financial assistance, their interest in a hearing *prior* to termination of benefits was found to outweigh the interest argued by the state and local authorities, conserving fiscal and administrative resources (by stopping payments promptly on discovering reasons to believe recipients were no longer eligible, and reducing expenditures on hearings that would not otherwise be demanded by recipients).

The decision is remarkable for its holding that due process required a full oral hearing (personal appearance, right to be represented by counsel, cross examination, impartial decision maker, determination based solely on evidence addressed at the hearing) *before* termination. But the more important aspect of the decision was Justice Brennan's broad opinion on the applicability of due process generally. Though the applicability of due process to the case was not challenged, Justice Brennan nevertheless took the occasion to elaborate on some broad principles for the application of due process in the modern welfare state. Noting first that the particular benefits at stake in this case were a matter of statutory entitlement, Justice Brennan suggested that all such

welfare entitlements might be regarded as a species of "property" protected by
due process:

> It may be realistic today to regard welfare entitlements as more like "property"
> than a "gratuity." Much of the existing wealth in this country takes the form
> of rights that do not fall within traditional common-law concepts of property.
> It has been aptly noted that
>
> "[s]ociety today is built around entitlement. The automobile dealer has his
> franchise, the doctor and lawyer their professional licenses, the worker his
> union membership, contract, and pension rights, the executive his contract
> and stock options; all are devices to aid security and independence. Many of
> the most important of these entitlements now flow from government: subsi-
> dies to farmers and businessmen, routes and airlines and channels for televi-
> sion stations; long term contracts for defense, space, and education; social
> security pensions for individuals. Such sources of security, whether private or
> public, are no longer regarded as luxuries or gratuities; to the recipients they
> are essentials, fully deserved, and in no sense a form of charity. It is only the
> poor whose entitlements, although recognized by public policy, have not
> been effectively enforced." Reich, Individual Rights and Social Welfare: The
> Emerging Legal Issues, 74 Yale L.J. 1245, 1255 (1965). See also Reich, The
> New Property, 73 Yale L.J. 733 (1964).[62]

Whether the entitlements are labeled "property" appears to be only a matter of
formalism for Justice Brennan, since the real criterion of due process applicability lies not in labels—"right" or "privilege"—but in the practical importance of the individual interest weighed against that of the government. A
general balancing test is embraced but with a strong suggestion of greatly
different weights for the respective individual and governmental interests.

    Goldberg is a pivotal case in the evolution (some say "revolution") of
modern due process. Building on a broad conception of entitlements—what
Charles Reich styled the "New Property"—it promised a new era of constitutional protection not only for individuals on public assistance but for virtually
everyone with some colorable claim of expectation interest: public employees,
licensees, Social Security claimants, pensioners...The list is as long as the
welfare state is broad. *Goldberg* supporters heralded this liberal solicitude for
welfare claimants. Critics were appalled; *Goldberg* could only enlarge the scope
of the welfare state itself, by transforming every welfare claim into a claim of
right.

    The liberal promise of *Goldberg* turned out to be short-lived. Only two
years later in *Board of Regents v. Roth,*[63] the Court declined to follow the path
that Justice Brennan had charted for it in *Goldberg.* In *Roth* an untenured
public university teacher claimed due process entitled him to a hearing on the
university's refusal to rehire him at the end of his one-year appointment term.
Under state law an untenured teacher had no procedural protection in case of a
simple refusal to rehire, and Roth had been given no reason for, nor any

opportunity to contest, the university's decision. Applying a simple balancing test, a la *Goldberg*, the district court found a violation of due process, a finding affirmed by the court of appeals. However, the Supreme Court rejected simple interest balancing as the dispositive criterion of due process. For *any* due process protection to apply, the Court ruled, it must first be shown that there was a deprivation of property and liberty. Roth had shown no such protected interest in this case. His liberty was not impaired, since Roth's ability to be employed elsewhere had not been jeopardized. No property right was implicated because Roth had no "legitimate claim of entitlement." The state law gave untenured teachers no such entitlement by contract or otherwise; at most Roth had a mere "unilateral expectation," which was insufficient. *Goldberg* was distinguished by the fact that there the benefits were a matter of expressed statutory entitlement.

In a companion to *Roth, Perry v. Sindermann,*[64] the Court reached a different result in the case of another university teacher who had been employed for four successive one-year terms and had been let go at the end of the last. In *Sindermann* the university had no formal tenure system, but its guidelines, on which Sindermann claimed reliance, had promised permanent tenure to teachers so long as their service was satisfactory. The Court held that this promise might be sufficient to create a "legitimate expectation of entitlement to continued employment"—hence a property right protected by due process. (Whether it did in fact create such an expectation was a question to be determined by the trial court.)

Although the Court in *Roth* purported to reject the old right-privilege distinction, specifically as used in *Bailey v. Richardson*, critics have claimed it did no such thing.[65] In truth it is not easy to articulate the difference between *Roth* and *Bailey*; the fact that *Roth* eschews the simplistic and question-begging term "privilege" does not alter the fact that it adheres to the operative part of the right-privilege distinction. Under *Roth* it is still necessary to locate an independent "right" to which due process can attach. Where such a right does not exist, it matters not whether we label the individual's unprotected interests a privilege or label them "nothing" (as in the ancient argot of contract interpretation, where the absence of the conditions of an enforceable contract was described as "*nudum pactum*").

III. Changing Conceptions of Liberty and Property

The Higher Law Tradition

Roth was faithful to the text of the Fifth and Fourteenth Amendments; so too, of course, was *Bailey*: due process is required only when a person is threatened with deprivation of "life, liberty or property." Unfortunately the Constitution is silent as to what these concepts mean. 'Life' is straightforward for the most part (allowing for the usual complications for the unborn fetus). But it is also nonproblematical in the usual, noncriminal, context of procedural due process. Despite recurrent provocation no one has yet suggested we deal with the shortcomings of public employees by shooting them, and notwithstanding Justice Brennan's claim in *Goldberg* that welfare payments are a "brutal need," the case has not yet arisen in which termination literally threatened the recipient's life. However, 'liberty' and 'property' are full of ambiguities that pure canonical interpretation cannot resolve.

It has been doubted that the Framers of the Amendment conceived of property and liberty in the capacious sense that these terms acquired in the early nineteenth century and have, to a degree, retained since. Contrary to Justice McReynolds's expansive view of 'liberty' in *Meyer,* which we saw earlier, most constitutional scholars have supposed that the original understanding of the concept followed Blackstone's exegesis of Magna Charta and denoted only freedom from imprisonment or, by extension, freedom from physical restraint.[66]

Accepting this as a reasonable historical interpretation (for want of any substantial evidence to the contrary), it should not be given much weight even within an interpretivist perspective. Inasmuch as the due process clause was designed for criminal prosecutions, it is not surprising that *for this purpose* liberty would be conceived in terms associated with criminal punishment. Had the Framers of the Fifth Amendment considered the present range of due process applications to administrative proceedings (which apparently even interpretivists do not dispute are legitimate and necessary applications), it seems plain that they would not have embraced Blackstone's narrow view.

However, the question of how broadly the Framers might have defined liberty in the modern context of due process is largely made moot in any event by the apparently capacious meaning given to "property." Certainly Madison, whose views on constitutional meaning are accorded great respect by most constitutionalists, had an expansive conception of property:

> This term in its particular application means "that dominion which one man claims and exercises over the external things of the world, in exclusion of every other individual."
>
> In its larger and juster meaning, it embraces every thing to which a man may attach a value and have a right; and which leaves to every one else the like advantage.
>
> In the former sense, a man's land, or merchandize, or money is called his property.
>
> In the latter sense, a man has property in his opinions and the free communication of them ....
>
> Government is instituted to protect property of every sort; as well that which lies in the various rights of individuals, as that which the term particularly expresses. This being the end of government, that alone is just government, which impartially secures to every man, whatever is his own.[67]

No doubt there is in Madison's essay an element of rhetoric to which we are properly cautious in attaching the weight of legal authority. And, rhetoric aside, I am mindful that it can be misleading to assume that specific words and phrases in the Constitution necessarily encapsulate general philosophical conceptions. Still, in matters of constitutional interpretation the line between legal meaning and philosophical, even rhetorical, statement is not a clear one. Even today, constitutional glossarists, the Supreme Court included, regularly consult the heavily rhetorical *Federalist* for pertinent "legislative history" concerning the Framers' intent—despite Madison's own cautions about relying on the *Federalist* inasmuch as the "authors might be sometimes influened by the zeal of advocates."[68] Madison's essay on property ought to command roughly comparable respect.

Madison's expansive view of property was consistent with the prevailing liberal view of property, an essentially Lockean conception.[69] For Locke property rights arise from human effort, from the mixing of labor with resources given by God to all persons. Property rights are the means by which human effort is legally recognized and secured against interference from others—including the state. Lockean property is a "natural right" of man, anterior to the state. The state gives *particular content* to property rights and enforces them through positive law. However, at bottom the ultimate authority for property derives not from positive law but from antecedent natural rights, the protection of which is the animating force of the social contract.

Locke's theory is not free of ambiguity or contradiction. Locke himself was obscure about the interrelationship between natural right and positive law and that ambiguity persists in American adaptations of Locke.[70] Also, the notion that property attaches itself to human efforts—"labor" broadly defined—is more than a little confused.[71] However, the general idea of property as a basic security for individual activity had, and has continued to have, a strong hold on western liberal political thought. That idea has survived attacks on Locke's particular formulation of natural rights and social contractarianism. Hume, for example, repudiated both natural rights and contractarianism but still embraced the substance of Locke's theory on a different premise. Like Adam Smith and the later utilitarians, Hume reached more or less the same result through arguments from utility: security for the fruits of individual activity was necessary (useful) to provide incentives for beneficial activity and thereby to promote "the convenience and necessities of mankind."[72]

Inasmuch as they were not tied to abstract natural rights concepts, the utilitarian arguments gave a broader sweep to the idea of property rights as security for individual freedom, and were influential with some early American thinkers. However, Locke's appeal to natural rights and social contractarianism appears to have been more influential in early American constitutional theory. "Natural law" and "natural rights" were the common vocabulary of political writing in the colonial and constitutional period;[73] natural rights to life, liberty, and property were explicitly declared by state bills of rights that were adopted after Independence.[74] Natural rights theory, of course, eventually succumbed to more modern positivist conceptions, but the appeal to fundamental rights, as something implicit in the very notion of an ordered society, persisted in writings on constitutional theory and in occasional judicial opinions well into the nineteenth century.[75]

Whatever its philosophical underpinnings, property was expansively conceived. Consistent with the view that it provided a security interest in the fruits of labor, property rights extended beyond tangible things capable of possessory interest. Madison's expansive definition is faithful to Locke for whom property was coextensive with the natural right to "lives, liberties and estates." In this view property is, indeed, mostly atmospheric—a kind of shorthand for the full range of liberty implied by Lockean liberalism, particularly economic liberty. It is, as Alan Ryan puts it, not "three acres and a cow" but the opportunity to seek work, "to make a living."[76]

How far this expansive Lockean-Madisonian concept of property was embraced by the early courts confronted with concrete constitutional controversies is not easy to determine; there is not an abundance of pertinent early precedents for the simple reason that there were not many occasions for addressing the question. Neither the states nor the federal government was vigorous in applying their respective powers in ways that encountered individual liberty or property rights. Such precedent as there is consists mainly of state cases, construing state constitutional due process clauses. (The Fifth Amendment's due process clause, of course, was inapplicable to the states until it was included in the Fourteenth Amendment.)[77]

Judicial Interpretations

Perhaps the most noteworthy early decision in support of an expansive, Lockean-Madisonian concept of property is an 1833 decision of the North Carolina Supreme Court in *Hoke v. Henderson*,[78] holding that a court clerk had a property right in his public office. Justice Ruffin, a leading judge of the period, explained:

> [Property] means ... whatever a person can possess or enjoy by right .... That an office is the subject of property thus explained, is well understood by everyone, as well as distinctly stated in the law books from the earliest times .... The office is created for public purpose; but it is conferred on a particular man and accepted by him as a source of emolument. To the extent of the emolument it is private property, as much as the land which he tills, or the horse he rides or the debt which is owing to him.[79]

Five years later the Alabama Supreme Court, in *Ex Parte Dorsey*,[80] gave a comparably broad interpretation to property. An applicant to the bar challenged the constitutionality of a state statute requiring all persons seeking public office to take an oath that they had not engaged in or invited a duel and would not do so while in office. Interpreting "public office" to include membership in the bar, the court, in a split decision, held that the oath requirement violated the due process clause of state constitution. Of particular importance, one of the two judges writing separately for the majority specifically addressed the question whether the underlying interest in practicing a profession qualified as liberty or property. Without considering whether it was liberty, Judge Ormond held that it was certainly property. (He went on to conclude that because the disqualifying conduct was not related to professional responsibilities the statute was unconstitutional; the other member of the majority rested more on the oath requirement. A dissent challenged both the conclusion that professional practice was a property right—he labeled it a mere "privilege" —and the conclusion that the state could not condition the "privilege" on the taking of such an oath.)

The most famous pre-Civil War state decisions on the scope of due process and the related interpretation of "property" is *Wynehamer v. The People*.[81] *Wynehamer* was one of a series of state court decisions passing on the constitutionality of liquor prohibition laws that enjoyed uncommon political popularity in the mid-nineteenth century, and which provided repeated occasions for testing the emerging notion of substantive due process in the state courts.[82] In *Wynehamer* the court held that the statute was invalid insofar as it interfered with a property right to possess and/or dispose of liquor. The judges were not unanimous in how far the property extended, whether to mere possession or also to sale. Judge Comstock, whose opinion is the one most often cited, thought the right extended to a power of disposition and sale as well as private use and enjoyment.

Hoke, Dorsey and*Wynehamer* all spoke to the question of property rights, finessing the question whether there was a liberty interest of corresponding scope. This usage, of course, is faithful to the broad, "atmospheric" Lockean concept of property as economic liberty, and reinforces the conclusion that the distinction between liberty and property did not have the importance later constitutional semanticists (*e.g.,* the Supreme Court in *Roth*) gave it, for any freedoms that did not entail physical liberty could be classed as "property."

Herman v. State[83] in 1855 appears to have been the first case to address property and liberty distinctively. The occasion was a state liquor-prohibition law similar to the New York law in *Wynehamer*. The court found the law to violate both liberty and property interests protected by the state under its equivalent of the federal due process clause. Of property the court said:

> Chancellor Kent, following Blackstone, says: (vol. 2, p. 1.) "The absolute [or natural] rights of individuals may be resolved into the right of personal security, the right of personal liberty, and the right to acquire and enjoy property;" not some property, or one kind of property, but, at least, what-

soever the society organizing government, recognizes as property. How much does this right embrace, how far does it extend? It undoubtedly extends to the right of pursuing the trades of manufacturing, buying, and selling, and to the practice of using. These acts are but means of acquiring and enjoying, and are absolutely necessary and incidental to them.[84]

As to liberty:

> We lay down this proposition, then, as applicable to the present case; that the right of liberty and pursuing happiness secured by the constitution, embraces the right, in each compos mentis individual, of selecting what he will eat and drink, in short, his beverages, so far as he may be capable of producing them, or they may be within his reach, and that the legislature cannot take away that right by direct enactment.... If we are right in this, that the Constitution restrains the legislature from passing a law regulating the diet of the people, a sumptuary law, (for that under consideration is such, no matter whether its objects be morals or economy, or both,) then the legislature cannot prohibit the manufacture and sale, for use as a beverage, of ale, porter, beer, etc., and cannot declare those manufactured, kept and sold for that purpose, a nuisance, if such is the use to which those articles are put by the people.[85]

Both property and liberty were, for the court, "natural rights" "anterior to the constitution ... we did not derive them from it, but established it to secure to us the enjoyment of them."[86]

Constitutional scholars critical of the expansion of due process have been wont to dismiss these decisions as exceptional. Edward Corwin, for example, notes that the Alabama Supreme Court appears to have subsequently retreated from its holding in *Hoke,* and that *Wynehamer* and *Herman* were not followed by any state court decisions confronting similar prohibition laws in this period.[87] If the point is simply that few courts went so far as, say, *Wynehamer* or *Herman* in invalidating state legislation under the due process concept, Corwin is surely correct. However, his more general inference that state courts repudiated the use of due process clauses to impose *substantive* restraints on legislation is not supported by a careful reading of the cases.[88] The general thrust of the decisions upholding state liquor prohibition statutes, for example, is that the legislation was a valid use of the state's police power to enact laws for the benefit of public health and welfare.[89] There is no necessary implication from these holdings that the due process clause imposes *no* restraints on legislative powers. More to the point of the present essay, there is no implication that the underlying interests at stake did not qualify as property or liberty for purposes of some kind of constitutional due process—particularly procedural due process.[90]

It is important here to distinguish several distinct questions. One is the question whether due process should be interpreted to impose substantial restraints on legislative action or whether it should be purely a limitation on judicial processes. A second question is, given some substantive content, what are the standards of purpose or rationality imposed by substantive due process. A third question is what interests qualify for protection, that is, how are "property" and "liberty" defined? This third question is obviously independent of the first two since, whatever else it does or does not protect, due process accords procedural protections against arbitrary government (nonlegislative) actions. A fourth question is a counterpart to the second: what particular protections are accorded by procedural due process? However, this fourth question is only tangentially relevant to the present discussion.

Failing to distinguish these questions, Corwin and some other constitutional scholars have given us a somewhat misleading view of due process history. In fairness, however, it should be noted that the courts themselves frequently confused the different questions. For example, in both the substantive and procedural due process contexts there was a tendency to invoke the terms property and liberty to describe interests that have been improperly invaded. Thus, where a legislative action is deemed an unacceptable use of the police power or government process is considered arbitrary, the interest invaded will be described as "property" or "liberty," but where the action or process is affirmed as reasonable, one commonly finds courts dismissing the underlying rights as mere privileges. We already noted that this was a common tendency of courts construing procedural due process until quite recently. A similar tendency can be found in substantive due process decisions as well.

This is one reason why it is difficult to make confident statements about judicial conceptions of property and liberty apart from the particular adjudicatory context. Where a court upholds the state interest against that of the individual, one cannot always be sure from the opinion whether it is because the individual interest had *no* constitutional dignity as property or liberty, or because the state's interest in public welfare overrode the admitted property or liberty right. The uncertainty is compounded by the fact that the pre-Civil War case law does not have much density. Most of the state cases are accounted for by a single series of legislative enactments: liquor prohibition. There was little occasion for either state courts or the United States Supreme Court to pronounce the definition of property or liberty in such contexts, since neither state nor federal government was deeply into regulating matters that would raise problems of due process interpretation.

It was not until in the nineteenth century that the Supreme Court had important occasion to consider what kinds of interests implicated due process. The first occasion was in the *Slaughterhouse Cases*[91] in 1873. The Court was asked to hold that a Louisiana state law creating local monopolies in slaughterhouses violated the due process and the privileges and immunities clauses of the Fourteenth Amendment. The Court, by a 5 to 4 vote, held that neither constitutional provision was violated. The privileges and immunities clause was held to ensure protection of certain rights secured to individuals as citizens of the United States, but this did not embrace all civil rights. The due process clause was summarily dismissed as not protecting trade or occupational opportunities. Justice Field (joined by Chief Justice Chase and Justices Swayne and Bradley) and Justice Bradley separately dissented from the Court's interpretation. Both dissenting opinions argued that the right to pursue an occupation or trade was both property and liberty protected by the Fourteenth Amendment.

Though the majority refused to apply the Fourteenth Amendment to protect a claim of occupational freedom, they did not hold that occupational freedom could not qualify as liberty or as property, but merely that the state's power to regulate such freedom was not *substantively* constrained by the Fourteenth Amendment. In fact, in the same year as the *Slaughterhouse Cases* the Supreme Court, in a procedural due process case, *Ex Parte Robinson,*[92] held that an attorney could not be disbarred without prior notice of the grounds of the complaint and an opportunity to defend against them. The Court appeared to regard the attorney's "right to practice his profession" as an aspect of property rather than liberty, though this is not clearly indicated. Supreme Court and state court decisions following *Robinson* generally recognized that due process protects against arbitrary denial of the "right" to practice a profession, but as in *Robinson* they were vague as to the nature of the right.[93] It appears to have been thought unimportant how the right was characterized—unimportant, that is, so long as the basic interest at stake was recognized as a "right."[94]

When the Court embarked upon substantive due process with *Allgeyer* in 1897, it characterized occupational pursuits as liberty.[95] So too in *Meyer,* where occupational pursuits were specified as merely one of a series of endeavors essential to the "pursuit of happiness by free men," which are protected by due process.[96] However, occupational pursuits could be also characterized as property, as in *Coppage v. Kansas,*[97] and it does not appear that the Court in this period gave much, if any, thought to property and liberty as distinctive rights with separate fields of application.

In this respect, the Court was reasonably faithful to the "original understanding" considered as a set of values and principles. In the philosophical spirit of natural rights that inspired it, the phrase "life, liberty and property" was, as I noted earlier, mostly atmospheric; liberty and property were not terms of art, at least not artful precision. If these terms had any specific meaning in the collective consciousness of the Framers, it probably was incidental to the context in which due process was envisioned to play a role, and not a carefully deliberated definition.

The Demise of Natural Law

The shift from a natural rights to a positivist perspective in the law in modern times obviously implied a change in the conception of property and liberty. Recall that in the "higher law" tradition rights are a set of claims anterior to the state, claims preserved by the social contract itself (read, Constitution) but not created by it. In the modern positivist state the individual still has claims against the state, but increasingly the claims do not rest on natural right embedded in the social contract; they derive from social conventions as embodied in laws enacted or recognized (as in the common law) by the state. Although the connotations may be misleading, it would not be inaccurate to say that we have shifted from a Lockean to a Hobbesian conception of rights, from natural rights to positivism.

The shift to positivism has necessarily implied a diminution in the strength of rights protection, but it has also introduced greater potential scope to definition of rights. So long as rights were grounded in natural law, they were fixed to stable conceptions, both secular and religious, of the natural "order" of things. A positivist conception is inherently more flexible by being attached to shifting expectations based on changing circumstance.

This is particularly the case with property, less so with liberty. Liberty has been expanded from its restrictive meaning of freedom from incarceration, as exemplified most fully by *Meyer's* extraordinary catalogue of liberties.[98] However, modern applications of liberty adhere at least to the traditional negative form, freedom *from* government interference.[99] As broad as the *Meyer* catalogue of liberties is, it retains the spirit of Lockean liberalism in this respect. By contrast, modern positivism has transformed property into an almost free-form protection for all manner of claims that individuals may assert against the state pursuant to some "entitlement" conferred by contract or statutory instrument or some other amorphous source like the common law.[100]

It was the important contribution of Charles Reich to translate these new claims into the old vocabulary of property in lieu of the "privilege" label that had been affixed by courts unwilling to give full legal protection to the claims. Reich sought thereby to give to the new positivist claims the dignity and respect (via due process) that the Framers had accorded to fundamental, "natural" rights. One might say that Reich's "New Property" replaced Locke's old property as the lodestar of the due process clause. However, this characterization misses an important point; the "old property" is not so much replaced as it is given a new dimension, one that fits the demands of contemporary society.

This revised translation of property was appealingly modern. It had (has still) the virtue of extending some of the constitutional security associated with classical property to the new claims that the welfare state had created and to do so within the same linguistic framework the Framers gave us, thereby preserving the image of constitutional stability and continuity of meaning.

I say this extended "some" of the constitutional security advisedly, for the purpose of this move was to extend procedural, not substantive, protections to these claims. The Court has resisted the suggestion of Reich, and more recently of Justice Marshall, to treat the new property substantively the same as the old.[101] The sense of maintaining different degrees of substantive constitutional protection for new and old property may be debated but I won't debate it here. It is enough simply to anticipate my later argument that the due process protection for either should not turn on whether the label 'property' has been affixed to the underlying interest.

IV. Property and Liberty: Legal Positivism and Legal Rights

This brings us back to *Goldberg v. Kelly.* The Court's embrace of Reich's New Property expanded protection for important claims against the state —claims that had heretofore been subject to summary treatment as mere "privileges." That was its obvious virtue. Its apparent vice was, in the pertinent words of Macaulay's impertinent quip about the *original* American Constitution, "it is all sail and no anchor."[102] If the old concepts of property and liberty were vague, what must be said of the new ones—especially property? At least with the older idea of property we could appeal to some *fundamental* norms that were thought to be embedded in the ideas of individual freedoms vis-à-vis state interference. But what is the domain of the New Property and of the due process that attends it?

Goldberg was not instructive on the point. It did point to the fact that in this case the welfare entitlement—the "property"—had been explicitly created by Congress in the Social Security Act. However, the Court also intimated that constitutional protection would not be confined to interests clearly denominated as "entitlements" or as "property" or as "liberty" but would extend to all *important* interests. That possibility was soon realized in *Boddie v. Connecticut,*[103] where the Court held that due process required that indigents be given free access to the courts for purposes of obtaining a divorce; though it implied that denial of such access infringed "liberty," the Court finessed any consideration of the question of what the underlying right was.

The possibility of such a full-sail application of due process was cut short in *Roth.* However, *Roth* did not anchor "property" in anything much more specific. In *Roth,* Justice Stewart said for the Court that a property right entails more than a "unilateral expectation of it"; it requires a "legitimate claim of entitlement." In the companion *Sindermann* case this was elaborated slightly: a person has a property interest in a benefit "if there are such rules or mutually explicit understandings that support this claim of entitlement."[104]

It requires no great analytical sophistication to see that this formulation is question-begging. What does support a "legitimate claim" of entitlement? The above language suggests either a contractual or quasi-contractual approach: property arises out of mutual understandings or at least an implied promise by the state on which the individual justifiably relies. This theory of "legitimate expectations" essentially follows Bentham's theory of property, except that Bentham did not tie the source of the expectations to law alone, but conceived of a broader category of "natural expectations" that the law should honor.[105] This broader notion of social expectations can be derived from Locke's view, and in that philosophical context it is entirely coherent and sensible. Property entitlements do represent a general set of expectations grounded in social and political, as well as legal, understandings of the time.

However, inasmuch as the modern version of expectations is tied to specific legal instruments, it is circular. As Stephen Williams has observed: "Insofar as promises, expectations and reliance are the bases of a property or a liberty interest, the statute or rule which generates the expectation or reliance is its proper measure."[106] There is, in short, no basis for going behind the law being challenged as unconstitutional: what it promises is what it gives; what it does not give it did not promise.

The problem of defining property according to specific legal expectations is especially problematic given the modern conception of property. The new property is functionally limited. This is true of old property too, at least according to the modern revised translation. For better and for worse the realists taught us to think of rights generally in functional, flexible terms. A property right, for example, is not a singular thing but, in a now clichéd metaphor, a "bundle-of-sticks," a collection of legal powers and remedies. The powers and remedies are not uniform across all kinds of "property."[107] For example, conventional property—sometimes misleadingly called "common law" property—is usually characterized by two major elements: the right to exclusive possession/use and transferability. However, these elements are subject to various legal conditions that limit their realization or their enforcement. For example, the right of exclusive possession/use is limited by the enforcement remedies provided: it may be protected by injunctive relief against interference or only by an award for damages.[108] In some cases it may not be enforceable at all against certain persons — those who have special easements or use privileges. In functional terms, then, the "property" right describes some set of legal attributes that are protected and how they are protected. This is elementary to the point of triteness as far as common property law is concerned. However, when this elementary idea is transposed to due process property concepts, it has been the subject of sharp controversy on and off the Court.[109]

I think at bottom the controversy is really over the propriety of a positivist view of constitutional due process more than it is over conceptions of property. Despite arguments by Justices Brennan and Marshall that "property" has a constitutional dimension, the rest of the Court has repeatedly emphasized that the *definition* of property for due process purposes is purely a matter of positive (nonconstitutional) law—though liberty has both constitutional and nonconstitutional sources.[110] In the case of property, due process protection is thus a matter of blending positive and constitutional law, the former being employed to identify the basic right, the latter to prescribe the degree of protection—the "remedy," if you will.

The separation of property right and remedial protection is internally inconsistent insofar as it purports to rely on the positive law to define property but then rejects the basic tenet of positive law, that right and remedy are interdependent. (Indeed, following the realist tradition we can say that the remedy is the right.) That fact in itself would not be so troubling if we were dealing with property that was well defined and widely accepted as such—a car, a house, or a Swiss army knife. Unfortunately, the nature of the due process problem virtually limits its application to less tangible and less well-established notions of property rights such as the "right" to employment, the "right" to education, the "right" to welfare benefits, and the like. It is precisely here that an underlying *property* right is difficult to identify apart from a set of prescribed processes, *so long as one adheres to a positivist conception of property.*

To give the question concrete illustration, imagine a civil service statute that provides as follows: (a) an individual in the competitive service may be removed or suspended only for such cause as will promote the efficiency of the service; (b) removal or suspension for cause shall be determined only after written notice to that individual, containing reasons for such action, and an opportunity to file a written response; (c) examination of witnesses or a hearing is not required, but may be provided at the sole discretion of the person directing the removal or suspension. What "entitlement" does an employee have under such a statute? Does the employee have a due process right to have a full hearing notwithstanding subsections (b) or (c)? What would be the basis for such a right: subsection (a)? Does that subsection *by itself* create a "legitimate claim of entitlement" (*Roth*) supported by "rules or mutually explicit understandings" (*Sindermann*)?

The above hypothetical statute is essentially a summary of pertinent provisions of the Lloyd-LaFollette Act applicable to the federal civil service. In *Arnett v. Kennedy,*[111] a federal employee discharged under that act for falsely accusing his supervisor of bribery claimed a denial of due process because he was not awarded a full hearing *before* his removal. In this regard it is pertinent to note that under regulations of the Civil Service Commission and the agency for which the employee worked, a full trial-type hearing was available on appeal from an adverse decision, that is, *after* removal. The Court rejected the due process attack but the multiple opinions of the justices gave no clear rationale. Writing for a plurality of three members of the Court, Justice (now Chief Justice) Rehnquist wrote:

> Here appellee did have a statutory expectancy that he not be removed other than for 'such cause as will promote the efficiency of [the] service.' But the very section of the statute which granted him that right, a right which had

previously existed only by virtue of administrative regulation, expressly provided also for the procedure by which 'cause' was to be determined, and expressly omitted the procedural guarantees which appellee insists are mandated by the Constitution. Only by bifurcating the very sentence of the Act of Congress which conferred upon appellee the right not to be removed save for cause could it be said that he had an expectancy of that substantive right without the procedural limitations which Congress attached to it ... The employee's statutorily defined right is not a guarantee against removal without cause in the abstract, but such a guarantee as enforced by the procedures which Congress has designated for the determination of the cause... [w]here the grant of substantive right is inextricably intertwined with the limitations on the procedures which are to be employed in determining that right, a litigant in the position of appellee must take the bitter with the sweet.[112]

Justice Rehnquist's positivist-functionalist interpretation of 'property' did not command the assent of the majority in *Arnett,* and for a time there was confusion as to where the majority of the Court stood on the definition of "property." I think the matter is still not entirely free of confusion as a conceptual matter, but a majority of the Court has openly repudiated the Rehnquist view in several recent cases, the most recent of which is *Cleveland Board of Education v. Loudermill.*[113]

Loudermill involved the discharge of public employees without a pretermination hearing. Affirming a decision by the court of appeals that this violated due process, the Court rejected appellant's argument that employees had only such property as the state legislature conferred and that such property was "defined by, and conditioned on, the legislature's choice of procedures for its deprivation." In speaking for the majority, Justice White noted that the argument was identical to Justice Rehnquist's view in *Arnett* which the Court on two more recent occasions had rejected:

> In light of these holdings, it is settled that the "bitter with the sweet" approach misconceives the constitutional guarantee. If a clearer holding is needed, we provide it today. The point is straightforward: the Due Process Clause provides that certain substantive rights—life, liberty, and property —cannot be deprived except pursuant to constitutionally adequate procedures. The categories of substance and procedure are distinct. Were the rule otherwise, the Clause would be reduced to a mere tautology. "Property" cannot be defined by the procedures provided for its deprivation any more than can life or liberty. The right to due process "is conferred, not by legislative grace, but by constitutional guarantee. While the legislature may elect not to confer a property interest in [public] employment, it may not constitutionally authorize the deprivation of such an interest, once conferred, without appropriate procedural safeguards."[114]

Justice White's argument about "reducing the Clause...to a mere tautology" is unanswerable. If the legislative definition is dispositive as to both the existence and the content of "property," the due process clause has no function. This is the "positivist trap" about which too much has been written. However, Justice Rehnquist's argument (repeated in a dissent in *Loudermill*) is equally unanswerable. So long as the Court eschews a *constitutional* definition of what constitutes property, it has no warrant to manipulate the statutory or common law definition so as to take only part of it. Recalling the bundle-of-sticks concept, if the state of federal law confers a set of rights, remedies, and conditions, X, Y, and Z, and calls the *bundle* "property," the Court has no basis on which to take one of the "sticks," say X, and declare it to be a property right protected by its own due process requirements. Only if the Court is willing to take from the state or federal government the power to define what is property, can it legitimately unbundle the package. I might add that it makes no difference whether the state/federal law defines X, Y and Z as property in a single instrument, for it is the *totality* of the law that determines the appropriate legal characterization. Indeed, as *Sindermann* teaches, it is the set of legal practices that counts even if the practices are not fixed in any formal instrument.

Critics of the positivist approach, both on and off the Court, have interpreted it as a return to the right-privilege notion or, more precisely, to the argument underlying the conditioned benefits jurisprudence, that the greater power includes the lesser: the power of the states to create (or not create) property carries with it the power to define all the attributes thereof, procedural and substantive. Rehnquist himself lends support to this interpretation; his "bitter-with-the-sweet" phrase in *Arnett* evokes Justice Holmes's discredited quip in *McAuliffe v. Mayor of New Bedford* that the public employee "takes his employment on the terms which are offered him."[115]

But whether this interpretation is what Justice Rehnquist had in mind or not, it is not the correct—that is, the truest—view of the positivist logic.[116] Whether or not a positivist conception of rights provides an appropriate ground for due process, it misses the point to relate it to the greater-includes-the-lesser notion. That notion is an argument from power. The positivist concept is not one of power but of interpretation. To the extent 'property' (or, equally, 'liberty') is a predicate of due process, it is necessary to have a definition, a means of identifying what it is. For most conventional property interests in things, the definitional problem is essentially nonproblematic. At the very least we can fall back on more or less accepted common-law conceptions that will identify the existence of the property right and specify its content. But it has been recognized from ancient times that property rights extend beyond interests in things to an array of legal relationships and obligations.

The definition of property rights was always indeterminate, but in an era when it was conceived largely in terms of natural law, anterior to the state, there were some plausible limits given by the range of what were regarded as basic economic activities by the individual to which a claim of right could be made. The rise of the modern state altered our concept of property by replacing natural law with positive law. In doing so it partly constricted and partly expanded protection of property rights. Older forms of property were fettered by new social conditions and obligations, but the *range* of protection was expanded with the creation of Reich's New Property.

The Court has recognized the extension of property but has ignored its underlying *functional* meaning. Put it this way: in *Loudermill* the Court found that the state had created a "property" right. But how did it know this? The statute did not say that public employees had a "property right." What it said was that employees had a right to certain discharge procedures, which did not include a pretermination hearing. Respondents probably put the case badly by arguing that the statute created a "conditional right," insofar as that label evoked Holmes's discredited edict in *McAuliffe*. Suppose instead respondents had argued that the statute created *no* property right to employment, but did create a property in specified discharge procedures? Essentially that was Rehnquist's interpretation of what the statute did. How can the Court say otherwise, *if* it is the *statute* that is the source of the right?

The debate in *Loudermill* between Justice Rehnquist and the current majority of the Court over conceptions of property is confused by the fact that each seems to be talking past the other. Rehnquist's view of property is, in one sense, a perfectly logical application of the Reichean conception of property embraced by the Court in *Goldberg*. The New Property celebrated by Charles Reich, and by Justice Brennan in *Goldberg,* is a positivist conception in which the right is defined in terms of the cluster of instrumental powers and remedies created by legal or social convention. Put somewhat oversimply, the right doesn't define the powers and the remedies that attend it; rather the powers and remedies define the right. Reich discovered a New Property in the array of benefits (employment, licenses, pensions, Social Security, etc.) conferred by the welfare state based on the fact that these benefits required, and to considerable extent had received, legal security against arbitrary withdrawal by the state. As I interpret it this is Rehnquist's view as well. (If it isn't, it should have been.)

To suggest agreement between Rehnquist and Reich is surely to invite ridicule from anyone passingly familiar with their respective writings. But the agreement is only in the logic of argument, not in the underlying philosophy of due process (or of anything else). For Reich the New Property concept was only a means to an end, and a largely rhetorical one at that. The objective was to obtain legal protection, legal security for social benefits—to get beyond the idea that government benefits were simply a privileged largess to be conferred or withheld or conditioned at will. And, of course, it was in this same spirit that Justice Brennan embraced the idea of *Goldberg.* Faithful to the *spirit* of Reich's argument, Justice Brennan was concerned with the importance of the interest at stake in terms of the need for securing it against arbitrary action. *Roth* and *Sindermann* redirected the Court back to the older idea of defining the threshold right first, then ordering the process that was due. *Roth* and *Sindermann* did not repudiate the new property concept; they merely tried to anchor it in "concrete" entitlements as opposed to a free-floating individual adjudication of "need."

Unfortunately, the Court has never really quite come to grips with the tension between the spirit of the New Property invention and the logic of the argument that was used to gain it recognition. While Justice Brennan would embrace the spirit, Justice Rehnquist wants the logic, and Justice White seems to want both.

The debate over property (and, to a lesser extent, liberty) is only partly over different conceptions of what constitutes the "right." It is also a debate over the sources of the right. As I mentioned earlier, a majority of the Court since *Roth* has insisted that property is defined only by positive law—statutes or common law—and not by the Constitution itself. Justices Brennan and Marshall have suggested that property rights can be grounded in the Constitution itself, though their suggestion is somewhat muted and hesitant.[117] Some scholars have been more forthright and clear in arguing for Constitution-based property.[118] I agree with their argument. Despite Justice Stevens's off-hand dismissal of the idea of a Constitutional common law of property as "remarkably innovative,"[119] it isn't obvious why it is any more remarkable than constitutionally grounded 'liberty', which the Court has accepted for ninety years.[120] Treating the Constitution as a source of property does present the difficult problem of defining the right without any textual guidance. However, one could make essentially the same point about 'liberty', yet the task of giving substantive content to that concept has not noticeably daunted the Court. Indeed, as we observed earlier, throughout most of the history of due process the Court has been largely indifferent to any careful differentiation of property and liberty, an indifference I interpret to be a recognition of their similar purpose as expressions of fundamental rights.

We are brought back, at long last, to the problem with which this essay began: the source of constitutional principle, more specifically whether and how far constitutional adjudication should be (can be) a matter of interpretation as opposed to an admittedly open-ended search for basic constitutional values. In at least one respect, however, the search for property and liberty rights *in* the Constitution is consistent with conservative interpretivism, to the extent one defines interpretivism as fidelity to the basic values of the Framers. Although we do not have textual authority for constitutionally defined concepts of property and liberty, we do know that the Framers thought of these concepts as the product of natural rights, secured by the Constitution, and not the product of positive law. The natural rights-higher law assumptions that underlay the Framers' ideas about constitutionalism are at war with the modern positivist view that regards such rights (property at least) as the artifact of legislatures or common-law courts.

Grounding property, along with liberty, *in* the Constitution (or in some "higher law" reflected therein) gets us out of the positivist trap and gives a more secure foundation for what appears presently to be the prevailing view of the Court (represented by Justice White). It is hardly uncontroversial support, for all the reasons that inhere in constitutional interpretation generally. In effect we trade the awkwardness of positivism for the nebulosity of natural law or, what comes to the same, the vagaries of creative judicial review—though originalists can perhaps be appeased by reminding them that this vagueness is inherent in value concepts that the Framers embraced.

Despite the inference one might draw from the fact that the Court's two most liberal members argue for it, a constitutional (i.e. judicial) definition of property does not imply the instant transformation of all welfare benefits, contracts, or dispensations into property. Certainly it does not if the appeal to "higher law" is taken seriously, for such an appeal demands that only "fundamental" interests be recognized as constitutional rights.

V. Legal Rights and Legal Stakes

We return, yet again, to *Goldberg v. Kelly,* this time with a nonpositivist perspective. Without implying that this new perspective should be limited by the Framers' exact understanding of liberty and property, we may think of a revised opinion in *Goldberg* drawing more on the Framers' natural rights view of property than Reich's positivism. Is the return to *Goldberg,* by way of Madison (or to Madison by way of *Goldberg;* it comes to the same) worthwhile?

When all is said and done about competing conceptions of due-process property and liberty interests, it appears more is said than done. Both within the Court and outside it the debate over the question of what property and liberty are turns out to be more about symbols than practical consequences. Particularly (but not exclusively) in the context of procedural due process, what turns on finding that a particular interest is a right is only whether to proceed to a further stage of judicial scrutiny wherein most of the critical (albeit theoretically less interesting) questions are asked.

In the context of substantive due process, one examines the governmental action according to standards of rational purpose, which as generally employed are so undemanding that one can fairly describe the very inquiry as *pro forma.* In special cases, where fundamental rights or suspect classifications are implicated, the constitutional thresholds are necessarily met, for the very nature of such cases (*e.g.,* freedom of speech or of association, racial equality) implies that a basic 'liberty' is at issue.

In the case of procedural due process, a finding of property or liberty is only a preface for a judicial inquiry on which almost everything of real substance rests. Once a property or liberty right is identified, the due process claimant still faces the burden of showing that the particular procedures he received were insufficient; more was "due." There are, however, virtually no fixed standards for defining what is due. The Court has a formula, enumerated in *Mathews v. Eldridge*,[121] that, essentially, calls for a utilitarian balancing of government and individual interests.

To say that this test can yield a range of specific procedures is an understatement. At one end of the range, the process due is truly minimal. For example, a year before *Eldridge*, the Court in *Goss v. Lopez*[122] held that a high school student who was briefly suspended for disruptive conduct "must be given *some* kind of notice and afforded some kind of hearing." However, the emphasis was on "some"; it would be sufficient, the Court said, to discuss with the student the basis for official actions, with "opportunity to explain his version of the facts at the discussion."[123] A year after *Eldridge*, in a second student-disciplinary case, *Ingraham v. Wright*,[124] involving an impromptu "paddling" of an unruly student, the Court ruled that due process was satisfied by an opportunity to pursue, after the fact, a civil damage action for excessive punishment!

At the other end of the process range, *Goldberg* required a full evidentiary hearing *before* the government action in question. The Court in *Eldridge* essentially made *Goldberg* an exceptional case limited to its particular facts; however, the exceptional character of *Goldberg* probably was more in the timing than the content of the hearing.

The Court's application of *Eldridge* has been criticized as erratic, even incoherent. Jerry Mashaw, for example, argues that "although promising transparency and generality, it has produced instead an opaque and Balkanized jurisprudence that can only hope to be understood within the particular context of specific programs or substantive fields of activity (education, public employment, or the like)."[125] Mashaw may be right, though his criticism appears to expect a lot from what purports to be only a very general formula. It is the nature of such a formula that it will not yield a clear set of outcomes, particularly not where it is designed to give liberal room for administrative variation in different contexts. To expect more is to demand a closer judicial surveillance of agencies than is probably desirable or to assume a greater degree of uniformity among administrative situations with respect to relevant due process criteria than is realistic.

Mashaw's stronger criticism is directed not to the Court's enforcement of the *Eldridge* criteria so much as to the criteria themselves. Or rather it is the normative basis of the criteria, for Mashaw challenges the basic utilitarian model (which, in somewhat Pickwickian fashion, he calls a "model of competence"). While important on some practical level of legislative policy judgment, he argues the model is inappropriate to constitutional adjudication precisely because there is no basis for preferring the Court's utilitarian determinations over those made by the legislature. Mashaw is cautious about embracing a rights-based approach to due process to the extent it might suggest a kind of absolutism that would override or at least obscure the need to balance competing claims of right. At bottom, however, his conception of due process is one of individual rights, defined essentially in terms of dignitary values such as autonomy, self-respect, and equality.[126]

Mashaw is surely correct that a utilitarian system provides an infirm base for judicial correction of legislative judgments. But so too does any other system. It is by no means obvious to me that courts cannot in fact make "better" utilitarian calculations than legislatures, if one is willing to assume the possibility of a general public interest that is other than what the political process generates. Nevertheless, grant that the courts are unqualified to define the public interest on utilitarian grounds; are they more qualified to do so on other grounds? It is not at all obvious that judges are better as moral theorists than as political engineers.[127] In fact the experience of most judges prior to their appointment better equips them to be the latter than the former. Most judges come to the bench from active participation in the same political world wherein legislators dwell.

Mashaw's critique of utilitarian judicial review might be understood to rest not on relative competence but on constitutional appropriateness: the notion is that the Constitution is not "about" utilitarian values. Maybe, but any argument based on what the Constitution is "about" quickly leads us into the proverbial Serbonian bog into which whole armies disappear. The fact is that the Constitution is no more about "dignity" than it is about "utility." All we know from constitutional text and its immediate history is that the Framers wanted to protect certain interests—life, liberty and property—from arbitrary government interference, by subjecting government action affecting those interests to due process restraints. Everything else is invention. I do not say inappropriate invention, but certainly invention that permits wide-ranging philosophical perspective of what the Constitution is "about." To rule out utilitarianism as a constitutional value one must essentially rule it out as a philosophical argument of moral or political theory. Many have tried to do so, but we cannot pause even to consider their efforts.[128] It must be enough simply to say that in such a wide-ranging philosophical inquiry over what "counts" as a legitimate moral *cum* political template, due process considerations tend to get lost as a special concern.

However, the matter of moral and political values is rather tangential to my main purpose; whatever the proper values that should inform due process, I think those values are not well served by continued preoccupation with 'property' and 'liberty' thresholds. Critics of *Roth* and its progeny have proposed to bypass any threshold requirement of a property right or liberty interest as a prerequisite for procedural due process.[129] There is much to be said for doing so for both procedural and substantive due process. The argument for an independent due process right is slightly embarrassed by having no textual support in the written constitution. But it is a commonplace that constitutional law has not been greatly handicapped by want of clear textual support. Terms have been added to promote essential constitutional purposes. Illustrative are First Amendment cases that include within the ambit of "speech" speech-related activity and "expressive" conduct that would not be considered in any ordinary-language sense to be speech.[130] More to the point of the present argument, terms have been ignored where they are deemed inessential to the central function of constitutional protection. The Fourth Amendment jurisprudence provides an apt example. Like the due process clause, the Fourth Amendment nominally comes in two parts, an identification of protected rights and a specification of how they are protected. The first part defines the right of the people to be secure in their "persons, houses, papers, and effects"; the second part protects these rights against "unreasonable searches and seizures." The Court's Fourth Amendment jurisprudence has focussed on the second part and, with rare exception, ignored the first.[131] Given the breadth of the protected threshold interests (particularly "persons" and "effects") the Court has wisely chosen not to devote close attention to those terms but to look directly to the scope of protection to which the inquiry invariably must lead: what is a "reasonable" search or seizure?

In the case of procedural due process, a due process unanchored to any specific right or interest would presumably closely resemble the English concept of "natural justice" which, being derived from England's unwritten constitution, is purely a common law creature of protean shape, tailored to the circumstances of each situation.[132] Those who find the already protean character of due process unsettling will find the English doctrine an imprudent model to say the least. However, the protean character of natural justice already inheres in American due process. The Supreme Court is constantly reminding us that the process is a "flexible" concept whose particular procedural requirements must be responsive to the different circumstances and interests involved. Indeed, flexibility is the essence of *Eldridge*. The threshold requirements of property or liberty do not in fact give any firmness or clarity to the present law.

What these thresholds do supposedly give is some baseline for determining when courts must intervene in the administrative process. The real fear is not that unanchored due process would lack specificity and clarity but that it would lack restraint: without a property or liberty anchor, the courts would be invited to intervene in situations where the nature of the interests at stake simply does not call for judicial surveillance.

This has been a concern since *Goldberg v. Kelly* brought due process to the welfare state. The courts have been asked to intervene in what seems to be an ever-increasing number of variety of disputes involving welfare benefits, public employment, student discipline, prison administration ... the list is long. The Supreme Court's growing hostility to being asked to formulate due process rules for such disputes is evident in numerous recent opinions, most notably in student discipline and public employee disputes. On the assumption that the Constitution should not be interpreted to constitute the Supreme Court as a roving superintendent of schools or a chief personnel manager (etc.), the Court's fear of being dragged into everyday conflicts in the name of ensuring individual dignity or fairness or what have you is a legitimate reason to place some limitations on the reach of due process.

It has been suggested to me that elimination of the rights threshold will only throw the burden of screening access to the courts on to the amorphous doctrine of standing. It is not possible here to delve into the arcana of judicial standing in order to evaluate this possibility.[133] A few brief summary comments will have to suffice.

First, a review of due process cases will quickly reveal that few, if any, present significant standing problems. Obviously, cases in which a "right" is found are nonproblematical, since standing to seek review should be understood as an intrinsic attribute of the right protected. Only those cases where the personal interest at stake is not a protected right present a potential standing problem. However, even in these latter cases standing is unlikely to present a real problem, for the personal interest involved typically satisfies the "injury in fact" criterion of current standing rules.[134] It is conceivable that removal of any "right" requirement as a threshold of due process protection might encourage claims based on interests too ephemeral to meet standing requirements, but I doubt such claims would materially add to the burden of claims that already flow from constitutional and nonconstitutional provisions other than the due process clause.

Second, insofar as the underlying concern of screening judicial claims is to protect courts, and constitutional adjudication, from being overwhelmed by trivial or ephemeral controversies, that function is not now being served in due process cases by the requirement of threshold rights. As those rights have been defined, they neither screen out the trivial nor serve as a useful guide to ensure wise and restrained judicial intervention. The two school-disciplinary cases mentioned earlier illustrate the point.

Recall that in the first case, *Goss,* the Court held that public high school students were entitled to "some kind of notice" and "some kind of hearing" before being suspended from school. The threshold requirement of an entitlement to public education was found in relevant state law; the Court also found a liberty interest affected by virtue of the fact that disciplinary suspension affected the students' "good name, reputation, honor, or integrity." Given the definitions of property entitlements and liberty interests by the Court at least since *Goldberg,* the Court's finding of such interests here is unexceptionable. What is debatable—and four dissenting justices did debate it—is whether the nature of the dispute really warranted judicial intervention by way of the due process clause.

The Court essentially abandoned *Goss* two years later in *Ingraham*. By a shift in one vote the *Goss* dissenters became a majority. In *Ingraham* the discipline took the form of corporal punishment rather than suspension, but in practical effect the *educational* deprivation was the same (one student suffered physical injuries that kept him out of school for eleven days—one more than the suspension period in *Goss*). The Court could not distinguish *Goss* on the issue of threshold interests; it found a liberty interest in being free of punishment. (It found no deprivation of a property interest in public education because the punishment was not intended to disrupt the student's education!) Conceding that the requisite threshold interest was present, the Court nevertheless held that due process required no special procedural prerequisites to punishment. Purporting to apply *Eldridge* (which had intervened between *Goss* and *Ingraham*), the Court found that the student's interest was adequately protected by a common law tort suit, in case punishment proved excessive or unwarranted, and that special *administrative* procedures were not warranted.

What did the Court's due process *pas de deux* in *Goss* and *Ingraham* accomplish? It cannot have been a ringing vindication of property and liberty rights. Whether the Court was correct in *Ingraham* or in *Goss* in its assessment of the need for judicial surveillance of school discipline, it seems plain that such an assessment cannot turn importantly on whether the student's interests constitute property or liberty. At least it cannot turn importantly on *present* conceptions of property and liberty.

If this judgment is correct, perhaps the evolution of property and liberty has come to its logical terminus so far as due process is concerned.[135] These rights have now become so expansive, so protean, that they no longer serve much practical purpose in defining the occasions for due process inquiry. This is the lesson I derive from the *Goss* and *Ingraham* cases (among others) with respect to procedural due process in particular. If the 'rational basis test' of substantive due process had importance, much the same point could be made there also.[136] Possibly the terms still carry symbolic importance and may on that account be retained to give added weight to due process deliberations. But if symbolism is the rationale for adhering to familiar terminology, the contemporary positivist perspective cannot be retained without trivializing the ideals that give force to the symbolism.

VI. Conclusion

The "original intent" of this essay was to sketch the historical evolution of property and liberty concepts in the context of constitutional due process.

Mindful of what I wrote about original intent in Part I, I have to concede that this is not a controlling guide to interpretation; and in fact history, in the sense of simple narrative in the past tense, was never my entire concern, as is evident both from comments on constitutional interpretation in Part I and those in Part V on due process. Nevertheless, some notion of the historical evolution is important; as Justice Holmes said: it "fixes our vocabulary" and "limits our imagination."

As to the vocabulary, we do, of course, use the operative terms of due process—notably 'life', 'liberty', 'property', and 'due process'—employed by the Framers; whether our meaning is the same as theirs is more problematic. This is not merely a question of historical evidence. Even within contemporary legal discourse the terms have a surprising degree of indeterminacy, and we could reasonably expect a corresponding degree of vagueness in the "original understanding." It is important to emphasize at this point that we are not concerned with the core of such concepts as 'property' and 'liberty', which have a fairly stable meaning over time. There probably has never been a time in Anglo-American law when "three acres and a cow" (to draw again on Alan Ryan's phrase) was not property, though the indicia of ownership have doubtless changed. So too it is hard to imagine any real dispute over freedom of physical movement being 'liberty'. The serious problems of interpretation involve such questions as whether raising a cow or farming three acres is property or liberty.

In Part III I argued that the Framers conceived of property and liberty in broader terms than many contemporary constitutionalists believe. The evidence is not, I concede, unequivocally supportive, particularly on the question of liberty. However, it is important that the question of meaning be addressed in the context of the Framers' broad philosophical perspective and purpose. I suppose this observation is trite, but it needs saying if only as a counter to strict constructionists who want to read this Bill of Rights as if it were a bill of lading.

That the Framers had a broad view of both property and liberty is strongly suggested by their view of what government was all about. Government existed to protect rights, not to create them. Property and liberty are anterior to the state; they embody the full range of freedoms that individuals possess by "natural law." The common usage of property and liberty accords with this broad interpretation, as does the philosophical literature (most notably, but not exclusively, Locke) on which the Framers drew. Madison's famous essay on property is illustrative.

Of course, it was the task of courts to give legal definition to philosophical generality. There is not an abundance of early precedent, but what there is appears consistent with a broad understanding of property and liberty. State cases in the pre-Civil War period follow Madison in interpreting 'property' as virtually synonymous with economic freedom. Rather curiously, 'liberty' appears to occupy a secondary role in due process rights prior to the Supreme Court's first foray into substantive due process in 1897 in the *Allgeyer* case.

However, the most striking fact is judicial indifference to whether a right is 'property' or 'liberty'; the important concern is whether it is a protected right. I believe this conforms to the Framers' usage of the terms as more atmospheric than artful.

Legal conceptions are, of course, shaped by philosophical fashion and by social conditions. The "higher law" foundations that shaped the Framers' views became increasingly anachronistic by the close of the nineteenth century; so too did the idea of social contractarianism and the notion of individual rights grounded therein. Increasingly, the fashion of philosophical and legal discourse was towards a positivist conception of rights and law— rights as the creation of the state and law as its instrument. To be sure, the rhetoric of natural rights did not disappear with the advent of the twentieth century, as the Supreme Court's opinion in *Meyer v. Nebraska* illustrates. Indeed, appeals to something essentially the same as natural rights can still be found in the privacy jurisprudence of cases like *Roe v. Wade* or *Moore v. City of Eastlake*.

However, the "realist" tenor of modern thought is hostile to the idea of natural law. While some rights may be "fundamental" in something approaching a higher law conception, the source of most rights is nothing more exalted than the changing secular convenience of the state. This new positivist view has diminished the strength of rights, but it has also broadened their scope. The changing character and scope of rights also introduced a fresh source of uncertainty and controversy into the definition of rights for purposes of constitutional due process. Much of the uncertainty and controversy is due to the Supreme Court's melding of nonconstitutional sources of rights creation with constitutional definition of rights protection.

Two possible solutions to the difficulty suggest themselves. One is a return to something like the earlier tradition of the Court, defining due process rights according to its own interpretation of a "higher law." If one changes the term "higher law" to "constitutional common law"—a change of no substance—this suggestion is not radical; nearly the entire corpus of contemporary constitutional law rests on constitutional common law. A second approach might be just to abandon the idea of a rights-based due process, focusing constitutional adjudication solely on the situational needs of the individual and the government. The second approach will doubtless appear to many to be ad hoc if not unprincipled, just as the former will seem artificial and conceptualistic. However, the present jurisprudence contains both sets of faults.

Notes

1. *Learning and Science,* in COLLECTED LEGAL PAPERS 139 (1920).

2. *See, e.g.,* M. PERRY THE CONSTITUTION, THE COURTS AND HUMAN RIGHTS (1982); L. TRIBE, AMERICAN CONSTITUTIONAL LAW 886-90 (1978); Wellington, *Common Law Rules and Constitutional Double Standards: Some Notes on Adjudication,* 83 YALE L. J. 221 (1973). Citing the foregoing under simple labels such as "fundamental moral principles" or "shared social values" obscures the considerable variation in this vein of constitutional scholarship. For example, Perry and Wellington both embrace morality as a basis for constitutional principle, but diverge substantially in the sources to be consulted for moral enlightenment. Tribe, along with many other constitutionalists, argues for basic personal "rights" such as a right of privacy that are more or less independent of specific textual or historic authority; however, the precise source of principles by which the protected rights are defined is unclear. It is precisely the variability of this entire perspective that is central to Ely's criticism. *See* J. ELY, DEMOCRACY AND DISTRUST: A THEORY OF JUDICIAL REVIEW (1980). For a critical review of the fundamental rights/values perspective *and* its critics, *see, e.g.,* Brest, *The Fundamental Rights Controversy: The Essential Contradictions of Normative Constitutional Scholarship,* 90 YALE L. J. 1063 (1981). For Brest the entire debate over constitutional principles between those who want active judicial surveillance of political majorities and those who do not reveals an inherent contradiction in liberal political theory. As with other Critical Legal Theorists Brest's answer to the conflict is radical social change in the direction of a more communitarian society.

3. Standard references include R. BERGER, GOVERNMENT BY JUDICIARY (1977); Monaghan, *Our Perfect Constitution,* 52 N.Y.U. L. REV. 353 (1981); Bork, *Neutral Principles and Some First Amendment Problems,* 47 IND. L. J. 1 (1971).

4. This is a prominent theme of modern Critical Legal Scholars. *See, e.g.,* R. Gordon, *Critical Legal Histories,* 36 STAN L. REV. 57, 70-71, 98-102 (1984). Of course, this perspective is not unique to Critical Legal Theory, nor is it special to a historical perspective—as the obligatory reference to Thomas Kuhn (*See,* THE STRUCTURE OF SCIENTIFIC REVOLUTIONS (2d ed. 1970)) indicates. *See generally,* R. RORTY, CONSEQUENCES OF PRAGMATISM xiii-xvii (1982).

5. *Learning and Science, supra* note 1.

6. *See* Schauer, *Precedent,* 39 STAN. L. REV. 571 (1987).

7. J. AUSTIN, PROVINCE OF JURISPRUDENCE DETERMINED (1832).

8. H. L. A. HART, THE CONCEPT OF LAW 20-25 (1961).

9. I do not argue that this legitimacy requires, as Lon Fuller insisted, congruence with some fixed ("natural") moral principles. Fuller, *Positivism and Fidelity in Law—A Reply to Professor Hart,* 71 HARV. L. REV. 630 (1958). I think H. L. A. Hart's pragmatic rebuttal of the mixture of law and morals is convincing. *See,* HART, *supra* note 8 at 181-207. Nevertheless, implicit in Hart's argument that legal authority requires a "rule of recognition" by which legal obligation is separated from mere command is a notion of public assent that is grounded in *principle* even if the principle does not have a set moral content.

10. Weber, *Politics As A Vocation,* in H. GERTH & C. MILLS, eds., FROM MAX WEBER: ESSAYS IN SOCIOLOGY 77, 78 (1958).

11. For an excellent review of the Court's uses, and misuses, of history *see*, C. MILLER, THE SUPREME COURT AND THE USES OF HISTORY (1972). On the use, and misuse, of history by courts and legal advocates generally *see* Powell, *Rules for Originalists,* 73 VA. L. REV. 659, 661 (1987). Powell's "rules" are an excellent prescription for responsible use of history.

12. One of the abler critiques along these lines is ELY, *supra* note 2 at 43-72. Unfortunately, Ely did not employ his powerful skepticism to his own claim that the Constitution is essentially designed (or, more precisely, should be interpreted) to reinforce democratic processes, leaving substantive outcomes to be governed only by the constraints of process. That claim is at odds with a simple reading of the constitutional text and with what history teaches us the Framers were about. It is also unconvincing as a normative argument about the role of constitutionalism generally. *See, e.g.,* Tushnet, *Darkness on the Edge of Town: The Contributions of John Hart Ely to Constitutional Theory,* 89 YALE. L. J. 1037 (1980); L. Tribe, *The Puzzling Persistence of Process-Based Constitutional Theories,* 89 YALE L. J. 1063 (1980). Tribe rejects Ely's process theory in favor of a substantive-values view of the Constitution, but does not specify how the values are derived. Tushnet rejects both the process and substantive value views. Like Brest, *supra* note 2, Tushnet uses the conflict in other scholarly perspectives to support his own Critical Theory perspective: liberal political theory is unable to formulate a coherent theory of constitutionalism.

13. A fascinating account of the deficiencies in the records of the Constitutional Convention concludes that it would be impossible to derive reliably the intent of the Framers from those records: Hutson, *The Creation of the Constitution: The Integrity of the Documentary Record,* 65 TEX. L. REV. 1 (1986).

14. Quoted in F. MCDONALD, NOVUS ORDO SECLORUM: THE INTELLECTUAL ORIGINS OF THE CONSTITUTION 255 (1985).

15. The differences between Federalists and Antifederalists on the basic question of national versus state power is only illustrative of divergent interests and ideologies (which, of course, existed within as well as between these two major groups). For an excellent recent discussion of these interests and ideologies see MCDONALD, *supra* note 14 at 57-96, 185-224.

16. An important example is the range of interpretations among the Framers about the scope of the contracts clause (Article I, Section 10). *See* MCDONALD, *supra* note 14 at 270-75; Boyd, *The Contract Clause and the Evolution of American Federalism, 1789-1815,* 44 WM. & MARY Q. (3d ser.) 529 (1987). *See generally* Powell, *supra* note 11 at 684-87.

17. *See,* Powell, *The Original Understanding of Original Intent,* 98 HARV. L. REV. 885 (1985).

18. *See, e.g.,* Monaghan, *supra* note 3 and Monaghan, *Stare Decisis in Constitutional Adjudication,* 88 COLUM. L. REV. 723, 724-26 (1988).

19. The volume of the historical literature frustrates any attempt to capture it in a footnote. MCDONALD, *supra* note 14 at pp. 57-96 gives an overview of republican and

other theoretical influences. Other important references on republican influence include J. POCOCK, THE MACHIAVELLIAN MOMENT: FLORENTINE POLITICAL THOUGHT AND THE ATLANTIC TRADITION (1975); G. WOOD, THE CREATION OF THE AMERICAN REPUBLIC—1776-1787 49-75 (1969); B. BAILYN, THE IDEOLOGICAL ORIGINS OF THE AMERICAN REVOLUTION (1967). The discovery of republican influence by constitutional law scholars is more recent. Good discussions include Sunstein, *Interest Groups in American Public Law,* 38 STAN. L. REV. 29 (1985); Michelman, *The Supreme Court, 1985 Term—Foreword: Traces of Self-Government,* 100 HARV. L. REV. 4 (1986).

20. A recent symposium on Gordon Wood's seminal book, *supra* note 19, illustrates the character of the controversy. *See, Forum,* 44 WM. & MARY Q. (3d ser.) 549-640 (1987).

21. *See,* WOOD, *supra* note 19 at 421.

22. Among the most cogent of Jefferson Powell's "rules for originalists" *supra* note 11, at 672-74, is not to treat historical figures as our contemporaries merely because they use familiar modern words and phrases. As Powell points out, the Framers' discussion of constitutional politics "took place in a thought-world, and were conducted in a political language, distinct from our own." *Id.* at 673. A notorious example of the common disregard of this lesson is the frequent identification of Madison as a progenitor of modern interest group theory. There is doubtless some kinship between Madison's analysis of factions (most notably in his FEDERALIST No. 10 essay) and contemporary analyses of interest groups. But the translation of Madison into contemporary terms has resulted in a significant loss of Madison's political conceptions, most notably his republican ideals. *See,* WOOD, *supra* note 19 at 505; Sunstein, *supra* note 19 at 42.

23. R. DWORKIN, LAW'S EMPIRE, 56-59 (1986); Cavell, *A Matter of Meaning It,* in S. CAVELL, MUST WE MEAN WHAT WE SAY? 213, 225-37 (1969). I do not mean that the legal and literary interpretations have the same purpose and effect. Manifestly they do not. *See,* Posner, *Law and Literature: A Relation Reargued,* 72 VA. L. REV. 1351 (1986). I do intend to suggest that, if one is willing to free legal interpretation (constitutional interpretation in particular) from its strict historical environment, Cavell's interpretive technique has an appeal in the realm of law no less than in the realm of literature.

24. *See* Rorty, *The Historiography of Philosophy: Four Genres,* in PHILOSOPHY IN HISTORY 49-75 (R. Rorty *et al. eds. 1984).*

25. 5 U.S. (1 Cranch) 137 (1803). Although the Framers' views on judicial review (nowhere expressed in the Constitution) have been the subject of much debate, it now is generally accepted that they contemplated some form of review. *See, e.g.,* A. BICKEL, THE LEAST DANGEROUS BRANCH: THE SUPREME COURT AT THE BAR OF POLITICS 14-15 (1962); WOOD, *supra* note 19 at 453-63.

26. There were 55 delegates to the Convention, most of them men of social distinction and privilege (an "assembly of demi-gods" Jefferson called them). *See,* M. FARRAND, THE FRAMING OF THE CONSTITUTION 39 (1913). DWORKIN, *supra* note 23, makes a similar point about the Framers and about the argument from democratic choice generally.

27. The "over one hundred years" is based on the date of Murray's Lessee v. Hoboken Land and Improvement Co., 59 U.S. (18 How.) 272 (1855), where the Court assumed that due process applied to a distress warrant issued by the Solicitor of the Treasury. The Court ignored defendant's argument that the warrant was not a judicial act to which due process applied. However, the Court went on to find that defendant received all the process that was due.

28. The rhetorical tone of the question is intended to invite a negative answer. *See,* Monaghan, *supra* note 18 (respect for *stare decisis* and stability precludes restoration of original intent). Nevertheless, the prospect of rolling back over one hundred years of history (i.e., since *Murray's Lessee*) is apparently quite conceivable to some. Frank Easterbrook, first as professor of law and more recently as judge, has suggested returning to the original intent of the due process clause, which he thinks was simply a restraint on courts, not legislatures. Easterbrook, *Substance and Due Process,* 1982 SUP. CT. REV. 85 (1982); Gumz v. Morrissette, 772 F. 2d 1395, 1404-6 (7th Cir., 1985).

29. Madison himself provides confirming testimony on this point. He warned against expansive interpretations that might undermine the constitutional structure fixed by the Framers. But he also accepted the fact that the Constitution would receive interpretations different from those originally intended, and to the extent that those later interpretations acquired public acceptance, he thought they should not be disturbed. *See,* Powell, *supra* note 17 at 939-41.

30. The textual point is stressed by ELY, *supra* note 2 at 18, despite his rejection of strict ("clause-bound") interpretivism. Ely's literalism seems to me more than a little simplistic. No violence is done to language by construing the phrase "due process" to include substantive restraints of the kind that have been incorporated therein. From ancient times the common law imparted notions of rationality and purpose into its conception of fair adjudication. And it strains no imagination to think of "due process of law" as implying more than merely mechanical procedures. Whether the Framers *intended* such an interpretation is another point, of course. On this the historical account of the due process clause traces its origin to the "law of the land" provisions of Magna Charta which were adopted first by state constitutional draftsmen, then by the Framers of the Federal Constitution. Accepted interpretation of English constitutional history (transmitted to colonial America via Blackstone) assigns to the Magna Charta provisions no ambition to limit the power of Parliament (and hence to impose no restraint on substantive law), but only to prescribe the processes of the courts in adjudicating individual rights (life, liberty and property). *See, e.g.,* Reeder, *The Due Process Clause and the Substance of Individual Rights,* 58 U. PA. L. REV. 191, 214 (1910); Corwin, *The Doctrine of Due Process Before the Civil War,* 24 HARV. L. REV. 366, 370-73 (1911). However, the Framers did not accept the basic premise of English constitutionalism—the supremacy of Parliament—(*see* note 32 *infra*) which undercuts the assumption that they necessarily accepted the English content of Magna Charta's "law of the land" by accepting its form.

31. *See, e.g.,* WOOD, *supra* note 19, *passim.* Specifically on the natural law/social contract theory influences *see* Corwin, *The Higher Law Background of American Constitutional Law,* 42 HARV. L. REV. 149; 365 (1928, 1929).

32. As WOOD, *supra* note 19 at 259-305, observes, the Americans embraced the Lockean *social* contract theory, a contract among people, not simply between government and people, which was committed to a view of natural rights that was beyond the power of government. In contrast to the English tradition, in the Lockean social contract full sovereignty of the people is not transferred to the legislature, and the legislature holds its power only as trustee. *Id.* at 344-89. Most importantly, the trustee can be held to account in ordinary law courts for enactments that are inconsistent with natural right—with principles of "right reason" and "justice." As Wood points out, this merging of fundamental law with positive law was the foremost innovation of American political thought. It was also the source of basic conflict between the ideals of natural right on the one hand and democratic governance on the other. *Id.* at 295-305. It is, of course, a conflict that has never been resolved, as the never-ending debate over judicial review attests.

33. 83 U.S. (16 Wall) 36 (1873). A Louisiana law granting a monopoly charter to maintain slaughterhouses in three parishes was challenged by the butchers, whose right to practice their trade was allegedly curtailed by the monopoly. They claimed that the exclusion created an involuntary servitude in violation of the Thirteenth Amendment, and deprived them of their privileges and immunities, of due process and of equal protection, all in violation of the Fourteenth Amendment. The Court rejected all of the claims. It devoted most of its time to privileges and immunities, which it construed as applying to certain rights created *by the Constitution* for citizens of the *United States* (as prescribed by Article IV) and not the entire domain of civil rights "heretofore belonging exclusively to the States." The due process claim was given short shrift: the restraint on the exercise of trade was not "a deprivation of property within the meaning of that provision." The equal protection clause was found inapplicable inasmuch as it was designed to prevent discrimination on account of race.

34. 165 U.S. 578 (1897). A Louisiana law that required that all marine insurance on property in the state be obtained only from companies complying with Louisiana law was challenged by defendants who were found guilty of violating the statute by obtaining out-of-state insurance on cotton to be exported from New Orleans. Defendants claimed the law deprived them of liberty in violation of the Fourteenth Amendment's due process clause. The Court unanimously agreed; in an opinion by Justice Peckham, the Court construed "liberty" to embrace:

> not only the right of the citizen to be free from the mere physical restraint of his person, as by incarceration, but ... the right of the citizen to be free in the enjoyment of all his faculties; to be free to use them in all lawful ways; to live and work where he will ... to pursue any livelihood or avocation, and for that purpose to enter into all contracts which may be proper, necessary and essential to his carrying out to a successful conclusion the purposes above mentioned.

Id. at 589.

35. 198 U.S. 45 (1905). A New York law setting maximum hourly and weekly hours of employment of bakery employees was challenged as a violation of the Fourteenth

Amendment. The Court upheld the challenge. Justice Peckham, for a majority of the Court, followed *Allgeyer* in holding that the right to conduct business is part of the liberty protected by due process, and that the law here exceeded the proper boundaries of the police power in infringing that liberty. Justice Harlan (joined by Justices White and Day) and Justice Holmes wrote separate dissents each challenging the Court's finding that the law was not reasonably related to legitimate state ends. Importantly, for all the attention given to Justice Holmes's celebrated dissent ("the 14th Amendment does not enact Mr. Herbert Spencer's Social Statics") neither Holmes nor Harlan challenged Justice Peckham's premise that due process did have some substantive application and that "liberty" embraced economic freedoms.

36. *See generally*, TRIBE, *supra* note 2 at 434-49.

37. 262 U.S. 390 (1923). Notice that it was the teacher's right, not that of the child, that was determined by the Court; however, the teacher's right logically implied some kind of right on the part of the child, as Justice Holmes observed in dissent.

38. *Id.* at 399 (citations omitted).

39. In dissenting to *Meyer* and to a companion case, Holmes observed that it was reasonable to provide that a young child "shall hear and speak only English at school," and this being reasonable it could not violate the "liberty" of the teacher to prohibit him from teaching a foreign language.

40. 268 U.S. 510 (1925).

41. 300 U.S. 379 (1937). It was abandoned insofar as the Court no longer treated the rational basis test as a meaningful limitation on legislative choices. Williamson v. Lee Optical Co., 348 U.S. 483 (1955), is the standard reference. *See also,* United States v. Carolene Products Co., 304 U.S. 144 (1938); Daniel v. Family Security Life Ins. Co. 336 U.S. 220 (1949); Ferguson v. Skrupa, 372 U.S. 726 (1963). *See generally,* Gunther, *The Supreme Court, 1971 Term—Foreword: In Search of Evolving Doctrine on a Changing Court: A Model for a Newer Equal Protection,* 86 HARV. L. REV. 1 (1972).

42. 381 U.S. 479 (1965). Justice Douglas's opinion for the Court studiously avoids grounding the decision on due process, invoking instead the concept of a general right of privacy based on "emanations" from the First, Third, Fourth and Fifth (self incrimination, not due process) and Ninth Amendments. Justice Goldberg, joined by the Chief Justice and Justice Brennan, accepted due process as the basis of the decision, relying, *inter alia,* on *Meyer.* So, too, Justices Harlan and White, in separate concurring opinions, acknowledged due process as the proper ground for the privacy right. Justices Black and Stewart, dissenting, both understood the case to be a revival of substantive due process à la *Lochner.*

43. 410 U.S. 113 (1973). Justice Blackman's opinion for the Court tracks Justice Douglas's opinion in *Griswold* in citing various provisions of the Bill of Rights as supporting a right of privacy. Unlike Douglas, Blackman, however, does not recognize that the privacy right is textually grounded in the due process clause albeit without much discussion of substantive due process as a doctrinal foundation. *Id.* at 64. Interestingly Justice Stewart, who dissented in *Griswold,* concurred separately in *Roe*

and explicitly accepted substantive due process (à la *Griswold, Meyer, Pierce* and other cases) as the basis for the decision. In a concurring opinion to a companion case, Justice Douglas continued to insist that recognition of the right of privacy was not a matter of substantive due process. Doe v. Bolton, 410 U.S. 179, 209, 212 (1973). This was nothing more than disingenuous word play on the part of Justice Douglas, insofar as he relied on such cases as *Meyer* and *Pierce.*

44. 431 U.S. 494 (1977). Justice Powell, writing for the Court, relies on *Meyer* and *Pierce* as well as on an array of other decisions involving what have come to be called "privacy rights," for example, Griswold v. Connecticut, 381 U.S. 479 (1965); Roe v. Wade, 410 U.S. 113 (1973); Skinner v. Oklahoma, 316 U.S. 535 (1942). Justice Powell's opinion expresses the usual concern about reviving *Lochner,* but emphasizes that "Appropriate limits on substantive due process come not from drawing arbitrary lines but rather from careful 'respect for the teachings of history [and] solid recognition of the basic values that underlie our society'." 431 U.S. at 503 (quoting *Griswold*). It is noteworthy that Justice White, dissenting to the Court's decision, and also expressing the view that substantive due process should be narrowly circumscribed, conceded that it had some role to play in constitutional review:

> No case that I know of ... has announced that there is some legislation with respect to which there no longer exists a means-ends test as a matter of substantive due process law. This is not surprising, for otherwise a protected liberty could be infringed by a law having no purpose or utility whatsoever.

Id. at 548. White concluded, however, that the liberty here in issue required only a minimal rationality standard and, on that standard, the ordinance passed muster.

45. 106 S. Ct. 2841 (1986). In *Bowers,* Justice White, for a majority of the Court, followed his opinion in *Moore* (*supra* note 44) about narrowly circumscribing substantive due process; the so-called privacy right was thus confined to matters of "family, marriages or procreation," and did not embrace sexual preferences. It is important to emphasize, however, that his opinion is addressed to the question whether private sexual activity is a fundamental right that requires "strict scrutiny"; it was conceded that the law still required a "rational basis" (which the Court, following its usual pattern, found without difficulty).

46. *See, e.g.,* D. TRUMAN, THE GOVERNMENTAL PROCESS: POLITICAL INTERESTS AND PUBLIC OPINION (1951); E. LATHAM, THE GROUP BASIS OF POLITICS (1952). It is conventional to trace interest group theory back to A. BENTLEY, THE PROCESS OF GOVERNMENT: A STUDY OF SOCIAL PRESSURES (1908). However, this interest in interest groups did not really become a common perspective of political science until the 1940s and 1950s. In more recent times, the interest group perspective has been refined by "public choice" theory, which is heavily indebted to economic models and analysis. *See, e.g.,* D. MUELLER, PUBLIC CHOICE (1979).

47. ELY, *supra* note 2.

48. *See, id.* at 73-179.

49. Judge Hans Linde has argued that legislatures are bound by some standards. Linde, *Due Process of Lawmaking*, 55 NEB. L. REV. 197, 222-51 (1976). However, apart from procedural requirements and standards for "legitimate lawmaking" (*id.* at 228-29), he is hard pressed to identify any particular requirements other than the formal mechanics for enacting laws. The kinds of due process formalities required of courts and agencies are not binding on legislatures, as Linde concedes. *See* Gellhorn and Robinson, *Rulemaking Due Process: An Inconclusive Dialogue*, 48 U. CHI. L. REV. 201, 222-26 (1981). Examples of institutional/separation-of-powers constraints include Bowsher v. Synar, 106 S. Ct. 3181 (1986) (exercise of "executive" prerogatives by legislative officer unconstitutional); INS v. Chadha, 462 U.S. 919 (1983) (legislative veto of executive rules or orders unconstitutional).

50. The literature on procedural due process is too immense even to catalogue here. Two recent works exhaustively and ably canvass the subject. J. MASHAW, DUE PROCESS IN THE ADMINISTRATIVE STATE (1985); Rubin, *Due Process and the Administrative State*, 72 CALIF. L. REV. 1044 (1984).

51. *See, e.g.,* Board of Regents v. Roth, 408 U.S. 564 (1972).

52. Murray's Lessee v. Hoboken Land and Improvement Co., 59 U.S. (18 How.) 272 (1855). A congressional statute providing for the issuance of distress warrants to collect debts owed the government was challenged as a violation of due process inasmuch as the warrants were issued without a hearing. The Court held that the use of summary proceedings in this context was in accordance with historic usage accepted at the time the Constitution was drafted; hence due process was satisfied.

53. On the right-privilege notion generally *see* Van Alstyne, *The Demise of the Right-Privilege Distinction in Constitutional Law*, 81 HARV. L. REV. 1439 (1968).

54. *See generally*, Kreimer, *Allocational Sanctions: The Problem of Negative Rights in a Positive State*, 132, U. PA. L. REV. 1293 (1984). There are really two distinct, though related, ideas here: one is that the state's affirmative power as employer or "welfare agent" is almost wholly discretionary; individual beneficiaries do not have enforceable "rights" to the benefits conferred, or have only such rights as the government itself concedes in creating the employment or benefit programs; a second notion is that the government may impose as a condition of granting such benefits restraints on the exercise of other rights the individual possess. Kreimer, *supra*, uses the phrase "allocational sanctions" to describe both of these concepts. This is misleading in suggesting a specific purpose of using the allocation of benefits in order to impose external constraints. No doubt this is sometimes the case; but often the conditions are simply regarded as a necessary characteristic of the benefit conferred, *e.g.*, welfare benefits conditioned on residency, *see* Shapiro v. Thompson, 394 U.S. 618 (1969) (invalidating such a condition insofar as it interfered with the right to travel).

55. Kreimer, *supra* note 54, discusses numerous recent cases. Two illustrations suffice here. In United States Civil Service Comm'n v. National Ass'n of Letter Carriers, 413 U.S. 548 (1973), the Court held that the special circumstances of public employment justified prohibition against civil servants participating in political campaign activity, a prohibition that, by the Court's own acknowledgment, could not have been

sustained against ordinary citizens. In United States Postal Service v. Council of Greenburgh Civic Ass'ns, 453 U.S. 114 (1981), the Court held that the needs of the federal postal service justified imposing special restraints on the use of mailboxes to receive material other than regular mail. Again, such a restraint on receiving information could not have been sustained without the link to a special government purpose.

56. Some generalizations can be made by way of classifying, if not rationalizing, the cases. For example, pursuit of professional occupation, such as law or medicine, was almost always treated as a matter of right; occupations commonly touted as matters of mere privilege typically involved "less respectable" services such as operating a tavern or retail liquor store. *See* W. GELLHORN & C. BYSE, ADMINISTRATIVE LAW, CASES AND COMMENTS 768-770 (1954).

57. *See, e.g.,* Columbia Auto Loan v. Jordan, 196 F.2d 568 (D.C. Cir. 1952).

58. 182 F.2d 46 (D.C. Cir. 1950), *aff'd by evenly divided court,* 341 U.S. 918 (1951).

59. *See, e.g.,* Speiser v. Randall, 357 U.S. 513 (1958) (invalidating a loyalty oath); Sherbert v. Verner, 374 U.S. 398 (1963) (conditions on unemployment benefits invalid insofar as they interfered with recipient's religious beliefs); Keyishian v. Board of Regents, 385 U.S. 589 (1967) (loyalty oath for public teachers unconstitutional).

60. In 1959, in Greene v. McElroy, 360 U.S. 474 (1959), the Court invalidated summary revocation of a security clearance needed for private employment in defense-related work. Although the decision was grounded on the absence of statutory authority for the summary procedures, the Court's opinion bristles with warnings that such summary procedures might violate due process. Two years later in Cafeteria Workers Union v. McElroy, 367 U.S. 886 (1961), the Court mooted the warning of *Greene* by refusing to invalidate summary revocation of a security clearance. Noteworthy, however, is the Court's refusal to place its decision on a simple right-privilege dichotomy. Instead, it purported to balance the individual's interest against that of the government and found the latter outweighed the former, particularly insofar as it found no stigma effect which would impair the individual's pursuit of a similar job elsewhere (the individual here was an employee of a private concessionaire that operated a cafeteria in a naval gun factory; the Court reasoned that she was free to work in other locations for the same employer or another; she was denied the opportunity to work at only this one location). Setting aside the result, the *Cafeteria Workers'* balancing test was unmistakably a step away from *Bailey* and towards a due process more sensitive to individual interest and less driven by labels.

61. 397 U.S. 254 (1970).

62. *Id.* at 262 n.8.

63. 408 U.S. 564 (1972).

64. 408 U.S. 593 (1972).

65. Most commentators have criticized *Roth* and its general premise that due process should turn on formally established "rights," at least rights defined separately from the due process clause itself. While the precise arguments differ in detail, all

essentially concur that the test of the due process clause should not be construed literally but interpreted broadly to protect important interests, or what is the same, to confer a right in the process itself. *See, e.g.,* MASHAW, *supra* note 50 at 163-64; Rubin, *supra* note 50 at 1046; Van Alstyne, *Cracks in the New Property: Adjudicative Due Process in the Administrative State,* 62 CORNELL L. REV. 445, 483 (1977); Michelman, *Formal and Associational Aims in Procedural Due Process,* in 18 NOMOS: DUE PROCESS 126 (1977). Some commentators, however, insist on stricter adherence to the rights language of the text. *See,* Williams, *Liberty and Property: The Problem of Government Benefits,* 12 J. LEGAL STUD. 3, 4-19 (1983); Easterbrook, *supra* note 28.

66. *See, e.g.,* Monaghan, *Of "Liberty" and "Property",* 62 CORNELL L. REV., 405, 411-52 (1977); Reeder, *supra* note 30.

67. Madison, *Property,* in 6 THE WRITINGS OF JAMES MADISON 101-3 (G. Hunt, ed. 1906).

68. Letter from Madison to Edward Livingston (Apr. 17, 1824), quoted in Powell, *supra* note 17, at 936. Madison's caution is consistent with his and other Framers' view that constitutional interpretation should be a matter of textual exegesis and should not rely on external sources of "legislative interest." Indeed, it was for just this reason that Madison delayed publication of his notes of the Convention. *Id.* at 936 and *passim.*

69. *See* R. SCHLATTER, PRIVATE PROPERTY: THE HISTORY OF AN IDEA, 187-205 (1951). For the original statement *see,* J. LOCKE, TWO TREATISES OF GOVERNMENT 329-44 (P. Laslett ed. 1965).

70. On the confusing intermixture of natural law and the positivist conceptions by Locke and others, see SCHLATTER, *supra* at 159 (Locke); 166-71 (Blackstone); 182-83 (Smith); 188-200 (Adams, Madison, Jefferson, among others). Jefferson's views in this regard are noteworthy. While he resisted the natural rights theory of property to the extent it opposed the state's prerogative to promote equality and social welfare, he seems to have accepted the basic Lockean concept of property as security for man's labor, and at various times he described this as a natural right. *See,* SCHLATTER, *supra* note 69, at 196-99. Morton White interprets Jefferson's views as derived from Burlamaqui's theory of property as a kind of "secondary," as opposed to a "primary" natural right such as the right to life. The point of the distinction is more than a little obscure, but in general terms it appears to imply that property is shaped by, and subject to, social circumstances and other rights or liberties. Nevertheless, as White points out, the right is still "natural" in the sense of being prior to the state. *See,* M. WHITE, THE PHILOSOPHY OF THE AMERICAN REVOLUTION 213-28 (1978). The similarity of Jefferson's view of natural rights and that of Burlamaqui (as well as Grotius) is also noted by A. KOCH, THE PHILOSOPHY OF THOMAS JEFFERSON 148 (1957).

71. The difficulties with a labor theory of property are discussed in A. RYAN, PROPERTY AND POLITICAL THEORY 32-48 (1984). Illustratively: if I pick apples from a tree, do I obtain a property right to the apples, the whole tree, the stand of trees or the land?

72. *See,* D. Hume, *An Inquiry Concerning the Principles of Morals* (1751), in 4 PHILOSOPHICAL WORKS 258 (1854). On the utilitarian view of property generally *see* SCHLATTER, *supra* note 69, at 239-51; RYAN, *supra* note 71, at 91-117.

73. *See, e.g.,* WOOD and BAILYN references, *supra* note 19, and Corwin, *supra* note 30.

74. *See, e.g.,* Section 1 of the Virginia Declaration of Rights (1776):

> That all men are by nature equally free and independent, and have certain inherent rights, of which, when they enter into a state of society, they cannot by any compact deprive or divest their posterity; namely the enjoyment of life and liberty with the means of acquiring and possessing property, and pursuing and obtaining happiness and safety.

For text and commentary *see* A. HOWARD, 1 COMMENTARIES ON THE CONSTITUTION OF VIRGINIA 58-69 (1974). The Virginia Declaration of 1776 was a model for other states; even today the bill of rights in most states has a clause similar to the above. *See, id.* at pp. 68-69. It is noteworthy that while these state bills track the rhetorical tone of the Declaration of Independence, they specifically mention "property," thus reverting to the declaration of the first Continental Congress whose "immutable laws of nature" were specified, after Locke, as "life, liberty and property." *See,* SCHLATTER, *supra* note 69 at 188-89.

75. *See,* B. WRIGHT, AMERICAN INTERPRETATIONS OF NATURAL LAW 149-326 (1931). For examples of judicial opinions embracing natural law, *see, e.g.,* Vanhorne's Lessee v. Dorrance, 2 Dall. 304 (C.C.D.Pa. 1795); Calder v. Bull, 3 Dall (U.S.) 386 (1798); Herman v. State, 8 Ind. 545 (1855). Even Chief Justice Marshall, who did not appeal often to natural law, sometimes gave evidence of a belief in it. *See, e.g.,* Fletcher v. Peck, 6 Cranch 87, 135 (1910) ("nature of society" may prescribe some limits to legislative power); Johnson and Graham's Lessee v. McIntosh, 8 Wheaton 543, 572 (1823) ("principles of abstract justice" which regulate the "rights of civilized nations").

76. RYAN, *supra,* note 71 at 45-46. It is in this broad functional interpretation that the Lockean view adumbrates a utilitarian argument. (On the instrumentalist proto-utilitarianism in Locke *see, id.* at 30.)

77. The inapplicability of the Fifth Amendment to the states was not determined until 1833, in Barron v. Baltimore, 32 U.S. (7 Pet.) 243 (1833). Technically, therefore, there was a period of more than forty years between the time of the ratification of the Fifth (1791) and of the Fourteenth (1867) when federal due process might have been applied to the states. Be that as it may, it wasn't, and the effect was to leave due process adjudications primarily to state constitutions, there being little federal government activity providing occasion for Fifth Amendment due process. Despite the limited precedent in the pre-Civil-War period, Edward Corwin concluded that an expansive view of property, in particular its extention to occupational liberty, "found little or no support from the Common Law, and had in consequence before the Civil War little influence upon judges." *The Basic Doctrine of American Constitutional Law,* 12 MICH. L. REV. 247 (1914). *See also,* Corwin, *supra* note 30. As I will discuss below, I think Corwin misreads some of the cases and confuses the question of rights definition with that of the degree of protection.

78. 15 N.C. (4 Dec.) 1 (1833).

79. Id. at 17.

80. 7 Porter (Ala.) 293 (1838).

81. 13 N.Y. 378 (1856).

82. The cases are discussed in Corwin, *supra* note 30.

83. 8 Ind. 545 (1855).

84. *Id.* at 557.

85. *Id.* at 558-59.

86. *Id.* at 557.

87. Corwin, *supra* note 30 at 60-75. *See also,* Warren, *The New Liberty Under the Fourteenth Amendment,* 39 HARV. L. REV. 431, 442-43 (1926); Williams, *"Liberty" in the Due Process Clauses of the Fifth and Fourteenth Amendments: The Framers' Intentions,* 53 COLO. L. REV., 117, 127 (1981).

88. In one of the cases cited by Corwin, State v. Kieran, 5 R.I. 497 (1858), there is a strong suggestion that the court conceived of due process only in procedural terms (*see* 5 R.I. at 506-7). There is no plain holding to this effect, however, in *Kieran* or any of the other cases.

89. The following cases, cited by Corwin, seem to me particularly clear on this point: Goddard v. Jacksonville, 15 Ill, 589 (1854); People v. Gallagher, 4 Mich. 243 (1856); State v. Paul, 5 R.I. 185 (1858); State v. Kieran, 5 R.I. 497 (1858); Lincoln v. Smith, 27 Vt. 328 (1854).

90. The one case that comes closest to denying the existence of a property or liberty right in the sale of liquor is People v. Gallagher, 4 Mich. 243 (1856). However, even here the majority opinion lays paramount stress on the reasonableness of the legislative prohibition in light of public health needs.

91. 83 U.S. 36 (1873).

92. 86 U.S. 505 (1873). *Robinson* cites an earlier state decision, Ex Parte Heyfron, 5 Miss. (7 How.) 127 (1843); applying due process to a disbarment proceeding.

93. *See, e.g.,* Gage v. Censor of the New Hampshire Eclectic Medical Society, 63 N.H. 92 (1884); State v. State Medical Examining Bd., 32 Minn. 324, 20 N.W. 238 (1884); People v. McCoy, 125 Ill., 289, 17 N.E. 786 (1888); State v. Schultz, 11 Mont. 429, 28 Pac. 643 (1892); Goldsmith v. United States Board of Tax Appeals, 270 U.S. 117 (1926).

94. This reflects a more general indifference, prior to *Roth* in 1972, to defining separate domains for liberty and property for purposes of procedural or substantive due process. *See,* Monaghan, *supra* note 66, at 409.

95. *See,* 165 U.S. at 589.

96. *See,* 262 U.S. at 399.

97. 236 U.S. 1, 14 (1915) (the right to work partakes of both liberty and property).

98. This is not to say that the Court has been entirely faithful to the breadth of *Meyer's* formulation. Nevertheless, it has recognized most of the "liberties" specifically identified by *Meyer. See, e.g.,* Willner v. Committee on Character, 373 U.S. 96 (1963) (professional occupation); Loving v. Virginia 388 U.S. 1, 12 (1967) (marriage); Skinner v. Oklahoma, 316 U.S. 535 (1942) (procreation). Indeed, the Court has added to the specific items listed in *Meyer.* For example, free speech rights were added to the list by virtue of the assumption in Gitlow v. New York, 268 U.S. 652 (1925), that the First Amendment was incorporated into the Fourteenth via the protection of "liberty." *See,* Board of Regents v. Roth, 408 U.S. 564 (1972) (dictum). That incorporation brings in religious liberty as well, of course. *See,* Wisconsin v. Yoder, 406 U.S. 205 (1972). Access to the courts (for purposes of obtaining a divorce) was, by implication, treated as liberty in Boddie v. Connecticut, 401 U.S. 371 (1971), though the Court was basically indifferent to characterization of the underlying interest or right. Even racial equality became an implied liberty by reason of the anachronistic "reverse incorporation" of the equal protection clause into the Fifth Amendment (where, of course, it does not appear in the text) in Bolling v. Sharpe, 347 U.S. 497 (1954).

99. Boddie v. Connecticut, *supra* note 98, might be interpreted as an affirmative liberty case. However, the Court's opinion (by Justice Harlan) emphasized the fact that the individuals were not free to act without court action—marriage could not be dissolved (and remarriage was illegal) without court approval. Hence the state was in a posture of constraining individual liberty.

On negative vs. "affirmative" liberty generally, *see,* I. BERLIN, FOUR ESSAYS ON LIBERTY, 118-72 (1969). This purely negative form of the concept of liberty is not beyond challenge; a deeper examination of its philosophical premises suggests room for a more positive conception. *See,* C. Taylor, *What's Wrong With Negative Liberty, in* THE IDEA OF FREEDOM: ESSAYS IN HONOR OF ISAIAH BERLIN 175-93 (A. Ryan ed. 1979). However, the negative form of liberty remains conventional in ordinary social discourse, despite occasional rhetorical inventions, such as FDR's famous "four freedoms" ("freedom from want," "freedom from fear," etc.), for political purposes. Given what we know about the corrupting effects of semantic manipulation for political expediency, there is wisdom in keeping legal usage as close as possible to conventional understandings. *See* G. ORWELL, 1984 (1949); *see also,* Orwell, *Politics and the English Language, in* INSIDE THE WHALE AND OTHER ESSAYS 143 (1971).

100. *See, e.g.,* Goldberg v. Kelly, 397 U.S. 254 (1970) (welfare benefits; entitlement by statute); Perry v. Sindermann, 408 U.S. 593 (1972) (public employment; entitlement by "implied" contract and "unwritten common law"); Goss v. Lopez, 419 U.S. 565 (1975) (public education; entitlement by statute); Memphis Light, Gas & Water Division v. Craft, 436 U.S. 1 (1978) (public utility service; entitlement by contract).

101. *See,* Flemming v. Nestor 363 U.S. 603 (1960), holding that retroactive congressional termination of plaintiff's retirement benefits was not a violation of due process because the beneficiary had no "accrued property right" under the Social Security system. Interestingly, the Court conceded that the legislation was subject to

the 'rational basis test' (which it found satisfied here). On the latter point *see,* Dandridge v. Williams, 397 U.S. 471 (1970) (applying equal protection analysis; minimal rationality test applicable to Social Security AFDC program). Justice Marshall's suggestion appears in his dissent in Board of Regents v. Roth, 408 U.S. 564, (1972). For Reich's argument *see, The New Property,* 73 YALE L.J. 733, 768-71 (1964) (criticizing *Nestor*). Both Marshall and Reich are very general in their discussions; neither squarely confronts the question whether, for example, the takings clause should be applied to New Property. Interestingly, part of the burden of Reich's discussion of substantive protection is devoted to criticizing not merely the distinction between old and new property but between personal and economic rights, *id.* at 772-73. *Compare,* Justice Marshall's dissent in *Dandridge, supra,* arguing for a closer judicial scrutiny of government regulation of economic interests in the welfare context than in the occupation context (à la *Lee Optical* and its progeny, *see, supra* note 41). Marshall seems to be arguing for *greater* protection of New Property than for the old!

102. Letter from Lord Macaulay to H. S. Randall, May 23, 1857, quoted in Cinderella Career & Finishing Schools, Inc. v. FTC, 425 F.2d 583, 591 (D.C. Cir. 1970).

103. 401 U.S. 371 (1971). *See also* Bell v. Burson, 402 U.S. 535, 539 (1971), applying due process to suspension of a driver's license where the Court was content to find an "important interest." For a critique *see generally,* Williams, *supra* note 65 at 14-17.

104. 408 U.S. at 601.

105. *See,* J. BENTHAM, THEORY OF LEGISLATION, 112-13 (6th ed. 1890).

106. Williams, *supra* note 65, at 7.

107. The bundle-of-sticks/bundle-of-rights idea is the contribution of the legal realists who used it to undermine the classical notion of property as a sacrosanct right. *See,* Grey, *The Disintegration of Property,* in 22 NOMOS: PROPERTY, 69, 81, 85 (1980); *see also,* Rubin, *supra* note 50, at 1086. In this respect the evolution of property concepts mirrors the general transformation of American legal thought away from natural law and towards a utilitarian, positivist perspective.

108. *See,* Calabresi and Melamud, *Property Rules, Liability Rules and Inalienability: One View of the Cathedral,* 85 HARV. L. REV. 1089 (1972).

109. The judicial dispute can be traced through the following sequence of cases: Arnett v. Kennedy, 416 U.S. 134 (1974); Bishop v. Wood, 426 U.S. 341 (1976); Vitek v. Jones, 445 U.S. 480, 490-91 (1980); Logan v. Zimmerman Brush Co., 455 U.S. 422 (1982); Cleveland Bd. of Educ. v. Loudermill, 470 U.S. 532 (1985). For a sample of the academic controversy see the sources cited in note 65 *supra. See also,* Cass, *The Meaning of Liberty: Notes on Problems Within the Fraternity,* 1 NOTRE DAME J. LAW, ETHICS & PUB. POL. 777, 791-96 (1985).

110. The distinction between property and liberty as to the source of the right is noted in *Roth* and in virtually all of the post-*Roth* cases, *supra* note 107. The positive-law basis for property appears in the due process jurisprudence; so far as I am aware the Court has never decided whether for other purposes, say, takings, property has a

constitutional basis. Of course, there is no textual basis for distinguishing due process from takings, and it is not easy to construct a logical argument for doing so. Yet, I think it almost certain that were the question squarely put to the Court, it would not permit positive law to circumvent the takings clause by legislative redefinition of those "things" conventionally regarded as property.

111. 416 U.S. 134 (1974).

112. *Id.* at 151-54.

113. 470 U.S. 532 (1985).

114. *Id.* at 541.

115. 155 Mass. 216, 220, 29 N.E. 517, 518 (1892).

116. I do not mean to imply that one cannot make a sensible argument from power, which is, I believe, the thrust of Grey, *Procedural Fairness and Substantive Rights,* in 18 NOMOS: DUE PROCESS 182 (1977). However, for reasons fully examined in Kreimer, *supra* note 54, I believe the argument from power is not persuasive as a matter of logic or constitutional principle. As to logic, there is no necessity for construing a government power to grant or deny benefits to carry with it a power to impose "lesser" conditions: legal power is what "we the people" make it and there is no incoherence in shaping it so that it can only be exercised in certain defined ways. As to constitutional principle, limiting the ways in which the government can use its power is a means of preventing strategic manipulation by the government in order to pursue certain objectives that it could not, or would not, otherwise pursue *directly.* The point is illustrated with remarkable clarity by Nollan v. California Coastal Com'n, 107 S. Ct. 3141 (1987), where a state zoning authority sought to condition a development permit on provision of a public easement. The Court correctly perceived the condition to be an attempt to avoid the takings clause and invalidated it. On the facts of the case I believe the Court was clearly correct both in its perception and its decision.

117. *See,* Board of Regents v. Roth, 408 U.S. 564 (1972).

118. *See, e.g.,* Monaghan, *supra* note 66.

119. In Bishop v. Wood, 426 U.S. 341, 349-50 n. 14 (1976), Justice Stevens, for the Court's majority, sarcastically rejected "Mr. Justice Brennan's remarkably innovative suggestion that we develop a federal common law of property rights."

120. It has been accepted since Allgeyer v. Louisiana, 165 U.S. 578 (1897). Liberty may also be created by positive, nonconstitutional law. *See, e.g.,* Vitek v. Jones, 445 U.S. 480 (1980). Where no liberty right can be "found" in the Constitution, the same positivist trap that exists for property ensnares "liberty." *See,* Meachum v. Fano, 427 U.S. 215 (1976).

121. 424 U.S. 319, 335 (1976).

122. 419 U.S. 565 (1975).

123. *Id.* at 579-82.

124. 430 U.S. 651 (1977).

125. MASHAW, *supra* note 50, at 153.

126. Mashaw explores, *id.* at 172–82, several core values that a dignitary approach should serve, notably: equality of treatment, predictability, transparency, rationality, participation, and privacy. These values do not point unequivocally to any single set of procedures, as Mashaw recognizes. Moreover, he recognizes that they do point to a quite modest set of constitutionally required precedures—in many instances, little more than a neutrally applied set of criteria and a requirement for reasons. Given the fact that the dispute in these cases typically involves not due process in the abstract, but whether certain specific procedures should be followed, the practical question is how well a dignity test resolves these disputes. Diver, *Book Review, The Wrath of "Roth"*, 94 YALE L. J. 1529 (185), is critical of Mashaw's approach on these grounds. *See also* the criticism of Rubin, *supra* note 50 at 1098, who regards the idea of a dignitary theory as an attempt to reconstruct an independent rights threshold when what is needed is to escape from the notion of rights altogether. I am not sure Rubin's characterization of the dignitary theory is entirely fair to its exponents, but I agree with Diver that the notion has little operational usefulness. Such value as it has is largely symbolic, which probably does not warrant the attention it has received.

127. Grey, *The Constitution as Scripture*, 37 STAN. L. REV. 1, 23–25 (1984), expresses a similar sentiment in admonishing us not to think of federal judges—including Supreme Court justices—as our national priesthood:

> We should not see federal judges as priests, but as officials given more job security than other civil servants so that they can decide disputes fairly, taking account of a mass of institutionalized rules and precedents ... Much less than as priests should we imagine Supreme Court justices as prophets. They are comfortably middle-of-the-road, senatorially confirmable lawyer-politicians.... It does not overcorrect much to think of the Justices of the United States Supreme Court, in the exercise of their majestic power of judicial review, as members of a nine-member committee reviewing the decisions of a dispute-resolution bureaucracy, deciding many minor political issues and a few important ones, guided in those decisions by what their committee has said and done before, by their sense of the professional and the popular culture, and, in a relatively few cases, by the words of the Constitution.

128. For an extremely interesting and diverse set of perspectives on utilitarianism *see*, UTILITARIANISM AND BEYOND (A. Sen & B. Williams eds. 1982).

129. *See, e.g.*, MASHAW, *supra* note 50 at 163-64; Rubin, *supra* note 50 at 1158-78; Monaghan, *supra* note 66 at 485-90.

130. *See, e.g.*, Buckley v. Valeo, 424 U.S. 1 (1976) (campaign spending protected as instrumental to protected free speech); Tinker v. Des Moines Independent Community School Dist., 393 U.S. 503 (1969) (armbands are protected symbolic speech).

131. I am indebted to my colleague Bill Stuntz for drawing my attention to this parallel. Katz v. United States, 389 U.S. 347 (1967), applying the Fourth Amendment protection to eavesdropping on a telephone conversation, illustrates the Court's traditional emphasis on the scope of the protection rather than the specified nature of the right. On the broad and vague character of the terms of the Fourth Amendment generally see Amsterdam, *Perspectives on the Fourth Amendment,* 58 MINN. L. REV. 349, 395-96 (1974). Oliver v. United States, 466 U.S. 170 (1984) can be taken as an exceptional case where the Court concerned itself with the threshold right in the context of denying protection to observation of persons in "open fields." However, it is noteworthy even here that the Court went on to apply the general *Katz* test of "reasonable expectation of privacy" as specification of the right protected. Of course, privacy is nowhere mentioned in the constitutional text as a protected right.

132. On the English concept of natural justice *see, e.g.,* J. BEATSON & M. H. MATHEWS, ADMINISTRATIVE LAW: CASES AND MATERIALS 191-286 (1983).

133. To say that standing doctrine is "arcane " is perhaps misleading, for there is a certain simplicity to the concept of limiting access to the courts to litigants who have more or less distinct interests that are plausibly within a zone of interest protected by the law on which they rely. What is mysterious is the Supreme Court's application of this doctrine. Illustrations of the confusion can be found almost by random sampling of recent cases. *Compare, e.g.,* Village of Arlington Heights v. Metropolitan Housing Development Corp. 429 U.S. 252 (1977) (standing to challenge exclusionary zoning granted to individual seeking to purchase housing foreclosed by zoning) *with* Warth v. Seldin, 422 U.S. 490 (1975) (standing to challenge exclusionary zoning denied to group alleging interest in housing foreclosed by zoning). *See generally,* Tribe, *supra* note 2, at 79-114.

134. On injury in fact *see, e.g.,* Sierra Club v. Morton, 405 U.S. 727 (1972); United States v. SCRAP, 412 U.S. 669 (1973). Injury in fact is not the sole criterion of standing. It is also necessary that the injury be causally related to the government action challenged, *see, e.g.,* Allen v. Wright, 468 U.S. 737 (1984). The Court has also required that the interest be presumptively within a "zone of interests" protected by the statute or constitutional provision from which the litigant claims protection. *See,* Clark v. Securities Industry Ass'n, 479 U.S. 388 (1987).

135. Grey, *supra* note 127, at 81, suggests that the substitution of a modern bundle of rights for a "thing-ownership" conception of property "has the ultimate consequence that property ceases to be an important category in legal and political theory." If I understand the point, Grey is suggesting that the bundle conception forces us to focus on the functional purposes of property rights, and this implies that the desideratum for legal and political judgments is no longer something called "property" but ulterior referents—utility, freedom, security, or what have you. Whether this is true in the context of takings I am inclined to doubt, but in *due process* jurisprudence I think it is almost unarguable that "property" has lost most of its significance as a touchstone for protecting basic rights.

136. In Flemming v. Nestor, 363 U.S. 603 (1960), the Court was willing to apply

the minimum rationality standard to legislation terminating retirement benefits even though it held that the beneficiary had no property right in the benefits. *Cf.* Dandridge v. Williams, 397 U.S. 471 (1970) (equal protection analysis; minimum rationality test applied to state eligibility standards of AFDC benefits).

The Proper Scope of The Commerce Power
RICHARD A. EPSTEIN*

"The Congress shall have Power . . . To regulate Commerce with foreign Nations, and among the several States, and with the Indian Tribes"[1]—such is the clause in the Constitution to which most federal power can be traced in today's general welfare state. The labor statutes, the civil rights statutes, the farm and agricultural statutes, and countless others rest on the commerce power, or—more accurately—on a construction of the commerce clause that grants the federal government jurisdiction so long as it can show (as it always can) that the regulated activity burdens, obstructs, or affects interstate commerce, however indirectly. Is this underlying interpretation of the commerce clause correct?[2]

The entire inquiry may be idle theoretical speculation, or it may have profound practical importance. I cannot say which, although at present I should guess the former; too much water has passed over the dam for there to be a candid judicial reexamination, that looks only to first principles, of the commerce clause. Still, in an age in which the theory of government is again subject to general theoretical discussion, it is instructive to ask, as a matter both of first principle and of Supreme Court precedent: what is the proper construction of the grant of congressional power contained within Article I, Section 8, Clause 3?

In Part I of this article, I introduce the question of the scope of the commerce power by discussing its intended role in limiting government power and its relation to the individual rights protections of the Constitution. In Parts II and III, I analyze the text of the commerce clause and look at the place of the commerce clause in the overall constitutional structure. Finally, in Parts IV and V, I analyze the clause in light of the cases that have construed and

---

* I wish to give thanks to Professor Edmund Kitch of the University of Virginia School of Law and my colleague David Currie for their especially insightful comments on an earlier draft of this paper. I have also benefitted from discussions with Dennis Hutchinson and Michael McConnell. A somewhat different version of this article appeared in Epstein, *The Proper Scope of the Commerce Clause*, 73 VA. L. REV. 1387 (1987).

extended its scope during our entire constitutional history. My analysis places special emphasis on the fifty-year period of the rise of the administrative state, from the onset of the Interstate Commerce Commission in 1887 to the height of the New Deal. My conclusion is clear enough. I think that the expansive construction of the clause accepted by the New Deal Supreme Court is wrong, and clearly so, and that a host of other interpretations are more consistent with both the text and the structure of our constitutional government.

I. The Problem: Structure And Individual Rights

The commerce power is not a comprehensive grant of federal power. It does not convert the Constitution from a system of government with enumerated federal powers into one in which the only subject matter limitations placed on Congress are those which it chooses to impose upon itself. Nor does the "necessary and proper" clause work to change this basic design; although it seeks to insure that the federal power may be exercised upon its appropriate targets, it is not designed to run roughshod over the entire scheme of enumerated powers that precedes it in the Constitution.[3] If forced to summarize what the commerce clause means, I would say that it refers more to "commerce" as that term has been developed in connection with the "negative" or "dormant" commerce clause cases.[4] These cases are concerned with the scope of the commerce power in those instances where Congress has passed no legislation. The unique, and most problematic, feature of the dormant power is that it converts an ostensible grant of power to Congress into a limitation on the power of the states. Clearly the dormant power could not extend to all productive activities within the states, for then the states could not act at all even on the most routine matters of domestic governance. Accordingly, the dormant power has been construed to cover only state regulations involving the use of the roads, rails, rivers and airspace, and the goods and services shipped thereby. The dormant power has remained relatively constant since its inception, as commerce has been used largely in the ordinary meaning of the term.

The term commerce also has had a stable usage in other contexts. Zoning for "commercial" uses, for example, is often used in opposition to zoning for "manufacturing" uses. The Uniform Commercial Code does not cover the law of manufacturers. More generally, the idea of commerce seems closer to the idea of "trade" than to other economic activities. It is in just this sense that the term was used in ordinary discourse at the time of the founding. Hume's essay *Of Commerce*, for example, explicitly places the idea of commerce in opposition to that of manufacturing.[5] The same usage, restrictive by modern standards, was adopted by Hamilton, who for example in *Federalist* No. 11 uses commerce as a synonym for trade and navigation, and links his discussion of the commerce power with the need to have an American navy to police and protect the seas.[6] But whatever the uncertainties, commerce does not comprise the sum of all productive activities in which individuals may engage. There is at least a slight irony here, for the Uniform Commercial Code is enacted under state law, whereas everything from manufacturing to welfare is regulated comprehensively at the federal level.

Finding the proper interpretation is of course no easy task. One great problem has to do with the function of the commerce clause itself. The Constitution contains two general types of provisions; the first class is structural and was designed to divide powers between state and federal government and, at the federal level, between the different branches of government. The second class was designed to protect individual rights against wrongdoing by government. The two types of provisions are in some sense parts of an integral strategy to ensure that the government, state or federal, does not become the enemy of the very people whom it is organized to protect. But the provisions work in very different ways, and their proper construction proceeds along rather different paths.

In considering guaranties of individual rights, we address the highest ends of government and civilization. Generally it is possible to look to the common law, to a rich political theory, and to a long political tradition in order to gather hints about what these provisions mean and how they should function. The Framers understood the protection of speech, contract, and property as ends good in themselves, as rights so "natural" and ends so clear that they did not receive the intellectual justification they so desperately needed—and still need. In reading these provisions, we can draw upon a large body of materials to guide our interpretation: Hobbes, Locke, Hume, Montesquieu, and a host of lesser, but still able, writers.[7] The differences that emerge in dealing with these questions are often attributable to the richness and the centrality of their subject, not to the want of speculation about them.

Provisions that go to the question of jurisdiction are no less important to sound governance than those that govern individual rights. Yet jurisdiction principles have a very different intellectual pedigree. Jurisdiction is not part of ordinary moral discourse, or of our common understanding of right and wrong. Instead, jurisdiction is always regarded as a means towards an end rather than as an end in itself. Hamilton treated jurisdiction as a more effective guarantor of individual rights than a bill of rights, because he believed that it provided clear and powerful lines to keep government from straying beyond its appointed limits.[8] Hamilton's judgment was, I think, wrong to the extent that it relied on jurisdictional provisions as the sole limit to government power.[9] But it contained a fair measure of good sense in using jurisdictional limitations as an important, indeed indispensable, limitation upon government power.

The difficulty lies in construing jurisdictional provisions to achieve this political end. Here there is no comparable tradition of political philosophy upon which to draw. The classical writers who extolled the virtues of liberty and property did not have the practical experience of the Founders in forming governments. The great debates over political theory always asked the question of how individuals in a state of nature could enter into a social contract for their mutual advantage. They never considered the possibility that, in practice, social contract theory would be tested in a world in which it was hardly clear whether Sovereign States or ordinary persons were the contracting parties. It is not surprising, therefore, that the classical writers never addressed federalism, enumerated powers, or jurisdiction, even though these form fundamental features of our constitutional system.[10]

We must, therefore, examine this question in an artificial world devoid of theories of natural rights. We must take our cue from more immediate, technical considerations. Or so it seems. Appearances are deceiving, however, and I shall argue throughout this article that the reasons for the expansion of the commerce clause were strongly substantive. The rationale for limited government became obscure in an age when the Progressive tradition of good government came to dominate American intellectual life. Judges who were persuaded that national solutions were needed for national problems could hardly be expected to invoke the commerce clause as a barrier to federal action when they believed in the importance of popular democracy, the soundness of the underlying legislation, the need for national uniformity, or all three. A judge's view of the commerce clause might be very different, however, if the perils of collective choice and the wisdom of the underlying substantive legislation were called into question. A court which shared the Framers' view of government as a necessary evil could, if it so chose, put more teeth into the commerce clause than has existing case law.

Cases from both the Progressive Era and the New Deal showed a close fusion between issues of substantive rights and questions of federal jurisdiction. The very attitudes that led to the demise of substantive due process protection of economic liberties lay behind judicial interpretation of the commerce clause.[11] To trace this history, it is necessary to discard the aura of inevitability that modern courts and writers have placed around the commerce clause.[12] At each stage in the historical analysis, the right question to ask is: Was this extension of federal power justified by the text and structure of the Constitution? There are no shortcuts in the journey. Let us start with the text.

II. The Text

The first place to look, to find the meaning of the commerce clause, is the text of the clause itself. Here one notices that the word "commerce" governs three separate sets of relations—those with foreign nations, among the states, and with Indian tribes.[13] One should assume that the word commerce applies with equal force to all three cases, and bears the same meaning with respect to each of its objects. One cannot, for example, assign a meaning to "commerce" which is intelligible only with respect to foreign nations. The asserted construction must make equally good sense for commerce among the states and for commerce with the Indian tribes.

Similarly, one does not want a meaning of the term commerce which renders any one of these three heads of the commerce power redundant or unnecessary. The modern view—which says that commerce among the several states includes all manufacture and other productive activity within each and every state, because of the effect that such manufacture has upon commerce—violates this constraint. If commerce includes all that precedes trade with foreign nations, among the states, and with Indian tribes, then the three heads of jurisdiction cover the same ground; that is, each by itself covers manufacturing or agriculture within each of the states. The scope of the clause would thus be plenary even if it said only that Congress shall have power to regulate commerce with foreign nations, or even with the Indian tribes, and remained silent about commerce among the several states. The level of industrial production within each state, after all, influences the amount, type, and price of goods available for export or Indian trade. Granting Congress the power over commerce among the states thus accomplishes nothing that has not been already provided for elsewhere in the document. What possible sense does it make as a matter of ordinary English to say that Congress can regulate "manufacturing with foreign nations, or with Indian tribes," or for that matter "manufacturing among the several states," when the particular fabrication or production takes place in one state, even with goods purchased from another?

Taking the alternative position, that commerce means trade, or as Chief, Justice Marshall said, "intercourse,"[14] with or among the parties named, changes the situation dramatically. By Chief Justice Marshall's account, "intercourse" covered both shipping and navigation, and the contracts regulating buying and selling. Using that two-part definition it becomes clear that trade with foreign nations is not trade among the several states or with the Indian tribes. Each part of the clause attributes the same meaning to the term commerce, and each of the objects of the clause—foreign nations, the states, and Indian tribes—becomes an indispensable part of the constitutional structure. The power to regulate commerce with foreign nations, for example, is needed to ensure that trade negotiations with foreign nations are not conducted by each of the several states in its own individual capacity.[15]

It is worth noting that this view of commerce as trade is consistent with the other prominent mention of the word commerce in the Constitution. Article I also states that "[n]o preference shall be given by any Regulation of Commerce or Revenue to the Ports of one State over those of another . . . ."[16] The term "commerce" is used in opposition to the term "revenue," and seems clearly to refer to shipping and its incidental activities; this much seems evident from the use of the term "port." The clause itself would sound odd if it referred, for example, to preferences "given by any Regulation of Commerce, Manufacture or Revenue to the ports of one State." The term "commerce" in this commerce provision does not carry with it the extensive baggage placed upon it by the better-known New Deal cases concerning the commerce clause.

III. The Structure

One obtains the same interpretation of the commerce clause when considering the clause in light of the overall constitutional structure. Article I, Section 8, contains an extensive list of separate, discrete, and enumerated powers granted to Congress, whereas Article I, Section 9, contains a comparable list of powers specifically denied to it. These two lists—one of powers and the other of prohibitions—are not written in a vacuum. Both suggest that the basic architecture of Article I contemplates a division of power between the states and the federal government. There are limitations at both levels of government, from which there is a clear implication that certain matters lie wholly outside the scope of congressional power.

This view certainly appears to agree with the original theory of the Constitution. The federal government received delegated powers from the states and the individuals within the states. The exact source of the granting power might be somewhat unclear; after all, the preamble begins with "We the People,"[17] yet ratification was by nine of the thirteen sovereign states.[18] Yet whatever the pedigree of the Constitution, there was clearly no sense that either grantor conferred upon the Congress the plenary power to act as a roving commission, in order to do whatever it thought best for the common good. The looseness of vague grants of power would have given rise to the possibility of massive abuse, a possibility the Framers seemed determined to control. The federal government was to have supremacy in the areas under its control, but the *quid pro quo* was that these areas were to be limited by specific jurisdictional grants. A system which says that the commerce clause essentially allows the government to regulate anything that even indirectly burdens or affects commerce does away with the key understanding that the federal government has received only enumerated powers. The doctrine of "internal relations" is not only a philosophical creed that says every event is related to every other separate event; it is also something of an economic truth in a world in which the price of any given commodity depends upon the costs of its inputs and upon the alternatives available to potential buyers. To say that Congress may regulate X because of its price effects upon any quantity of goods so shipped, is to say that Congress may regulate whatever it pleases, a result that cases such as *Wickard v. Filburn*[19] have eagerly inferred.

On this score, moreover, there is no reason to distinguish the commerce of the eighteenth and nineteenth centuries from that of the twentieth. Business in one state has always had profound economic effects upon the fortunes of other states. The pre-Civil War battles between North and South over the tariff show just how much the fate of each state has always depended upon national economic policies.[20] There was no economic revolution during the Progressive Era or the New Deal that justifies the convenient escape of saying that it is only the nature of business and trade that has changed, not the appropriate construction of the commerce clause.[21] The intimate interdependence between trade and national economic conditions was as clear to the Phoenicians and the Romans as it is to ourselves. There has been no basic transformation of the economy that requires, or allows, a parallel transformation in the scope of the commerce clause. International trade is driven by the principle of comparative advantage and the costs of reaching distant markets. It did not begin with either the steamship or the railroad.

If the constitutional limitations on federal powers were designed to act as a substitute Bill of Rights, then the expansive interpretation of the commerce clause has done away with any possibility that limitations on federal jurisdiction can provide indirect protection for individual liberties. The necessary effect is that greater burdens are placed upon the substantive limitations, such as the Bill of Rights, found elsewhere in the Constitution. These limitations have met with varying fates themselves; one need only contrast the takings clause of the Fifth Amendment with the First Amendment protection of the freedom of speech. Speech is, for example, regarded as a "preferred freedom," so that limitations upon it must be strictly justified, as by showing an imminent and violent peril to public order. In contrast, limitations upon economic liberties are routinely sustained as a proper exercise of the police power, even on the flimsiest demonstration of some public benefit. Private rights in this domain have been left to the mercy of the "good faith" of Congress, whose mischief the Bill of Rights was meant to contain.

Nor is this understanding of the commerce power upset by the "necessary and proper" clause of the Constitution, which may expand the power of Congress, but does not provide for an unlimited grant of federal power. The necessary and proper clause provides that Congress shall have the power "[t]o make all Laws which shall be necessary and proper for carrying into Execution the foregoing Powers, and all other Powers vested by this Constitution in the Government of the United States, or in any Department or Officer thereof."[22] As drafted, the clause does nothing to upset the balance of power between the federal and the state governments, nor to contravene the principle of enumerated powers on which the structure of Article I, Section 8 rests. What the necessary and proper clause does is to ensure that the Congress shall have all means at its disposal to reach the heads of power that admittedly fall within its grasp. Such is the import of the phrase "for carrying into Execution": Congress shall not fail because it lacks the means of implementation. The clause does not, however, authorize the creation of new and independent heads of power, such as over local manufacture or agriculture, that obliterate the distinction between a federal and a national government. The necessary and proper clause thus permits the regulation of local affairs that are in a sense separable from national ones, as happens when local and interstate cars, for example, move along the same line.[23] But it is hardly "necessary" to regulate every form of local activity in order to regulate the three heads of commerce over which Congress has power. And it is surely not "proper" to do so.[24]

This reading of the necessary and proper clause may appear somewhat narrower than that given by Chief Justice Marshall in *McCulloch v. Maryland:* "Let the end be legitimate, let it be within the scope of the constitution, and all means which are appropriate, which are plainly adapted to that end, which are not prohibited, but consist with the letter and spirit of the constitution, are constitutional."[25] Yet Chief Justice Marshall's broad reading of the clause does take into account the risks of overinclusion, by reference to matters which "consist with the letter and spirit of the constitution," which surely includes respect for the principle of enumerated powers (which he acknowledged as being preserved in the Tenth Amendment).[26] More to the point, he adopted just this limited interpretation of "necessary and proper" in *Gibbons v. Ogden:* "In the last of the enumerated powers, that which grants, expressly, the means for carrying all others into execution, Congress is authorized 'to make laws which shall be necessary and proper' for the purpose. But this limitation on the means which may be used, is not extended to the powers which are conferred."[27] In essence, Marshall treats the necessary and proper clause as though it imposes limitations only upon the *means* that Congress can use to reach the *permitted* ends set out elsewhere in Article I. It does not, however, expand the class of ends on which Congress may legislate. So understood, the necessary and proper clause places a small but important weight upon the jurisdictional scales. But it is far from an automatic trump that overrides other jurisdictional limitations. Its historical role in the explication of the commerce clause is relatively small, and deservedly so.[28]

IV. The Case Law Before The New Deal: 1824-1936

The elaborate case law under the commerce clause can be profitably interpreted in light of the above understandings. Thus, it is often said today that the New Deal does not represent violent revolution but prudent reformation[29] (one thinks of Martin Luther and that other reformation). More precisely, the newer cases are said only to have returned to the wisdom of Chief Justice Marshall, who understood the importance of an expansive interpretation of the commerce clause to the maintenance of the Union.[30] In between, in such cases as *United States v. E.C. Knight Co.*,[31] the courts are said to have strayed from the original understanding to a view that effectively hampered the power of Congress to impose much-needed social and economic regulation. This set of insights has even been dressed up in plausible philosophical garb. Professor Tribe's treatise, *American Constitutional Law*, tells us that the Supreme Court between 1887 and 1937 substituted a "formal classification" of economic activities for the "empiricism"[32] that characterized Chief Justice Marshall's great judgment in the pivotal case of *Gibbons v. Ogden.*[33]

The New Deal was not a reformation, but a sharp departure from previous case law, and one that moved federal power far beyond anything Chief Justice Marshall had in mind. *Gibbons* is often regarded as an expansive interpretation, and for its time so it was. Yet when the critical passages of the opinion are read as a whole, it seems quite clear that the case strongly adumbrated the subsequent holding in *E.C. Knight,* with which it is said to contrast so clearly. It is worth a minute to describe Chief Justice Marshall's logic, for the key to understanding his view is to understand that he found in the rigid and formal structures of the Constitution the materials that enabled it to be the foundation on which a perpetual Union could rest. His vision of the Constitution was not that of a living and changing organism, but of a great temple of government that, properly understood, could endure for the ages.[34]

Gibbons v. Ogden

At issue in *Gibbons v. Ogden* was whether New York could grant an exclusive franchise that permitted steamships to ply between New Jersey and New York only with the franchisees' permission.[35] New Jersey had passed a retaliatory law; citizens of New Jersey sued in New York for violating New York law could recoup treble damages against the New Yorker in a New Jersey court.[36] The New York statute threatened massive commercial balkanization.[37] Chief Justice Marshall decided, first, that navigation among the several states was interstate commerce, and second (in order to avoid the question of the dormant commerce clause, i.e., whether the clause alone struck down this state law even when Congress was silent), that a 1793 federal statute that licensed ships in the "coasting trade" had preempted the New York statute.[38]

Professor Tribe has summarized his view of the broad scope of *Gibbons* as follows:

> [I]n an elaborate preliminary discussion, Marshall indicated that, in his view, congressional power to regulate "commercial intercourse" extended to all activity having any interstate impact—however indirect. Acting under the commerce clause, Congress could legislate with respect to all "commerce which concerns more states than one." This power would be plenary: absolute within its sphere, subject only to the Constitution's affirmative prohibitions on the exercise of federal authority.[39]

This passage suggests that Chief Justice Marshall in *Gibbons* gave a very extensive reading to the reach of the commerce clause. But that is only because of the redactor's power of selection. Consider the fuller context of the quotation from *Gibbons:*

> Commerce among the States, cannot stop at the external boundary line of each State, but may be introduced into the interior.

> It is not intended to say that these words comprehend that commerce, which is completely internal, which is carried on between man and man in a State, or between different parts of the same State, and which does not extend to or affect other States. Such a power would be inconvenient, and is certainly unnecessary.

> Comprehensive as the word "among" is, it may very properly be restricted to that commerce which concerns more States than one. The phrase is not one which would probably have been selected to indicate the completely interior traffic of a State, because it is not an apt phrase for that purpose; and the enumeration of the particular classes of commerce to which the power was to be extended would not have been made, had the intention been to extend the power to every description. The enumeration presupposes something not enumerated; and that something, if we regard the language or the subject of the sentence, must be the exclusively internal commerce of a State.[40]

The passage gives a quite different sense of the commerce clause's scope than the one that Tribe suggests. It is hard to find in the phrase "commerce which concerns more states than one" a total jurisdiction over all commercial activity, especially when the phrase is preceded by the word "restricted."[41] Quite the opposite; it looks as though Chief Justice Marshall wanted only to refute the argument (see his first sentence quoted) that interstate commerce can only take place on the narrow boundary between the two states.[42] Such a position, if carried into law, would have rendered the commerce clause a dead letter. Commerce between two states, or among many, must take place within the physical confines of one or both of them. It is therefore the nature of a transaction, rather than its location, that stamps it as part of interstate commerce. Navigation between states takes place at one instant in one state, and at another instant in another. Both portions of the journey are covered by the commerce clause, even if purely intrastate navigation is excluded. The power may be plenary, but it is surely limited as to its objects. Matters outside its scope are fully reserved to the states. Chief Justice Marshall did write, as Tribe suggests, of the "plenary" nature of the commerce power. But again his words must be set in context. Chief Justice Marshall thus wrote: "This power, like all others vested in Congress, is complete in itself, may be exercised to its utmost extent, and acknowledges no limitations other than are prescribed in the constitution."[43] But he continued:

If, as has always been understood, the sovereignty of Congress, though limited to specified objects, is plenary as to those objects, the power over commerce with foreign nations, and among the several states, is vested in Congress as absolutely as it would be in a single government, having in its constitution the same restrictions on the exercise of the power as are found in the constitution of the United States.[44]

It follows therefore that "plenary" powers were understood by Chief Justice Marshall to be wholly consistent with powers "limited to specified objects."

This view is, moreover, reinforced when we take into account Marshall's principles of construction, which should give caution both to advocates of judicial restraint and of judicial activism. His attitude was essentially that the Constitution should be construed in its "natural sense." He was rightly suspicious of any effort to impose principles of "strict construction," but by the same token did not wish to give words an extravagant meaning given their function and purpose within the framework of the constitution.[45] He followed a middle course on the issue of construction, that of ordinary meaning, no different from that which a good contracts judge follows when he attaches ordinary meaning to contractual provisions.[46] Even with an explicit reference to the necessary and proper clause,[47] Chief Justice Marshall acknowledged that the commerce clause was itself directed toward specific ends, as was captured by the distinction between "internal" and "external" commerce, where internal commerce was that trade "between man and man in a State, or between different parts of the same State."[48] By that definition internal commerce is as commonplace in our own time as it was in Marshall's: every purchase at a supermarket is internal commerce, even if the market itself acquired its own goods from a supplier out of state.

Nor is this balance between internal and external commerce undone because Chief Justice Marshall used the word "affects" to round out the scope of Congress's power. Those references to activities that "affect" interstate commerce cannot be read in isolation from the rest of the text, as an effort to nullify the basic doctrine of enumerated powers. Instead, his purpose was to counter prior contentions about the scope of internal commerce that had been stated by the New York court in *Livingston v. Van Ingen*.[49] There, New York Chief Justice Kent gave the commerce clause its narrowest possible construction, and thus treated as part of internal commerce any portion of an interstate journey that was undertaken wholly within local waters.[50] When Chief Justice Marshall spoke of local regulations that "affect" interstate commerce, he did so to reject the argument that New York could insist that all rival carriers be required to use sails in New York waters, even if they used steam elsewhere. So long as this restriction "affected" the journey as a whole, the regulation reached commerce among the several states, notwithstanding that its "direct" impact was on New York waters alone. There is not the slightest hint that Chief

Justice Marshall meant to have the "affects" qualification expand the specific objects to which the "plenary" commerce clause applies, beyond the control of interstate commercial transactions and the instrumentalities of interstate commerce.

Further elaboration of Chief Justice Marshall's meaning appeared elsewhere in his opinion. At one point he addressed whether the states could pass inspection laws, or whether these laws fell solely within the domain of the congressional commerce power.[51] He finessed that question by giving a very narrow definition of what interstate commerce included:

> That inspection laws may have a remote and a considerable influence on commerce, will not be denied; but that a power to regulate commerce is the source from which the right to pass them is derived, cannot be admitted. The object of inspection laws, is to improve the quality of articles produced by the labour of a country; to fit them for exportation; or, it may be, for domestic use. They act upon the subject before it becomes an article of foreign commerce, or of commerce among the States, and prepare it for that purpose.[52]

It is instructive to compare this passage with the most famous sentence of *E.C. Knight,* which has been cited as a sign of its narrow and indefensible rigidity: "Commerce succeeds to manufacture, and is not a part of it."[53] Chief Justice Marshall himself could have written that sentence, citing *Gibbons* as authority. His style was anything but "empirical," if that term is used to identify the necessary economic connection between intrastate and interstate commerce. Indeed the passage just quoted is wholly inconsistent with the indirect burden on interstate commerce approach taken in the modern law. Chief Justice Marshall's greatness rests upon his appreciation of the boundaries which should dominate the constitutional playing field. Individual cases may fall close to the boundary lines, and must be placed on one side or the other. Yet the position of the boundary lines must remain fixed if the power to adjudicate is to remain. Things cannot be partly in and partly out of interstate commerce. As long as one government or the other must regulate, the boundaries must be sharp—such as the foul lines in baseball—and not fuzzy. It has been said that modern constitutional law represents the triumph of "formalism" over "realism."[54] If this is true, then Chief Justice Marshall was the great formalist, not the precursor of the modern realists.

There is a good deal to be said for Marshall's categorical approach. If pressed to give a common law analogy to Marshall's way of thinking, I would offer the common law trilogy of the liabilities of a landowner to the trespasser, the licensee, and the invitee. Everyone agrees on the broad outlines of this tripartite distinction: the trespasser is a person who enters the land of another without legal permission or justification, the licensee is a guest who typically enters residential premises for social reasons, and the invitee is the customer on business premises. Even with this broad agreement, however, no judge ever thought that these categories were crystal clear, nor that individual cases would not give rise to honest disagreements of opinion. But it was thought that the categories were fixed and limited as a matter of principle: "There is no half-way house, no no-man's land between adjacent territories. When I say rigid, I mean rigid in law."[55] And the modern disintegration of the categories has done little to produce any coherent law of occupiers' liability.[56] So it is with interstate commerce. The principle that the power of Congress *did not* extend to the internal commerce of the state was as important to the overall scheme as the recognition that the power of Congress extended to interstate commerce. Marshall well understood the fact that local events affected interstate commerce, but he rejected it as a basis for extension of congressional power over internal matters. *Gibbons* thus stands in sharp opposition to the very assertion of federal power that characterizes such cases as *United States v. Darby*[57] and *Wickard v. Filburn.*[58] In *Wickard*, Justice Jackson captured the transformation of *Gibbons* when he wrote: "At the beginning Chief Justice Marshall described the federal commerce power with a breadth never yet exceeded."[59] No way.

The Expansion of Commerce Clause Jurisdiction

There is a long road from *Gibbons* to the modern doctrine of the broad reach of congressional power under the commerce clause. This section will trace the twists and turns in that road. In one sense *Gibbons*, for all its importance, is an odd place from which to begin the journey, because the case itself as much concerned the limitation of state power as it did the extent of congressional power under the coastal trading statute. Indeed, the negative, or dormant, commerce clause power that prohibits states from intruding on the federal authority over interstate commerce, even absent any congressional legislation on the subject of the state action, dates from *Gibbons* as well; Justice Johnson's concurring opinion argued that the commerce clause standing alone prohibited New York from passing the statute in question.[60] The primary purpose of this section is not, however, to trace the negative side of the clause,[61] which has proven quite stable in recent times. Rather, the purpose is to follow the expansion of the affirmative power of the clause. This development took place along three separate lines.[62] The first line took its cue from the narrow holding of *Gibbons* that navigation counted as commerce under the clause, and concerned the "instrumentalities of commerce." This section follows the expansion of the clause, briefly in connection with navigable waterways, and more extensively with the systematic and inexorable expansion of the federal power to regulate the railroads under the Interstate Commerce Act of 1887, as amended.[63]

The second line of cases involved the regulation of goods admittedly in interstate commerce (that is, goods in transit across state lines) in order to control the primary conduct of persons in either the sending or receiving state. In these cases Congress has sought to exercise a kind of federal police power, with control over lotteries, prostitution, adulterated food, and working conditions within the various states. This line of cases might be called the "indirect regulation" cases. The third line of cases, emanating from *E.C. Knight* itself, explored the distinction between manufacture and commerce among the several states.

Between 1870 and 1937 the scope of federal power under these three lines of case law continued to expand, but in ways that still left an extensive area of economic life outside the power of Congress. In particular, the distinction between manufacture and commerce laid down in *E.C. Knight* in 1895 retained its validity until it was at last overturned in 1937 by *NLRB v. Jones & Laughlin Steel Corp.*[64] In general, the expansion of the first and second heads of the commerce power fall within the general scheme set out by Chief Justice Marshall in *Gibbons,* in that they address both the power of Congress to regulate the means by which goods are shipped in interstate commerce and the types of goods that can be shipped. In my judgment, the scope of the federal power under these two heads moved, prior to 1937, a step or two beyond where proper argument would take them. But although these difficult cases can be argued at the margin, nothing in the case law under these two heads undermined the essential validity of the line between commerce, on the one hand, and manufacture and agriculture on the other, clearly adumbrated in *Gibbons* and accepted in *E.C. Knight.* It is only when the last distinction is rejected that a system of enumerated powers is dismantled. Yet it is not conceptually necessary to say that power to regulate commerce among the several states must reach everything if it is to reach anything. The modern generation of negative commerce clause cases is instructive because it proves that it is possible, and sensible, to articulate an enduring conception of interstate commerce—just as Chief Justice Marshall had insisted.

1. The Instrumentalities of Commerce

Gibbons itself laid down the distinction between the "internal commerce" or "interior traffic" of a state and commerce among the states.[65] Although Chief Justice Marshall articulated the distinction with confident assurance, its limits were not really tested until 1870, when the Court in *The Daniel Ball*[66] considered an 1852 inspection statute for steam passenger vessels operating on the navigable waters of the United States. The appellant questioned whether Congress had the power to inspect a ship that remained within a single state, even though it carried goods that had been shipped from other states, or were eventually destined for shipment into other states.[67] As framed, the case offered an instructive counterpoint to *Gibbons,* which had decided that the federal commerce power reached a single, continuous journey that started in one state and ended in another. The Court in *The Daniel Ball* asked what happened when the same journey involved two ships instead of one. If Chief Justice Marshall's view of the commerce clause was as expansive as the received wisdom has it—if "plenary" had meant "wholly unbounded"—then it is unintelligible why the Supreme Court should have paused a second to decide *The Daniel Ball.* It is only because *Gibbons* extended the scope of the commerce power to "intercourse," and kept it there, that there was any occasion to deliberate on the loose ends left open by *Gibbons.*

Relative to the understandings of its time, *The Daniel Ball* gave *Gibbons* a modestly expansive interpretation. The opinion by Justice Field—no friend of big government—upheld the 1852 inspection statute because of the Court's explicit fear that any other interpretation of the commerce clause would strip the federal government of its fundamental powers. "Several agencies combining, each taking up the commodity transported at the boundary line at one end of a State, and leaving it at the boundary line at the other end," he wrote, "the Federal jurisdiction would be entirely ousted, and the constitutional provision would become a dead letter."[68]

Justice Field's conclusion has assumed the status of a necessary truth. Nonetheless, there is reason to ask whether the decision is as impregnable as it seems. It appears that the commerce clause could well apply to *goods* destined for sale in another state as part of a continuous transaction, even if they are shipped by boats that operate solely within the territorial waters of one state. Where the transfer of goods from boat to boat is part of a comprehensive plan—as when the various carriers have coordinated travel schedules—then Congress should have jurisdiction. But it is far from self-evident that because the goods are in the interstate market the ships which carry them on parts of the journey are in interstate commerce as well. The states could regulate the safety of the boats on which the goods are carried, while the federal government could (as it has never seen fit to do) pass a statute dealing with the rights and duties of common carriers and their customers, as well as maintain jurisdiction over any ship that did cross a state line. There need be no gap in the system of regulation. And as long as ships remain within a single state, shipowners hardly need the federal power to protect them from inconsistent regulation. If state regulation became overly onerous, a shipowner could escape it by explicitly organizing his business to specialize in interstate transport, or by moving to another state. Deciding *The Daniel Ball* the other way would have promoted competition between state governments. Such an outcome would hardly have made the commerce clause a dead letter, as Justice Field insisted, even if it would have stopped the further expansion of federal power.

There is a danger in this alternative analysis of *The Daniel Ball* that federal jurisdiction will be less comprehensive than is needed to perform a particular regulatory task. The Court in *The Daniel Ball* and subsequent decisions reacted to this danger by weighing the risk of underinclusion within the federal power more heavily than the reverse danger of overinclusion. With the vantage of hindsight, *The Daniel Ball* originated the "protective principle" which, when pushed to its limit, finds that the use of federal power in a doubtful case is *always* "necessary," perhaps in the sense of the "necessary and proper" clause.[69] But there are some risks to the strategy that, although not evident here, must be kept in mind. Unless the countervailing principle of enumerated powers is brought to the fore, then the basic structure may be lost in a series of small accretions, each one palatable on its own, even though the whole structure is not.

It is precisely that form of incrementalism that characterized the later cases involving the use of railroads in interstate commerce. The impetus for national regulation clearly came from the famous decision in *Wabash, St. Louis & Pacific Railway v. Illinois*.[70] That case prevented state governments from regulating railroad fares from points within a state to points outside it.[71] There was a functional reason for the decision, given the risk that separate states could impose inconsistent obligations upon carriers. Congress attempted to solve this problem by passing the Interstate Commerce Act (ICA) in 1887. The statute marked the most ambitious use of federal power until that time. Congress created a new administrative agency, the Interstate Commerce Commission (ICC), and delegated to it the power to enforce a system of regulation that extended to all aspects of interstate railroad traffic, including rates, rebates, preferences, scheduling, and pooling.[72]

Sensible economic concerns led to the passage of the first ICA, which was designed to prevent discrimination against short-haul carriers. The problem arose because of the structure of the railroad lines. Different carriers went by different routes from one population center to another. Thus there was competition on the long-haul routes (such as San Francisco to Chicago), because shippers had many choices. But once out in the plains, any given line had a local monopoly that it could exploit against farmers and others. When it exacted monopoly profit, its short-haul rates could easily exceed its long-haul rates, even if the actual cost of long-haul shipment was greater. But simply preventing the price per segment from exceeding the price for the whole trip would have gone a long way toward eliminating monopoly profit. It would also have avoided involving the government in the ratemaking that characterized the ICC after the "reforms" of this century, including the Transportation Act of 1920, which gave the ICC power to implement comprehensive rate-of-return regulation.[73]

One question was whether the ICC's authority reached trips that began and ended within a single state. In essence, this was the land-based version of the question raised (and answered in the affirmative) in *The Daniel Ball*. Nonetheless, as a matter of first principle, one could forcefully insist that the proper answer should have been "no." The obvious response is that unprincipled exploitation of short-haul users would have continued on a limited scale even after the passage of the ICA. But that need not have been the case. The states could have had exclusive jurisdiction over these short-haul runs, and their local laws could have replicated the key substantive provision of the ICA, thereby protecting purely intrastate shippers: the railroad could not charge more for the intrastate run than it charged for any longer interstate run of which the intrastate segment was a part. The danger of radical state restrictions on the power of carriers to cover their costs for internal runs could have been avoided by constitutional protections against confiscation, such as those invoked during this period in *Smyth v. Ames*.[74] The jurisdictional balance between federal and state governments could have been quite stable if left where *Gibbons* had placed it. More to the point, *Gibbons's* limits on the extent of the commerce clause would have been important because they would have limited the degree to which Congress could have used its commerce power to cartelize the entire railroad industry, as it did by amending the ICA after World War I.[75]

Historically, however, the dividing line between interstate and intrastate journeys did not endure. It is instructive to trace the expansion of the commerce clause in the railroad cases. At each point the Supreme Court seemed aware that there must be some limit to the commerce power, but on virtually every occasion it found the federal legislation at issue not to exceed the limit. The Court failed to understand that too much federal jurisdiction was as dangerous as too little. In this regard, *Houston, East & West Texas Railway v. United States (The Shreveport Rate Case)*,[76] decided in 1914 marked an especially instructive watershed. This case has been read as an important step forward (the bias is implicit) for the commerce power. The facts were complicated, and the details have unfortunately been forgotten in modern times. Nonetheless, they deserve close attention today.

Various points in East Texas were served by interstate carriers operating out of Shreveport, Louisiana on one end, and Dallas and Houston on the other.[77] Before the intercession of the ICC, the prices charged by these railroad lines were far higher for shipping goods from Shreveport to Texas than were the rates for shipping goods within Texas, where rates were set by a state body, the Texas Railroad Commission.[78] The ICC ordered that the railroads adjust rate structures that "unjustly discriminated in favor of traffic within the State of Texas and against similar traffic between Louisiana and Texas."[79]

The commission proposed a compound remedy to alleviate the perceived ills. The first part of the ICC order imposed specific maximum rates that the carriers could charge on their interstate, i.e., Louisiana-Texas, routes.[80] The second part was a general nondiscrimination provision which held that the rates in interstate traffic could not be higher than those in intrastate traffic.[81] The order, however, left it to the railroads to decide whether they raised intrastate rates, lowered interstate ones, or did a little of both. All that was required was equalization of rates within the ceilings set by the first part of the ICC order. Given the structure of the order, it was possible for the railroads to comply in full with the ICC order without changing their intrastate rates: the railroads simply had to reduce their interstate rates until they equaled the rates charged on the intrastate runs. Accordingly, the decision upholding the ICC order could be read not to involve a conflict between the rates established by the ICC for interstate traffic and those set by the Texas Railroad Commission for intrastate traffic. As such, the decision does not appear to have extended the scope of the commerce clause very far.

This narrow reading of the case, however, is belied in at least two respects. First, the *Shreveport Rate Case* protected the railroads if they chose to raise their intrastate rates in defiance of the rates set by the Texas Railroad Commission. Although there was no necessary regulation of intrastate rates, the remedy envisioned made the state powerless to set any intrastate maximum below the ICC maximum if the railroads chose to raise their local rates to the ICC levels. The unmistakable thrust of the opinion was to make the congressional power paramount over state authority:

> Wherever the interstate and intrastate transactions of carriers are so related that the government of the one involves the control of the other, it is Congress, and not the State, that is entitled to prescribe the final and dominant rule, for otherwise Congress would be denied the exercise of its constitutional authority and the State, and not the Nation, would be supreme within the national field.[82]

Second, the *Shreveport Rate Case* relied upon and extended earlier decisions that had sustained the power of Congress to regulate railroad safety, even when there was a "commingling of duties relating to interstate and intrastate operations."[83] *Southern Railway v. United States*[84] had sustained the Safety Appliance Act[85] with respect to cars in interstate travel, even though it necessarily embraced cars that were used in intrastate travel as well. In the *Second Employer's Liability Cases,*[86] the Court had sustained Congress's authority to allocate liability for accidents caused to employees in interstate commerce, even when they were caused by employees engaged in intrastate commerce. These cases arguably could be justified under some protective principle as a response to the same hard choice faced by the Court in *The Daniel Ball:* if Congress were confined to matters that were purely in interstate commerce, then it could never legislate to the limit of its jurisdiction.[87] Yet for Congress to reach the full limits of its jurisdiction it must on some occasions go beyond it. The choice is necessarily either over- or underinclusion. It is hard to gainsay a judicial decision that opts for the former over the latter, at least in cases where interstate and intrastate commerce are inextricable—such as different railroad cars on the same train. A necessary and proper clause argument has evident force here.[88]

Justice Hughes (the same Justice Hughes who later, as Chief Justice, wrote *NLRB v. Jones & Laughlin Steel Corp.*)[89] made it appear in the *Shreveport Rate Case* that there was a seamless web encompassing both the safety cases and the rate regulation cases. But the rate regulation case marked an expansion of the commerce power, although perhaps an inadvertent one, beyond the safety cases that preceded it. The commerce clause was at issue in the safety cases because railroad cars were used for both interstate and intrastate runs at different times, and were often mixed on the same train. There was thus a "commingling of duties relating to interstate and intrastate operations."[90] Yet no such commingling existed with respect to the rate structures, as it was surely possible to regulate interstate fares without regulating intrastate fares. The various rate schedules were distinct; it was possible for the ICC to set rates on the interstate runs without having to set them on intrastate activities. Indeed, it appears that this was Congress's intention in passing the original statute.[91] In order to uphold the expanded jurisdiction sought by the ICC, the "commingled" approach of the safety cases had to yield to a broader formulation whereby Congress could extend "its control over the interstate carrier in all matters having . . . a close and substantial relation to interstate commerce."[92] At this point the Justices should have considered whether the risks of overextension of federal power were worth running. But, lacking an underlying theory of the risks of regulation, the Court acted as though any exercise of the congressional jurisdiction were benign. The path of broad construction and social virtue again coincided, in the Court's view.

For all their nimble footwork, the authors of the *Shreveport Rate Case* did not necessarily commit the Court to an all-inclusive view of the commerce clause. The regulations in question were imposed upon the intrastate business of interstate carriers. Congress's commerce power did not yet necessarily reach intrastate carriers that did not engage in interstate business. In addition, the *Shreveport Rate Case* tied federal regulation of local business to proof of discrimination against interstate commerce. The ICC could not have comprehensively regulated the entire railway business under its authority alone, for some local rates, at least, were not set in conjunction with discriminatory interstate rates. Yet this barrier too was quickly overrun by the Court in *Wisconsin Railroad Commission v. Chicago, Burlington & Quincy Railroad,*[93] which upheld the constitutionality of one of the worst pieces of modern economic legislation, the Transportation Act of 1920.[94] The Act replaced specific control of long-haul/short-haul problems with comprehensive regulation of the railroad industry, and helped cartelize an entire industry by imposing comprehensive rate of return regulation.[95] Yet, under the rationale of the *Shreveport Rate Case,* the statute could *not* have been sustained in its entirety under the commerce clause, because it reached local railroad runs that by no stretch of the imagination competed with interstate runs.[96] On these local routes a showing of nondiscrimination, so critical to the *Shreveport Rate Case*, could not be made. But the Court again took a benevolent view of an expansive statute,[97] finding that Congress could ensure that the costs of running railroads were properly distributed between interstate and intrastate carriers.[98]

The connection between federal jurisdiction, interest group politics, and substantive entitlements is clear. The Court adopted a benevolent, public interest interpretation of the 1920 statute, and hence saw no risk in extending federal power farther than prior law had taken it. But too much regulation is always at least as risky as too little.[99] Furthermore, the Court's extension of the commerce clause in the *Shreveport Rate Case* dictated the likely structure of future regulation, to which the Court also was to acquiesce. It was not possible (or at least less possible) to have comprehensive rate-of-return regulation, complete with control over entry, if Congress could not touch the local portions of the railroad business. If the emphasis had remained on the long-haul/short-haul problem, then a system of federal and state regulation that limited congressional control to wholly interstate trips would have been adequate to the task. The original ICA thus was clearly superior to its 1920 version. It was only the judicial expansion of the commerce clause that made it possible for Congress to adopt its own unfortunate substantive provisions.

The game has still not run its course, for even the decisions of the Court in rate cases after the *Shreveport Rate Case* do not mandate the conclusion that the commerce clause is all-embracing. To see the remaining distinctions, consider the fate of one critical passage from the *Shreveport Rate Case:*

> Congress is empowered to regulate,—that is, to provide the law for the government of interstate commerce; to enact 'all appropriate legislation' for its 'protection and advancement;' to adopt measures 'to promote its growth and insure its safety;' 'to foster, protect, control and restrain.' Its authority, extending to these interstate carriers as instruments of interstate commerce, necessarily embraces the right to control their operations in all matters having such a close and substantial relation to interstate traffic that the control is essential or appropriate to the security of that traffic, to the efficiency of the interstate service, and to the maintenance of conditions under which interstate commerce may be conducted upon fair terms and without molestation or hindrance.[100]

This passage appears to say that the commerce clause supports congressional power over the *instruments of commerce*—railroads and the highways—because of the impossibility of disentangling the various threads of interstate and intrastate business, but extends no further. Federal jurisdiction over commerce would end at the railroad station, with the already bloated ICC of the 1920 Act. This judgment implies no preference for regulated, overcompetitive industries. The railroads have serious long-haul/short-haul problems that make the competitive solution difficult. In any event, the conflict is not between federal regulation and market competition. Instead it is a conflict between state and federal regulation, and there is no reason to think *a priori* that one will be superior, by whatever measure, to the other.

One could therefore find a stable stopping point to the commerce power by limiting its reach to transportation by rail, river, road, and, today, by air. Congressional power would be limited to commerce as traditionally understood, even though it would reach intrastate as well as interstate commerce with respect to those transportation facilities that were devoted to both.

It is possible, however, to unhinge the last fragment of the previous passage from the whole so as to make it appear that any competition, from whatever source, justifies federal regulation. Just that step was taken during the New Deal. But before we turn to this ultimate transformation of the *Shreveport Rate Case* line of cases,[101] it will be instructive to examine the other two lines of commerce clause cases.

2. What Goods May Be Shipped in Interstate Commerce?

The pre-New Deal expansion of the commerce clause did not stem solely from the federal regulation of the instrumentalities of interstate commerce. It was also intimately connected to the types of goods that could be shipped in interstate commerce at all. These cases, it seems clear, did not necessarily involve only commerce among the several states, although the regulated goods were in transit from one state to another. But the relevant questions were, and remain, intractable because both the motive and effect of congressional regulation concerned matters that were themselves not within the "stream of commerce," at least as the phrase was understood before 1937. The true goal of these regulations was to govern—"influence" is not a strong enough word—the behavior of individuals and firms before their goods entered commerce or after they left it. In evaluating the statutes, the Court was required to consider the interaction between the commerce clause and the rest of the constitutional structure, in particular the principle that Congress possessed only the limited and enumerated powers conferred upon it by Article I—powers that did not allow it to intrude upon the reserved powers of the states. The drawing of the relevant lines is by no means an easy task. But there is, on balance, good reason to believe that the Court, even before the 1937 revolution, construed the commerce clause in ways that extended the power of Congress beyond its proper scope.

The first case in the line was *Champion v. Ames*[102] in 1903. The question before the Court was whether Congress could prohibit the transportation of lottery tickets across state lines under the commerce clause.[103] The first Justice Harlan's opinion upheld the statute as a proper application of the commerce power.[104] But Justice Harlan's defense of federal power in *Champion* is problematic. Although the statute in question operated on articles of interstate commerce, its purpose surely was not to protect or to facilitate interstate commerce. Quite the opposite—its purpose was designed to influence the primary conduct of individuals, either before the goods entered interstate commerce or before it left them. One telltale sign of the new aggressiveness to which the commerce power was turned that Congress sought to *prohibit*, not to regulate, the transfer of lottery tickets in interstate commerce. In and of itself, this fact hardly seems dispositive, for it is doubtful that the commerce clause could be read so that "regulation" occupies a domain so narrow that all types of prohibition fall outside the power of Congress. Hamilton himself spoke of "prohibitory regulation" when addressing in *Federalist* No. 11 the need to regulate commerce with foreign nations.[105] If these prohibitions are (regrettably) proper in the foreign context, then they cannot be wholly banished in the domestic one.

Analytically, too, it seems that regulations comprehend prohibitions. To be sure, regulation and prohibition do not mean the same thing, and the Constitution itself uses the two terms in clear opposition to each other.[106] It would be very odd indeed to say that Congress had the power "to prohibit all commerce with foreign nations, among the states, or with the Indian tribes," for the total elimination of all trade seems hard to reconcile with the original vision of vibrant national markets unimpeded by petty local regulations.[107] But it is difficult to have the extreme case determine the principle, given the massive overlap between regulations and prohibitions in ordinary speech. The class of conditional prohibitions—of the sort which say that no goods may travel in interstate commerce unless evidenced by a bill of lading—is so extensive and benign that it is difficult to see how any jurisdictional limitation on congressional power could be erected on the strength of the verbal distinction alone.

The source of the uneasiness with *Champion* does not, however, disappear even if we acknowledge (however uneasily) that all prohibitions are regulations, within the meaning of the commerce clause. Instead, the common concern with both regulations and prohibitions of the sort found in *Champion* and its progeny is that Congress will use its powers of regulation to upset the doctrine of enumerated powers. Stated otherwise, *Champion* is perhaps the first case in which Congress had consciously sought to exploit the outer reaches of the commerce clause in ways that might trench upon the power of the states. In one sense, the Congress stayed within the commerce clause, because Chief Justice Marshall told us that the commerce power is "plenary" over everything that comes within its specified limits. But, in another sense, Congress used its plenary power to arrogate to itself matters reserved to the states. The uneasiness that one thus feels with *Champion* is quite similar to that which is provoked by the troublesome doctrine of unconstitutional conditions, which no one quite understands, but which, nonetheless, no one can ignore.[108] One way to read unconstitutional conditions is an effort by the state to expand its power over the private activities of individuals by conditioning their access to public facilities, most typically roads: thus the doctrine has been invoked to hold that the state cannot allow a private carrier to use the public highways unless it first agrees (without compensation) to be regulated as a public carrier.[109] The clear function of the doctrine is to curb the state desire to use its power of public instrumentalities to control private behavior, even though it is allowed to exclude vehicles of certain classes from the highways altogether.

The *Champion* line of cases shows the same type of tensions at work, as the Court struggled to find the line that allowed the power of Congress to remain plenary, without undermining the reserved powers of the state. Some forms of regulations, and indeed prohibitions, seem not to threaten the delicate balance of the federal system. As the dissent in *Champion* suggested, for example, a clear instance of an acceptable prohibition is one preventing the shipment in interstate commerce of goods that are themselves a peril to interstate commerce:

> The power to prohibit the transportation of diseased animals and infected goods over railroads or on steamboats is an entirely different thing, for they would be in themselves injurious to the transaction of interstate commerce, and, moreover, are essentially commercial in their nature. And the exclusion of diseased persons rests on different ground, for nobody would pretend that persons could be kept off the trains because they were going from one State to another to engage in the lottery business.[110]

Here there is no concern that Congress, by the use of a single enumerated power, is trying to dominate the states in the exercise of their reserved powers.

Similarly, a somewhat broader but wholly defensible line could stress the harmony between federal and state regulation. Suppose that the statute at issue in *Champion* prohibited the shipment of lottery tickets from any state in which their production was illegal or into any state in which their possession was illegal. Here the congressional statute would be *in aid of* valid legislation at the state level. It would reinforce, rather than contradict, state law. In *Champion,* however, the tie between state and federal regulation was nonexistent, or even negative. The shipment of lottery tickets was forbidden in interstate commerce, although their use may have been wholly legal in the states from which and to which they were sent. To be sure, if congressional power under the commerce clause had been clearly established, the supremacy clause would have resolved the conflict between state and federal laws in Congress's favor.[111] But the supremacy clause is of no help until the proper scope of the commerce clause has been first determined, in light of the concerns raised by the doctrine of unconstitutional conditions. The narrower tests previously discussed would not seem to allow the *Champion* prohibition. The "in aid of" test would allow Congress to impose restrictions on interstate transportation only where it worked to assist an existing state prohibition against the production or consumption of the product in question. A "noxious use" test is somewhat broader because it allows Congress to impose restrictions on the interstate shipment of noxious goods—adulterated foods, poisons, dangerous drugs, and perhaps even lottery tickets. It is possible to object to both these formulations on the ground that the Constitution nowhere provides for any independent federal police power. But even if these exercises of legislative power are accepted, they would still respect the independent power of the states.

There was yet a third line of argument that could have prevailed in *Champion*. The case could have rested on a peculiar amalgam of the police power and the commerce clause, showing yet again the affinity between jurisdictional and substantive concerns. Lottery tickets were an issue toward which states had long taken a quite schizophrenic attitude. Sometimes the states prohibited lotteries; sometimes they allowed private firms to run them under state charter; sometimes they ran the lotteries themselves.[112] Generally speaking, gambling fell within the class of dubious private activities subject to police power regulation along with, for example, prostitution. One possible stopping point under the commerce clause would provide that Congress could prohibit the transmission in interstate commerce of those goods which a state *could* ban under its police power, as it was then understood, even if the state had not actually prohibited their use. Justice Harlan, who wrote the majority opinion in *Champion*, always gave an expansive,[113] and occasionally maddeningly extravagant,[114] scope to the police power whenever supposed issues of health and morals arose, though otherwise he was a tiger in defense of individual liberty and freedom of contract.[115] Justice Harlan's opinion in *Champion* emphasized the police power, stressing the iniquitous nature of lotteries and asking, "why may not Congress, invested with the power to regulate commerce among the several States, provide that such commerce shall not be polluted by the carrying of lottery tickets from one State to another?"[116] Harlan rejected the idea that the commerce clause "countenances the suggestion that one may, of right, carry or cause to be carried from one State to another that which will harm the public morals."[117]

The question then arises: Could the argument equating prohibition under the police power with prohibition under the commerce clause survive? Why not? It is an argument that could permit the federal government to regulate the transport of prostitutes across state lines,[118] whether or not prostitution was legal in the state to which they were sent, or to prohibit the sale of adulterated foods and drugs.[119] Note that each of these examples would be far more secure if the sale of the ultimate product or service were illegal in the state to which the goods were shipped, as was typically the case. This broader conception, although perhaps less preferable than the more limited versions of the commerce clause discussed above, would still have left its scope less than comprehensive.

It was just this conception of the relationship between the commerce clause and the police power that held the line against federal power in *Hammer v. Dagenhart*.[120] In *Hammer*, federal legislation forbade the shipment in interstate commerce of any goods manufactured in any plant that used child labor in ways prohibited by the statute within a thirty-day period prior to the shipment.[121] There was no requirement that the actual goods shipped in interstate commerce had to have been made by child labor—only that some goods made at the plant had been made with the use of child labor. The validity of the statute was hardly compelled by *Champion*, for the sale of ordinary clothing could not be prohibited as an illicit item of commerce under the most extravagant version of the police power. Indeed, the Court understood the statute for what it was; it was not an effort to control the goods themselves, but to prescribe the internal rules governing their manufacture within the state.[122] The delicacy of this legislation was manifest in an age when direct federal regulation of manufacture had been precluded by the Supreme Court in *United States v. E.C. Knight*.[123] In *Hammer* the Supreme Court stuck to its guns, and by a narrow five-four decision refused to extend *Champion* beyond the noxious or dangerous products to which it applied.

On balance, *Hammer* was correctly decided, assuming that the commerce clause must be understood within the larger structural context of the Constitution. Thus, if the child labor statute in *Hammer* had been good law, one can envision the following cycle of evasion and response: a firm using child labor now divides its business into two halves, subject to common stock ownership. One half makes goods for intrastate commerce using child labor, while the other half makes goods for interstate commerce without using child labor. Congress then passes a new statute which says that no firm whose shareholders have a dominant interest in a second firm that uses child labor may send its goods into interstate commerce. The firm decides to go out of the interstate business altogether. Congress next passes a statute which says that no firm that acquires part of its supplies from any firm that uses child labor may ship its goods in interstate commerce, whether or not the goods made with child labor are incorporated into its own goods shipped interstate.

Why stop here? If the political will exists, Congress can pass a law which states that no firm in any state may ship its goods in interstate commerce unless every other firm within that state forswears the use of child labor. In each case the statute technically regulates only goods within the stream of interstate commerce. If prohibitions are simply forms of regulation, then Congress can raise the price of state independence so high that even the foolhardy must capitulate. Congress can make any use of child labor a federal issue by redefining the keys that unlock the gates to interstate commerce. If child labor can be reached by Congress, then so can everything else reserved to the states. A "Congressional Marriage Act" could provide that "no manufacturer can ship its goods in interstate commerce unless its state legislature passes a statute under which all local marriages conform to the federal requirements." These concerns were indeed raised by Justice Day, who wrote that majority opinion in *Hammer*.[124] Justice Day correctly noted that prior cases were limited to cases in which the "use of interstate transportation was necessary to the accomplishment of harmful results,"[125] and held that only the limited version of the commerce clause was consistent with the Tenth Amendment.[126] He noted that competition within the federal system was essential to the original constitutional design.[127]

Justice Holmes, in dissent, wrote a spirited and perceptive defense of the congressional power:

> The act does not meddle with anything belonging to the States. They may regulate their internal affairs and their domestic commerce as they like. But when they seek to send their products across the state line they are no longer within their rights. If there were no Constitution and no Congress their power to cross the line would depend upon their neighbors. Under the Constitution such commerce belongs not to the States but to Congress to regulate.[128]

Holmes surely overstated his point. No one doubted that Congress had the power to override any state effort to block the shipment of goods in interstate commerce. But the justification of one use of that power hardly demanded acceptance of any use of it. The child labor statute in *Hammer* was invalid because Congress had used its admitted powers over interstate commerce to eliminate a state's "internal affairs" completely. Holmes never addressed this limit to his principles, nor identified the expansive statutes that his views necessarily tolerated—even though he had previously warned against interpreting the commerce clause so as to allow Congress to reach every productive endeavor of human life.[129] His observation that no statute should be upset because it has "indirect effects" upon the domestic affairs of the state[130] simply failed to address the structural threats that the child labor statutes posed to the distribution of state and federal power.

Justice Day's majority opinion in *Hammer* was strong on the jurisdictional side, but apologetic on the substantive side.[131] The issue of child labor laws had long been an emotional one, and there was a powerful consensus in the Progressive movement that these statutes were absolutely necessary to counteract the evils of an unrestrained laissez-faire economic system which tolerated, and indeed encouraged, child labor. The Solicitor General, John W. Davis (who later represented the southern states in *Brown v. Board of Education*[132]), insisted that, although the need was pressing, individual states were reluctant to enact their own child labor statutes because they feared that their manufacturers would be harmed by competition from industries in states still employing child labor:

> The shipment of child-made goods outside of one State directly induces similar employment of children in competing States. It is not enough to answer that each State theoretically may regulate conditions of manufacturing within its own borders. As Congress saw the situation, the States were not entirely free agents. For salutary statutes had been replaced, legislative action on their part had been defeated and postponed time and again, solely by reason of the argument (valid or not) that interstate competition could not be withstood.[133]

The quoted passage was something of an overstatement, as every state in the Union, including North Carolina (the state at issue in *Hammer*), had some statute regulating child labor on its books.[134] The real question was whether the weaker North Carolina statute, which forbade child labor below the age of twelve, was preferable to the federal minimum of fourteen.[135]

Justice Day made no substantive attack on the child labor laws—rather, he sympathized with them.[136] Justice Day was in the awkward position of having to defend jurisdictional limitations that worked against what he thought to be highly desirable social regulation.

The case takes on a different complexion, however, if one looks with even modest suspicion on child labor statutes, as I do, and thinks that as a general rule the only proper grounds for government intervention in family relations are abuse or neglect. Any reader of Laura Ingalls Wilder's *Farmer Boy* knows that child labor was not a creature of the industrial revolution.[137] Arduous labor, day and night, without any employer to regulate or to sue, has always been the lot of farm children. The children in the factories were certainly not as well off as we would like, but they were probably better off than they would have been back on the farm, or than if they had been left in the city without any opportunity to sell their labor. Their families had voted to leave the farm or the old country with their feet, as a matter of life and death.[138] Under this view, the substantive reforms may well have been misguided initiatives that inflicted harm upon the very persons they were ostensibly intended to benefit. Child labor changes in its character and intensity as changes occur in the means of production, the income level of parents, and the returns to children from more education. Restrictions on child labor may be proposed as ways to prevent child neglect and abuse, but the case for them is far from self-evident. Even if the police power is thought to be extensive enought to "protect" children from their parents as a constitutional matter, as it surely was by 1918,[139] there is a clear risk that the proper limits of the police power will be exceeded when legislation is used by interest groups that do not rely upon child labor to undercut rivals who do. Stated otherwise, child labor legislation could well be misguided paternalism or interest-group politics.

This skeptical view of the substantive issues in *Hammer* should caution one against reading more into the commerce clause than its language—or its place in the overall constitutional structure—allows. There is no obvious reason to approach the jurisdiction question with the assumption that child labor laws are intrinsically good if only we knew how to enact them. Their strength, far from being a given, should be tested in competition between states. Such competition would show the true importance of child labor laws to the state: will a state impose the restriction even when local firms may be hampered in interstate competition? The legislative question surely is not an all-or-nothing one. Indeed, the difference between North Carolina's twelve-year limit and Congress's fourteen is surely only one of degree. It is far from self-evident which minimum is better, assuming there should be child labor laws at all.

The relatively clean line in *Hammer* prevented Congress from using its power over the movement of goods in interstate commerce to regulate the terms and conditions of their production. The line of cases regarding what types of goods could be shipped in interstate commerce thus imposed real limitations on the power of Congress. To be sure, the ICC cases afforded Congress powerful jurisdiction over the instrumentalities of interstate commerce.[140] But even when broadly construed, these still stopped with the railroads and navigable waters (and, by obvious extension, interstate highways and interstate airplane transportation). The line between state police power and the commerce clause had shifted, and there is reason to think that some of the shifts had already placed too many matters on the federal side of the line. But the case law was still a long way from giving Congress comprehensive powers to regulate all productive activities.

3. Manufacturing and Commerce

I now turn to the last line of cases necessary to complete the overall picture—those that drew the sharp and structural line between commerce on one hand and manufacture (or production and agriculture) on the other. This line of cases began with *United States v. E.C. Knight Co.*[141] in 1895, and retained its overall validity until the 1937 term. What follows is an account of how that line of cases developed and retained its distinct position from the two groups of cases just considered.

E.C. Knight was the first constitutional challenge to the Sherman Act.[142] At issue was the acquisition by the American Sugar Refining Company, a New Jersey corporation, of four Pennsylvania corporations that manufactured refined sugar. The United States challenged the merger under the Sherman Act as "a combination or contract in restraint of trade or commerce among the several states."[143] The Court held that the merger could not be reached by the Sherman Act because it was not part of interstate commerce and had no "direct" effect upon it.[144] Chief Justice Fuller made a conscious effort to delineate the respective spheres of the state police power and the commerce clause in his majority opinion in ways that harken back to *Gibbons v. Ogden:*

> Commerce succeeds to manufacture, and is not a part of it. The power to regulate commerce is the power to prescribe the rule by which commerce shall be governed, and is a power independent of the power to suppress monopoly. But it may operate in repression of monopoly whenever that comes within the rules by which commerce is governed or whenever the transaction is itself a monopoly of commerce.

> It is vital that the independence of the commercial power and of the police power, and the delimitation between them, however sometimes perplexing, should always be recognized and observed, for while the one furnishes the strongest bond of union, the other is essential to the preservation of the autonomy of the States as required by our dual form of government; and acknowledged evils, however grave and urgent they may appear to be, had better be borne, than the risk be run, in the effort to suppress them, of more serious consequences by resort to expedients of even doubtful constitutionality.

> Contracts to buy, sell, or exchange goods to be transported among the several States, the transportation and its instrumentalities, and articles bought, sold, or exchanged for the purposes of such transit among the States, or put in the way of transit, may be regulated, but this is because they form part of interstate trade or commerce. The fact that an article is manufactured for export to another State does not of itself make it an article of interstate commerce, and the intent of the manufacturer does not determine the time when the article or product passes from the control of the State and belongs to commerce.[145]

Chief Justice Fuller tried to raise a barrier between manufacture, on the one hand, and sale or shipment of goods in interstate commerce, on the other. But the barrier was not as well-defined as Chief Justice Fuller made it out to be. Justice Harlan forcefully made this point in his dissent, noting that this merger was designed to regulate not only the manufacturing of refined sugar but also "selling sugar in different parts of the country."[146] The transaction in *E.C. Knight* had two purposes: manufacture, over which there could be a local monopoly that Congress could not reach, and a plan for restrictive interstate sale, designed to raise prices in interstate markets. The status of the sales plan element of the merger was the subject of dispute between the Justices. Chief Justice Fuller's majority opinion allowed federal regulation of the contracts by which the sugar was bought and sold.[147] Yet it reads as though it would not have allowed the regulation of a structural agreement made prior to actual

sales, by which the parties agreed to sell only certain amounts in interstate
commerce at certain prices. According to his view, this master agreement
would fall outside of the scope of the commerce clause. Justice Harlan's
dissent, on the other hand, did *not* attack Chief Justice Fuller's position that
"commerce succeeds manufacture." Instead he argued that manufacture
became commerce when the sugar was sold to be transported, not subsequently, when it actually was placed in interstate transport:

> It is said that manufacture precedes commerce and is not a part of it. But it is
> equally true that when manufacture ends, that which has been manufactured
> becomes a subject of commerce; that buying and selling succeed manufac-
> ture, come into existence after the process of manufacture is completed,
> precede transportation and are as much commercial intercourse, where
> articles are bought *to be* carried from one State to another, as is the manual
> transportation of such articles after they have been so purchased.[148]

Justice Harlan never quite closed in on the essential issue in the case. The
government did not attack the individual contracts for sale of sugar in interstate commerce, but only the prior structural arrangements that influenced the
terms on which the interstate sales were made. In most antitrust cases, the
contracts for the division of markets or the maintenance of prices are separate
and distinct from any contract arrangements for the manufacture or sale of
goods. But the transaction at issue in *E.C. Knight* was a merger that was quite
impossible for Congress to reach by a plan to regulate the interstate sales of the
combined sugar business (even if these preliminary merger agreements were
regarded as in interstate commerce) without necessarily intruding into the
regulation of manufacture, which *both* the majority and the dissent expressly
regarded as outside the scope of the commerce clause.[149] *E.C. Knight* was thus
an early version of the *Shreveport Rate Case* problem, in which the Court
recognized that the regulation of interstate commerce was necessarily either
over- or underinclusive.[150] The difference between the majority and dissenting
opinions in *E.C. Knight* is best explained as a response to the issue of whether
too much or too little regulation was desired. Justice Harlan in dissent thought
that the regulation was appropriate, for the peril of national monopolies was
too great to be ignored.[151] To Chief Justice Fuller, on the other hand, the
decisive consideration was that the expansion of the commerce power to meet
the danger of monopoly ran the far greater risk of upsetting the grand constitutional balance between the federal and the state governments.[152] That is why he
was so eager to strike down any statute "of even doubtful constitutionality."[153]

Unfortunately, these genuine substantive concerns were not incorporated
into a careful analysis of the error costs of alternative jurisdictional rules.
Instead the debate focused on the question whether the regulation had an
impact on interstate commerce that was "direct or immediate" or "remote or
indirect."[154] These abstract, largely nondescriptive terms simply could not

carry the vast institutional weight placed upon them in future years. The *E.C. Knight* opinions, in retrospect, seem in large part to be simple word games or metaphysical abstractions rather than debates about important principles.

The difference between the two sides, moreover, was not as great as might be supposed. The substantial common ground between Chief Justice Fuller and Justice Harlan is clearly borne out by looking at the next important case in the line, *Addyston Pipe & Steel Co. v. United States,* [155] written for a unanimous Supreme Court by Justice Peckham, who is today largely remembered for his opinion in *Lochner v. New York* striking down New York's ten-hour maximum daily labor law for bakers.[156] *Addyston Pipe* upheld a federal attack on an explicit contract by cast-iron pipe producers to divide the territorial market for their product among themselves in order to create a set of local monopolies.[157] At one level the case appears indistinguishable from *E.C. Knight,* from which it differed solely by the method chosen by the parties to obtain their monopoly prices. A merger of manufacturing businesses was the method of choice in *E.C. Knight,* while an explicit cartelization was chosen in *Addyston Pipe.* If the sole question was whether there was a "direct" or "indirect" effect upon commerce, whether by the price or volume of goods shipped, the two cases could hardly be distinguished. If a merger designed to raise prices has only an "indirect" effect upon commerce, then so too does a cartel arrangement with that same purpose and effect.

Yet if the distinction between the two cases is viewed in light of the underlying substantive concerns motivating the Court, then it makes perfect sense. *E.C. Knight* raised two questions: first, whether the preliminary step (be it merger or cartel) toward a proposed sale of goods in interstate commerce was itself part of interstate commerce; and second, even if a preliminary step was part of interstate commerce, could Congress reach it by regulating manufacture, which everyone conceded was not part of interstate commerce? Chief Justice Fuller found *E.C. Knight* an easy case because he was prepared to answer the second question in the negative, given his doubts about the first. Yet in *Addyston Pipe* the second question vanished, because the cartel arrangement reached only planned interstate sales and had no influence at all upon manufacturing. Only the first question had to be addressed. The difficult choice between necessary over- and necessary under-inclusion did not arise in *Addyston.* To apply the Sherman Act, it needed only to be said that preliminary agreements, designed by the parties to regulate their private sales in interstate commerce, were themselves part of interstate commerce.[158] It did not take a very inventive reading of *Gibbons* to say that these outward-looking contracts were not part of the purely internal commerce of the state. This refinement of *E.C. Knight* therefore did not challenge the view that manufacture and commerce were distinct spheres. Despite giving Congress its way in *Addyston Pipe,* the Court did not intrude upon the basic principle that the power to regulate commerce among the several states was only one of a list of enumerated powers. *Addyston Pipe* therefore hardly broke with the past. The Court reached a unanimous decision (with Fuller still Chief Justice) because the risk of excessive congressional power was not present.

The same can be said about the two other major early antitrust decisions that invoked the commerce clause. The issue in *Northern Securities Co. v. United States*[159] was whether Congress could reach a stock merger of two railroad lines. Congressional power was sustained by a five-four vote, with Justice Harlan writing for the Court and with Chief Justice Fuller and Justice Peckham (joined by Justices Holmes and White) in dissent. The latent disagreement that divided the Court in *E.C. Knight* again came to the fore, albeit in somewhat different form. Justice Harlan's basic posture was unchanged. If a merger of gigantic manufacturing concerns was of federal concern because of its direct influence on prices, he had no reason to pause simply because the antitrust laws were applied to a transaction in shares of stock that was local in origin and governed by the state law.[160] Indeed, the fact that the underlying assets were two interstate railroads could have only strengthened Justice Harlan's view that the transaction had to be reached by the antitrust laws. It was no longer necessary, after all, to tiptoe along the narrow line between manufacture and commerce, for the merger did not involve any regulation of manufacturing. If Congress could regulate the rates on interstate lines, then why should it not be able to stop the merger?

The four dissenting Justices took a very different position. To them, the appropriate balance between state and federal power was as primary an issue as it had been to Chief Justice Fuller in *E.C. Knight*, given that the regulation of state corporate ownership, a local matter, was inseparable from the regulation of interstate transport.[161] A passage from Justice Holmes's dissent shows the interplay between two dominant motifs of the early decisions:

> The point decided in [*E.C. Knight*] was that "the fact that trade or commerce might be indirectly affected was not enough to entitle complainants to a decree." Commerce depends upon population, but Congress could not, on that ground, undertake to regulate marriage and divorce. If the act before us is to be carried out according to what seems to me the logic of the argument for the Government, which I do not believe that it will be, I can see no part of the conduct of life with which on similar principles Congress might not interfere.[162]

In a single passage, Justice Holmes was able to merge and confuse two distinct ideas: first, that Congress could not regulate absent direct effects on interstate commerce; and second, that the federal-state balance of power under the Founders' plan required that the commerce clause be given some effective limits, lest the independent powers of the states be undermined. In a sense the five-four vote in *Northern Securities* is explained in that the case was a more powerful one for congressional action under the commerce power than was

E.C. Knight. But the differences between the majority and the dissenters on the question of principle were minor, and at best *Northern Securities* identified the tipping point at which the interstate elements start to dominate the overall transaction.

In *Swift & Co. v. United States,*[163] decided a year later, the consensus of *Addyston Pipe* reasserted itself. In *Swift,* the government brought an antitrust case against fresh food dealers who sought to organize bidding in livestock markets across the United States.[164] The distinction between this cartel and the one in *Addyston Pipe* was not worth pursuing, so Justice Holmes came out of his dissent in *Northern Securities* and wrote for a unanimous Court condemning this cartel for its effect on interstate commerce:

> [I]t is a direct object, it is that for the sake of which the several specific acts and courses of conduct are done and adopted. Therefore the case is not like [*E.C. Knight*], where the subject matter of the combination was manufacture and the direct object monopoly of manufacture within a State. However likely monopoly of commerce among the States in the article manufactured was to follow from the agreement it was not a necessary consequence nor a primary end. Here the subject matter is sales and the very point of the combination is to restrain and monopolize commerce among the States in respect of such sales.[165]

Holmes's distinction between direct and indirect consequences is unpersuasive, because it places too much weight on elusive notions of causation, without addressing the paramount institutional concerns raised by the case. What was needed in addition was an explicit acknowledgement that the doctrine of enumerated powers has an important structural role to play in constitutional interpretation. Once that principle is accepted, then there is good reason for tolerating some of the ambiguity that is invited by references to "direct and indirect objects," without fretting unduly over the metaphysical speculation that these terms invite. The line between commerce and manufacture makes good sense, given the structure of the commerce clause and Article I of the Constitution as a whole.

Whatever the weaknesses in Holmes's basic theory, *Swift* and its predecessors articulated a set of boundary lines that was reasonably easy to apply. The Court read *Swift* as the decisive precedent in favor of the federal power in both *Stafford v. Wallace*[166] and *Chicago Board of Trade v. Olsen.*[167] In neither case was the line between manufacture and commerce tested, let alone overthrown.

In *Stafford,* the court upheld the constitutionality of the Packers and Stockyards Act of 1921,[168] which regulated the middlemen who arranged the sale and shipment of cattle from the West to purchasers in the Chicago stockyards.[169] The Act gave to the Secretary of Agriculture the power to set maximum and minimum prices and to prohibit discriminatory and deceptive trade practices.[170] The Court relied heavily on an analogy to the "instrumentalities of interstate commerce":

> The stockyards are not a place of rest or final destination. Thousands of head of live stock arrive daily by carload and trainload lots, and must be promptly sold and disposed of and moved out to give place to the constantly flowing traffic that presses behind. The stockyards are but a throat through which the current flows, and the transactions which occur therein are only incident to this current from the West to the East, and from one State to another.[171]

Olsen upheld the Grain Futures Act,[172] which regulated the sale of grain for future delivery on boards of trade, under the rationale that manipulation of futures prices had burdened and obstructed interstate commerce.[173] Chief Justice Taft again emphasized the link between trade in goods and the railroads.[174]

These two decisions, by involving matters ancillary to the actual shipment of goods by the railroads, clearly expanded the scope of the commerce power. General concern about fraud and manipulation (both of which are wrongs under state law) is not an obvious reason to allow federal regulation. It is possible therefore to argue that the statutes themselves were unconstitutional, despite the unanimous decisions of the Supreme Court. For the purposes of this article, however, it is sufficient to note that *nothing* in either case challenged *E.C. Knight's* distinction between manufacture or production on the one hand, and interstate commerce on the other. As late as 1935 in *Schechter Poultry Corp. v. United States,*[175] Chief Justice Hughes wrote, in limiting the jurisdiction of Congress under the commerce clause, "The distinction between direct and indirect effects has been clearly recognized in the application of the Anti-Trust Act," and then used the distinction to strike down the National Industrial Recovery Act.[176] The next year, in *Carter v. Carter Coal Co.,*[177] a majority of the Supreme Court struck down various provisions of the Bituminous Coal Conservation Act of 1935[178] on the ground that the commerce clause did not allow the federal government to regulate the terms of employment within the mines.[179] The *Carter* Court correctly distinguished *Stafford* as a "flow of commerce" case, in which Congress had regulated the "throat" of interstate commerce, and nothing more.[180] Elsewhere in his majority opinion, Justice Sutherland wrote categorically that "[t]he relation of employer and employee is a local relation."[181]

E.C. Knight's basic distinction between manufacture and commerce thus held firm as late as *Carter* in 1936. The emerging pattern said, for example, that the Ford Motor Company did not manufacture goods in interstate commerce, but the Northern Pacific Railroad shipped them in interstate commerce. As constitutional principles go, this line was relatively clear. It is just the line that is observed today in the dormant commerce clause cases,[182] and it is as intelligible with the affirmative power cases as with the dormant power cases. This third line of cases under the commerce clause added to congressional power, but it surely did not lead to the conclusion that Congress should have the comprehensive power to regulate the entire business of life. The Court had expanded the reach of earlier cases involving the "instrumentalities of interstate commerce." This broadened scope of the commerce power allowed Congress to regulate matters actually outside the scope of commerce in order to regulate what fell within its admitted power. But the overbreadth doctrine was applied only in cases that did not involve common carriers. And Congress's power to prohibit the shipment of certain kinds of goods in commerce was sharply, but correctly, limited by *Hammer v. Dagenhart* to those things noxious in themselves.[183] The totality of commerce clause jurisprudence as it emerged before the New Deal may not have been perfect; indeed, it probably yielded a bit too much to federal power, at least under the power to regulate instrumentalities of commerce and the power to regulate the type of goods shipped in interstate commerce. But the set of rules was surely workable. This state of affairs was to change in the 1930s. The final part of this article will trace the rapid decline of the old distinctions, and will briefly note the regrettable social consequences that followed in the wake of departures from sound constitutional principle.

V. The New Deal Transformation of the Commerce Clause

The New Deal cases systematically removed each of the previous limitations on the scope of the commerce clause. This expansion of federal power was not driven by any textual necessity. Instead, it is better understood, but hardly justified, as a response to two separate but related forces. First, the 1936 Roosevelt mandate and the prospect of court packing could hardly have been lost on the Court.[184] Second, a narrow majority of the Court was in sympathy with the dominant intellectual belief of the time that national problems required national responses. The New Deal cases worked a revolution in constitutional theory as well as in textual interpretation. The original theory of the Constitution was based on the belief that government was not an unalloyed good, but was, at best, a necessary evil. The system of enumerated powers allowed state governments to compete among themselves, thus limiting the risks of governmental abuse even absent explicit, substantive limitations on the laws that states could pass. The various limitations upon the federal power helped achieve this end. The New Deal conception, on the other hand, saw no virtue in competition, whether between states or between firms. The old barriers were stripped away; in their place has emerged the vast and unwarranted concentration of power in Congress that remains the hallmark of the modern regulatory state.

The first major case to test the traditional analysis of the commerce clause was *NLRB v. Jones & Laughlin Steel Corp.*,[185] which involved a challenge to the National Labor Relations Act (Wagner Act).[186] The Wagner Act in essence removed employers' power to hire and fire at will, instead requiring extensive collective bargaining in good faith between employers and unions if the union is approved by a majority of employees.[187] The unions were selected by a majority of workers, but had the power to bind workers who dissented.[188] Individual contracts inconsistent with the master agreement were unenforceable, lest the union's power be undermined by dissatisfied workers.[189]

The Wagner Act was based squarely upon the commerce clause. The draftsmen sought to meet the fundamental challenge of jurisdiction by providing that federal jurisdiction extended not only to cases of "commerce" but also to cases "affecting commerce": "The term 'affecting commerce' means in commerce, or burdening or obstructing commerce or the free flow of commerce, or having led or tending to lead to a labor dispute burdening or obstructing commerce or the free flow of commerce."[190]

This extended definition proves that Congress used a legal fiction to expand federal jurisdiction beyond its original grant. The commerce clause does not say "Congress shall have the power to regulate commerce, and all matters affecting commerce with foreign nations, among the several states, and with the Indian tribes." The statutory text, moreover, invited a favorable outcome on the jurisdictional question by smuggling into its expanded definition of commerce the desirable effects that the labor statute was intended to achieve. Yet there was no real evidence that local regulation of employment markets was incapable of achieving desired economic goals. It was only the distinct New Deal bias for worker monopolies protected by explicit barriers to entry (here, against rival workers who would work for less) that could have led to the conclusion that the Wagner Act would improve the free flow of commerce. How cartelization of labor markets would remove barriers or obstructions to interstate commerce has never been explained. Labor cartelization generally raises the level of wages and reduces the quantity of goods produced. When a cartel is legally protected against new entrants into its market, the new entrants are no longer able to take advantage of the price "umbrella" that an unregulated cartel necessarily creates for enterprising rivals. The Wagner Act surely had an effect on commerce, and that effect was negative.

A system of limited government keeps local governments in competition with each other. This sensible institutional arrangement was wholly undermined by Congress's decision, in the teeth of the commerce clause, to subject all employment markets to nationally uniform regulation. As in the case of child labor laws, as previously discussed, the power of states to impose collective bargaining requirements on firms is effectively limited by the ability of old firms to leave the state and of new ones not to enter it. Also, since domestic firms can escape whatever misguided tariff barriers may be thrown up against international suppliers of goods and services, the level of state regulation is effectively curtailed, and the volume of goods and services in commerce increases.

The transformation in legislative and judicial thinking about the commerce clause is revealed by the reversal in substantive outcomes. *Gibbons v. Ogden* ensured free trade by overturning a state-granted legal monopoly.[191] The Sherman Act cases were also directed against private monopolies—a lesser peril—which were seen incorrectly, I believe, as "regulating" interstate commerce.[192] Both *Gibbons* and the Sherman Act cases were attempts to facilitate free trade in open markets—one at the constitutional, the other at the statutory, level. With the later expansion of congressional jurisdiction by such laws as the Transportation Act of 1920, however, the commerce clause became an instrument to suppress competition, rather than one to further it.[193] It is only if one thinks that government can neutrally determine when there is too much competition as well as when there is too little that the broader interpretation of the commerce power becomes plausible. And it is clear that the New Deal thinkers thought they understood the vices of competition.[194]

It is always, however, a precarious venture for judges to make independent normative judgments about the desirability of certain social arrangements when passing on the constitutionality of certain acts. In a sense, the task of interpretation should depend, as Chief Justice Marshall did in *Gibbons v. Ogden,* on the natural and ordinary sense of the word.[195] The approach also leads, however, to the conclusion that the Wagner Act goes beyond the scope of the commerce clause under the authority of *E. C. Knight* and, most notably, *Carter.*[196] The three decisions of the United States Courts of Appeals that passed upon the Wagner Act declared it unconstitutional by applying the precedents mechanically.[197] Recall that the hard question in *E.C. Knight* was whether prospective restraints of trade in interstate markets could justify an intrusion into manufacture, an area normally regulated by the states. *Jones & Laughlin,* of course, involved no effort to monopolize an interstate market. Quite the opposite; the contracts at issue concerned only matters of local employment which, as the Court's opinion in *Carter* had confirmed, had never been thought a federal matter under any prior conception of the commerce clause.[198]

To respond to this difficulty, the Court in *Jones & Laughlin* resurrected the losing argument of *Carter*—that anything which had a substantial effect upon interstate commerce could be regulated regardless of its source.[199] In so doing, the Court in effect borrowed the language of those cases concerned with the instrumentalities of interstate commerce[200] and applied it generally, as if the original subject-matter restriction had not been integral to the earlier decisions. Manufacture was no longer distinguishable from commerce, because the manufacturing process involved "a great movement of iron ore, coal and limestone along well-defined paths to the steel mills, thence through them, and thence in the form of steel products into the consuming centers of the country—a definite and well-understood course of business."[201]

To be sure, Chief Justice Hughes acknowledged in *Jones & Laughlin* that some "internal concerns" of the state remained outside the power of Congress to regulate.[202] But it was all lip service; the companion cases to *Jones & Laughlin* showed that the "internal concerns of a state" had become an empty vessel. *NLRB v. Fruehauf Co.* applied the Wagner Act to a manufacturer of commercial trailers that obtained more than fifty percent of its material out of state and sold eighty percent of its output to out-of-state customers.[203] *NLRB v. Friedman-Harry Marks Clothing Co.* used the same logic, applying the statute to a clothing manufacturer that purchased most of its raw cloth out of state, and sold a majority of its finished garments there as well.[204] The commerce clause was thus hardly limited to the integrated multistate firms like Jones & Laughlin. And beneath the legal analysis lay the ultimate policy reason for the decisions: Congress and the NLRB believed that industry-wide unionizations could not succeed without federal assistance, and the Court accepted this belief, and the desirability of the substantive conclusion, at face value.[205]

The cases that followed *Jones & Laughlin* continued to sustain the power of the federal government to regulate interstate commerce expansively, on the ground that any competition among states necessarily restricted the scope of government action. The government's argument in *United States v. Darby*[206] in defense of the Fair Labor Standards Act (FLSA),[207] for example, was essentially identical to that made unsuccessfully a generation before in *Hammer v. Dagenhart*:

> No State, acting alone, could require labor standards substantially higher than those obtaining in other States whose producers and manufacturers competed in the interstate market. Employers with lower labor standards possess an unfair advantage in interstate competition, and only the national government can deal with the problem.[208]

The Court's unanimous decision upholding the FLSA accepted the substantive case for the statute at face value, and regarded the FLSA as essentially public interest rather than interest-group legislation.[209] Arguments in favor of *Hammer's* limits on federal power were curtly dismissed: "The motive and purpose of a regulation of interstate commerce are matters for the legislative judgment upon the exercise of which the Constitution places no restriction and over which the courts are given no control."[210]

There remained only the question whether federal power extended to those goods of local manufacture which were not shipped in interstate commerce. In this regard Justice Stone cited the *Shreveport Rate Case* to support the proposition that a "familiar like exercise of power is the regulation of intrastate transactions which are so commingled with or related to interstate commerce that all must be regulated if the interstate commerce is to be effectively controlled."[211] Justice Stone omitted any reference to the desire to fight local discrimination against interstate commerce that was so critical to the earlier decision, or to any recognition that the *Shreveport Rate Case* did not apply to all "intrastate transactions" but only to the "instrumentalities" of interstate commerce—in particular to interstate railroad operations.[212] Nor did Justice Stone acknowledge that the *Shreveport Rate Case* never challenged the distinction between commerce and manufacture defended in *E.C. Knight.* Justice Holmes in his *Hammer* dissent defending federal authority still recognized that some manufacture was part of the purely internal commerce of that state.[213] Yet such was the strength of the federal tide that Justice Stone abandoned that vestige of state autonomy in *Darby.*[214] The question of state autonomy, so critical to *E.C. Knight,* also received back-of-the-hand treatment in *Darby;* the Court brushed aside the Tenth Amendment, and the principle of enumerated powers that it articulated, as "but a truism that all is retained which has not been surrendered."[215]

Justice Stone's cavalier treatment of jurisdictional objections to the FLSA resulted from his powerful belief in the soundness of the basic social legislation involved.[216] To him, the suppression of "unfair" competition from exploited labor was the dominant "evil" the FLSA attacked.[217] The possibility that the minimum wage law could be a barrier to the entry of unskilled labor into the labor market, and hence the very evil to be avoided, was never assessed. What failed in *Darby* was not the language of the Constitution, but the willingness of the Justices to accept the theory of limited government upon which it rested.

The same failure was repeated in cases that sustained the powerful system of agricultural price supports and acreage restrictions that was introduced by the New Deal. The question in *United States v. Wrightwood Dairy*[218] was whether Congress could authorize the Secretary of Agriculture to set minimum prices for milk that was produced and consumed within a single state. The usual language which spoke of a transaction "which directly burdens, obstructs, or affects, interstate or foreign commerce in such commodity or product thereof," was duly set out in the statutory language.[219] Ironically, the anticompetitive effect of federal interstate milk regulation became the justification for a further expansion of federal power:

> As the court below recognized, and as seems not to be disputed, the marketing of intrastate milk which competes with that shipped interstate would tend seriously to break down price regulation of the latter. Under the conditions prevailing in the milk industry, as the record shows, the unregulated sale of the intrastate milk tends to reduce the sales price received by handlers and the amount which they in turn pay to producers.[220]

Even after *Wrightwood* plugged the loophole of intrastate sales, another obstacle remained to comprehensive federal agricultural regulation. Farmers could still influence the price of agricultural products in interstate commerce simply by keeping and using them on their own farms. The scope of agricultural regulation expanded to meet this challenge. *Wickard v. Filburn*[221] upheld the statutory authority of the Secretary of Agriculture to limit the consumption of wheat on the very farms that grew it. Here there was no sale transaction at all, but this did not matter to the Court. The government's ability to maintain artificially high regulated prices for goods shipped across interstate lines would surely have been compromised if local consumption had been allowed to expand supply to meet demand. The economic interdependence of the various activities was held to preclude any watertight division between production and commerce.[222] The Court regarded the distinction between direct and indirect effects on interstate commerce as quite beside the point (as indeed it was), and the entire issue of enumerated powers and state autonomy disappeared from view.[223] Once the Court decided to ignore the limitations of the *Shreveport Rate Case*,[224] it saw *Wickard* as a natural extension of the *Shreveport Rate Case* doctrine. This is just the approach that Justice Jackson took:

> The opinion of Mr. Justice Hughes found federal intervention constitutionally authorized because of "matters having such a close and substantial relation to interstate traffic that the control is essential or appropriate to the security of that traffic, to the efficiency of the interstate service, and to the maintenance of conditions under which interstate commerce may be conducted upon fair terms without molestation or hindrance."[225]

Carefully excised from the quotation was the beginning of Justice Hughes's sentence: "[Congress's] authority, extending to these interstate carriers as intruments of interstate commerce, necessarily embraces the right to control their operations in all matters ...."[226] This excision, doubtless deliberate, completed the transformation of the commerce clause.

The question then arises as to how is it possible to stand a clause of the Constitution upon its head. I do not think that the explanation comes from any vagueness in the language of the commerce clause.[227] If a Court innocent of political theory or of any predilection on the merits of the underlying legislation approached a commerce case, it could not possibly parse the words of the clause so as to reach the extravagant interpretations of federal power accepted in *Jones & Laughlin, Darby, Wrightwood,* and *Wickard.* Could anyone say with a straight face that the consumption of homegrown wheat is "commerce among the several states?" A powerful principle must have led to so fanciful a conclusion. That principle has to go to the idea of what kind of government and social organization is thought to be just and proper for society at large.

I have no doubt that the Justices of the Supreme Court who forged so powerful a doctrine had such a conception in mind. At one level they rejected the idea of limited federal government and decentralized power. That idea only made sense if there was a risk that governments could misbehave. If it was thought that they always acted in the public interest, then any effort to deny them substantive power would have hobbled the forces of virtue and enhanced those of wickedness. It is noticeable that all the key New Deal commerce clause opinions took the substantive findings of Congress at face value. None was prepared to identify the powerful interest group politics that were so evident in both the labor and agricultural cases—the very policy areas in which the commerce clause reached its present scope. Once government is thought to be the source of risk, however, then competition between governments makes sense, and there is good reason to uphold the ideas of limited government and enumerated federal powers that were part of the original design. The New Deal's change in attitude toward the commerce clause thus depended upon a radical reorientation of judicial views toward the role of government that, in the end, overwhelmed the relatively clean lines of the commerce clause.

In addition, the key federal laws of the New Deal cartelized either labor or product markets that would otherwise have been highly competitive absent government regulation.[228] Indeed, there were substantive challenges to each of these laws, usually under the due process clause.[229] These developments were not unrelated, for jurisdictional limitations upon the power of Congress only made sense if there was reason to think that use of the power would have been harmful. Once the idea that markets performed useful functions was cast aside, however, the jurisdictional limitations ceased to make any sense. The war cry became a call for Congress to act because, in an age of economic interdependence, national problems demanded national solutions.[230]

Yet the point about economic interdependence mistakes the disease for the cure. It is precisely because markets are interdependent that there is reason to fear comprehensive federal regulation.[231] Competitive markets are the best way to allocate scarce goods and services. They promise to bring price into line with the marginal cost of production, and they hold out some hope that all the possible gains from trade will be achieved by voluntary transactions. Markets are not just a good in themselves. They are powerful instruments for human happiness and well-being.

Legal monopolies have precisely the opposite effect. They raise price above marginal cost and they prevent many voluntary transactions from taking place, so that the total social output is reduced by the deadweight loss that they cause. Worse still, the ability to obtain legal protection against competition invites individuals and groups to spend valuable resources in order to obtain (or resist obtaining) economic rents.[232] Even though no market is an ideal competitive market, there is absolutely no reason to impose economic regulations, such as minimum price laws or cartelization of labor markets, whose only effect is to drive quantity and price further from the competitive equilibrium. When viewed from this perspective, the Wagner Act, the Fair Labor Standards Act, and the Agricultural Marketing Acts appear to be longstanding social disasters that could not long have survived with their present vigor solely at the state level.

There is a dangerous tendency to assume that physical injury and competitive injury form part of a seamless web, so that the power to regulate the one necessarily confers the authority to regulate the other. It is as though the power to protect interstate commerce against robbers and thieves[233] is sufficient warrant for the far more extensive social controls that treat competitive activities undertaken within different states, when the social consequences of violence and competition are so radically different.[234] Virtually any form of commercial activity will yield not only satisfied customers but disappointed rivals. In an integrated economy, some of these rivals will do business in the same state as the winners, while some will do business elsewhere. Once the protection of competitive losers becomes a valid object of government power, then the potential scope of government activity expands far beyond what is required to prevent the use of force or fraud. The connection between jurisdiction and substance is very close, perhaps unavoidably so. The ability to conceive of competitive injury as a justification for the exercise of federal power lies at the root of all the modern commerce clause decisions. The ability to perceive the essential difference between violence and competition is *all* that is needed to respect the limitation on federal power that is implicit in the commerce clause.

VI. Conclusion

I thus return to my original theme: Although questions of jurisdiction and substantive rights appear to be distinct, the unfortunate history of decision-making under the commerce clause shows how unbreakable is the link between them. The very distinction between violence and competitive harm that is necessary for organizing the private and public substantive law is critical to an understanding of the proper principles of federal jurisdiction. Hamilton may not have had it all correct when he said that sound limitations on government jurisdiction obviated the need for a bill of rights.[235] But he was surely correct when he said that the maintenance of those jurisdictional limitations is one essential bulwark to sound constitutional government.[236]

The problem of sovereignty remains: How do the people compel the holders of governmental monopoly power to act as though they could only obtain a competitive return for their services?[237] Federalism facilitates a solution by allowing easy exit, as well as by allowing voice. National regulation prevents unhealthy types of competition among jurisdictions, such as were present in *Gibbons*. Under this view, the old construction of the commerce clause makes sense: it facilitates national markets by preventing state balkanization. This was the achievement of *Gibbons*. The great peril of national regulation is that it may be taken too far, to impose national uniformity which frustrates, rather than facilitates, markets. This was the New Deal. I cannot help thinking that a sound view of the commerce clause is one that returns to *Gibbons*. The affirmative scope of the commerce power should be limited to those matters that today are governed by the dormant commerce clause: interstate transportation, navigation and sales, and the activities closely incident to them. All else should be left to the states.

I realize that this conclusion seems radical because of the way the clock has turned. One is hesitant to require dismantling of large portions of the modern federal government, given the enormous reliance interests that have been created. And I do not have, nor do I know of anyone who has, a good theory that explains when it is appropriate to correct past errors that have become embedded in the legal system. It is far easier to keep power from the hands of government officials than it is to wrest it back from them once it has been conferred. We had our chance with the commerce clause, and we have lost it.

Still, the argument from principle seems clear enough, even if one is left at a loss as to what should be done about it. And, in a sense, that is just the point. Congress and the courts can proceed merrily on their way, if they are convinced that the basis for an extensive federal commerce power is rooted firmly in the original constitutional text or structure. But uneasiness necessarily creeps into the legislative picture if, as I have argued, the commerce clause is far narrower in scope than modern courts have held. There is a powerful tension between the legacy of the past fifty years and the original constitutional understanding. It is a tension that we must face, even if we cannot resolve it.

Notes

1. U.S. CONST. Art. I, § 8.

2. More accurately, the inquiry might be stated: How should the grant to Congress be understood when the commerce clause is construed in light of the necessary and proper clause? See *infra* notes 22-28 and accompanying text.

3. This theme of limited and enumerated powers was central to the distinction between a federal and national government. It is evident on the face of Article I, which begins with the words "All legislative powers herein granted" (without specifying who the grantor was), and it was reiterated in all the ratification debates. *See, e.g.,* 2 THE DEBATES IN THE SEVERAL STATE CONVENTIONS ON THE ADOPTION OF THE FEDERAL CONSTITUTION 435-36, 454, 540 (J. Elliot 2d ed. 1836) (dialogue of Wilson and McKean); 3 *id* at 95, 246, 444, 553; 4 *id.* at 147-49, 259-60 (dialogue of Iredell and Pinckney).

4. The origins of the doctrine lie in Cooley v. Board of Port Wardens, 53 U.S. (12

How.) 299 (1851); for later applications *see, e.g.,* South Carolina State Highway Department v. Barnwell Bros. 303 U.S. 177 (1938); Southern Pacific Co. v. Arizona 325 U.S. 761 (1945); Regan, *The Supreme Court and State Protectionism: Making Sense of the Dormant Commerce Clause,* 84 MICH. L. REV. 1091 (1986). For further discussion see *infra* at text accompanying notes 60-61.

5. *See,* D. HUME, OF COMMERCE (1752), *reprinted in* ESSAYS: MORAL, POLITICAL, AND LITERARY 252, 263-64 (Liberty Classics ed. 1985). Hume's basic theory was that nations that tolerate foreign commerce are able to realize gains from trade that permit them to accumulate greater wealth, and to achieve greater prosperity and political stability, than those that rely upon domestic manufacture and agriculture alone. Hume's essay mixes historical example with analytical propositions in a style that anticipates the *Federalist.*

6. FEDERALIST No. 11 (A. Hamilton) ("Concerning Commerce and a Navy"). The opposition between commerce on the one hand, and agriculture and manufacture on the other, seems clear enough. Thus in speaking of the control over foreign commerce, Hamilton wrote:

> By prohibitory regulations, extending, at the same Time throughout the States, we may oblige foreign countries to bid against each other, for the privileges of our markets. This assertion will not appear chimerical to those who are able to appreciate the importance of the markets of three millions of people—increasing in rapid progression, for the most part exclusively addicted to agriculture, and likely from local circumstances to remain so—to any manufacturing nation.

Id. at 63 (Modern Library College ed. 1937).

7. *See, e.g.,* T. HOBBES, LEVIATHAN (Everyman's Library ed. 1950); D. HUME, *supra* note 4; J. LOCKE, AN ESSAY CONCERNING HUMAN UNDERSTANDING (R. Wilburn ed. 1947); MONTESQUIEU, THE SPIRIT OF THE LAWS (T. Nugent trans. 1949).

8. FEDERALIST No. 84 (A. Hamilton). Hamilton continued:

> I go further, and affirm that bills of rights . . . are not only unnecessary in the proposed Constitution, but would even be dangerous. They would contain various exceptions to powers not granted; and, on this very account, would afford a colorable pretext to claim more than were granted. For why declare that things shall not be done which there is no power to do? Why, for instance, should it be said that the liberty of the press shall not be restrained, by which restrictions may be imposed?

Id. at 559 (Modern Library College ed. 1937). Hamilton's argument presupposes that the doctrine of enumerated powers places substantial limitations upon all grants of power to the federal government, including those under the commerce power.

9. Thus Hamilton thought that the principle of freedom of speech could not protect the press from arbitrary taxation:

> It cannot certainly be pretended that any degree of duties, however low, would be
> an abridgment of the liberty of the press . . . And if duties of any kind may be laid
> without a violation of that liberty, it is evident that the extent must depend on
> legislative discretion, regulated by public opinion, so that, after all, general
> declarations respecting the liberty of the press, will give it no greater security
> than it will have without them.

Id. at 560 n.

Hamilton was clearly wrong on this issue. It may not be possible to use the First
Amendment to insist that the press be free of all general taxes, but it is possible to limit
the nature of the taxes that are imposed. Special taxes placed upon the press, but not
other industries, may be prohibited, or special taxes placed on some portions of the
press, but not others, may be prohibited. Courts have intervened to prevent dispropor-
tionate taxation when public opinion has failed to do so. *See, e.g.,* Minneapolis Star &
Tribune Co. v. Minnesota Comm'r of Revenue, 460 U.S. 575 (1983); Grosjean v.
American Press Co., 297 U.S. 233 (1936). *Grosjean* has had little development because
its holding was clear enough to stop most forms of abusive taxes in their tracks.

10. Some sense of the twist of history is found in Patrick Henry's speech in
opposition to the ratification of the Constitution in the Virginia debates:

> [W]hat right had they to say, We, the People? My political curiosity, exclusive of
> my anxious solicitude for the public welfare, leads me to ask, who authorized
> them to speak the language of, We, the People instead of We, the States? States
> are the characteristics, and the soul of a confederation. If the states be not the
> agents of this compact, it must be one great consolidated National Government
> of the people of all the States.

H. STORING, WHAT THE ANTIFEDERALISTS WERE FOR 12 (181) (quoting Henry). Henry was a
better prophet than even his supporters would have allowed at the time. Storing rightly
notes that the Anti-Federalists were on their strongest ground when they opposed a
principle of ratification that put the Constitution into effect; at least as between the
parties, when nine states ratified it. Under the Articles of the Confederation, each state
had a blocking position against the changes, and Rhode Island had not bothered to send
a delegate to the Philadelphia Convention.

11. It is no coincidence, for example, that West Coast Hotel Co. v. Parrish, 300 U.S.
379 (1937) (upholding minimum wage law for women), was decided in the same term as
NLRB v. Jones & Laughlin Steel Corp., 301 U.S. 1 (1937). This is discussed *infra* notes
185-202 and accompanying text.

12. *See, e.g.,* Cohen, *The Inevitable Constitutional Revolution of 1937* (speech to
the AALS Constitutional Law Meeting, Washington, D.C., Oct. 8, 1987) written in
response to my short paper, *The Mistakes of 1937,* GEORGE MASON L. REV. (1988) (forthcoming). Cohen places heavy reliance upon the Roosevelt landslide of 1936 as justification for the expanded construction of the commerce clause.

13. U.S. CONST. Art. I, § 8.

14. Gibbons v. Ogden, 22 U.S. (9 Wheat) 1, 189 (1824). Chief Justice Marshall continued:

> Commerce, undoubtedly, is traffic, but it is something more: it is intercourse. It describes the commercial intercourse between nations, and parts of nations, in all its branches, and is regulated by prescribing rules for carrying on that intercourse. The mind can scarcely conceive of a system for regulating commerce between nations, which shall exclude all laws concerning navigation, which shall be silent on the admission of the vessels of the one nation into the ports of the other, and be confined to prescribing rules for the conduct of individuals, in the actual employment of buying and selling, or of barter.

Id. at 189-90. Chief Justice Marshall may well have borrowed the term "intercourse" from Hamilton, who in speaking of "The importance of the Union, in a commercial light," also spoke of "our intercourse with foreign countries as well as with each other." FEDERALIST No. 11, at 62 (A. Hamilton) (Modern Library College ed. 1937). Note too that in FEDERALIST No. 11, Hamilton repeatedly stressed that navigation was comprehended in commerce, the very point that Chief Justice Marshall had emphasized in his decision.

15. This point was stressed by Hamilton in FEDERALIST No. 11, as in the sentence quoted *supra* note 5. For those of us who believe in free trade, the powers given Congress seem far too broad, as the debates over the current protectionist trade bills reveal. *See also* Kitch, *Regulation and the American Common Market,* in REGULATION, FEDERALISM, AND INTERSTATE COMMERCE 16, 51 (A. Tarlock ed. 1981).

16. U.S. CONST. Art. I, § 9.

17. *Id.* preamble.

18. *See id.,* Art. VII.

19. 317 U.S. 111 (1942). For further elaboration, *see infra* notes 221-26 and accompanying text.

20. *See,* S. MORRISON, H. COMMAGER & LEUTCHENBURG, A CONCISE HISTORY OF THE AMERICAN REPUBLIC 188-91 (1977).

21. See, for one illustration of this escape, a superb new casebook:

> The Civil War and its aftermath inaugurated an era in which Congress began to act more vigorously. The very success of the national economy created problems. The economy became obviously interconnected; problems were no longer localized, so that it became difficult to imagine a purely internal commerce that affected no other states.

G. STONE, L. SEIDMAN, C. SUNSTEIN & M. TUSHNET, CONSTITUTIONAL LAW 138 (1986).

22. U.S. CONST. Art. I, § 8.

23. *See infra,* notes 83-88 and accompanying text.

24. *See,* FEDERALIST No. 33, in which Hamilton gives a relatively narrow reading of the necessary and proper clause; he tries to allay the fear that it will allow the national government to run roughshod over the states:

> But SUSPICION may ask, Why then was it introduced? The answer is, that it could only have been done for greater caution, and to guard against all cavilling refinements in those who might hereafter feel a disposition to curtail and evade the legitimate authorities of the Union.

FEDERALIST No. 33, at 200 (A. Hamilton) (Modern Library College ed. 1937). In the subsequent dispute over the clause in connection with the creation of a national bank, Hamilton gave a broader interpretation, similar to that put forward by Chief Justice Marshall. *See,* D. CURRIE, THE CONSTITUTION IN THE SUPREME COURT: THE FIRST HUNDRED YEARS, 1789-1888, at 160-69.

25. McCulloch v. Maryland, 17 U.S. (4 Wheat.) 316, 421 (1819).

26. *Id.* at 406.

27. Gibbons v. Ogden, 22 U.S. (9 Wheat.) 1, 187 (1824). Note too that Chief Justice Marshall addressed the necessary and proper clause in order to show that it does not require a rule of strict construction.

28. Thus, Professor Tribe gives but one brief connection between the two clauses, where they are discussed in connection with the so-called protective principle. This principle allows Congress to reach matters outside the scope of the commerce clause in order to govern those matters that fall within it. *See,* L. TRIBE, AMERICAN CONSTITUTIONAL LAW § 5-7, at 240 (1978). The threat this principle poses to the doctrine of enumerated powers is ignored by Professor Tribe, but is discussed herein. *See infra,* notes 69-73 and accompanying text.

29. *See, e.g.,* L. TRIBE, *supra* note 28, § 5-4, at 232-35.

30. *See id.*

31. 156 U.S. 1 (1895).

32. L. TRIBE, *supra* note 28, § 5-4, at 234-35. He continued: "But with its watershed decision in NLRB v. Jones & Laughlin Steel Corp. [301 U.S. 1 (1937)], the Court acceded to political pressure and to its own sense of its doctrine's irrelevance and manipulability, abandoning the formally analytical approach to the commerce clause, and returning to Chief Justice Marshall's original empiricism." *Id.* at 235. Professor Tribe was not the first to develop this line of thought. It was documented in great detail in Stern, *The Commerce Clause and the National Economy 1933-1946,* 59 HARV. L. REV. 645 (1946), a highly readable and happily partisan defense of the New Deal decisions written by a member of the Solicitor General's office, who had participated actively on the government's side.

33. 22 U.S. (9 Wheat.) 1 (1824).

34. See Chief Justice Marshall's discussion in *McCulloch,* where his famous phrase, "we must never forget, that it is a *constitution* we are expounding," was designed to show only the opposition between a document which spoke in great outlines and the detailed positions of, say, a commercial code. McCulloch v. Maryland, 17 U.S. (4 Wheat.) 316, 407 (1819). See also his dissent in Ogden v. Saunders, 25 U.S. (12 Wheat.) 213 (1827) (Marshall, C.J., dissenting), where his argument for the *prospective* application of the contract clause rested in part on his vision that individuals preserve in civil society the rights to contract that they have in the state of nature. *Id.* at 345-49. Chief Justice Marshall also wrote:

> In framing an instrument, which was intended to be perpetual, the presumption is strong, that every important principle introduced into it is intended to be perpetual also; that a principle expressed in terms to operate in all future time, is intended so to operate. But if the construction for which the plaintiff's counsel contend be the true one [i.e. retroactive legislation only], the constitution will have imposed a restriction in language indicating perpetuity, which every State in the Union may elude at pleasure. The obligation of contracts in force, at any given time, is but of short duration; and, if the inhibition be of retroactive laws only, a very short lapse of time will remove every subject on which the act is forbidden to operate, and make this provision of the constitution so far useless.

Id. at 355.

It is at least a little ironic that Chief Justice Hughes refers to the Chief Justice Marshall of *McCulloch* in Home Bldg. & Loan Ass'n v. Blaisdell, 290 U.S. 398, 442-43 (1934), while ignoring the Chief Justice Marshall of *Ogden.*

I have given a modified defense of Chief Justice Marshall's position in Epstein, *Toward a Revitalization of the Commerce Clause,* 51 U. CHI. L. REV. 703, 723-30 (1984). For criticism, see Kmiec & McGinnis, *The Contract Clause: A Return to the Original Understanding,* 14 HASTINGS CONST. L.Q. 525, 557-59 (1987).

35. Gibbons v. Ogden, 22 U.S. (9 Wheat.) 1, 1-2 (1824). Ogden was the assignee of the original franchisees. Robert Livingston and Robert Fulton.

36. *Id.* at 4-5 (argument of Daniel Webster for appellant).

37. Also at issue was whether the exclusive franchise was an impairment of contract by the state of New York. The conclusion that it was would seem quite plausible if the contracts clause was given the prospective interpretation that Chief Justice Marshall urged three years after *Gibbons. See,* Ogden v. Saunders, 25 U.S. (12 Wheat.) 213, 354-56 (1827) (Marshall, C.J., dissenting). But Chief Justice Marshall was in dissent in *Saunders* and the interpretation was lost. One might also note that *Gibbons* involved the conversion of public property (to which access is open and equal) to private property. It was a taking, albeit of public and not private property. The public trust issue surfaced in Livingston v. Van Ingen, 9 Johns. 507 572-73 (N.Y. 1812), in which New York Chief Justice Kent brushed aside the argument that there was an impropriety in the grant under state law doctrine. On the vexing use of the public trust doctrine, *see* Illinois Central R.R. v. Illinois, 146 U.S. 387 (1892); Rose, *The Comedy of the Commons: Custom, Commerce and Inherently Public Property,* 53 U. CHI. L. REV. 711

(1986); Sax, *The Public Trust Doctrine in Natural Resource Law: Effective Judicial Intervention,* 68 MICH L. REV. 471 (1970). For my views, *see* Epstein, *The Public Trust Doctrine,* 7 CATO J. 411 (1987).

38. *Gibbons,* 22 U.S. (9 Wheat.) at 190-91, 213-17.

39. L. TRIBE, *supra* note 28, § 5-4, at 232 (footnotes omitted).

40. *Gibbons,* 22 U.S. (9 Wheat.) at 195 (emphasis added).

41. *Id.* Stern used the same selective powers of quotation, stating that "the Commerce Clause comprehended 'that commerce which concerns more states than one.' " Stern, *supra* note 32, at 648 (quoting *Gibbons,* 22 U.S. at 194-95). He then dropped the rest of the material quoted above and continued with the remainder of the passage, beginning "[t]he genius and character of the whole government seem to be, that its action is to be applied to all the external concerns of the nation, and to those internal concerns which affect the states generally." *Id.* The passage reads more broadly without the omitted language.

42. Marshall emphasized this point elsewhere in *Gibbons:*

> But, in regulating commerce with foreign nations, the power of Congress does not stop at the jurisdictional lines of the several States. It would be a very useless power, if it could not pass those lines. The commerce of the United States with foreign nations, is that of the whole United States. Every district has a right to participate in it. The deep streams which penetrate our country in every direction, pass through the interior of almost every State in the Union, and furnish the means of exercising this right.

Gibbons, 22 U.S. at 195. Note that Marshall assigned to commerce a uniform meaning with regard to both commerce with foreign nations and among the several states.

43. *Gibbons,* 22 U.S. (9 Wheat.) at 196.

44. *Id.* at 197.

45. Chief Justice Marshall wrote:

> What do gentlemen mean, by a strict construction? If they contend only against that enlarged construction, which would extend words beyond their natural and obvious import, we might question the application of the term, but should not controvert the principle. If they contend for that narrow construction which, in support of some theory not to be found in the constitution, would deny to the government those powers which the words of the grant, as usually understood, import, and which are consistent with the general views and objects of the instrument; for that narrow construction, which would cripple the government, and render it unequal to the objects for which it is declared to be instituted, and to which the powers given, as fairly understood, render it competent; then we cannot perceive the propriety of this strict construction, nor adopt it as the rule by which the constitution is to be expounded.

Id. at 188.

46. Farnsworth writes: "An especially common rule of construction is that if language supplied by one party is reasonably susceptible to two interpretations, one of which favors each party, the one that is less favorable to the party who supplied the language is preferred." E. FARNSWORTH, CONTRACTS § 7.11, at 499 (1982). The rule is widely used with standard form contracts, and even beyond them. Its major cost is that it biases the way in which the original documents are drafted, rendering them more complicated and less clear than they would under a rule of ordinary and natural meaning, without the presumption.

47. *Gibbons,* 22 U.S. (9 Wheat.) at 187; *see supra,* notes 22-28 for a discussion of the clause.

48. *Gibbons,* 22 U.S. (9 Wheat.) at 194.

49. 9 Johns. 506 (N.Y. 1812).

50. New York Chief Justice Kent wrote:

Our turnpike roads, our toll-bridges, the exclusive grant to run stage-wagons, our laws relating to paupers from other states, our *Sunday* laws, our rights of ferriage over navigable rivers and lakes, our auction licenses, our licenses to retail spiritous liquors, the laws to restrain hawkers and pedlars; what are all these provisions but regulations of internal commerce, affecting as well the intercourse between the citizens of this and other states, as between our own citizens.

Id. at 579.

51. *See Gibbons,* 22 U.S. (9 Wheat.) at 203.

52. *Id.*

53. United States v. E.C. Knight Co., 156 U.S. 1, 12 (1895).

54. One new casebook states: "Under the *formal* approach, the Court examines the statute and the regulated activity to determine whether certain objective criteria are satisfied. . . . In contrast, the *realist* approach attempts to determine the actual economic impact of the regulation or the actual motivation of Congress." G. STONE, L. SEIDMAN, C. SUNSTEIN & M. TUSHNET, *supra* note 21, at 139.

55. Robert Addie & Sons (Collieries), Ltd. v. Dumbreck, 1929 App. Cas. 358, 371 (H.L.). The passage continues:

When you come to the facts it may well be that there is great difficulty—such difficulty as may give rise to difference of judicial opinion—in deciding into which category a particular case falls, but a judge must decide and, having decided, then the law of that category will rule and there must be no looking to the law of the adjoining category. I cannot help thinking that the use of epithets, "bare licenses," "pure trespassers" and so on, has much to answer for in obscuring what I think is a vital proposition; that, in deciding cases of the class we are considering, the first duty of the tribunal is to fix once and for all into which of the three classes the person in question falls.

Id. at 371-72.

56. The key case is still Rowland v. Christian, 69 Cal.2d 108, 443 P .2d 561, 70 Cal. Rptr. 97 (1968). *Rowland* was in a sense wholly gratuitous, as recovery could have been awarded under the traditional view holding hosts responsible for latent defects causing harm under ordinary usage. *See id.* at 115, 443 P.2d at 566, 70 CAL. REP. at 102. For a criticism of the modern tendency of balancing in the tort area, *see* Epstein, *The Risks of Risk/Utility,* 47 OHIO ST. L.J. 469, 473 (1987).

57. 312 U.S. 100 (1941); *see* discussion *infra* notes 206-17 and accompanying text. Note too that *Darby's* view of the clause makes hash of the reserved powers clause of the Tenth Amendment. If jurisdiction under the commerce clause is both plenary and unlimited, then there is nothing left to reserve. The Tenth Amendment thus really becomes a truism. Yet the amendment sharply confirms that the federal government has only delegated powers: "The powers not delegated to the United States by the Constitution, nor prohibited by it to the States, are reserved to the States respectively, or to the people." U.S. CONST., Tenth Amendment. Why bother with amendment if *Darby is* correct? By contrast, the Tenth Amendment makes good sense if Chief Justice Marshall's view in *Gibbons* is followed.

58. 317 U.S. 111 (1942); *see* discussion *infra* notes 221-27 and accompanying text.

59. *Id.* at 120. Justice Jackson went on to note that Chief Justice Marshall in *Gibbons* warned that "effective restraints on its exercise must proceed from political rather than from judicial processes." *Id.* The passage in *Gibbons* reads in full:

The wisdom and the discretion of Congress, their identity with the people, and the influence which their constituents possess at elections, are, in this, as in many other instances, as that, for example, of declaring war, the sole restraints on which they have relied, to secure them from its abuse. They are the restraints on which the people must often rely solely, in all representative governments.

The power of Congress, then, comprehends navigation, within the limits of every State in the Union; so far as that navigation may be, in any manner, connected with "commerce with foreign nations, or among the several States, or with the Indian tribes." It may, of consequence, pass the jurisdictional line of New-York, and act upon the very waters to which the prohibition now under consideration applies.

Gibbons, 22 U.S. (9 Wheat.) at 197. Justice Jackson thus confused two points. First, the need for political decisions for matters properly within the scope of the commerce powers, and, second, the scope of the clause itself. The latter was only held to "comprehend navigation" in New York waters, not all productive activities within the state.

60. Justice Johnson wrote:

The power of a sovereign state over commerce, therefore, amounts to nothing more than a power to limit and restrain it at pleasure. And since the power to prescribe the limits to its freedom, necessarily implies the power to determine what shall remain unrestrained, it follows, that the power must be exclusive; it can reside but in one potentate; and hence, the grant of this power carries with it the whole subject, leaving nothing for the State to act upon.

It is impossible, with the views which I entertain of the principle on which the commercial privileges of the people of the United States, among themselves, rests, to concur in the view which this Court takes of the effect of the coasting license in this cause. I do not regard it as the foundation of the right set up in behalf of the appellant. . . . And I cannot overcome the conviction, that if the licensing act was repealed to-morrow, the rights of the appellant to a reversal of the decision complained of, would be as strong as it is under this license.

Gibbons, 22 U.S. at 227-32 (Johnson, J., concurring).

61. It is strange to think of how little the commerce power moved in the decades that followed *Gibbons.* Cooley v. Board of Wardens, 53 U.S. (12 How.) 299 (1851), stood for the principle that the federal jurisdiction under the commerce clause comes in two parts. For those matters, such as pilotage in local waters, that fall within interstate commerce but that are of great local concern as well, the federal and state jurisdictions are concurrent. *Id.* at 319-20. For those matters for which there should be a uniform rule, the power of Congress is exclusive. *Id.* at 319. This delicate compromise is somewhat tricky to reconcile with the constitutional text, even if greater feats of legerdemain have been done in the name of constitutional construction. The power granted by the commerce clause seems to be unitary for all objects that fall within it; how then can federal jurisdiction be exclusive for some areas and concurrent for others?

Nonetheless the *Cooley* solution does have a structural sense that makes it more durable than might appear at first blush. Local conditions easily could demand separate treatments, which do not threaten interstate commerce in the same way as did the New York statute at issue in *Gibbons.* Local practices shown to discriminate against outsiders could be addressed by the privileges and immunities clause of the Constitution, and arguably by other substantive provisions as well. U.S. CONST. Art. IV, § 2, cl. 1.

62. In analyzing this division, I do not discuss in depth United States v. Coombs, 37 U.S. (13 Pet.) 71 (1838), which upheld the constitutionality of a statute that imposed criminal penalties against "any person who shall plunder, steal or destroy any money, goods," etc. from a ship under the admiralty jurisdiction of the United States. Justice Story sustained the constitutionality of that statute, writing that the commerce clause "extends to such acts, done on land, which interfere with, obstruct, or prevent the due exercise of the power to regulate commerce and navigation with foreign nations and among the states." *Id.* at 78. Note that there are actions outside of interstate commerce that have evident effects upon interstate commerce. Yet the decision does little to threaten the system of enumerated powers found in the Constitution; the train of physical effects is quite limited, and another case for which the necessary and proper clause could sensibly make the difference. But, given its limited extent, it is not surprising that *Coombs* was not invoked in the subsequent expansionary period of the commerce clause.

63. Ch. 104, 24 Stat. 379 (1887) (current version at 49 U.S.C.A. §§ 10101-11917 (Supp. 1987)).

64. 301 U.S. 1 (1937).

65. *Gibbons,* 22 U.S. (9 Wheat.) at 194-95.

66. 77 U.S. (10 Wall.) 557 (1870).

67. *Id.* at 562 (argument of appellant).

68. *Id.* at 566.

69. *See infra,* notes 22-28; L. TRIBE, *supra* note 28, § 5-6, 238-39.

70. 118 U.S. 557 (1886).

71. *Id.* at 577.

72. Ch. 104, 24 Stat. 379 (1887) (current version at 49 U.S.C.A. §§ 10101-11917 (Supp. 1987). Section 4 of the statute provided:

> That it shall be unlawful for any common carrier subject to the provisions of this act to charge or receive any greater compensation in the aggregate for the transportation of passengers or of like kind of property, under substantially similar circumstances and conditions, for shorter than for a longer distance over the same line, in the same direction, the shorter being included within the longer distance; but this shall not be construed as authorizing any common carrier within the terms of this act to charge and receive as great compensation for a shorter as for a longer distance.

Id. § 4, 24 Stat. at 380.

A proviso to the section then gave the ICC the power to relieve carriers from this obligation "in special cases," but did not set out any standards which indicated when this general obligation should be suspended, and none are apparent as a general matter. Section 3 of the Act contained a prohibition against undue preferences, and § 5 prevented certain kinds of pooling of freight. Section 6 dealt with the obligation of common carriers to print schedules complete with routes and charges, required these to be placed on file with the commission, and prohibited any deviations from the schedules as printed.

The powers of the ICC were expanded first by the Elkins Act of 1903 (32 Stat. 847, c. 708), which increased the power of the ICC to prevent secret rebates, the Hepburn Act of 1906 (34 Stat. 584, c. 3591), which clearly empowered the ICC to set maximum rates on the rails, and the Mann-Elkins of 1910 (36 Stat. 539, c. 309), which brought telegraph, telephone and cable companies under the Act, and strengthened the power of the ICC under section 4 of the original act by eliminating the phrase "under substantially similar circumstances and conditions." For a general account of these early changes, *see* Aitchison, *The Evolution of the Interstate Commerce Act: 1887-1937,* 5 GEO. WASH. L. REV. 289, 302-40 (1937).

73. Transportation Act of 1920, ch. 91, 41 Stat. 456 (current version at scattered

sections of 49 U.S.C.A. (Supp. 1987); *see infra* notes 93–101 and accompanying text. The most controversial provisions of the statute were those which allowed the ICC to initiate rate proceedings in order to insure that the railroads would only obtain a fair return from their operations. One-half the railroad profits in excess of 6 percent were put into an ICC fund, the funds from which could be loaned to various railroads to allow them to improve their property. *See generally,* Aitchison, *supra* note 73, at 356-59.

74. 169 U.S. 466 (1898). The question raised in this case was whether there were any constitutional limitations upon the power of a state (in this instance, Nebraska) to set the rates that railroads could charge for carrying both persons and freight within the state. The Court held that the railroad was a "person" under the due process clause of the Fourteenth Amendment, entitled to a just return on its investment. In essence the decision tried to steer a fine line between two risks. If the railroad was allowed to charge rates without any limitation, then it could reap monopoly profits from its consumers. If the state was allowed to regulate without limitation, then it could essentially take the money that had been invested in the line by stripping shareholders of any return. The Court, in *Smyth,* applied a reasonably strict standard of review to protect the railroad. The standard of *Smyth* was considerably relaxed, but not wholly eliminated in the aftermath of the New Deal. *See,* Federal Power Commission v. Hope Natural Gas Co., 320 U.S. 591 (1944).

75. *See* Transportation Act of 1920, ch. 91, 41 Stat. 456 (current version at scattered sections of 49 U.S.C.A. (Supp. 1987)).

76. 234 U.S. 342 (1914). I am most indebted to Professor Edmund Kitch for pointing out to me the genuine complexities that this case raises, and for insisting that I deal more fully with the matter.

77. *Id.* at 346.

78. *Id.*

79. *Id.* at 345. One example of the discrimination was that "a rate of 60 cents carried first class traffic a distance of 160 miles to the eastward from Dallas, while the same rate would carry the same class of traffic only 55 miles into Texas from Shreveport." *Id.* at 346.

80. *Id.* at 346-47.

81. *Id.* at 347.

82. *Id.* at 351-52.

83. *Id.* at 352.

84. 222 U.S. 20 (1911).

85. Ch. 196, 27 Stat. 531 (1893) (current version at 45 U.S.C. §§ 1-7 (1982)).

86. 223 U.S. 1 (1912).

87. *See supra,* notes 65-69 and accompanying text.

88. *See supra,* notes 22-28 and accompanying text.

89. 301 U.S. 1 (1937); *See infra,* notes 185-205 and accompanying text.

90. *The Shreveport Rate Case,* 234 U.S. at 352.

91. The actual language of the Interstate Commerce Act appears to have precluded the regulations that were sustained in the case. Section 3, which prevented "undue or unreasonable preference or advantage" to one person over another, was subject to a proviso that read:

> *Provided, however,* that the provisions of this act shall not apply to the transportation of passengers or property, or to the receiving, delivering, storage, or handling of property, wholly within one State, and not shipped to or from a foreign country or to any State or Territory as aforesaid.

The Shreveport Rate Case, 234 U.S. at 356-57 (quoting the Interstate Commerce Act). Yet this remnant of Chief Justice Marshall's "internal commerce" of the several states did not long survive. The Court concluded that the proviso did not apply "when the Commission finds that unjust discrimination against interstate trade arises from the relation of intrastate to interstate rates as maintained by a carrier subject to the act," *Id.* at 358. Certainly there was no reference to unjust discrimination in the proviso, which would have been wholly redundant if it reached only those cases in which no discrimination was present, for these were precisely the cases lacking conduct which the ICC could find unlawful.

92. *Id.* at 355.

93. 257 U.S. 563 (1922).

94. Transportation Act of 1920, ch. 91, 41 Stat. 456 (current version at scattered sections of 49 U.S.C.A. (Supp. 1987)).

95. "The . . . most novel and most important feature of the act, requires the Commission so to prescribe rates as to enable the carriers as a whole, or in groups selected by the Commission, to earn an aggregate annual net railway operating income equal to a fair return on the aggregate value of the railway property used in transportation." *Wisconsin R.R. Comm'n,* 257 U.S. at 584. This is merely a nice way to describe cartelization of the railroad industry.

96. *See id.* at 579-80.

97. *See id.* at 583. Typically, expanded government authority during the First World War set the stage for expanded government authority after peace had returned.

98. The Court wrote:

> Congress in its control of its interstate commerce system is seeking in the Transportation Act to make the system adequate to the needs of the country by securing for it a reasonable compensatory return for all the work it does. The States are seeking to use that same system for intrastate traffic. That entails large duties and expenditures on the interstate commerce system which may burden it unless compensation is received for the intrastate

business reasonably proportionate to that for the interstate business. Congress as the dominant controller of interstate commerce may, therefore, restrain undue limitation of the earning power of the interstate commerce system in doing state work. The affirmative power of Congress in developing interstate commerce agencies is clear.

Id. at 589-90.

99. "Capture," whether by railroads wishing to cartelize their industry, or by shippers wishing to ship their goods below cost, is an inherent risk of all forms of regulation. The basic insight here is that regulation of all forms constitutes an implicit transfer of wealth among private individuals. The difficult question is to determine which interest group or groups will be able to take over, or capture the process. *See* McChesney, *Rent Extraction and Rent Creation in the Economic Theory of Regulation*, 16 J. LEGAL STUD. 101 (1987); Peltzman, *Toward a More General Theory of Regulation*, 19 J. LAW & ECON. 211 (1976); Posner, *Taxation by Regulation*, 2 BELL J. ECON. & MGMT. SCI. 22 (1971); Stigler, *The Theory of Economic Regulation*, 2 BELL J. ECON. & MGMT. SCI. 3 (1971).

100. *The Shreveport Rate Case*, 234 U.S. at 351 (citation omitted).

101. *See infra* notes 185-234 and accompanying text.

102. 188 U.S. 321 (1903). The appellants attempted as an initial maneuver to keep the case outside the commerce clause altogether by arguing that lottery tickets were not articles of commerce at all but were instead "mere evidences of contract made wholly within the boundaries of a State, which contracts are valid or invalid according to the municipal law of the State where made or attempted to be enforced." *Id.* at 327. This argument seems weak. If the writing has a tangible form, and if the ticket can be brought or sold, then something, rather than nothing, is working its way through the channels of interstate commerce.

103. *Id.* at 327.

104. *See id.* at 353-54.

105. *See supra* note 14.

106. See U.S. CONST. Art. I, § 9, cl. 1 ("The Migration or Importation of such Persons as any States now existing shall think proper to admit, shall not be prohibited by the Congress prior to the Year one thousand eight hundred and eight, but a Tax or duty may be imposed on such Importation, not exceeding ten dollars for each Person."). Clearly any regulation that made it impossible to import slaves (note the euphemism in the text) into the United States was prohibited as well. For the vexed relationship of this clause to the commerce power, *see* Berns, *The Constitution and the Migration of Slaves*, 78 YALE L.J. 198 (1968). Note, however, that although the commerce clause might have given Congress the power to regulate (or even prohibit) the slave trade, it did not give it the power to regulate the position of the slaves located within the state, much less to prohibit slavery.

107. This argument was well made by the appellant's counsel in oral argument. *Champion,* 188 U.S. at 329-30 (argument of appellant). There the point was limited to the transfer of "promisory notes, of deed, of bonds, of contracts for personal services, etc." *Id.* In principle, however, it could extend to the underlying goods shipped in interstate commerce as well.

108. The principle states that "a state is without power to impose an unconstitutional requirement as a condition for granting a privilege." Frost & Frost Trucking Co. v. Railroad Comm'n, 271 U.S. 583, 598 (1926). The most exhaustive treatment of the subject is found in Kreimer, *Allocation Sanctions: The Problem of Negative Rights in a Positive State,* 132 U. PA. L. REV. 1293 (1984). I have addressed the use of the doctrine of unconstitutional conditions in the context of eminent domain in Epstein, *Takings: Descent and Resurrection,* 1987 SUP. CT. REV. 1 (1987); Epstein, *Foreword: Unconstitutional Conditions, State Power, and the Limits of Consent,* 102 HARV. L. REV. 4 (1988).

109. This connection between the commerce clause and the Fifth Amendment was noted by counsel for appellees in Hammer v. Dagenhart, 247 U.S. 251 (1917), who insisted that there was a higher level of judicial review under the commerce clause. *See id.* at 267.

110. *Champion,* 188 U.S. at 374 (Fuller, C.J., dissenting).

111. *See* U.S. CONST. Art. VI.

112. For a checkered history of lotteries passing in and out of favor in one state, *see* Stone v. Mississippi, 101 U.S. 814 (1881).

113. Thus, in Mugler v. Kansas 123 U.S. 623, 661, 662 Harlan J. wrote:

> It belongs to that department [i.e. the legislature] to exert what are known as the police powers of the State, and to determine, primarily, what measures are appropriate or needful for the protection of the public morals, the public health, or the public safety. . . .
>
> [I]t is difficult to perceive any ground for judiciary to declare that the prohibition by Kansas of the manufacture or sale, within her limits, of intoxicating liquors for general use there as a beverage, is not fairly adopted to the end of protecting the community against the evils which confessedly result from the excessive use of ardent spirits. There is no justification for holding that the State, under the guise merely of police regulations, is here aiming to deprive the citizen of his constitutional rights; for we cannot shut out of view the fact, within the knowledge of all, that the public health, the public morals, and the public safety, may be endangered by the general use of intoxicated drinks; nor the fact, established by statistics accessible to everyone, that the idleness, disorder, pauperism, and crime existing in the country are, in some degree at least, traceable to this evil.

See also his opinions in Jacobson v. Massachusetts, 197 U.S. 11 (1905) (upholding compulsory vaccination); Lochner v. New York, 198 U.S. 45, 65 (1905) (Harlan, J., dissenting from holding that New York could not limit bakers' working hours).

114. Thus, in Powell v. Pennsylvania, 127 U.S. 678 (1888), Harlan professed to follow his earlier opinion in *Mugler* in sustaining under the police power a state statute that prohibited the manufacture or sale of any "oleaginous substance." The statute was a rank form of special interest regulation to protect the dairy interests against competition from margarine producers. Harlan nonetheless refused to allow the defendants to prove that their products were wholesome as sold.

It will be observed that the offer in the court below was to show by proof that the particular articles the defendant sold, and those in his possession for sale, in violation of the statute, were, in fact, wholesome or nutritious articles of food. It is entirely consistent with that offer that many, indeed, that most kinds of oleomargarine butter in the market contain ingredients that are or may become injurious to health. The court cannot say, from anything of which it may take judicial cognizance, that such is not the fact. Under the circumstances disclosed in the record, and in obedience to settled rules of constitutional construction, it must be assumed that such is the fact. 'Every possible presumption. . . is in favor of the validity of a statute, and this continues until the contrary is shown beyond a rational doubt.'

By this logic the state could ban all dairy products as well as their substitutes. Note the progression from *Mugler* to *Powell*. In the former case Harlan knew of the perils of drink. In the later he allowed the state to presume some imagined perils to margarine, without allowing the defendant to introduce evidence to the contrary.

115. *See, e.g.,* Adair v. United States, 208 U.S. 161 (1908) (upholding freedom of contract between employer and employee); Smyth v. Ames, 169 U.S. 466 (1898) (holding confiscatory state railroad rate regulations to be violations of the 14th Amendment); Berea College v. Kentucky, 211 U.S. 45, 58-70 (1908) (Harlan, J., dissenting) (criticizing racial segregation).

116. *Champion,* 188 U.S. at 356.

117. *Id.*

118. *See,* Caminetti v. United States, 242 U.S. 470 (1917); Hoke v. United States, 227 U.S. 308, 322 (1913) (noting the link between the police power and the commerce clause).

119. *See,* Hipolite Egg Co. v. United States, 220 U.S. 45 (1911). *Hipolite* was confined to "illicit articles—articles which the law seeks to keep out of commerce because, they are debased by adulteration," *id.* at 57, and which were "at their point of destination in the original, unbroken packages," *id.* at 58.

120. 247 U.S. 251 (1918).

121. Act of Sept. 1, 1916, ch. 432, 39 Stat. 675. This act prohibited all labor by children under 14, and allowed children between the ages of 14 and 16 to work only eight-hour days, six days per week.

122. *Hammer,* 247 U.S. at 272.

123. 156 U.S. 1 (1895); *see infra* notes 141-58 and accompanying text.

124. *Hammer,* 247 U.S. at 271.

125. *Id.*

126. *Id.* at 273-74.

127. Justice Day wrote:

> There is no power vested in Congress to require the States to exercise their police power so as to prevent possible unfair competition. Many causes may cooperate to give one State by reason of local laws or conditions, an economic advantage over others. The Commerce Clause was not intended to give to Congress a general authority to equalize such conditions.

Id. at 273.

128. *Id.* at 281 (Holmes, J., dissenting).

129. *See,* Northern Secs. Co. v. United States, 193 U.S. 197, 402-3 (1904) (Holmes, J., dissenting).

130. *Hammer,* 247 U.S. at 277.

131. *See id.* at 276-77.

132. 347 U.S. 483 (1954).

133. *Hammer,* 247 U.S. at 256-57 (argument of appellant).

134. *Id.* at 275 ("That such employment [e.g., child labor] is generally deemed to require regulation is shown by the fact that the brief of counsel states that every State in the Union has a law upon the subject, limiting the right to thus employ children.").

135. *Hammer,* 247 U.S. at 268-69 n.1.

136. "That there should be limitations upon the right to employ children in mines and factories in the interest of their own and the public welfare, all will admit." *Id.* at 275.

137. *See,* L. WILDER, FARMER BOY (1933).

138. *See,* I. HOWE, THE WORLD OF OUR FATHERS (1976). Howe's book is notable for its discussion of the unintended harmful consequences of turn-of-the-century social legislation on the very people it was supposed to protect. Howe himself is a social democrat who supports such legislation, but his accounts reveal his obvious sense of puzzlement about the issue, although he was not moved to change his substantive positions. *See e.g., id.* at 150-53 (discussing the mixed results of housing legislation in New York, including the 1901 statute that forbade further construction of the so-called "dumbbell" tenements).

139. *See, e.g.,* the account of the police power given in New York Cent. R.R. v. White, 243 U.S. 188, 207 (1917).

140. *See, supra,* notes 74-101 and accompanying text.

141. 156 U.S. 1 (1895).

142. Ch. 647, 26 Stat. 209 (1980) (current version at 15 U.S.C. §§ 1-8 (1982)).

143. *E.C. Knight,* 156 U.S. at 9.

144. *Id.* at 16-17.

145. *Id.* at 12-13.

146. *Id.* at 18 (Harlan, J., dissenting).

147. *See id.* at 12-13.

148. *Id.* at 35-36 (Harlan, J., dissenting).

149. *See, id.* at 12, 36-37 (Harlan, J., dissenting).

150. *See supra* note 87 and accompanying text.

151. Justice Harlan wrote:

> If this combination, so far as its operations necessarily or directly affect
> interstate commerce, cannot be restrained or suppressed under some power
> granted to Congress, it will be cause for regret that the patriotic statemen who
> framed the Constitution did not foresee the necessity of investing the
> national government with power to deal with gigantic monopolies holding in
> their grasp, and injuriously controlling in their own interest, the entire trade
> *among the States* in food products that are essential to the comfort of every
> household in the land.

E.C. Knight, 156 U.S. at 19 (Harlan, J., dissenting).

152. *Id.* at 13.

153. *Id.*

154. *Id.* at 15-16.

155. 175 U.S. 211 (1899).

156. 198 U.S. 45 (1905). Yet Justice Peckham did not simply use "freedom of
contract" as a phrase to conceal all understanding of regulatory issues. In *Addyston
Pipe,* for example, he was explicit about the limits of freedom of contract in its
constitutional guise:

> It has been held that the word "liberty," as used in the Constitution, was not
> to be confined to the mere liberty of person, but included, among others, a
> right to enter into certain classes of contracts for the purpose of enabling the
> citizen to carry on his business. But it has never been, and in our opinion
> ought not to be, held that the word included the right of an individual to
> enter into private contracts upon all subjects, no matter what their nature

and wholly irrespective (among other things) of the fact that they would, if performed, result in the regulation of interstate commerce and in the violation of an act of Congress upon that subject.

Addyston Pipe, 175 U.S. at 228-29 (citation omitted).

The passage is odd in the sense that it treats private contracts as the equivalent of public regulation, and because it inverts the relationship between constitutional principle and legislative action. But otherwise stated, the principle of freedom of contract does not protect contracts in restraint of trade. The explanation for the distinction lies in the external effects of two kinds of contracts. Contracts in restraint of trade may well have negative, systematic, economic effects; ordinary commercial contracts have positive systematic effects. The issue could be understood, although it was not by Justice Peckham, in terms of the just compensation requirements associated with limitation of both contract and property rights. See R. EPSTEIN, TAKINGS: PRIVATE PROPERTY AND THE POWER OF EMINENT DOMAIN 202-3 (1985).

157. *See, Addyston Pipe,* 175 U.S. at 248.

158. *Id.* at 226-27.

159. 193 U.S. 197 (1904).

160. *See id.* at 327-28.

161. *Id.* at 402 (Holmes, J., dissenting).

162. *Id.* at 402-3 (Holmes, J., dissenting) (citation omitted).

163. 196 U.S. 375 (1905).

164. *Id.* at 388.

165. *Id.* at 397.

166. 258 U.S. 495, 517 (1922) ("The judgment in [Swift] gives a clear and comprehensive exposition which leaves to us in this case little but the obvious application of the principles there declared.").

167. 262 U.S. 1, 35 (1923) ("[Swift] merely fitted the commerce clause to the real and practical essence of modern business growth. It applies to the case before us just as it did in [Stafford].").

168. Ch. 64, 42 Stat. 159 (current version at 7 U.S.C. §§ 181-231 (1982)).

169. *Stafford,* 258 U.S. at 514.

170. *Id.* at 513-14.

171. *Id.* at 515-16.

172. Ch. 369, 42 Stat. 998 (1922) (current version codified as part of the Commodity Exchange Act, 7 U.S.C. §§ 1-24 (1982 & Supp. III 1985)).

173. *Olsen,* 262 U.S. at 32.

174. Chief Justice Taft wrote:

> The railroads of the country accommodate themselves to the interstate function of the Chicago market by giving shippers from western States bills of lading through Chicago. . . for temporary purposes of storing, inspecting, weighing, grading, or mixing, and changing the ownership, consignee or destination and then to continue the shipment under the same contract and at a through rate. . . . The fact that the grain shipped from the west and taken from the cars may have been stored in warehouses and mixed with other grain, so that the owner receives other grain when presenting his receipt for continuing the shipment, does not take away from the interstate character of the through shipment . . . .

Id. at 33-34.

175. 295 U.S. 495 (1935).

176. *Id.* at 521, 547, 551 (citing the National Industrial Recovery Act, ch. 90, 48 Stat. 195 (1933)).

177. 298 U.S. 238 (1936).

178. Ch. 824, 49 Stat. 991 (1935).

179. *Carter,* 298 U.S. at 239.

180. *Id.* at 305.

181. *Id.* at 308.

182. *See supra* notes 60-61 and accompanying text.

183. Hammer v. Dagenhart, 247 U.S. 25, 271 (1918); *see supra* notes 120-40.

184. *See,* G. GUNTHER, CONSTITUTIONAL LAW 128-30 (11th ed. 1985).

185. 301 U.S. 1 (1937). Companion cases to *Jones & Laughlin* were NLRB v. Friedman-Harry Marks Clothing Co., 301 U.S. 58 (1937), and NLRB v. Fruehauf Trailer Co., 301 U.S. 49 (1937).

186. Ch. 372, 49 Stat. 449 (1935) (current version at 29 U.S.C. §§ 151-69 (1982 & Supp. III 1985)).

187. *See id.* § 8(a)(5), 29 U.S.C. § 158 (a)(5).

188. *See id.* § 9(a), 29 U.S.C. § 159 (a).

189. *See,* J.I. Case Co. v. NLRB, 321 U.S. 332 (1944).

190. *Id.* at 450.

191. *See, supra* notes 35-59 and accompanying text.

192. *See, supra* notes 141-83 and accompanying text.

193. *See, supra* notes 93-101 and accompanying text.

194. "There would appear to be no difference in the constitutional power to protect interstate commerce against unduly high prices, as in the Sherman Act, and excessively low prices, as in the New Deal legislation." Stern, *supra* note 32, at 651. The economic error is to think that price levels, rather than economic structure, are the source of any misallocation of resources.

195. *See,* Gibbons v. Ogden, 22 U.S. (9 Wheat.) 1, 188 (1824).

196. *See,* Carter v. Carter Coal Co., 298 U.S. 238 (1936); E.C. Knight Co. v. United States, 156 U.S. 1 (1895).

197. *See* NLRB v. Fruehauf Trailer Co., 85 F.2d 391 (6th Cir. 1936), rev'd, 301 U.S. 49 (1937); NLRB v. Jones & Laughlin Steel Corp., 83 F.2d 998 (5th Cir. 1936), re'vd 301 U.S. 1 (1937). The circuit opinions were reprinted in full in Justice McReynolds's dissent to all three of these cases. *See* Labor Board Cases, 301 U.S. 76, 79–84 (1937) (McReynolds, J., dissenting).

198. *Carter,* 298 U.S. at 308-9.

199. *Jones & Laughlin,* 301 U.S. at 37; *see, Carter,* 298 U.S. at 317 (Cardozo, J., dissenting).

200. *See, Jones & Laughlin,* 301 U.S. at 36-37 (quoting Second Employers' Liability Cases, 233 U.S. 1, 47 (1911); The Daniel Ball, 77 U.S. (10 Wall.) 557, 564 (1870)).

201. *Jones & Laughlin,* 301 U.S. at 34-35 (quoting the government's argument).

202. Chief Justice Hughes wrote:

> The authority of the federal government may not be pushed to such an extreme as to destroy the distinction, which the commerce clause itself establishes, between commerce "among the several States" and the internal concerns of a State. That distinction between what is national and what is local in the activities of commerce is vital to the maintenance of our federal system.

Id. at 30.

203. NLRB v. Fruehauf Co., 301 U.S. 49, 50 (1937).

204. NLRB v. Friedman-Harry Marks Clothing Co., 301 U.S. 58, 73 (1937).

205. The Court in *Friedman-Harry Marks* wrote:

> With effective competition between the industry's enterprises an accepted fact regardless of location, and bearing in mind the purpose and effect of the migration of enterprises, it seems unavoidable that the members of the Amalgamated Clothing Workers should, as they do, regard the industry as one whose

> economic organization is not based on the interests of each individual enterprise, but is one in which union conditions, to be maintained at all, must prevail generally.

Id. at 59.

206. 312 U.S. 100 (1941).

207. Ch. 676, 52 Stat. 1060 (1938) (current version at 29 U.S.C. §§ 201-9 (1982) & Supp. III 1985)). The statute empowered Congress to set both minimum wages and maximum hours to cover all employers who were engaged in the production of goods for the interstate market, and to enact sanctions, including fines and imprisonment, to punish violators of the act.

208. *Darby,* 312 U.S. at 102 (the government's argument).

209. *Id.* at 115.

210. *Id.*

211. *Id.* at 121.

212. *Id.* at 109 n.1. Justice Stone's version of The Shreveport Rate Case, 234 U.S. 342 (1914), was adopted by Justice Jackson in Wickard v. Filburn, 317 U.S. 111, 123-34 (1942). *See infra* notes 221-26 and accompanying text.

213. Hammer v. Dagenhart, 247 U.S. 251, 281 (1918) (Holmes, J., dissenting).

214. *See, Darby,* 312 U.S. at 115.

215. *Id.* at 124.

216. *See id.* at 122.

217. *Id.*

218. 315 U.S. 110 (1942).

219. *See id.* at 116 (quoting the Agricultural Marketing Agreement Act of 1937, ch. 296, 50 Stat. 246 (current version at scattered sections of 7 U.S.C. (1982 & Supp. III 1985))).

220. *Id.* at 120.

221. 317 U.S. 111 (1942).

222. *See id.* at 120.

223. *See id.*

224. The Shreveport Rate Case, 234 U.S. 342 (1914).

225. *Wickard,* 317 U.S. at 123 (quoting *The Shreveport Rate Case,* 234 U.S. at 351).

226. *The Shreveport Rate Case,* 234 U.S. at 351. Professor Tribe's rendition of *The Shreveport Rate Case's* sentence suppresses this first clause as well, with the exception of keeping the word "control" and dropping the words "their operations in." TRIBE, *supra* note 28, § 5-4, at 235 (quoting *The Shreveport Rate Case,* 234, U.S. at 351).

227. *See, supra* notes 13-16 and accompanying text.

228. Descriptively, one reason why there is little federal regulation of land use, for example, is that the markets for land tend to be more local than national. For these markets federal regulation is of little assistance, so regulation is apt to take place at the local level. But where the economics change, as with strip-mining, the regulation becomes federal. For my views on how the eminent domain clause of the Fifth Amendment (as applied to both federal and state governments) should function, *see* R. EPSTEIN, *supra* note 156; Epstein, *supra* note 34.

229. *See, e.g., Wickard,* 317 U.S. at 129-33; *Darby,* 312 U.S. at 125; *Jones & Laughlin,* 301 U.S. at 43-49. *Wrightwood Dairy,* 315 U.S. at 110, is an apparent exception, but only because the question of whether the state could control the price of milk had already been resolved in favor of the state. See Nebbia v. New York, 291 U.S. 502 (1934).

230. Professor Tribe has written that

> *Hammer v. Dagenhart* highlights the tension that existed between the Supreme Court's taxonomic approach to the commerce clause in the early 20th century—an approach grounded in the theory of dual sovereignty and sustained by a faith in the market as the proper mechanism for distributing wealth—and the increasingly undeniable consequences of economic inter-dependence.

TRIBE, supra note 28, § 5-7, at 238 n.l. The word "creating" should be inserted in place of "distributing" to understand the economic case.

231. Moreover, there is reason to fear local regulation that is designed to preclude external competition, as in *Gibbons.* Indeed, the great achievement of the commerce clause has been its negative side, which has precluded state regulation even when the federal government has not acted. Perhaps the ideal form of the commerce clause should have been negative: "No state shall have any power to pass legislation that interferes with the freedom of commerce among the several states." There are of course difficulties to this proposal. For example, it makes any sensible response to the long-haul/short-haul problem difficult. The mischief of excessive federal action, however, is far greater.

232. See Tullock, *The Welfare Costs of Tariffs, Monopolies, and Theft,* 5 W. ECON. J. 224, 232 (1967), for the first demonstration of the point. I have addressed some of these problems in Epstein, *supra* note 34.

233. *See, supra* note 62.

234. For the modern analogue, *see* Garcia v. San Antonio Metro. Transit Auth., 469 U.S. 528 (1985), dealing with the ability of the federal government to regulate the states themselves under the commerce clause.

235. *See,* THE FEDERALIST No. 84 (A. Hamilton); *supra* notes 5-8 and accompanying text.

236. *See id.*

237. *See,* R. EPSTEIN, *supra* note 156, ch. 2.

Economic Liberty, Antitrust, and the Constitution, 1880-1925

TONY FREYER*

James Madison and the Framers of the Constitution fervently believed that the preservation of "republican liberty" depended upon the "security of private rights." Yet the Constitution did not state precisely the scope and nature of these rights. As Madison argued in *Federalist* No. 10, the Framers expected economic liberty to emerge from social and political conflict. Accordingly, Americans have primarily relied upon constitutional process to resolve struggles over the sanctity of property and the freedom of contract. More particularly, it was the interaction between this process and wider values and interests which shaped the constitutional principles governing economic rights.[1]

The Constitution says nothing directly about anticompetitive or restrictive agreements among giant corporations or small businessmen. Antitrust, the body of law which has grown up since the late nineteenth century to regulate these practices, is not mentioned in the Constitution either. But few fields of law encompass more broadly the interaction between constitutional processes and conflicting values and interests. Arising out of government response to big business, antitrust reflected the lawmakers' struggle either to encourage or to limit the businessman's private right to enter contracts which created a new form of heavily-capitalized, centrally-managed, large corporate property. During the formative era of antitrust, state and federal policy makers attempted to control the development of such property. Ironically, the result was to facilitate the establishment of certain large business structures while prohibiting others. This ambiguity arose in part because big business challenged the established, independent, unincorporated small enterprisers who

* I wish to thank the following: National Endowment for the Humanities; Earhart Foundation; Research Grants Committee, University of Alabama; University of Alabama Law School Foundation. I am also indebted to Francis N. Stites and the Word Processing Center for Social Sciences and Humanities at UCLA.

had been central to the nation's economy throughout the nineteenth century. Because small businessmen were a significant political constituency, they and other groups pressured legislatures and courts to use antitrust to meet the threat of bigness. As a result, state and federal governments, and ultimately the Supreme Court, developed antitrust principles, thereby adapting constitutional guarantees of private rights and economic liberty to a changing business order. At the same time, however, lawmakers also responded to various other pressures, often fostering the very outcome that the small business interests opposed.[2]

From the 1880s to the 1920s, this process of adaptation significantly influenced American political and social life.[3] During that period big business was a new phenomenon, but the rhetoric its supporters and opponents used to defend or attack it was often old. Spokesmen for both sides expressed themselves in language similar to that employed during the making of the Constitution. Undoubtedly the leading influence on both the framing of the Constitution and policies aimed at controlling big business was the common law. Yet, as Forrest McDonald and Gordon Wood have shown, the belief in republicanism also shaped the Framers' work. Central to eighteenth-century republicanism was the conviction that true liberty depended upon the individual remaining economically independent in order to participate in public affairs, which in turn fostered the good of the commonwealth and public virtue. In public discourse, the ideological linkage between virtue and commonwealth did not persist beyond the 1830s. The idea, however, that economic dependency threatened self-government and the moral welfare of the community, was a separate republican value that found its way into Populist, and to some extent even Progressive, rhetoric. Small businessmen and their supporters also often defined the challenge of big business in terms of these values. Public officials, lawyers, and judges, moreover, appealed to the same values as they struggled to mold constitutional guarantees of private rights to the demands of a new economic order.[4]

To be sure, laissez-faire ideas associated with individual or economic liberty may have dominated the formative era of big business.[5] And the actual substantive content of republican values changed between the early nineteenth and early twentieth century, as Americans applied old words to new purposes. Nevertheless, as lawmakers looked to the common law to formulate antitrust rules governing the constitutional status of large corporations, they were also influenced by the older republican tradition. The interplay between republican values and the process of constitutional adaptation to economic change is my primary focus. In the larger study of which this is a part,[6] I explore the relation between these values and laissez-faire ideas. Here, I attempt merely to describe and analyze how lawmakers, responding to the emergence of big business, used the republican heritage to establish a theoretical interdependence between private rights and the public interest.

Americans were ambivalent about large corporations. They craved the benefits bigness made possible because of organizational efficiency and scale economies; but they also remained tenaciously committed to the ideal of small enterprise. Legislators and judges infused antitrust with republican values in an effort to resolve this tension, culminating eventually in the Supreme Court's "rule of reason." Although the rule of reason had a technical meaning derived from the English common law, it also possessed a broader policy content incorporating moralistic and economic assumptions. Since at least the early eighteenth century, the common law recognized that certain anticompetitive contracts, agreements, or combinations were lawful if found not to be unreasonable. Such reasonable restraints included anticompetitive agreements which were "ancillary to" an otherwise lawful contract, or those that were made for "a good consideration." Responding to growing popular criticism of giant corporations, many states from the 1880s on initiated prosecutions on the basis of these common-law rules. But the most famous result of discontent was the Sherman Antitrust Act of 1890, which made unlawful "every contract, combination in the form of trust or otherwise, or conspiracy, in restraint of trade or commerce among the several states, or with foreign nations." Under these provisions the Justice Department could prosecute individuals or corporations engaged in monopolistic practices. The attorney generals of the states as well as private citizens could also bring suit to enforce the law. Yet not until Chief Justice Edward D. White's decision in the famous *Standard Oil Case* (1911), did the rule of reason become the leading legal doctrine governing the interpretation of the Sherman Act, which in turn absorbed implicit moral presumptions regarding "good" versus "bad" anticompetitive arrangements and their impact upon "fair competition." It was this element of the rule of reason and the enforcement of the Sherman Act which was influenced by the republican values inherited from the Founding Fathers. [7]

I. The Framers' Ambivalent Original Intent

The Framers did not establish a particular economic system in the Constitution they drafted in 1787. It is, McDonald said, "meaningless to say that the Framers intended this or that.... [T]heir propositions were diverse and, in many particulars, incompatible. Some had firm, well-rounded plans, some had strong convictions on only a few points, some had self-contradictory ideas, some were guided only by vague ideals." Moreover, some of their "differences were subject to compromise; others were not." It was not surprising, then, that the Framers were ambivalent about the degree to which government should control property rights. A belief in property rights coexisted with an equally firm commitment to the public interest, McDonald concluded. The "crucial fact" was that property "ownership did not include the absolute right to buy or sell one's property in a free market; that was not part of the scheme of things in eighteenth-century England and America."[8]

The ambivalence about government control of property rights was rooted in the ambivalent character of liberty. The fundamental motive of both the patriots of the Revolution and the Framers of the Constitution was that proclaimed in the Declaration of Independence: the preservation of republican liberty. But there was an inherent tension in this idea. Republicanism conceived of liberty in terms of individual political action, the cultivation of civic virtue, and the good of the commonwealth. Another influence was the Lockean faith in the need to limit government to protect individual freedom, particularly the use of property. The Constitution's power to tax for the general welfare reflected the commonwealths' faith in government intervention for the benefit of the public. The limits the Constitution placed upon state authority to interfere with contracts embodied the commitment to property rights.[9]

The Framers sought to protect republican liberty by creating two distinct spheres of government authority. The national government operated upon individual American citizens under its jurisdiction, while within their constitutionally defined sphere the states retained their sovereignty. This division created two levels of government which exercised control over property rights. And, despite such constitutional limitations as the contracts clause, states retained ample authority to restrict the individual's buying and selling of property. The question was whether the Constitution, through the taxing power and commerce clause, granted the *federal* government a similar power to regulate economic liberty.[10]

In the ratification debates this question arose as one facet of the crucial issue of centralization. Antifederalists asserted that the Federalists wanted to replace the states' control over property rights with that of the national government. The Federalists denied that such displacement would result from the exercise of the taxing power and commerce clause or other federal powers, because the state and federal governments would share policymaking authority. Thus, both groups supported decentralized regulatory controls; they disagreed about the extent to which such controls should be vested in a central government. The central issue of the ratification debate was whether private rights and public-interest values embodied in republican liberty could survive without a strengthened Union.

The Federalists believed that government should encourage individual commercial activity. They wanted the strengthened central government to use its authority over property rights to promote trade and thereby increase individual opportunity. At the same time, they hoped that virtuous leaders would emerge who could maintain a balance between private rights and the public welfare. The Federalists sought to fulfill these goals by enlarging, through a national government, the sphere in which individuals and groups struggled to pursue their economic self-interest, subject, of course, to appropriate federal regulation.

The Antifederalists both concurred and dissented. "A comparison of our country...with other parts of the world, will prove, beyond a doubt," said *"Agrippa,"* "that the greatest share of freedom is enjoyed by citizens, so much more does commerce flourish." This was so because in America's state governments "every citizen has an influence in making the laws, and thus they are conformed to the general interests of the state; but in every other kind of government they are frequently made in favor of a part of the community at the expense of the rest." There could not "from the history of mankind, be produced an instance of rapid growth in extent, in numbers, in arts, and in trade, that will bear any comparison with our country."[11] But if the Antifederalists favored commercial prosperity, they also feared its implications for preserving individual and public virtue. Too much economic liberty encouraged individuals to place their own interest above the public welfare. Hence, as "people become more luxurious, they become more incapacitated of governing themselves."[12]

The Constitution's centralized government, the Antifederalists believed, threatened both republican virtue and disciplined commercial enterprise. The national government challenged the traditional belief that virtue could survive only in republics encompassing small territories. In addition, the centralized legislative and judicial power extended to "all cases respecting property." With the "unlimited right to regulate commerce, external and *internal,*" Congress could "create monopolies which have been universally injurious to all subjects of the countries that have adopted them, excepting the monopolists themselves.[13] The implication was, then, that by destroying virtue, centralization spawned an extravagant pursuit of wealth. As a result, the Antifederalists predicted, "Indolence will increase, and with it crimes cannot but increase. The springs of honesty will gradually grow lax, and chaste and severe manners be succeeded by those that are dissolute and vicious."[14]

The ratification of the Constitution did not end controversy over the relationship between government and economic liberty. A fundamental issue was the degree to which state and federal authorities should restrict or promote business enterprise and property rights through legal rules regulating contracts. Two categories of legal doctrine controlled most contractual obligations, though, admittedly, the legal rules making up these categories were always in a state of flux. The common law that Americans inherited from England governed contracts and combinations which restrained trade, established monopolies, unlawfully interfered with competition, or raised prices. Corporation law regulated the rights, obligations, and structure of companies chartered by the state. This law included the particular provisions contained in a given incorporation charter, the interpretation of those provisions by courts, and various other judicial doctrines. Despite some consistency in general principles, the common law and statutory provisions regulating contracts often differed from state to state. There were significant distinctions, too, between state and federal law pertaining to contracts.[15]

In addition, after the Constitution's ratification the rules governing contractual obligation evolved in a volatile political and economic environment. State legislatures governed individual enterprise through a wide range of regulations, including wage, price, and market controls. The federal government's impact was often less direct. Nevertheless, changing tariff, banking, and land policy, as well as federal court decisions, exercised a significant influence upon contract rights. These rights regulated access to and use of property within an economic order dominated by localism. Prior to the mid-nineteenth century, the typical American did not live in an ideal competitive world guided by Adam Smith's Invisible Hand. Most Americans were producers who operated in relatively self-contained local markets in which a few businesses dominated trade. The grass roots of industrial growth developed along streams in small rural communities whose workshops, mills, and factories served the same limited locality. To be sure, certain articles such as British textiles and other quality imports were distributed nationally, but the market for most manufactured goods and foodstuffs rarely extended beyond regional limits.[16]

During the years before the Civil War this economic order gradually changed. Since colonial days a relatively small group of general merchants living in a few seaboard commercial centers had dominated the national economy. After 1815, with the coincident termination of the Napoleonic Wars and the War of 1812, these merchants increasingly lost their influence to a new, nationally dispersed, and growing class of specialized middlemen. The proliferation of these new small businessmen resulted from an expanded national market that made possible a volume business. Market growth in turn provided incentives for enterprisers to invest in manufacturing and transportation facilities, which produced the nation's first big business—the railroads. But despite such changes, the traditional, locally oriented economy persisted beyond the Civil War.

A pronounced commercial rivalry characterized the changing economic order. As the nation grew, states and localities competed for immigrants, investments, entrepreneurial skills, and other scarce human and material resources. Responding to these pressures, state legislatures and courts fashioned policies designed to give their people a competitive edge in transportation, banking, and debtor-creditor relations. Small business and corporations gained much from such policies, while the opportunistic motivations underlying governmental action surely impeded long-term planning. Simultaneously the pervasive localism and the spread of franchise democracy that triumphed during the Jacksonian Era shaped policy making. To maintain their constituents' support, lawmakers attempted to distribute the costs and benefits of protection and development among as many political groups as possible. This distribution was rarely if ever equitable; but as a manifestation of intense private and public competition it encouraged a tenacious attachment to local control.

These tensions both shaped and were shaped by constitutional and legal rules governing economic liberty. The Framers of the Constitution had created a government in which both state and federal lawmakers possessed authority to regulate contract and property rights. The Federalists and Antifederalists had disagreed over the issue of centralization. Yet they both were committed to republican liberty and the belief that private and public interests were interdependent. Similarly, they had recognized that government should promote commercial prosperity, though the degree to which such promotion should subject private conduct and public power to the temptations of a free market was much disputed. These diverse values reflected a constitutional order which by the mid-nineteenth century had fostered a changing business system. Yet, although the railroads presaged an economy based on large corporations, small business and local control remained dominant.

II. The Challenge of Big Business and Republican Values

By 1900 a new economy dominated by large corporations had emerged. Driving the shift from small to big enterprise was the desire to reduce the costs of competition, thereby achieving greater economic efficiency. Both economic groups struggled to mobilize political support, generating controversy over the relationship between government and economic liberty. Those who favored corporate consolidation demanded that lawmakers should defer to constitutional guarantees of property rights and freedom of contract. Their opponents argued that these private rights and the public interest were interdependent, subject to the popular control of a disciplined, morally responsible, citizenry.

From the 1870s on, a rapid rise in urban population, the spread of technological innovation, and a tremendous expansion of transportation facilities sustained and stimulated corporate growth. The factory system and mass production enabled a single firm to greatly increase its potential rate of production, and thereby supply the rapidly expanding urban market. Simultaneously, however, the decades following the Civil War witnessed a precipitous decline in prices. The wholesale price index for all commodities in 1865 was 185; by the early 1890s it declined to around 80. Industrialists looked for ways to adjust output to the changing market and to influence prices. One way was to more efficiently exploit economies of scale through various organizational forms which in turn required a bigger business structure. Simultaneously, some manufacturers developed their own wholesale distribution networks. As a result, the need for the independent middleman and small competitor declined.[17]

The comparatively small, unincorporated businessmen were essential to the old, locally-oriented economic order. They brought buyers and sellers together, despite distance and poor communications. Generally, these middlemen were wholesalers who throughout most of the nineteenth century dominated the distribution of traditional consumer goods, including hardware, machine tools, drugs, groceries, leather goods, tobacco, liquor, jewelry, furs, furniture and other wood products, china and glassware, stationery, oil, varnish, and paint. As corporations grew through consolidation, however, the size of buyers and sellers in many industries increased, while their numbers decreased. Efficient transportation, a growing urban population, and centralized management organization fostered a radically different and far more concentrated market than that which had existed before the Civil War. By building their own marketing organizations, manufacturers were able to handle their buying and selling more effectively than could the specialized middlemen. So, to exploit economies of scale and establish greater control over prices, firms developed centralized management structures which subsumed the traditional roles of the smaller independent, unincorporated businessmen. And ultimately, consolidation meant that what William Jennings Bryan called this "broader class of businessmen" lost control of the nation's economy.[18]

The corporation was essential to the emerging new industrial order. The corporate form was, of course, not new, but between 1870 and 1890 increasing numbers of transportation and manufacturing companies had used it to consolidate new business functions and to establish greater centralized managerial control. There were, however, degrees in the level of centralization. Many big firms were little more than loose confederations or cartels formed to eliminate competition and to fix prices. Cartels had been and remained common among comparatively small enterprises, so their use by managerial capitalists merely represented the transfer of an established organizational form from small to big business. But the greater autonomy characteristic of the cartel meant that its contractual relations were often difficult to maintain if the interests of its members changed. The fundamental problem was that cartel members might seek to gain advantage by undercutting agreed prices, thereby unleashing the very competition the cartel had sought to prevent. Courts in England and America encouraged this instability because they refused to enforce agreements to fix prices or wages or to otherwise limit competition between employers, workers and employers, or workers themselves, even if those agreements were otherwise lawful.[19]

Another, tighter structure was the merger, in which companies turned over their independent control to a centralized board of directors. This managerial centralization had important advantages. Since mergers eliminated the independence of the firms absorbed, internal interference with enforcement of contractual agreements was not a problem. Moreover, mergers gave the managing directors of the parent firm direct control over assets and earnings of subsidiaries, which were usually located in different states.

Managerial control facilitated a wide range of inter-company contractual transactions, including the sale of assets of one subsidiary to another, the routing of profitable business to one subsidiary in preference to another, the concealment of losses, or the appearance of nonexistent deficits.[20] These considerations encouraged periods of intense merger activity, the most significant of which peaked in 1899, when 1,208 firms valued at over 2,064 million dollars were absorbed.[21]

Thus, to achieve economies of scale, consolidation was as essential as the elimination of competition. The "American workingman produces more, and he produces more because he has been supplied with the most perfect system of labor-saving machinery on earth," observed a defender of corporate concentration. "To supply this machinery large capital is necessary, the individual manufacturer, standing alone, is not in a position to perfect his machinery in the same measure as the consolidated enterprise."[22] At the same time, competition reduced the profit margins that were needed to cover the heavy fixed costs which arose from maintaining the huge capital investment the new, large organizational structure represented. Or, as a leading political economist put it, the "waste of competition...which comes from the inability of adapting one's plants and output to the needs of the market...can be partly saved by combination of many manufacturing establishments in one industry under one management."[23]

Companies established through merger also had difficulties. One observer said only half of the 328 mergers of the period 1888-1905 were successful. Shortly after these mergers took place, fifty-three failed outright; the rest earned profits that consistently were less than expected at the time the merger originally occurred. A major reason for low earnings was that often the new corporate entities had been overcapitalized with watered stock. This was so in part because new underwriting methods developed on the New York Stock Exchange after 1897 increased the market for merger issues, which in turn encouraged the demand for speculative investment in these issues. But, whatever the reason, it was apparent that centrally managed corporations were not immune to uncertainty and failure.[24]

These developments generated widespread opposition to virtually all forms of corporate consolidation, opposition articulated in terms of appeals to republican values. Thus, when Standard Oil used trust agreements to transfer ownership and managerial control from independent firms to a centralized board of directors, it created the first formal trust. Public opinion, however, ignored the narrow legal definition, equating all large combinations with trusts, which in turn were perceived as simply another form of monopoly.

The rhetoric about consolidation during Missouri's state-wide elections in 1888 was typical. Both Democrats and Republicans condemned trusts and monopolies, while the victorious Democratic governor warned his follow citizens that corporate centralization threatened the public interest. "Unchecked by any feeling of individual responsibility," he said, trusts, "moved solely by a love of gain, unfettered by the duties of citizenship...are enabled to perpetuate themselves by the adoption of methods and the use of agents which scruple at no means to accomplish their ends."[25] By the mid-1890s, such sentiments remained strong. President Grover Cleveland exclaimed that the trusts threatened the virtuous citizenry upon which republican government depended. "Whatever may be their incidental economic advantages, their general effect upon personal character, prospects, and usefulness cannot be otherwise than injurious," to workers, small businessmen, and farmers, who then possessed "little hope or opportunity of rising in the scale of responsible... citizenship."[26]

Many lawyers also perceived that the trusts threatened these same republican values. The legal profession's view was important because if reflected the emergence of a new market for legal services, including not only the big corporations but also the interests they threatened. Alexis de Tocqueville, moreover, identified lawyers as the bastion of conservatism in American society. Yet by the 1880s lawyers representing smaller, unincorporated enterprise had good reason to be concerned about competition with the growing corporate bar. The attorney serving corporate clients possessed financial and other resources which the lawyer representing small businessmen lacked. Significantly, the critics of the corporate lawyers appealed to the values of individual responsibility, self-denial, and moral accountability. As one lawyer proclaimed in 1888, traditional regard for "industry, patience, and perseverance" was giving way to the lust for "gold and silver." He blamed the "Trusts" forming in "all lines of business" and the lawyers whose technique and skill facilitated their development. "If the bar yields to this craze for gold, individual character will be lost in corporate enterprise and the bright escutcheon give place to the flaming sign-board. Degrade the bar to a business, and at least some of its members will sink to the lowest depths."[27]

Moreover, many lawyers perceived a connection between the threat to traditional values, and a perceived growing maldistribution of wealth among corporate capitalists, small businessmen, and wage earners. Since the Revolution, Americans had regarded the bar as a bastion of social order. This image diminished when the public perceived big corporations as undermining the public interest and responsible government. Indeed, it seemed as if "astute practitioners" had gained "advantage over their more scrupulous brethren ...enabling designing men to make contracts which...[were] understood in one sense and interpreted in another."[28] At the same time, the Illinois attorney general protested in 1894, the trusts fostered an inequitable concentration of wealth which repudiated popular government. "We may talk of democracy and equal rights all we please," he said, "but this country is today in danger from an evil...the evil of raising up a privileged class to prosper and grow rich at the unfair expense of the masses."[29]

Finally, critics of the big corporations linked the trusts to the social disorder which plagued the late nineteenth century. Thus, another lawyer feared that the trusts were destroying the legal profession as a bulwark against urban and agrarian unrest. "Anarchy" was "openly avowed, even under oath in the courts of justice. Fiends ready to apply the torch and throw the bomb, who laugh at wholesale murder, who would swim in gore, who abhor religion and repudiate God..." were gathering, he said, "in the thousands in great cities cursing the law and vowing vengeance on its officers." For now, he concluded, this nightmare was "but a dark speck, [which] may e'er long cover our skies and drench the land in blood." But with a "pure judiciary and bar inspired by honor, integrity, and independence, this apprehended horror...will pass, and our republic will outride every gale, and bear its countless blessings to distant generations."[30] Another observer was more subdued, but no less explicit. "Is it any wonder that anarchy thrives when rich and powerful combines violate the laws and defy state authority with impunity, and when they rob and oppress the people despite restraining laws?"[31]

Such criticism did not go unanswered. S.C.T. Dodd, the lawyer who developed Standard Oil's trust, noting the pernicious effect public opinion when aroused could have upon the judiciary's interpretation of state and federal antitrust legislation, nonetheless was confident that private rights would prevail. "If popular views are adopted in the construction" of these laws "and if they are held to be constitutional...they have made criminal all business of magnitude and all business conducted by means of association of persons and aggregation of capital. I have too much faith in our constitutions and our courts to believe such a result possible," he said.[32] A more persuasive response to the critics emphasized the economic efficiencies gained from corporate consolidation. "Perhaps the greatest of all benefits in the centralization is the concentration of technical knowledge and ability of the people connected with the business....When the Trust was organized, these gentlemen were brought together and this technical knowledge and skill was concentrated and utilized for the common good," said a director of the Sugar Trust in 1891.[33]

Ironically, the defenders of concentration had an ally in labor leader Samuel Gompers. After the federal government used the Sherman Act during the mid-1890s to prosecute unions for actions courts found to be unlawful interferences with trade, Gompers denounced those "who know little of statecraft and less of economics [who] urge[d] the adoption of laws to 'regulate' interstate commerce, [and to] 'prevent' combinations and trusts." He condemned such measures because, "when enacted, [they] have been the very instruments employed to deprive labor of the benefit of organized effort....The State is not capable of preventing the legitimate development of natural concentration of industry."[34]

Yet the arguments about big corporations had force in part because they drew upon republican values which had shaped the making and ratification of the Constitution. Like the Federalists and Antifederalists, neither the defenders nor opponents of corporate consolidation rejected private property or the need for government protection of economic liberty. What separated each group were disagreements about whose and what sorts of property and opportunity the government should protect. Arthur Hadley, a railroad authority who became president of Yale University, saw the American lawmakers' struggle as a:

> contradiction between our political theories and facts of industrial life. A republican government is organized on the assumption that all men are free and equal. If the political power is thus equally distributed while the industrial power is in the hands of a few, it creates danger of class struggles and class legislation which menace both our political and our industrial order.[35]

III. The Courts and Republican Values

Conflicts over government regulation of economic liberty inevitably involved the courts. During the 1880s and 1890s state attorney generals prosecuted corporate giants for violating common law prohibitions against corporations holding stock in other corporations. At the same time, private citizens brought their own suits challenging anticompetitive practices, which further influenced the legal rules governing big corporations. But because the large firms operated on a national scale, they could escape state prosecution by removing to a more friendly state. This problem encouraged Congress to intervene in 1890 with the Sherman Antitrust Act. This new federal law raised significant constitutional questions, however, concerning the degree to which it permitted the regulation of corporate operations which traditionally had been left to the states. A related but distinct issue involved what legal principles judges should use to interpret and apply the Sherman Act's ambiguous clauses. As state and federal judges grappled with these issues, they worked within the heritage of republican values; and the tension between private rights and the public interest reflected the conflict between small and large enterprise.

Public criticism and legal conflict focused initially on the trust, a controversial new legal device developed to facilitate managerial centralization. As noted above, technically, the trust was a form of merger in which various corporations contracted to transfer their securities to trustees who then ran the new corporate entity as one company. The first trust was Standard Oil, formed in 1882; by the 1890s mergers of this sort had been tried in several industries. But almost immediately the reliance upon private agreements ran afoul of state common law and statutory rules, which had existed at least since the eighteenth century, prohibiting contracts or combinations in restraint of trade. At the same time a few states saw an opportunity to attract business by abolishing these state restrictions upon contract rights. The first to do so was New Jersey, which in 1889 passed a statute permitting corporations to form holding companies. By establishing a holding company, a firm incorporated in one state could contract to purchase stock in companies incorporated in other states. Such a merger created a centralized enterprise which officially was based in one state but which in fact operated within a multi-state region or throughout the nation.[36]

The impact of the law on large firms was ambiguous. New Jersey's law made it relatively easy for big corporations to escape state prosecutions.[37] Yet it was possible for locals to defeat even those firms which merged to form a holding company. Texas public officials and lawmakers, responding to pressures from independent operators in the east Texas oil fields, passed antitrust legislation and initiated litigation defeating Standard Oil's attempt to take over the state's petroleum industry. Texas won its victory after Standard Oil had reconstituted itself as a New Jersey holding company.[38] A few other states achieved similar triumphs, which for a time enabled comparatively smaller enterprises in some industries to resist absorption by larger ones. Thus, by 1900, despite the proliferation of holding companies and other mergers throughout the American economy, the Constitution's federal system reinforced a republican faith in local control of economic liberty.[39]

State judges decided private suits against anticompetitive contracts. As Hans Thorelli has shown, because these decisions involved contracts in restraint of trade that were between residents of the same state, their impact was primarily local. Yet the results were clear: in the great majority of cases state courts favored competition.[40] An Alabama decision in 1900, *Tuscaloosa Ice MFG. Co. v. Williams,* was typical. Williams sued the Tuscaloosa Ice Company, arguing that the contractual agreement between them both in which Williams turned over his business, thus establishing the Company's monopoly, was void under common law rules prohibiting contracts in restraint of trade. As often happened in such agreements, Williams changed his mind, sued, and won at trial, whereupon the company appealed. The issue was whether a contract between the two ice manufacturers, in which one party granted the other a monopoly, was unlawful under the common law. The court found that the contract was a "vicious restraint of trade, and is therefore violative of the public policy of the state and void."[41]

The Alabama court's opinion suggested the values and interests it believed were at stake. Although the court admitted that it would uphold certain anticompetitive agreements if they seemed to be reasonable, the present contract was certainly not in this class. There was no doubt that the contract "tends to injure the public by stifling competition and creating a monopoly," the court said, giving one company the power "to arbitrarily fix prices...[thereby creating] a partial ice famine, upon which [it]...could batten and fatten at its own sweet will." Resorting to expressive language, the court observed that any defense of such practices was "exceedingly nude and bald." Yet, though the unfettered manufacture of ice in and of itself was undoubtedly important to the small town of Tuscaloosa during the hot, humid summer months during which the case was decided, the court stressed further considerations which it apparently regarded as equally compelling. Because of the contract to shut down one of the two firms, the "public loses a wealth producing instrumentality. Labor is thrown out of employment." This, the court claimed, forced workers upon the public welfare or drove them to become criminals. Hence, profits from a contract which established a monopoly were not "the just reward...[of] skill and energy and enterprise in building up a business, but...a mere bribery and seduction of... industry, and a pensioning of idleness." The "motives actuating such a transaction ...[were] always...sinister and baleful."[42]

The New Jersey holding company law, state prosecutions of consolidated corporations, and private suits against anti-competitive contracts reflected the ambivalent republican heritage. The New Jersey statute, by providing legal protection for the free exercise of property and contract rights, was consistent with the Constitution's sanction of private rights. And neither Texas nor Alabama public officials questioned the ultimate constitutional sanctity of contract and property rights. Yet, at the same time, many state legislators and judges believed prosperity depended upon protecting diverse, comparatively small-scale interests whose persistence and involvement in the community were considered essential to public welfare. In addition, as the *Tuscaloosa Ice MFG.* case suggested, state courts could link local economic well-being to broader concerns about individual moral accountability, unrestrained, exploitative behavior, and social stability. By drawings upon these values, state authorities enforced republican values which held that private rights and the public interest were interdependent.

The Sherman Act was Congress's response to this conflict on the state level. According to the law's preamble, its express purpose was to "protect trade and commerce against unlawful restraints and monopolies." To achieve this goal, Congress declared that every "contract, combination in the form of trust or otherwise, or conspiracy, in restraint of trade or commerce among the serveral states, or with foreign nations," was illegal. Although these phrases seemed straightforward, their meaning was subject to diverse construction and dispute. Lawmakers, judges, and commentators disagreed over what constituted a legal or illegal contract or combination "in restraint of trade." This was so in part because the language was taken from the common law, which in England and America had always been ambiguous. In both nations, as noted above, the principle governing anti-competitive or restraining contracts was "reasonableness," a standard open to interpretation.[43]

A particularly difficult issue was the reasonableness of the holding company. Given that the merger contracts forming a holding company made possible restrictive and anticompetitive practices, were these contracts none-theless reasonable and therefore lawful? The issue was complex because the internal structure of corporations was traditionally regulated under state common and statute law through charters of incorporation. Many incorporated firms were engaged in industrial production, such as manufacturing, rather than distribution or marketing. Yet the new corporate giants formed as holding companies often gained enough productive efficiency by merging that they could dominate, even if they did not directly control, the marketing carried on by other businessmen. Thus, holding companies raised a perplexing legal question: were the merger contracts made to establish improved productive efficiency reasonable and therefore lawful, if the control they permitted res-tricted the marketing operations of those doing business with the new corporation?[44]

This question raised further problems for the interpretation of the Sher-man Act. No one doubted Congress's power to regulate interstate and foreign commerce, including the contracts facilitating this trade. At this time, how-ever, authorities generally agreed that corporations involved in production confined principally within a single state were not subject to federal regulation under the commerce clause. By the late nineteenth century the Supreme Court had decided many cases defining the scope and limits of the commerce power along these lines. Thus, contractual agreements facilitating corporate produc-tion within one state generally were beyond the reach of the federal commerce power, whereas contracts directly touching interstate trade were subject to that power. How did this constitutional distinction between state and federal authority affect the contractual relations of holding companies whose control of production permitted a firm to compel others to accept anticompetitive or restrictive trade agreements? Where, in other words, did the state's control of production end, and the federal government's authority over commerce begin?[45]

The ultimate resolution of these questions was left to the Supreme Court. The Court's decisions, like those of state judges, shaped the relative status of small and big enterprise, and the impact of republican values. In the *Knight Sugar Trust* case of 1895, the Court narrowly construed the Sherman Act's provisions prohibiting contracts and combinations in restraint of trade. The majority held that the act applied only to restrictive combinations and con-tracts affecting trade, not to agreements among manufacturers involved in production. The Sugar Trust was a holding company whose production was confined principally to one state, Pennsylvania. Yet the merger of several competing Pennsylvania firms, in order to attain productive economies of scale, established a corporate entity with such economic power that it could virtually dictate the terms of interstate marketing agreements. When the federal government prosecuted the company, it made the constitutional argument that the Sherman Act applied to contracts creating production monopolies. But because such contracts were traditionally subject to state regulation, the Court decided, with only Justice John M. Harlan dissenting, that the Sherman Act did not reach those contractual agreements. Yet the Court also strongly implied that, had the government stressed the power the holding company exercised over interstate trade agreements, it would have won.[46]

The impact of the *Knight* case seemed equivocal. On one level it appeared that the Court had held that a holding company of the sort established by the sugar producers to achieve economies of scale did not violate the Sherman Act. Indeed, corporate lawyers so read the decision, thereby encouraging the turn-of-the-century merger wave. At the same time, the states, whose regulatory authority the Court had expressly confirmed, failed to deal effectively with the holding company. As long as states like New Jersey permitted the incorporation of holding companies, the regulatory authority of other states was ineffectual.[47] This suggested to contemporaries and many historians that the Court had subordinated the public interest to private rights, placed undisciplined acquisitiveness above moral accountability, favored consolidation over competition, and left small-scale enterprise defenseless against giant corporations. But the reality was more complex.

Within two years it became clear that the Court was deeply divided over how to interpret the Sherman Act. During the spring of 1895, shortly after deciding *E.C. Knight,* the Court, in order to halt the Pullman strike, upheld unanimously an injunction against Eugene V. Debs, who had attempted to support the Pullman workers with a secondary boycott imposed by his American Railway Union. The lower federal judges granted the injunction, holding that where labor unions interfered with trade they were acting as a combination in restraint of trade within the meaning of the Sherman Act. The framers of the law, however, had not intended to bring unions under the law. The Supreme Court, therefore, declined to accept this doubtful interpretation, basing its decision to sustain the injunction on the judiciary's general constitutional authority.[48] Not until December 1896, then, did the Court hear a case involving unequivocally the legal status of contractual agreements which impinged directly upon interstate commerce. The issue in *U.S. v. Trans-Missouri Freight Association* was whether a cartel agreement among competing railroads to fix rates violated the Sherman law. The Court divided five to four. For the majority, Justice Rufus W. Peckham held that the cartel's rate-fixing practices violated the act. Peckham reasoned that the law's provision should be read literally, without recourse to the ambiguities of the common law. Justice Edward D. White, however, argued for the dissenters that the common law's reasonableness standard should govern the application of the Sherman Act.[49]

The stakes in the Court's disagreement were high. The railroads contended that their anticompetitive practices were necessary to gain sufficient economies to offset high fixed costs. Competition drove rates so low that profit was inadequate to cover these costs, causing bankruptcy, the railroads claimed. The federal district court, which White and the dissenters wanted to affirm, accepted these arguments and found the cartel agreements to be reasonable. Thus, by rejecting the common law as the basis for construing the Sherman Act, Peckham refused to give priority to economic efficiency and private rights. "It is true the results of trusts, or combinations...may be different in different kinds of corporations," said Peckham, "and yet they all have an essential similarity, and have been induced by motives of individual or corporate aggrandizement as against the public interest."[50]

But it was not considerations of economic efficiency *per se* which Peckham rejected. He conceded that certain large corporations, such as the Knight Sugar Company, operating principally within a single state, were legal under the Sherman Act. What most concerned him were the social consequences of the changing economic order. There were, he admitted, "misfortunes" resulting from "all great industrial changes," which were the "inevitable accompaniment of...improvement." Particularly, it took time for "those who are thrown out of their old employment...[to] find opportunities for labor in other departments than those to which they have been accustomed." But such displacement was wrong when "effected by combinations of capital, whose purpose in combining is to control the production or manufacture of any...article in the market and by such control dictate the price at which the article shall be sold, the effect being to drive out of business all small dealers in the commodity and to render the public subject to the decisions of the combination as to what price shall be paid for the article."

The survival of "small dealers" and public benefit resulting from competition were, Peckham emphasized, entwined. When a "combination" controlled prices, the "country" lost the "services of a large number of small but independent dealers who were familiar with the business and who had spent their lives in it, and who supported themselves and their families from the small profits realized therein." Even lower prices gained from corporate consolidation did not justify destroying these independent enterprisers. The "real prosperity of any country" was lost if corporate bigness forced "an independent businessman, the head of his establishment, small though it might be, into a mere servant or agent of a corporation for selling the commodities which he once manufactured or dealt in, having no voice in shaping the business policy of the company and bound to obey orders issued by others." Consequently, when "any one commodity should be within the sole power and subject to the sole will of one powerful combination of capital" it was against the "substantial interests of the country."[51] Thus, whereas White and the dissenters wanted private rights to prevail, the majority upheld the public-interest principle of republican values.

Peckham did not have the last word. By 1899 the Court acknowledged

that to a limited extent the common law could provide guidelines for construing the Sherman Act.[52] Yet division among the justices persisted as to how far
or even whether they should adhere to the interpretive principles set down in
the *Trans-Missouri Freight Association* decision. In addition, federal regulation and restrictive agreements impinging upon interstate trade, and its
relation to the legal status of the holding company, remained open questions.
These issues, in turn, reflected continuing tension between republican values
and the conflicting interests of big corporations, workers, and small enterprise.
Because of this struggle it was another quarter century before coherent
antitrust principles emerged.

IV. Republican Values, "Fair Competition," and
the Triumph of the Rule of Reason

During the Progressive era, the first two decades of the twentieth century,
antitrust was a dominant issue in American life. In response to the turn-of-the-
century merger movement, the administrations of Theodore Roosevelt and
William H. Taft prosecuted and won major victories against giant holding
companies. As a result, the Court established the common law's rule of reason
as the basic doctrine governing the interpretation of the Sherman law. White's
dissent in *Trans-Missouri Freight Association* thus became the fundamental
antitrust principle. The Court's decisions shaped the federal government's
aproach to corporate consolidation, as federal superseded state authority in the
development of antitrust policy. From Wilson's election in 1912 to the mid-
1920s, federal officials applied the reasonableness standard in their efforts to
balance the interests of big and small business, with republican values
influencing the outcome.

White's rule of reason triumphed in part because Americans remained
ambivalent about corporate consolidation. Theodore Roosevelt and Wilson
reflected the public's divided mind. Although the "captains of industry...have
on the whole done a great good to our people," Roosevelt exclaimed, "yet it is
also true that there are real and grave evils...and a resolute and practical effort
must be made to correct these evils." As a result, "combinations and concentration should be, not prohibited, but supervised and within reasonable limits
controlled...."[53] Wilson said, "I, for one, don't care how big any business gets
by efficiency, but I am jealous of any bigness that comes by monopoly." This
meant, he asserted, "I am for big business, and I am against the trusts."[54]

To many observers the concentrated economy emerging from the merger
wave was the result of natural evolution, which paradoxically facilitated the
need for increased regulation. Corporate consolidation "has earned the right,"
said former U.S. Attorney General Richard Olney in 1906, "to be regarded as an
economic evolution."[55] Despite enormous "popular prejudice" from the

general public, "bitter condemnation" from the press, "denunciation by political demagogues," and "unrelenting har[assment] by legislature and courts," the corporate giants remained "unimpaired." To Olney this was yet another "instance of the ineffectiveness of artificial restraints when opposed to the operation of natural laws." A primary casualty of "natural" combination was the "hoary axiom—'Competition is the life of Trade.' " To reap the benefits arising from consolidation, Olney concluded, "competition regulated by law" was necessary, guided by such "meritorious objects" as "fair play, justice, and equality of opportunity and treatment."[56]

Ironically, even the "People's Lawyer," Louis Brandeis, the adamant foe of bigness, wanted the law to allow certain anticompetitive combinations. Brandeis opposed giant corporations because they threatened the ideal of participatory democracy, which depended upon independent enterprise. The "proposition that mere bigness can not be an offense against society is false," he said, "because...our society which rests upon democracy, can not endure under such conditions."[57] But implicit in this preference for small business were economic assumptions regarding the need for "fair competition" protected by law. Corporate consolidation permitted control over markets and prices, and placed small dealers at a competitive disadvantage which Brandeis believed was unfair. Echoing Peckham's *Trans-Missouri Freight Association* opinion, Brandeis observed that "the displacement of the small independent businessman by the huge corporation with its myriad of employees, its absentee ownership, and its financial control, presents a grave danger to our democracy."[58]

What was to be done? The answer, Brandeis believed, was that the law should allow small enterprisers to fix prices. "The moment you allow the cutting of prices you are inviting the great, powerful men to get control of the business," he said. That the corporations were able to lower prices because of efficiencies arising from organizational and scale economies, Brandeis flatly denied. "It is not even in accord with the natural laws of business," he said. "It is largely the result of unwise, man made, privilege-creating law, which has stimulated existing tendencies to inequality instead of discouraging them. Shall we, under the guise of protecting competition, further foster monopoly by creating immunity for price-cutters?" Accordingly, Brandeis urged lawmakers to permit and enforce anticompetitive price agreements among members of trade associations composed of small dealers. National, state and local associations "have gone on record, demanding that this illegitimate competition be put to an end....Big business is not more efficient than little business," he concluded.[59] "Regulation is essential to the preservation and development of [fair] competition, just as it is necessary to the preservation and best development of liberty."[60]

The growing consensus favoring regulated competition gradually overshadowed the Brandeisian conviction that bigness was, *per se,* bad. By the

1912 Presidential election, Wilson, though campaigning with Brandeisian rhetoric against Roosevelt, never accepted Brandeis's absolute condemnation of giant corporations. Essentially, both Wilson and Roosevelt reflected growing popular opinion which wanted the benefits gained from large-scale enterprise but also hoped to avoid its abuses.[61] As a Kansas newspaper observed in 1913: "The question is becoming more and more important daily whether regulation and supervision of big corporations by the government will produce better results for the entire country than fruitless efforts at dissolution." Such comments suggested that Americans were distinguishing between "good" and "bad" corporations. Many, to be sure, steadfastly opposed the distinction, as did the Kansan who observed that "As well might you refer to a 'Good' burglar! Every combination was 'conceived in sin and born in inequity.' " But by Wilson's election this view was clearly on the decline.[62]

The growing willingness to make a moral distinction between large corporations did not mean Americans were rejecting the ideal of the small businessman. Although Wilson declined to accept the Brandeisian "curse-of-bigness" idea during his first presidential campaign, he nonetheless resolutely defended small enterprise because he believed that, generally, big and small business could coexist as long as the one did not use its power unfairly against the other. Moreover, it was not "unfair" for a corporation to displace the small dealer because of superior organizational or productive efficiency.[63] On this, Wilson and Roosevelt, Olney, the Supreme Court in cases like *Trans-Missouri Freight Association,* and probably a majority of Americans, agreed. Evil occurred when the corporation used illegal tactics or devices. Thus, the chief criteria for determining whether the corporation was good or bad became conduct, and the emphasis upon conduct led to viewing competition in moral terms. Brandeis, then, viewed all competition between corporate giants and the little man as wrong *per se,* but others distinguished between competition based on superior efficiency and that involving evil behavior. Yet in either case the legitimacy of competition depended upon a moral standard.

Popular acceptance of regulated competition reflected the continuing influence of republican values. American voters and their public leaders did not question the sanctity of property and contract rights. But when unrestrained acquisitiveness was permitted to determine the uses to which these rights were put—bringing about abuse and cut-throat competition—they believed that government regulation was essential. Moral accountability enforced by law was needed, therefore, to reestablish the interdependency of private and public interest. James C. McReynolds, Wilson's attorney general and successful nominee for the Supreme Court, suggested the degree to which belief in legally imposed moral restraint held sway. Responding to charges that a stringent dissolution decree he had won in an antitrust case amounted to confiscation, he replied, "Confiscation? What if it is! Since when has property illegally and criminally acquired come to have any rights?"[64]

The influence of republican values encouraged the triumph of the rule of reason. The *Knight Sugar Trust* opinion had construed the Sherman Act narrowly, excluding from its restrictions a holding company formed to achieve economies of production within a single state. The *Trans-Missouri Freight Association* decision had applied the Sherman Act to cartel agreements among parties engaged in interstate trade. These two decisions left unclear the legal status of a holding company whose managerial structure, operation, and business extended beyond a single state. The *Northern Securities* case partially resolved this problem by establishing that a railroad involved in interstate commerce, which had organized as a holding company expressly to avoid competition, was an unreasonable restraint of trade and had, therefore, violated the law.[65] The opinion left open, however, the question whether large mergers formed simply to achieve greater organizational efficiencies in order to engage in business throughout the nation were automatically unlawful.

White attempted to resolve this problem by applying a standard of reasonableness. Both Standard Oil and American Tobacco were holding companies doing business throughout the United States and around the world. Each firm had entered into anticompetitive contracts involving distribution and production, which they defended on grounds of efficiency. In both the *Standard Oil* and *American Tobacco* cases, White relied upon the common law to decide whether these contracts were lawful.[66] The Chief Justice acknowledged that "freedom to contract" was the "rule in English law," and under the Sherman Act "freedom to contract was the essence of freedom from the undue restraint on the right to contract." But what was an *undue* restraint? It was, he said, restraint arising from pernicious conduct or acts leading to the "acquisition" of "every efficient means by which competition could have been asserted," and the "system of marketing...by which the country was divided into districts and the trade in each...was turned over to a designated corporation within the combination and others were excluded."[67] Using this "rule of reason" to interpret the Sherman Act, White held that its phrase " 'restraint of trade' only embraced acts...which operated to the prejudice of the public interests by unduly restricting competition...or which, either because of their inherent nature or effect or because of the evident purpose of the acts...injuriously restrained trade."[68]

This emphasis upon undesirable consequences resulting from pernicious conduct establishes a legal standard permitting considerable flexibility. If the court discovered questionable corporate behavior which produced restrictive results, it was contrary to the public interest and unlawful. Accordingly, in the *Standard Oil* case the Court found that the corporation had engaged in wrongful anticompetitive practices and therefore ordered the firm's dissolution. The American Tobacco Company suffered a similar fate. Yet White's decisions also expressly acknowledged that the law could find other examples of restraining conduct to be reasonable. In such cases, he said, the "words restraint of trade should be given a meaning which would not destroy the individual right to contract and render difficult if not impossible any movement of trade in the channels of interstate commerce—the free movement of which it was the purpose of the [Sherman] statute to protect.[69] With these words White recognized that many contractual agreements, though clearly anticompetitive in their result, nonetheless were entered into solely to achieve desirable economic efficiencies and therefore were lawful. Moral considerations blended with economic, then, to separate reasonable from unreasonable conduct.

Between the Wilson administration and the mid-1920s the impact of the Court's reasonableness standard was ambiguous. In the *U.S. Steel* case of 1920 the Court applied the rule of reason to uphold one of the largest corporations in the world. After examining thoroughly the conduct of the corporation's management, the Court found no evidence of unlawful anticompetitive practices. Of course, the firm's organizational structure, huge capitalization, and control of productive resources created efficiencies which impeded the entry of new companies. But with steel producers already in the business, U.S. Steel competed "fairly." Thus, in the record of the case, Youngstown Sheet & Tube Company, a competitor, asserted that U.S. Steel had engaged in "nothing but the fairest competition in every respect for the last seven or eight years."[70] To the Court this competitive behavior was more important than U.S. Steel's possession of the power to prevent new firms from entering the industry. The Court held, therefore, that as long as there was "no adventitious interference...to either fix or maintain prices" bigness was not in and of itself bad.[71]

At the same time, it became clear that federal rather than state government was better equipped to deal with the corporate giants. Although the states remained active in the antitrust field by successfully prosecuting anticompetitive agreements, this influence was confined primarily within the borders of each state, varying, of course, from state to state.[72] Meanwhile, the Court generally upheld the federal government's prosecution of anticompetitive agreements. Between 1890 and 1914 the Justice Department's antitrust suits rose steadily until they leveled off between 1915 and 1919. In about 80 percent of these cases the federal government won. Significantly, six out of seven of these suits were against cartel agreements among comparatively small enterprises in the furniture, lumber, and apparel, wholesale and retail trades. The government focused on these industries because it was easier to obtain testimony from customers and competitors proving unlawful conduct under the rule of reason. Thus, despite the occasional big case involving corporate giants like Standard Oil or U.S. Steel, the Justice Department devoted most of its energies to breaking up anticompetitive, cartel practices. Although the government's record of success in the cases involving such giants as Standard Oil was mixed, its record of success in the other class of cases clearly favored the sort of competition more characteristic of small-scale enterprise.[73] In one sense, then, on both the state and national level, the goal of antitrust policy to link competition to the public interest prevailed.

The rule of reason also had an ambiguous impact on the administrative enforcement of antitrust. Under the reasonableness standard the Wilson Administration and, later, Secretary of Commerce Herbert Hoover supported the wider use of consent decrees, whereby the government agreed to exempt business from antitrust prosecution in return for promises that it conform its conduct to antitrust policy. In some cases these decrees enabled relatively smaller firms to survive, while permitting corporate giants to achieve improved organizational efficiency.[74] At the same time, the Court applied the reasonableness standard virtually to emasculate the Wilson Administration's Clayton Antitrust Act* and the Federal Trade Commission. The Court construed the Clayton Act, despite its framers' admittedly ambiguous intent, to permit antitrust prosecutions of labor unions.[75] It also interpreted quite narrowly the Federal Trade Commission's powers to define unfair practices.[76]

But the flexibility inherent in the reasonableness standard reached its apex when applied to trade associations. As noted already, Brandeis favored trade associations because they provided comparatively small firms some of the economic efficiencies enjoyed by big corporations, while enabling those firms to remain independent. During the 1920s Hoover won widespread support for these organizations. "Probably the most compelling reason for maintaining proper trade associations," he exclaimed, "lies in the fact that through them small business is given facilities more or less equivalent to those which big business can accommodate for itself."[77] At first the Court restricted the associations on grounds that their activities resulted in price fixing.[78] But by 1925, in the *Maple Flooring Association* decision, the Court found many of their practices to be permissible. The "public interest is served," the Court held, "by the gathering and dissemination, in the widest possible manner, of information with respect to the production and distribution, cost and prices in actual sales, of market commodities." The distribution of "such information tends to stabilize trade and industry, to produce fairer price levels and to avoid the waste which inevitably attends the unintelligent conduct of economic enterprise."[79]

V. Conclusion

By the mid-1920s the Court had established that ambiguous if reasonable

---

*The Clayton Act was passed in 1914 as an amendment to the Sherman Antitrust Act. The Clayton Act prohibits certain practices the effect of which is to lessen competition or tend towards the creation of a monopoly. Prohibited activites include price discrimination, interlocking directorates, exclusive dealing contracts, and mergers (if monopolistic in effect).

legal rules governed the economic liberty of large and small business. The emergence of a consensus favoring regulated competition followed the Court's acceptance of White's rule of reason. Accordingly, from 1911 to 1925 the Justice Department and the administrative process applied this standard to determine the meaning of fair competition. The flexibility of the rule of reason permitted a wide range of results. Bigness triumphed in *U.S. Steel,* small enterprise gained some benefits in the trade association cases, competition prevailed in the Justice Department's cartel prosecutions, business-government cooperation was encouraged through the formulation of consent decrees, and Brandeisian trust-busting won in *Standard Oil.* The Court also undercut workers' rights by applying antitrust laws to labor unions. At the same time, the federal system left considerable power to the states to prosecute local anticompetitive practices.

But above all, the triumph of the rule of reason reflected the ambiguity inherent in republican values. Americans remained committed to private rights, yet they believed it was possible to hold the individual's use of them morally accountable, thereby preserving the public welfare. An abiding faith that these values were compatible led Americans to support the efficiencies associated with big corporations, while they tenaciously maintained the ideal of small enterprise. To be sure, big business was a new phenomenon. The Progressives responded to it, however, by infusing old republican values with a new meaning which blended faith in reasonable moral behavior with the commitment to economic efficiency and increased regulation enforced by enlarged government. Yet these new institutional and intellectual developments engendered tensions between public and private interests which were as old as the Constitution. The preservation of individual liberty and the welfare of society depended in no small degree upon this tension within the constitutional order inherited from the Founding Fathers.

Notes

1. Freyer, *Federalism* in ENCYCLOPEDIA OF AMERICAN POLITICAL HISTORY 546-64 (J. Greene ed. 1984), sets out the general analytical framework employed in this paper. Madison's phrase is quoted at page 549.

2. McCraw, *Rethinking the Trust Question,* in REGULATION IN PERSPECTIVE: HISTORICAL ESSAYS 25-55 (T. McCraw ed. 1981).

3. *Id. See also,* A. CHANDLER, THE VISIBLE HAND: THE MANAGERIAL REVOLUTION IN AMERICAN BUSINESS (1977).

4. Compare, for example, S. PIOTT, THE ANTI-MONOPOLY PERSUASION, POPULAR RESISTANCE TO THE RISE OF BIG BUSINESS IN THE MIDWEST (1985); MCDONALD, NOVUS ORDO SECLORUM, THE INTELLECTUAL ORIGINS OF THE CONSTITUTION (1985), and G. WOOD, THE CREATION OF THE AMERICAN REPUBLIC, 1776-1787 (1969).

5. Laissez-faire ideas are discussed in an enormous literature. *See* for example: McCurdy, *Justice Field and the Jurisprudence of Government-Business Relations: Some Parameters of Laissez-Faire Constitutionalism, 1863-1897,* 61 J. AM. HIST. 970 (1975); Benedict, *Laissez-Faire and Liberty: A Re-Evaluation of the Meaning of Origins of Laissez-Faire Constitutionalism,* 3 LAW AND HIST. REV. 293 (1985). Older works that are also helpful for understanding how certain groups used or rejected these ideas are: T. COCHRAN, RAILROAD LEADERS, 1845-1890: THE BUSINESS-MIND IN ACTION (1953); J. DORFMAN, THE ECONOMIC MIND IN AMERICAN CIVILIZATION, 1865-1918 (1949).

6. THE RESPONSE TO BIG BUSINESS: ANTITRUST IN BRITAIN AND AMERICA, THE 1880s TO THE 1980s (forthcoming).

7. That republican values were a significant factor in the development of antitrust is the burden of this essay. But the best study of the emergence of antitrust, including the evolution of common law principles, the drafting and development of the Sherman Act, and the making of the rule of reason, is: W. LETWIN, LAW AND ECONOMIC POLICY IN AMERICA: THE EVOLUTION OF THE SHERMAN ACT (1981). See also H. THORELLI, THE FEDERAL ANTITRUST POLICY, ORGANIZATION OF AN AMERICAN TRADITION (1955). For an early formulation of "reasonableness" in common law *see* Mitchell v. Reynolds 24 Eng. Rep. 347 (1711).

8. MCDONALD, *supra* note 4 at 14, 224.

9. *Id.,* 261, 264-65, 260-75. *See also,* Freyer, *supra,* note 1, at 546-50; and U.S. CONST. ART. I, § 7, cl.1; § 10, cl.2.

10. This and the following two paragraphs follow closely, Freyer, *supra,* note 1, at 547-49; and MCDONALD, *supra,* note 4 at 274, 279-82, 283, 284.

11. Agrippa, Kenyon, ed. THE ANTIFEDERALISTS 139 (1985).

12. As quoted, in H. STORING, WHAT THE ANTI-FEDERALISTS WERE FOR 21, n. 37 (1981).

13. Agrippa, *supra* note 11, at 142-43.

14. As quoted, STORING *supra* note 12 at 20, n. 35.

15. LETWIN, *supra* note 7 at 18-52, T. FREYER, FORUMS OF ORDER: THE FEDERAL COURTS AND BUSINESS IN AMERICAN HISTORY 1-19, 36-52 (1979).

16. This and the following two paragraphs follow closely Freyer, *supra* note 1 at 546-47, 551-53. *See also,* CHANDLER, *supra* note 3 at 1-146.

17. Material in this and the following paragraph draws upon G. PORTER & H. LIVESAY, MERCHANTS AND MANUFACTURERS: STUDIES IN THE CHANGING STRUCTURE ON NINETEENTH-CENTURY MARKETING (1971). The index was compiled by George F. Warren and Frank A. Pearson. *See* Bureau of the Census, Historical Statistics, 115.

18. William Jennings Bryan, as quoted in Livingston, *The Social Analysis of Economic History and Theory: Conjectures on Late Nineteenth-Century American Development,* 92 AM. HIST. REV. 64, 84 (1987).

19. Freyer, *supra* note 1 at 100, 104, 107; T. MCCRAW, PROPHETS OF REGULATION: CHARLES FRANCIS ADAMS, LOUIS D. BRANDEIS, JAMES M. LANDIS, ALFRED E. KAHN 48-52, 65-68, 98-99 (1985). The limited liability corporation is established by the legislature, though certain provisions governing its operation have roots in the common law. American legislatures established a few such corporations during the late eighteenth century, but they did not become widespread until early in the following century when they became the principal mode for creating banks, transportation companies, and to a lesser extent manufacturing firms. Generally, a cartel is distinguished from other organizational structures by the degree of centralized managerial control, and its ability to enforce its decisions upon the cartel members. In the nineteenth-century United States, various unincorporated businessmen as well as railroad and manufacturing corporations entered into cartel agreements, the primary purpose of which was the regulation of prices. For an incisive analysis of cartel structures and their operation *see* Chandler, *The United States: Seedbed of Managerial Capitalism,* in MANAGERIAL HIERARCHIES: COMPARATIVE PERSPECTIVES ON THE RISE OF THE MODERN INDUSTRIAL ENTERPRISE 9-40 (A. Chandler & H. Daems eds. 1980). At common law, in both the U.S. and U.K., cartel agreements were not enforceable; *see* for example Hilton v. Eckersley (6 Ellis & Blackburn, Q.B. 1855). As Chandler notes, the inability to enforce cartel agreements was a vital factor encouraging firms to merge into tighter corporate structures, thereby establishing the right to enforce contracts at law.

20. *Id.,* MCCRAW, 97-98, 325 n. 23, 326 n. 31, 331 n.38; Freyer, 101.

21. Hannah, *Mergers,* in ENCYCLOPEDIA OF AMERICAN ECONOMIC HISTORY 640-44 (G. Porter ed. 1981).

22. Charles R. Flint, founder of the U.S. Rubber Co., as quoted, Livingston, *supra* note 18 at 85.

23. Jeremiah Jenks, as quoted, *Id.* 84.

24. Hannah, *supra* note 21 at 642-44.

25. As quoted, PIOTT, *supra* note 4 at 31.

26. As quoted, DORFMAN, *supra* note 5 at 42-43.

27. As quoted, FREYER, HARMONY AND DISSONANCE: THE SWIFT AND ERIE CASES IN AMERICAN FEDERALISM 95 (1981).

28. *Id.*

29. As quoted, PIOTT, *supra* note 4 at 42-43.

30. As quoted, Freyer, *supra* note 1 at 95-96.

31. As quoted, PIOTT, *supra* note 4 at 34. For antitrust statutes, when they were passed, and their provisions *see infra,* text discussion and references note 35.

32. As quoted THORELLI, *supra* note 7 at 348 n. 154.

33. John E. Searles, as quoted, Livingston, *supra* note 18 at 86-87.

34. As quoted, DORFMAN, *supra* note 5 at 217, But see THORELLI, *supra* note 7 at 148-49 ns. 158 and 159.

35. Arthur Hadley, as quoted, Livingston, *supra* note 18 at 92.

36. FREYER, *supra* note 15 at 101, 107.

37. McCurdy, *The Knight Sugar Decision of 1895 and the Modernization of American Corporate Law, 1869-1903,* 53 BUS. HIST. REV. 304 (1979).

38. Pratt, *The Petroleum Industry in Transition: Antitrust and the Decline of Monopoly Control in Oil,* 40 J. ECON. HIST. 815 (1980).

39. McCurdy *supra* note 37; also THORELLI, *supra* note 7 at 254-64.

40. THORELLI, *supra* note 7 at 265-72.

41. 28 So. Rep. 669, 670 (Alabama, 1900).

42. *Id.,* 672-73.

43. On the common law *see* LETWIN, *supra* note 7 at 19-52. The phrases from the Sherman Act are taken from Letwin's reproduction of the law, *Appendix,* at 283-84.

44. N. A. LAMOREAUX, THE GREAT MERGER MOVEMENT IN AMERICAN BUSINESS, 1895-1904 159-86 (1985); and *see* references cited *infra* 45.

45. *Id.* McCurdy, *supra* note 37, 304-42; THORELLI, *supra* note 7 at 96-107; LETWIN, *supra* note 7 at 85-181.

46. U.S. v. E.C. Knight Co., 156 U.S. 1 (1895). For discussion see references given *infra* 47.

47. LAMOREAUX, *supra* note 44 at 164-69; LETWIN, *supra* note 7 at 121-22, 161-67; McCurdy, *supra* note 37.

48. In re Debs, 158 U.S. 564 (1895); LETWIN, *supra* note 7 at 123-28, 155-61.

49. U.S. v. Trans-Missouri Freight Association, 166 U.S. 290 (1896); LETWIN, *supra* note 7 at 167-72. Concerning the split between Justices White and Peckham, it seems likely that their disagreement did not reflect a fundamental cleavage between advocates of small unincorporated enterprise versus corporate big business. Rather, they disagreed over how much discretion judges should have in interpreting the Sherman Act. To be sure, the outcome of this issue influenced results in a given case, but neither judge wanted to either weaken small business or undermine the efficiencies gained from large corporations. Each judge wanted a balanced policy, but disagreed over how best to establish that balance.

50. 166 U.S. 290, 322-23.

51. *Id.,* 323, 324. But *see* R. BORK, THE ANTITRUST PARADOX: A POLICY AT WAR WITH ITSELF 25 (1978).

52. Addyston Pipe and Steel Co. v. U.S., 175 U.S. 211 (1899); U.S. v. Joint Traffic Association, 171 U.S. 505 (1898); Hopkins v. U.S., 171 U.S. 578 (1898). For discussion *see* LETWIN, *supra,* note 7 at 172-81.

53. As quoted, LETWIN, *supra* note 7 at 204-5.

54. As quoted, MCCRAW, *supra* note 19 at 112.

55. As quoted, LETWIN, *supra* note 7 at 119.

56. As quoted, *Id.*

57. As quoted, MCCRAW, *supra* note 19 at 109.

58. As quoted, *Id.*, 104.

59. As quoted, *Id.*

60. As quoted, *Id.*, 110.

61. As quoted, *Id.*, 112.

62. As quoted, PIOTT, *supra* note 4 at 146, 148-49.

63. McCraw, *supra* note 19 at 112.

64. As quoted, A BICKEL & B. SCHMIDT, THE JUDICIARY AND RESPONSIBLE GOVERNMENT, 1910-1921, 9 HISTORY OF THE SUPREME COURT 117 (1984).

65. U.S. v. Northern Securities Co., 193 U.S. 197 (1903); LETWIN *supra* note 7 at 182-237. U.S. v. Trans-Missouri Freight Association, 166 U.S. 290 (1896), U.S. v. E.C. Knight Co. 156 U.S. 1 (1895).

66. LETWIN, *supra* note 7 at 253-65.

67. U.S. v. Standard Oil, 221 U.S. 1, 56, 62, 75 (1911).

68. U.S. v. American Tobacco, 221 U.S. 106, 179 (1911).

69. *Id.*

70. As quoted, LAMOREAUX, *supra* note 44 at 176.

71. U.S. v. United States Steel Corp., 251 U.S. 427, 449 (1929). For discussion of barrier to entry *see* LAMOREAUX, *supra* note 44 at 175-77, 180-81.

72. *See* note 38.

73. MCCRAW, *supra* note 19 at 144-47.

74. U.S. v. Aluminum Co. of America (1912), in ANTITRUST CONSENT DECREES, 1906-1966 217 (1968); U.S. v. America Telephone and Telegraph Co. (1914), *id.* at 230; U.S. v. California Associated Raisin Co. (1922), *id.* at 275; U.S. v. General Outdoor Advertising Co., Inc. (1929), *id.* at 335.

75. LETWIN, *supra* note 7 at 275. This outcome resulted because the law's framers were unable to agree upon language which simply denied that the statute applied to labor. Instead, they resorted to ambiguous phraseology which said that the antitrust laws were not to be construed to prohibit labor unions or the lawful conduct thereof. For cases which construed the act's ambiguous language so as to defeat union activity *see:* Duplex Printing Press Co. v. Deering, 254 U.S. 443 (1921); American Steel Foundries v. Tri-City Central Trades Council, 257 U.S. 184 (1921). For a view of the

Clayton Act which differs sharply from Letwin's and that presented here *see:* A. MASON, ORGANIZED LABOR AND THE LAW, 119-31 (1925).

76. Keller, *The Pluralist State: American Economic Regulation in Comparative Perspective, 1900-1930,* in REGULATION IN PERSPECTIVE: HISTORICAL ESSAYS 76-78 (T. McCraw ed. 1981). BICKEL and SCHMIDT, *supra* note 64 at 662-63. The Federal Trade Commission Act of 1914 established a federal agency with power to forbid unfair competitive or deceptive practices; it left to the agency, however, the power to determine what "unfair" meant. Although Brandeis, who had influenced the law's passage, had hoped the commission would use its ambiguous authority to support the practices of small business and defeat those of big business, the Supreme Court, as it had with the Clayton Act, construed the grant of authority quite narrowly. As a result, the Commission was able primarily to research and publish information pertaining to "unfair practices," but lacked the power to actually prevent most such practices. *See* F.T.C. v. Gratz, 253 U.S. 421 (1920).

77. As quoted, Keller, *supra* note 76 at 79.

78. *Id.,* 78-80. *See also* BICKEL and SCHMIDT, *supra* note 64 at 180. *See also* American Column and Lumber Co. v. U.S., 257 U.S. 377 (1921).

79. 268 U.S. 563.

The Jurisprudence—and Mythology—
of Eminent Domain in American Legal History

HARRY N. SCHEIBER

American constitutional history is replete with durable myths. Few have proven so robust as the shibboleths associated with the doctrines of eminent domain, represented in "takings" theory and judicial interpretations of the Fifth Amendment. Scattered through the rhetorical landscape, in the history of our jurisprudence, are those well-known, well-worn phrases "the sacred rights of property," "the sanctity of vested rights," or, in the grandiloquent language of Blackstone, the "inviolable dominion of the property owner against invasion or damage by others."[1]

However we phrase it, "takings" analysis brings us back to the linked notions of sacrosanct property rights and fundamental law embedded time-lessly (as is usually argued) in the Fifth Amendment and, by a process of juridical incorporation, through the Fourteenth Amendment in regard to "life, liberty and property," back to a concept of due process that protects property owners from arbitrary governmental power.[2] In an era when conflicting ideologies have roiled the waters of constitutional and political discourse on matters of economic liberty, it is vital that we understand "takings" doctrine in light of the facts of history. That is, we must distinguish evidence from mere rhetoric—which is too often useful only as a manifestation of myth. The evidence that counts is that relating to how our law actually worked. Property rights, the scope of regulation, the line between the police power and a taking—all these are concepts that have been of importance to doctrine but also to practice, that is, to "law in action."

Today, those who champion the maxims of minimal government intervention—Professor Richard Epstein is a distinguished exemplar—make a wise move when they largely block history out of their analyses of property rights and takings, except to provide exegisis of the writings of Locke and other theorists.[3] The reason that this shrouding of the past is a shrewd maneuver for advocates of an extreme minimalism is a very simple one: the historical facts regarding eminent domain in national and state constitutional law would prove seriously embarrassing.[4] When they *do* pay any sustained attention to history, property-minded advocates of minimalism all too often portray the nineteenth century's constitutional doctrines as having religiously fostered entrepreneurial liberty and given sweeping protection to private rights in property as a matter of fundamental law (and, as a corollary proposition, as having thereby unleashed the private energies that conquered the continent and exploited its resources and produced the world's largest GNP).[5]

The evidence from history does not support such an argument. For one thing, despite the perdurable myths of laissez faire, there was strategic governmental intervention aplenty in nineteenth-century America. Government subsidies, immunities, tariffs, massive public enterprises (such as the state canal systems) involving millions in tax funds for transport and other infrastructure—all were essential elements in the record of that era, no less in the "laissez-faire" Gilded Age than before.[6] For another, judges gave a good deal of sustained attention to producing a theory of "public rights" (trenching seriously on private claims to property), and the law was responsive to the imperatives of that theory in balancing off claims of the public good against constitutional mandates for the protection of private "vested" rights.[7]

In the Constitution and the Bill of Rights—that is, in the "original understanding" of 1787-91—it is to the Fifth Amendment's takings and due process clauses that we must look to find explicit language about property (and, by extension, but only so, ideas about "economic liberty"). It is, therefore, ironic that no part of the historical record is more strikingly inconsistent with our hoary vested rights/laissez-faire myths than the development of eminent domain doctrines in the Republic's early history. There is little in the doctrine that American courts produced so far as eminent domain law is concerned—and also little in the actual record of American governmental practice of the 19th century—that will throw even a flimsy mantle of historical legitimacy over such views as those of Professor Bernard Siegan regarding what he sees as the pervasive concern of the Framers to protect private rights.[8] His foray is, one needs to conclude, one conducted onto thin historical ice which breaks dramatically under him, despite the astonishingly light evidentiary baggage that he chose to carry with him.

For Epstein, the record of eminent domain law, as opposed to its mythology, is probably of potential use as support for proposed constitutional norms only as evidence of how a conceptual or doctrinal muddle can be created when we seek to redistribute advantage or wealth through intervention. This, however, is not the point that he makes; instead, he invokes an ideal, which we are left to assume represents historical practice and not merely a fleeting idea or an eighteenth-century artifact that briefly captured the loyalty or imagination of American legislators. This ideal is prescriptive; it concerns the necessity of "making the property owner whole." It is this ideal, not anything in the actual record of American law in action, that provides Epstein with the standard by which to write off as unconstitutional nearly the entire legislation of the nation since 1933.

I do not mean to say that the legislatures and courts blatantly ignored or invariably trampled on property rights in the early Republic or in the nineteenth century. Undeniably, private rights in property and the ideal of economic liberty held a place of high respect in what may be termed the "legal culture" of the United States. But in counterpoint to vested-rights doctrines in American constitutionalism generally, and in the law of the states in particular, was a competing doctrine: the idea of "rights of the public," a standard by which courts would often validate legislation that expressed communal values and interests. This latter doctrine played a continuous and fascinating part in American property law; and it served as a conceptual bridge that covered issues of legitimacy in police power and taxation as well as eminent domain. It even went so far as to declare certain property a "public trust," beyond the reach of ordinary legislation by the government itself—a concept that Professor Joseph Sax rediscovered in the 1970s, and which he and fellow litigators then persuaded many courts to recognize as good law.[9]

It is difficult enough to read people's thoughts and motives, even for the pollsters dealing with the here-and-now; it is even more parlous to speculate on views that were held by the citizenry a hundred years ago, or at the nation's founding in that perilous terrain in which we regularly search for that Bigfoot of American law: "original intent." But the record of both politics and governmental action, on the one hand, and of doctrinal development in law, on the other, indicates that Americans have been pretty regularly concerned with community values—and with the mobilization of these values for purposes of pursuing what is regarded as being in the public interest, frequently to the detriment of important claims to private rights in property. The courts have sometimes reflected, sometimes led, and doubtless sometimes ignored public preferences as between public rights and private rights.[10] But in a variety of ways, and with varying degrees of faithfulness to what we may surmise (and *only* surmise) was the dominant or majority view, the courts, together with legislators and constitution-writers, have struggled regularly and openly with the problem for two hundred years.[11]

There have been some moments of high confrontation and doctrinal battle in the history of constitutional takings theory: among them were the Charles River Bridge Case; some of the state constitutional conventions that considered corporate privilege and regulation; the post-Civil War movement for economic liberty and equality; the New Deal dramas of political economy and law.[12] Social realities, formal doctrinal theory, and policy goals all have had their parts both in these moments of high confrontation and in the more routinized processes of the legal system since 1787. To deal with the jurisprudence of eminent domain and takings law is to embark, therefore, on an historical journey replete with the perils of seductive doctrinal intricacy. The jurisprudence has contributed to laissez-faire and vested-rights mythology by manufacturing a seductive rhetoric; but it has, also, regularly confounded the mythology in ingenious ways by undermining property claims of private owners under cover of various competing social claims, such as demands for material progress, the imperatives of egalitarian ideals, the quest for entrepreneurial advantage, and other legitimating goals and rationales.

Keeping this complexity in mind, I will deal in this essay with two issues in the history of eminent domain. The first section treats formal jurisprudence as it relates to the concept of economic liberty and the protection of property rights. In the second section I will consider some evidence from the history of eminent domain as a working system of law, a history that involved significant economic redistribution. The focus of the discussion there will be "law in action" rather than "law in books," with a view toward seeing to what degree the mythology of jurisprudence comported with the realities of governmental practice.

I. Property and the Idea of Liberty

Although the phrase "economic liberty" does not appear in the Constitution or its amendments, we are compelled by logic and intuition to acknowledge that it must have a place somewhere in the pantheon of constitutional ideals. Certainly it deserves such a place, as well as the concepts we term "privacy" or "individual dignity," both of which are today generally acknowledged as embedded in the document although the words are nowhere used in the Constitution.[13] But precisely how the concept of economic liberty connects with the document is a difficult matter. If even the contracts clause, with its explicit language, has given jurists such trouble for two centuries in the narrower task of defining the constitutional dimensions of "economic rights," it is no wonder that the work of correctly reading the meaning of economic liberty is so vexing an undertaking.

It is not my task here to spell out a full theory of economic liberty in American constitutional jurisprudence—a highly immodest undertaking that I have ventured elsewhere.[14] Indisputably, the starting point for any discussion of economic liberty must be in the Fifth Amendment—in which all these issues come to a focus—with its provisions that "no person shall . . . be deprived of life, liberty, or property, without due process of law; nor shall private property be taken for public use, without just compensation." (The former provision is referred to as the due process clause and the latter as the takings or eminent domain clause.)

Customarily this language in the Fifth Amendment is read in terms of the individual's right against the government. (As the Marshall Court affirmed in 1833, it was a right against the national government only; later, however, the Supreme Court would interpret the Fourteenth Amendment as incorporating and applying the Fifth Amendment to the states as well.[15]) That is, we tend to consider the issue in the context of economic liberty in the Lockean sense—in terms of economic individualism—in the sturdy tradition of English common law and its accommodation in the thought of American jurists such as Justice Paterson. In 1795, Paterson declared "the preservation of property . . . a primary object of the social compact."[16] Scholars long tended to seek, and to stress in the historical record, the evolution of doctrines that elaborated the "compensation" and "public use" requirements. Thus, in the conventional view—the interpretation long standard in our historical and legal literature—students of constitutional law interpreted that doctrinal evolution as evidence of how American law worked in the large to leave the private owner "with virtually uncontrolled dominion over the use and disposition of [his or her] property."[17] Widely accepted was Professor Corwin's view that the defense of vested property rights by postbellum courts was "the basic doctrine" of American constitutional law, with deep roots in the pre-Civil War's jurisprudential ground. Other learned commentators declared that property in America had become largely a "bundle" of private rights and liberties that far outweighed the importance of any residual "obligations" that formally remained part of that legal package.[18]

The scholarship of Willard Hurst and others, however, has broken new ground by showing how, in American property law generally, the legal system favored "dynamic" over "static" property interests. Eminent domain law's history is part of that record, and the ways in which eminent domain doctrines were developed and interpreted to clear the channels of enterprise, encourage new technologies, and allocate priorities among competing economic interests is a story once startling but now well accepted.[19]

From this newer scholarship comes not only a different perspective on the uses and impact of eminent domain, or its meaning in the full context of property law, but also a rather different slant on jurisprudential foundations. Instead of a quest to find the meaning of takings limitations in the matrix of the Constitution's economic-liberty values—still a worthy and relevant academic enterprise—we are alerted by the record, as we now understand it, to see the matrix of state powers, public rights doctrine, and positive government as equally relevant and important.[20]

The doctrines of American property law, including eminent domain law, are thus in large measure dualistic. They express the values of economic individualism and private ownership, with its allied precepts of reasonable expectations and quiet possession, but they are something more. These doctrines also embody notions of the sovereignty of the state and its legitimate reach. While governmental power is mobilized and constrained in our constitutional system, for the protection of private owners' "dominion" over their property, it is also mobilized in the name of rights of the public—the notion of *salus populi,* what we moderns usually term "the public interest." Insofar as property law, and especially eminent domain law, has served societal values and interests in a positive way, it is oriented against private interest and individualism. This raises the intriguing question: should we similarly view *economic liberty,* as a constitutional value, as being a dualistic concept, a concept reflecting the two faces of property law and eminent domain—one face expressive of economic individualism, the other of community values? Is economic liberty not also an ideal that can be understood as applying to the community as a whole, one that can be legitimately pursued and defended through laws that take prosperity of the whole society, rather than the narrow liberties of private owners, as the lodestone of constitutional validation?[21]

The natural law and civil law theorists, most notably Vattel and Grotius, had postulated that government's power to seize property was an inherent attribute of sovereignty.[22] In the early Republic, even the most property-minded, conservative Federalist jurists—the High Tories of jurisprudence in that day—recognized that the eminent domain power was a "despotic power . . . (that) exists in every government," for, as Justice Paterson admitted, "government could not subsist without it."[23] This reminder that individualistic, property-rights values, though deeply rooted in American constitutional doctrine, did not occupy the whole ground, is underscored by consideration of the early state cases.

Epstein has made much of the proposition that the takings clause was meant to protect property rights as they stood in the late eighteenth century— that is, as a bundle of rights that included the guarantees of prevailing common law as of 1787. But in the early cases, we find that the common law cited in relation to property rights was often the law of public rights, especially the notion of property *juris publici,* or the related idea of property private in ownership but public in purpose (such as rivers and streams under a navigational servitude, and inns and taverns or bridges and ferries as property "affected with a public interest").[24]

Operating from a doctrinal base in the common law that made ample room for public rights, many courts upheld important regulatory actions of the state legislatures which derogated private rights and which significantly damaged private firms and holdings.[25] In this light, common law and the postulates of the Continental lawyers converged. Thus, on matters "in which the whole community is interested," courts would validate significant trenching on private rights. The South Carolina court quoted Vattel as authority in one of the extreme cases of this sort from the early period:

> Every thing in the political society ought to turn to the good of the community, and if even the citizen's person is subject to this rule, their fortunes cannot be excepted. The State cannot subsist, or constantly administer public affairs in the most advantageous manner, if it has not the power of disposing, on occasion, of all kinds of goods, subject to its authority.[26]

The basic common law doctrine, Justice Colcock declared in this case, was that "the very act of civil or political association [means] that each citizen subjects himself to the authority of the entire body, in every thing that relates to the common welfare."[27] The tone of the rhetoric and the substance of the doctrine as it came down in such cases did not exclude strict indemnification for takings; but they stand as evidence militating against the highly individualistic reading of how a taking should be defined that some scholars have tried lately to derive from John Locke and other eighteenth-century theorists.[28]

Moreover, some of the early state decisions placed a heavy burden on property owners in locations where public improvements might be necessary. Owners were barred from making claims against the state, for example, by a Massachusetts high court ruling of 1832 that spoke in terms ironically reminiscent of earlier phrases about building "a City upon a Hill"—for the court there declared that "every one who purchases a lot upon the summit or on the decline of a hill, is presumed to foresee the changes which public necessity or convenience may require." (In this case, the public authorities had ordered a change of street grade that endangered the stability of a hillside building.) Recognizing that a governmental action affecting private rights might make an individual "involuntarily to contribute much more than his proportion to the public convenience," the court found no remedy except the willingness of the legislature voluntarily to provide relief.[29] In some jurisdictions, even where courts recognized an explicit abuse of power in one procedure or another (e.g., method of payment or even the basic requirement of compensation beyond nominal sums), they did not find a constitutional issue.[30]

It is of singular importance to recall that this situation in state law was no secret to John Marshall or to other conservative, property-minded jurists of the early national period. And yet Marshall, writing for the Court in *Barron v. Baltimore* in 1833, declared that the federal Constitution, which on other occasions of great moment he would interpret in a strongly nationalist mode, did not protect against the effects of such state actions. The Fifth Amendment did not apply to the states, Marshall declared; issues of takings compensation and inverse condemnation claims were within the jurisdiction of the state legislatures and courts alone.

How the eminent domain power was regarded in the state courts was reflected in the earliest American treatise on eminent domain law, written by J. B. Thayer—his first appearance in print, a prize essay from the "Law School at Cambridge."[31] This study appeared in 1856, at a time when the Massachusetts court had just made its great breakthrough, in *Commonwealth v. Alger,* in providing a reasoned jurisprudential statement of the states' police power— the landmark expression of "public rights" doctrine between the time of the Charles River Bridge Case and postbellum Fourteenth Amendment jurisprudence.[32] In eminent domain law, the state courts had begun much earlier to weave an elaborate tapestry of doctrine, but the law was in vital respects uncertain and confused. How Thayer used his opportunity to provide a treatise on a subject of burning importance, amidst the great spurt of railroad building in the late 1850s, is instructive indeed on the matter of how doctrine was founded, especially as to how he viewed the relationship of eminent domain to individualism and collective values in the law.

Thayer acknowledged the natural-law arguments for the necessity of compensation in takings: the requirement to compensate was founded in "the natural rights of the individual." But he also contended for a conceptually distinguishable source for the states' power to take property; this power rested in the sovereignty of government: it was an "attribute of sovereignty." When exigencies require a taking, according to this view, the sovereign merely does its duty to the community by expropriating property. An obligation to compensate follows "like a shadow," but if this obligation remains unfulfilled, the taking is not thereby invalidated. In the absence of compensation, the individual could not make a claim to have the property back; he would have only a theoretical remedy, "an eternal claim against the State, which can never be blotted out except only by satisfaction; but this claim is for compensation, and not for his former property."[33]

Thayer cited in support of this view—a view that William Stoebuck has termed the "inherent powers" doctrine—the writings of the natural law theorists Vattel, Grotius, Pufendorf, and Bynkershoek.[34] The eminent domain power, as Thayer portrayed it,

> attaches to the State as the right of property attaches to man; it is, so to speak, one of the natural rights of the State. . . . It is not, then, any common or technical doctrine of the law . . . but a sovereign right, coeval with the State itself[,] . . . a right whose sanction lies not in the authority of the State . . . but rather in that which is the source of the authority of the State; to wit, a necessity in the nature of man.[35]

Thayer himself was concerned to establish also, however, the equitable and natural-law limitations of the power; his analysis sought to provide a full rationale for limitations on the discretion of legislatures. His theory reflected the efforts already going forward, both in legal scholarship of the day and in the work of the state courts, which—with varying orientations, and with varying degrees of success—were struggling with the need to produce a full theoretical framework for the takings power and its limits. The Supreme Court, a few years before Thayer wrote, had in the case of *West River Bridge v. Dix* (1848) declared that it was up to the state governments "to protect their citizens from injustice and oppression" when the takings power was used abusively.[36] It left the property holder, as Daniel Webster argued, entirely to the states' mercy: the legislatures now exercised "unlimited despotisms over the private citizens."[37]

How did the state courts respond? The burden of the state courts' record, in the antebellum years and until the adoption of the Fourteenth Amendment, may be summarized in a few words: they interpreted "compensation" and "public use" as limitations on the eminent domain power. Some of them applied the Fifth Amendment specifically or else as a general limitation based on natural law. More generally, requirements of "due process" were incorporated into both eminent domain jurisprudence and emerging notions of inverse condemnation—the latter being the claim by a property owner adversely affected by a government's use of the police power that a taking has in fact occurred and that compensation is owed.[38]

And yet, while the state courts elaborated a theory of eminent domain that was protective of individual rights as an abstract matter, the practical consequences and meaning ran in a different direction from the emerging theory. In reality, the courts interpreted "public use" as a matter that would be left to legislative discretion. No less important, they interpreted "just compensation" in ways that made compensable mainly or exclusively physical takings. In many jurisdictions they permitted the offsetting of estimated benefits to a property owners' holdings not taken, so as to eliminate altogether any money payments in a great many cases—indeed, in cases probably involving very significant proportions of overall expropriation values.[39]

In sum, we know from the formal doctrines of the appellate courts, supported by the summaries of trial facts in their reports and in arguments of counsel, that the actual practice in eminent domain law was in stunning contrast to theory. As actually applied, eminent domain law supported enormous discretion in the legislature and strong state action—justified by doctrines of sovereignty and of "public rights"—usually with serious adverse effects upon claims of vested private property rights.[40]

Recently, a distinguished federal judge, James Oakes, remarked that when the Hughes Court in the 1930s adopted its famous "double standard," in accord with the doctrine of preferred rights expressed in the *Carolene* footnote,[41] the justices put traditional American property rights into a "dust-bin."[42] It seems more accurate to say, however, when we appraise the Court's renunciation of substantive economic due process in the 1930s, that the constitutional "dust-bin" was already nearly full to the brim with the artifacts of property claims which had fallen victim to eminent domain doctrines in prior eras of American legal history.

Even after adoption of the Fourteenth Amendment, moreover, neither the Supreme Court nor the state judiciaries renounced wholesale the broad interpretations of doctrines on what was "public use," what was compensable, and what was "justice" in the procedures and substance of compensation. There is far more continuity than discontinuity in eminent domain law, so far as these elements of formal doctrine and judicial interpretation are concerned.[43]

II. Administrative Perspectives and Political Contention

To recapture the wholeness and to test the mythology of eminent domain requires attention not only to grand constitutional phrases and the meanings immediately apparent in doctrinal formulations, but also to some of the more mundane administrative realities of eminent domain—of law in action, rather than law in books. It seems incontestable that these realities probably varied greatly from state to state as well as over time.

Tony Freyer has correctly warned of the narrow empirical basis on which we are operating. Little has been written on eminent domain, as Freyer points out, except on the basis of evidence from appellate reports; the small exceptions are writings by a few historians (myself included) which rely on constitutional convention debates and related newspaper and pamphlet materials, and of course Freyer's own more exhaustive exploration of business records and political sources for the Mid-Atlantic states.[44] Until thorough studies are attempted for other areas and time periods, we will not know whether American corporations were under great pressure—when governments devolved upon them the right to condemn property under the eminent domain power—to give in to the "utility. . . if not necessity, of conciliating neighborhood sentiment" by generously compensating property owners in eminent domain takings.[45] Or perhaps, instead, takings commonly were done, either by government itself or by corporate condemnors, in heavy-handed ways that left the property owner with compensation that no one would term fair or "just."[46] The truth is we simply do not have enough evidence as yet to say.

Glimpses of how entrepreneurs in the antebellum era viewed the travails of the takings process may occasionally be found in published railroad reports. Archival records are difficult to find, however, and generally they consist of dreary dockets and minutes from which it is hard to squeeze any important meaning. Even when condemnation judgments and prices are fully recorded, one confronts the problem that comparisons must be made with available records of market prices for land or other property.[47] In Massachusetts, the Western Railroad reported in a sarcastic vein to its stockholders in 1838 on how difficult it was to deal with landholders in laying out the right of way and negotiating takings of property. Once agents had ascertained the location of the line and the list of property owners, the company's land acquisitions agent reported, "The first attempts to negotiate generally prove[d] abortive."[48] What ensued, according to this report, was trying indeed to the patience of the busy railroad executive:

> Land owners, for the most part, are unwilling that their farms or lots should be cut up, and it generally so happens that the road, in their estimation, crosses their land just where they are the most unwilling to part with it. It is a new subject to them; they are not prepared to act then; they want a little time to consider it—to see how they are to be affected by the road, or to ascertain what damages their neighbor obtains.
>
> Their tale of grievances must be listened to: the descent of the property, the productiveness of the soil, the richness of the corporation, the arbitrary character of the law by which the Corporation are authorized to take the land

of the citizen without his consent. . . . Visit after visit must be made before negotiations can be closed.[49]

Interestingly, however, the Western Railroad agent found patience and forbearance "to be preferred on the ground of economy, to the calling out of the Commissioners," who would act as officers of the court in determining the land values and judgments.[50]

A report such as this one reveals that the negotiations involved some noteworthy transaction costs for the company; that the company clearly preferred dealing with private owners to turning matters over to the officers of local government; and that the railroad's agent found some owners "reasonable" and willing to deal at once, while others were "more unreasonable and [would] not agree at all."[51] It is difficult, however, to ascertain whether the company was paying market prices for the lands that it took, or whether, as seems more likely, it was enjoying—so long as it kept the commissioners out of the process—an effective below-market subsidy in its acquisition of many parcels. If, as Freyer reports for a Pennsylvania episode in takings, "numerous" landowners attempted to "extract every possible penny,"[52] we know with certainty that in other instances individual landowners made generous gifts of property for rights of way. Doubtless most such donors wanted canal or railroad lines to serve them close-by, a perceived selfish advantage; but old-fashioned public-spiritedness cannot be ruled out as a motive, especially in light of the way that local taxpayers voted in referenda for applying public revenue to the subsidy of public works during the course of the Transportation Revolution.[53]

In New Jersey, as in some other states, there was no compensation paid in most cases for takings of property to build public highways and roads. When a constitutional convention was called in 1843, the delegates debated the equitability of this practice; but they concluded by making no change in this element of their state law, instead continuing to leave it to the discretion of the legislature whether or not to provide for any compensation in takings for roads.[54]

The New Jersey debate took a different course, however, on the matter of what the state constitution should say with respect to chartered companies, when the legislature had devolved the eminent domain power upon them. The courts of the state had upheld such devolutions as within the ambit of "public use"; and the convention agreed upon constitutional language that by this time had become standard in many states: "Private property shall not be taken for public use, without just compensation. . . ."[55] This did not close out the issue: further argument turned on whether such companies should be permitted to build on the property they had condemned prior to actually making payment of compensation to the owners. Delegates cited numerous instances in which corporations had gone bankrupt before landowners had been paid for takings, either because the company had purposefully stalled or because a disputed compensation offer had become subject to lengthy legal proceedings. One strong faction in the convention demanded a new rule that would have required payment prior to actual seizure, so that a company could not "compel a man to part with his land, and get for it promises, or a line which is worth nothing, or a right of action [which would be] no equivalent at all."[56] Against this proposal were arrayed arguments that all progress would be halted—that a single owner could delay "important or necessary works."[57] The pragmatic view prevailed, and no prior payment requirement was written into the new constitution. That the law in action had previously worked so as to deny payments to owners who suffered from takings—the cases of the Delaware & Jobstown Railroad, the Somerville Road project, and the Trenton Water project were specifically cited[58]—and that the convention decided to perpetuate a system that had left citizens without recourse except at the legislature's mercy, is as important for us to recognize as the formal legal and constitutional terms of the discussion.

Debate on eminent domain issues in the New York constitutional convention of 1867-68 offers another intriguing, if fragmentary, glimpse of mundane administrative realities and their impact on the structure of rights and advantages. There was a move in the convention to require that local juries be impaneled to determine damages in railroad takings cases, in lieu of relying—as New York had done since 1846—upon court appointment of what were called "class commissions" to make the assessments.[59] These commissions, critics charged, were generally entirely pro-railroad, even "appointed under the dictation of the corporation."[60] The Rensselaer County representative declared, in this vein, that it was "wrong to go to a foreign county to bring in commissioners, and . . . in truth they are class men, they are men whose sympathies are expected to be with the corporation. . . ," appointed by a judge who may sit with "passes in his pocket from railroads which ask for the commissioners." The property owners who suffered were without power to challenge any judge or appointee on grounds of bias or conflict of interest. "The whole matter is left to the caprice of the judge," as one delegate complained, and no one could recall a single case in which a judge had increased any damage award set by commissioners so appointed.[61]

Opponents of the reform responded with the argument that it would become "impossible to make a public improvement," as any local jury would tend to be comprised of "fellow-sufferers with the party whose property is to be taken," and that the costs of not only railroad investments but also public streets and parks would be vastly increased.[62] Interestingly enough, however, there was also testimony that in the laying out of local public roads, juries had been used with the result that "fraud and unfairness" prevailed in many of those juries' judgments.[63] Apparently, the zeal of the local jurors to treat their neighbors well was not seen as an unmitigated public good: the effort to require local juries in eminent domain proceedings failed to gain a majority in the convention.[64]

In addition to such evidence from reported judicial cases and debates of eminent domain law in legislatures and constitutional conventions, we also can occasionally find commentary by informed observers. One such report is a book by Edward Watkin, a British railroad engineer. In *A Trip to the United States and Canada* (1851), Watkin reported on his investigation of comparative construction costs of U.S. and British railroads: the British promoters of railways, in his view, typically paid four to five times the market value of property purchased for rights of way. "In the United States, on the contrary," he wrote, "much of the land taken has cost the companies absolutely nothing."[65] Like the difference in requirements for construction materials and design of bridges, Watkin stated, the advantage enjoyed by the American promoter bespoke "the different spirit and temper in which the railways were . . . treated by the Legislature and the public, in the two countries."[66]

For Ohio, for New York before 1846, and for other jurisdictions, we have testimony that courts and assessors routinely would apply "offsetting" rules so as to find that "the increased value of the land [remaining] was more than any possible injury that could result to it," hence permitting railroads and the public canal agencies to take land without monetary compensation. This was a significant expression of the legislative and public attitudes on which Watkin remarked.[67]

Foreign observers in the early railroad period also found remarkable the way in which municipal authorities permitted railroads to build their lines "through populous streets of the largest cities, as of New York, Philadelphia, Baltimore, etc.," so as to facilitate delivery and exchange of goods and avoid "waste of time, . . . expensive transshipment of the goods" and other inconvenience and expense.[68] Little wonder that some intense public campaigns against the railroads' eminent domain powers made an issue of takings and railroad operations on the streets of major cities and not only in the agricultural districts of the countryside.[69] As Freyer's study reminds us, there were riots and numerous episodes of violent individual behavior in the Mid-Atlantic states, especially New Jersey, when railroad rights-of-way decisions or operations within town limits agitated the local citizenry.[70]

A particularly dramatic instance of popular revulsion against eminent domain came in New Hampshire in 1840, when what railroad leaders termed an era of "extortion" was inaugurated with a law that denied newly chartered railroads the power to employ the eminent domain power at all. Until repeal in 1844, the ban—which coincided in time, of course, with a serious depression that itself might have had the same effect—was said to have dampened or killed investor interest in new charters or construction. (There is, of course, the irony that once the depression ended, the law was repealed.)[71] More generally, quarrels over eminent domain issues—especially notorious delays in the railroad companies' payments on judgments or deeds of land—became a contributing factor in the enactment of general railroad statutes and in the establishment of New Hamphire's railroad commission, the second in New England.[72] Four decades later, echoes of similar controversies over similar abuses by railroads were heard in the 1879 California constitutional convention. A provision was adopted, after angry debate, requiring that "no right of way shall be appropriated to the use of any corporation other than municipal until full compensation therefore be first made in money, . . . irrespective of any benefit from any improvement proposed by such corporation."[73] Thus ended thirty years of takings in California in which courts had consistently applied the "offset" doctrine to authorize railroad takings without payment.[74]

In New York State, near the century's close, the issue of class commissioners to assess damages in takings resurfaced as a matter of lively debate. Some delegates to the 1894 convention for constitutional revision testified that the judges had routinely appointed "good commissioners, ...good, fair, competent men." Nonetheless, there were strong demands that the constitution should provide for juries to be appointed on petition by any injured landowners in railroad takings cases.[75] The debate that followed serves as a vivid reminder to us that labeling the winners and losers in regard to the actual impact of eminent domain law is no easy matter. This reminder militates against the arguments advanced by Morton Horwitz and others, arguments which I think are deeply flawed, that takings law consistently disadvantaged the poor and the dispossessed, always giving the advantage to the agents of industrialization.[76]

Thus, in the New York debate, one faction charged that the move to require juries was inspired by the railroad companies, especially the New York elevated railway corporations. Requiring juries, these critics charged, would be simply a means of "delaying and retarding litigation," always to the corporation's advantage against small property holders; and generally in urban centers the juries would be composed of citizens *not* resident directly along the line of the elevated railroad sytem, "believing it to be a great public benefit, and, therefore, . . . disposed to give rather small verdicts."[77] Here is grist aplenty for the mills of the public choice theorists!

Other delegates expressed a very different version of the realities of eminent domain in action. They rested their arguments on a strong populistic view that juries were the last resort of the small property owner against the arrogant "impositions and exactions of corporations" whose "hidden and sneaky methods" were responsible for many outrages in land condemnation awards.[78] One upstate New York delegate, however, denounced the jury requirement as "an absolutely socialistic proposition," suggesting that if New York City's judges and municipal officers were of such character as to merit checks by juries the solution was to cut New York "away from its moorings and carry it out into the Atlantic Ocean to be swept away by the winds and waves to be destroyed, as it ought to be, utterly and completely."[79]

Eminent domain was also discussed in the convention in relation to agricultural drainage projects. An amendment proposed for the benefit of "the earnest and progressive farmers" passed on a 63-43 vote, permitting devolution of the eminent domain power to farmers who needed drainage rights of way across neighboring lands. ("Progressive farmers," it should be noted, is a euphemism for highly capitalized operators, just as "self-subsistent farming" is a euphemism for rural poverty. Lest the reader leap to the conclusion that here is evidence that the elite had successfully manipulated the law so as to favor the "haves" over the "have-nots," it should be noted that the state Supreme Court promptly found this new takings power for drainage projects to be unconstitutional!)[80]

As had happened in New York's 1867 convention, the jury reform proposal as applied to railroad takings lost, this time by a close 70-67 vote—and there was no vote on cutting New York loose from its moorings. The convention, interestingly enough, also defeated a rider to the agricultural drainage provision that would have required jury determinations of damages in such cases; perhaps the capitalist farmers with the funds to undertake drainage projects shared an interest with some railroad promoters in keeping the damages process intact.[81] The nature of the debate—even discounting rhetorical excess of a lesser character than heard from the exponent of draconian measures for the City—suggests the accuracy of Tony Freyer's analysis. In his study of other Atlantic Coast states half a century earlier, he concluded that there were complex political cleavages rooted in regionalism, in functional differentiation (including intra-class entrepreneurial conflicts) of economic interests, and perhaps in ideological loyalties. "Pervasive social and political fragmentation," even atomization, is easier to read from this confusing record of constitutional debate than any simplied picture of "just how much of a benefit eminent-domain law was to transportation corporations, and who gained and who lost in the process."[82]

What is strikingly absent from the administrative record, however, is the property-minded law of eminent domain's mythology, let alone historical validation of what minimalists would prescribe as constitutional policy today. The law was rich in complexity and diverse in its effects. It was seen differently at different times, by a variety of interests in different jurisdictions. We find, therefore, no historical monolith that bespeaks a single-minded devotion to the sacred rights of private property.

Conclusion

The history of our eminent domain law has been one of tension between economic individualism and community values. The latter element of the duality—legal doctrines that were rooted in community values—was linked by iron juridical bonds to a powerful theory of the sovereign and its legitimate bounds of discretion. Like property law more generally, eminent domain law reflected a process of interplay among competing doctrines in the constitutional conventions, the legislatures, and the courts; it did not consist of a grand march with a linear theme—comparable to the "status-to-contract" drama of an earlier era. Nor did eminent domain law, either law in the books or law in action, represent a faithful adherence to a dominant doctrine and its progressive elaboration and perfection, whether that doctrine was instrumentalism and pragmatism, or public rights, or vested private rights.

It is indeed astonishing that the significance of the communal values in property law, let alone the specifics of eminent domain's administrative history, largely escapes the attention of some of today's notable analysts of property law.[83] If we want to measure contemporary jurisprudential "takings" doctrine against the values of the past or the historical record of law in action, we need to recognize that our law has been dualistic and has worked in a variety of ways—often bewilderingly so. Historically, American property law has expressed no single orthodoxy of either doctrine or economic preferences.

Notes

1. *See, inter alia,* two articles in the ENCYCLOPEDIA OF THE AMERICAN CONSTITUTION (ed. L. Levy and K. Karst 1986): Sax, *Takings,* and Scheiber, *Eminent Domain.* A general study of doctrine and a critique of modern eminent domain rulings in constitutional adjudication are provided in E. PAUL, PROPERTY RIGHTS AND EMINENT DOMAIN (1987).

2. There is great irony in the fact that historically property rights in this sense became protected by federal constitutional law through incorporation—the process of activist judicial interpretation that self-professed constitutional conservatives led by Attorney General Meese deplore today when it is used to mobilize other aspects of the Bill of Rights' guarantees against state action. (*See, e.g.,* speeches by Meese, Robert Bork, and others, reprinted in THE GREAT DEBATE: INTERPETING OUR CONSTITUTION [The Federalist Society, Occasional Paper No. 2, Washington, 1986]). The case in which incorporation brought the Fifth Amendment into play against the states was *Chicago, Burlington and Quincy Railroad v. Chicago,* 166 U.S. 226 (1897). *See* note 12, *infra.*

3. Reference in the text is to R. EPSTEIN, TAKINGS: PRIVATE PROPERTY AND THE POWER OF EMINENT DOMAIN (1986); *see,* on the matter of how accurately he represents Locke, the critiques in Note, *Richard Epstein on the Foundations of Takings Jurisprudence,* 99 HARV. L. REV. 791 (1986), and J. Balkin, *Learning Nothing and Forgetting Nothing: Richard Epstein and the Takings Clause,* 18 URBAN LAWYER 707 (1986).

4. Epstein does give brief attention to the history of the milldam acts, or at least a few cases (EPSTEIN, *supra* note 3, at 170-75), in order to inquire what went wrong, but compare with the discussion in L. LEVY, LAW OF THE COMMONWEALTH AND CHIEF JUSTICE SHAW 256ff. (1954). Bernard Siegan's work treats legal history in a narrow context as

federal constitutional law, thus offering a fragmented and consequently distorted portrayal of the legal system; and his interpretations of even national constitutional doctrine, however comforting modern-day "libertarians" may find them, are largely spurious, especially on the central issue treated here and in other works (see citations in note 1, *supra*); *see* SIEGAN, ECONOMIC LIBERTIES AND THE CONSTITUTION (1980). Professor Paul takes a different view altogether of Siegan's arguments; *see* PAUL *supra* note 1, at 118ff. et passim.

5. *See*, for example, the argument, a spurious one in my view, set forth in T. ANDERSON & P. HILL, THE BIRTH OF A TRANSFER SOCIETY, esp. at 44-45, 62-64 (1980).

6. Goodrich, *State In, State Out—A Pattern of Development Policy*, 2 JOURNAL OF ECONOMIC ISSUES 365 (1968); Scheiber, *State Law and 'Industrial Policy' In American Development*, 75 CALIF. L. REV. 415 (1987); and Scheiber, *The Impact of Technology on American Legal Development*, TECHNOLOGY, THE ECONOMY, AND SOCIETY (J. Colton and S. Bruchey ed. 1987).

7. I have made the argument for this view in Scheiber, *Public Rights and the Rule of Law in American Legal History*, 72 CALIF. L. REV. 217 (1984).

8. B. SIEGAN, ECONOMIC LIBERTIES AND THE CONSTITUTION (1980).

9. Scheiber, *supra* note 7; Selvin, *The Public Trust Doctrine in American Law and Economic Policy, 1789-1920*, WIS. L. REV. 1403ff. (1980); Sax, *The Public Trust Doctrine in Natural Resource Law: Effective Judicial Intervention*, 68 MICH. L. REV. 473 (1970).

10. An intriguing index of popular preferences—or of manipulable preferences of that segment of the public which has voted in a given election—is the initiative and referendum. At worst, the direct ballot on important issues of priorities, rights, and liberties gives us a check on what historians read from judges' decisions as an index of ideologies. Some surprises inhere in this history; *see, e.g.*, the fascinating episode of a California referendum vote on water rights, discussed in Scheiber, *supra* note 7, at 243-47. Mary Catherine Miller will provide a comprehensive discussion of this California example in a forthcoming article in the PACIFIC HISTORICAL REVIEW. Similar issues will be considered in the forthcoming book by Robert Kelley of the University of California, Santa Barbara, on political culture and regulatory issues in regard to California flood control; I am indebted to Kelley for discussion of this matter.

11. Scheiber, *Economic Liberty and the Constitution* (Seaver Endowed Lecture, 1986, Huntington Library), forthcoming in HUNTINGTON LIBRARY QUARTERLY (1988); *see also* Rose, *Comedy of the Commons: Custom, Commerce, and Inherently Public Property*, 53 U. CHI. L. REV. 711 (1986) and, for a perspective on colonial and nineteenth-century concepts, Vandevelde, *The New Property of the Nineteenth Century* 29 BUFFALO L. REV. 325 (1980). *See also*, Scheiber, *The Road to Munn: Eminent Domain and the Concept of Public Purpose in the State Courts*, 5 PERSPECTIVES IN AMERICAN HISTORY 327 (1971).

12. Charles River Bridge v. Warren Bridge, 11 Peters 420 (1837); H. HYMAN AND W. WIECEK, EQUAL JUSTICE UNDER LAW: CONSTITUTIONAL DEVELOPMENT, 1835-1875 passim (1982); Scheiber, *Economic Liberty, supra* note 11.

13. Even Judge Robert Bork, once so skeptical on the matter, found a niche for these ideas once the prospect of a Supreme Court seat was imminent.

14. Scheiber, *Economic Liberty, supra* note 11. Also, I address a few of these issues in Scheiber, *Original Intent, History, and Doctrine: The Constitution and Economic Liberty,* 78 AM. ECON. A. PAPERS AND PROCEEDINGS 140 (1988). *See also* Professor Robinson's essay in this volume.

15. Barron v. Baltimore (1833); CB&Q Railroad v. Chicago, 166 U.S. 226 (incorporating the Fifth Amendment through the Fourteenth Amendment, as a limitation on the states). *See* H. ABRAHAMS, FREEDOM AND THE COURT: CIVIL RIGHTS AND LIBERTIES IN THE UNITED STATES 33-34 (4th edition 1982); and also, Note, *The Public Use Limitations on Eminent Domain: An Advance Requiem* 56 YALE L. J. 599 (1949).

16. Van Horne's Lessee v. Dorrance, 2 Dall. 304 (1795).

17. B. SCHWARTZ, A COMMENTARY ON THE CONSTITUTION OF THE U.S., PART III: THE RIGHTS OF PROPERTY 231 (1965). Schwartz goes on to say: "So far, in fact, did American law go in this respect that it was characterized as conferring virtually sovereign power in the property owner." (231). See also Rose, *supra* note 11, at 711-16.

18. *See, e.g.,* J. COMMONS, LEGAL FOUNDATIONS OF CAPITALISM 328 (1924, 1959); and, *inter alia,* Scheiber, *Vested Rights,* in ENCYCLOPEDIA OF THE AMERICAN CONSTITUTION *supra* note 1. Corwin's famous formulation was set out in his article, *The Basic Doctrine of American Constitutional Law,* I SELECTED ESSAYS ON CONSTITUTIONAL LAW 101-27 (1938).

19. W. HURST, LAW AND THE CONDITIONS OF FREEDOM IN THE NINETEENTH CENTURY UNITED STATES (1956); Scheiber, *Property Law, Expropriation and Resource Allocation by Government, 1789-1910,* 33 JOURNAL OF ECONOMIC HISTORY 232 (1973) M. HORWITZ, THE TRANFORMATION OF AMERICAN LAW, 1790-1860 (1976); *see also* Scheiber, *Back to 'The Legal Mind'? Doctrinal Analysis and the History of Law,* 5 REVIEWS IN AMERICAN HISTORY 458-63 (1977). A reappraisal of the controversy, with important new evidence, is in Freyer, *Reassessing the Impact of Eminent Domain in Early American Economic Development,* WIS. L. REV. 1263-86 (1981).

20. *See* Zainaldin, *The New Legal History: A Review Essay,* 73 NORTHWESTERN U. L. REV. 202-18 (1973); R. Gordon, *Historicism in Legal Scholarship* 90 YALE L. J. 1017ff. (1981); Hurst, *Old and New Dimensions of Research in United States Legal History,* 23 AMERICAN JOURNAL OF LEGAL HISTORY 1-18 (1979). Also, Presser, *'Legal History' or the History of Law: A Primer on Bringing the Law's Past into the Present,* 35 VAND. L. REV. 849 (1982).

21. *See,* for fuller discussion and documentation, my *Economic Liberty supra* note 11; also, Scheiber, *The Takings Clause and the Fifth Amendment: Original Intent and Significance in American Legal Development,* a lecture at Vanderbilt University, 1987, to appear in a Center for Judicial Studies volume on original intent and the Bill of Rights.

22. For reviews of doctrine, *see* Lenhoff, *Development of the Concept of Eminent Domain,* 42 COLUM. L. REV. 596 (1942); and PAUL, *supra* note 1.

23. Paterson in Van Horne's Lessee v. Dorrance, 2 Dall. 304, 310 (1795).

24. Scheiber, *Road to Munn, supra* note 11, passim.

25. *Id. See esp.* Palmer v. Mulligan, 3 Caines 308 (N.Y. Sup. Ct., 1805); Shaw v. Crawford, 10 Johns. 236 (N.Y. Sup. Ct., 1813).

26. Quoted in Stark v. McGowen, 1 Nott & McC. 387, 392 (S. Carol. 1818).

27. *Id.* at 391, quoting Vattel's maxim, as one of the "fundamental principles of government."

28. *Supra* note 3.

29. Callendar v. Marsh, 1 Pick., 417, 430 (Mass. 1832).

30. *E.g.*, from South Carolina, the state with harshest regime of eminent domain, Partick and Mannigault v. Commissions, 4 McCord 541 (S.C. 1818). But see also Van Schrick v. Canal Co., Spencers Rep. 249 (New Jersey 1843). An important dimension of the doctrine is the definition of "public use" or "public purpose." If a court found there was no public purpose, in most jurisdictions, then there could be no taking at all; it was a prior question, settled at the threshold. But in fact the course of the law in every state left the legislatures with virtually unrestrained discretion. *See* Raleigh and Gaston Railroad v. Davis, 2 Dev. and Batt. 451, 456 (N.C. 1837); Harvey v. Thomas, 10 Watts 63 (Pa. 1840) (permitting takings for privately owned roads not open to the public in mining areas); and, for full discussion, Scheiber, *Road to Munn, supra* note 11 passim.

31. Quotation from editor's note to Thayer, *The Right of Eminent Domain*, n.s. 9 MONTHLY LAW REPORTER 241 (1856).

32. *See* discussion in L. LEVY, THE LAW OF THE COMMONWEALTH AND CHIEF JUSTICE SHAW (1954); *see also,* Scheiber, *supra* note 7, at 221-25.

33. Thayer, *supra* note 31, at 251.

34. *Id.* 241-43, 248-52 et passim. *See also* Lenhoff, *supra* note 22, at 596-97. Reference to Stoebuck is to his article, *A General Theory of Eminent Domain,* 47 WASH. L. REV. 553 (1972).

35. Thayer, *supra* note 31, at 242.

36. West River Bridge v. Dix, 6 How. 507 (1848).

37. Argument of counsel, 6 How. 507 at 520-21.

38. Scheiber, *Road to Munn, supra* note 11, at 360-76.

39. For California, *see* Scheiber and McCurdy, *Eminent Domain and Western Agriculture,* 49 AGRICULTURAL HISTORY 112 (1975); and for New York, Constitutional Convention, 1867-68, PROCEEDINGS, at 3256; for Ohio and other situations, Scheiber, *Property Law, Expropriation, supra* note 19, passim.

40. This argument follows closely from my *The Takings Clause and the Fifth Amendment, supra* note 21.

41. U.S. v. Carolene Products Co., 304 U.S. 144 (1938). The burden of the "preferred freedom" concept in the Carolene opinion was that the Court would give "more searching judicial inquiry" to any legislation that "restricts...political processes" or affects the fate of "discrete and insular minorities" than it would to legislation of other kinds, including economic regulatory legislation.

42. Judge Oakes is quoted from his lecture, *'Property Rights' in Constitutional Analysis Today*, 56 WASH. L. REV. 608 (1981).

43. There is a great paucity of information available on post-Fourteenth Amendment eminent domain law in the states, and I do not seek to recount the history of the last 120 years here. A brief summary dealing with constitutional conventions and appellate decisions was attempted in my *Property Law, Expropriation, supra* note 19; and more was said of the Far West in Scheiber and McCurdy, *supra* note 39. McCurdy treated the issue in national constitutional law in a splendid paper, *The Concept of Confiscation in the Industrial Age: General Theory and Industrial Strategy*, which remains unpublished though often used and cited, as, e.g., in PAUL, *supra* note 1, at 164. Legal historians generally still give their attention mainly to the antebellum era, and very little new material on the post-Civil War era has yet been brought to light. *See also* note 83, *infra*.

44. Freyer, *supra* note 19, at 1263-86. Freyer discusses the evidentiary basis of his own and earlier studies, at 1265-66.

45. Freyer, *id*, at 1273, quoting Letter of Thomas Fernon, president of the N. Penna. Railroad, ca. 1855.

46. As in cases cited in H. SCHEIBER, OHIO CANAL ERA: A CASE STUDY OF GOVERNMENT & THE ECONOMY, 1820-1861, 277-78 (1987).

47. Freyer is effective on this point by comparing voluntary agreements with directed judgments on costs. My only success in my Ohio research, with regard to archival sources, was in locating the records of one appraisal commission for Southwestern Ohio. (Reference is to the O'Brian Papers in the Cincinnati Historical Society, covering appraisals in Miami Canal takings.) These records offer an intriguing glimpse into the dreariness of the work—the slogging through marshes and into woods—that was required of the appraisers, but I could not draw out of them much hard data that bore on the major interpretive issues suggested by the language of statutes and appellate reports.

48. Western Railroad Co., FOURTH ANNUAL REPORT 28 (1828).

49. *Id.* at 29.

50. *Id.*

51. *Id.*

52. Quoted in Freyer, *supra* note 19, at 1275.

53. Documentation of gifts by Ohio landowners is scattered for 1825-31 in the Ohio Canal Commission Records, Ohio State Archives, Columbus. On local public aid

generally, *see also* C. GOODRICH, GOVERNMENT PROMOTION OF AMERICAN CANALS AND RAIL-ROADS, 1800-1890 passim (1960); and Scheiber, *The Transportation Revolution: Urban Dimensions,* in TOWARDS AN URBAN OHIO (J. Wunder ed. 1977).

54. New Jersey, State Constitutional Convention of 1843-44, PROCEEDINGS 414 (Delegate Vroom reported on the theory that "a certain percentage of all lands is reserved for public highways"). In Pennsylvania, the doctrine had held that when provincial lands had been granted originally, the proprietor had "reserved" the right to locate roads on property alienated. *See* M'Clenachan v. Curwin, 3 Yeates 362 (Pa. 1802).

55. New Jersey, *supra* note 54, at 615 (Section 16).

56. *Id.* at 416; *see also id.* at 159-61, 568.

57. *Id.* at 161.

58. *Id.* at 416.

59. New York State, V PROCEEDINGS OF THE CONSTITUTIONAL CONVENTION, 1867-68, 3247-48.

60. *Id.* at 3248.

61. *Id.* at 3251.

62. *Id.* at 3249, 3251.

63. *Id.* at 3253.

64. *Id.* at 3254.

65. WATKING, A TRIP TO THE UNITED STATES AND CANADA IN A SERIES OF LETTERS 121 (1852).

66. *Id.* at 121-22.

67. Scheiber, *Property Law, Expropriation, supra* note 19, passim; New York State, *supra* note 59, at 3256. On Ohio, *see* SCHEIBER, *supra* note 46.

68. Gerstner, *Letters from the U.S.,* new series, 26 JOURNAL OF THE FRANKLIN INSTITUTE 296ff. (1838).

69. EMINENT DOMAIN AND RAIL ROAD CORPORATIONS: SOME THOUGHTS ON THE SUBJECT—BY A FARMER (Philadelphia, 1873); cf. R. CUSHMAN, EXCESS CONDEMNATION (1917) (on how compensation requirements and procedures, as well as public use concepts, continued to be debated as urban land-use policies raised new challenges at the turn of the century).

70. *Freyer, supra* note 19, at 1276-77.

71. E. KIRKLAND, I MEN, CITIES, AND TRANSPORTATION 163-64, 275. (1948).

72. *Id.* at 274-76.

73. California Constitutional Convention, 1879, I DEBATES AND PROCEEDINGS 1024ff., 1189-90 (1880).

74. *See* Scheiber and McCurdy, *supra* note 39, passim.

75. New York State, 1894 Constitutional Convention, REVISED RECORD, 635.

76. Scheiber, *Law and American Agricultural Development,* 52 AGRICULTURAL HISTORY 439 (1978); and *supra* note 7. The "exploitation" view was presented by M. HORWITZ, in THE TRANSFORMATION OF AMERICAN LAW, 1790-1860 esp. at 63, 259-60 (1976).

77. New York State, 1894 REVISED RECORD 627, 651-53. The issue had come before the New York Court of Appeals in *Lynch v. Metropolitan Railroad Company,* 129 N.Y. 274 (1891), when the court rejected the contention that before being permitted to operate its railroad the company should be required to submit to a jury the determination of condemnation money judgments.

78. REVISED RECORD, *supra* note 75, at 631.

79. *Id.* at 647.

80. *Id.* at 847-56, 1050, 1061. The provision was found unconstitutional under the Fifth and Fourteenth Amendments of the Federal Constitution, in Matter of Tuthill, 163 N.Y. 133, 79 Amer. State Rep. 574 (N. Y., 1900). The court declared that such taking of private property for purposes which constituted "essentially a private benefit" amounted to impairment of "the obligation of the social compact" (79 Am. State Rep. at 582).

81. REVISED RECORD, at 849.

82. Freyer, *supra* note 19, at 1285.

83. A full analysis and critique, say, of Epstein's work would also require extensive consideration of the post-Fourteenth Amendment history, something I do not undertake here but on which *see* Scheiber, *Property Law, Expropriation, supra* note 19; McCurdy, *Justice Field and the Jurisprudence of Government-Business Relations, 1863-97,* 61 J. AM. HIST. 970-1005 (1975); Friedman, *The Constitutional Boundaries of Seizure: Pennsylvania Coal Co. v. Mahon,* 4 LAW & HIST. REV. 1 (1986); Sax, *Takings and the Police Power,* 74 YALE L. J. 37 (1964); F. BOSSELMAN et al., THE TAKING ISSUE (1973); Kanner, *Condemnation Blight: How Just is Just Compensation?* 48 NOTRE DAME LAWYER 765 (1973); Van Alstyne, *Just Compensation of Intangible Detriment,* 16 UCLA L. REV. 491 (1969), in addition to more recent writings, especially on the Court's struggle with the taking/police power line, e.g., Oakes, *supra* note 42; PAUL, *supra* note 1; and Sax, *The Decline of Private Property,* 58 WASH. L. REV. 481 (1983).

Republicanism, Railroads, And Nineteenth-Century Midwestern Constitutionalism

ALAN JONES*

Constitutional questions are primarily about power; economic growth as a constitutional question is primarily about power. And power is the unifying theme of the topics of this paper—republicanism as an ideology fearful of power, railroads as the technological and corporate power that transformed the growth of nineteenth-century America, and midwestern constitutionalism as an ambiguous effort to limit power and promote growth. My narrative covers the century from 1787 to 1887 and pays attention to patterns of republicanism in mid-century constitution making in the states of the Old Northwest (Illinois, Indiana, Michigan, Ohio, and Wisconsin) and the adjacent state of Iowa. The topic of railroads is narrowed to illustrations from the history of the Chicago, Burlington, and Quincy Railroad. These states constituted the great growth area of the nineteenth century, and the Burlington, while not atypical, was one of the most exemplary and successful railroads in the West.

The republican ideology that, in 1776, motivated Americans to fight for political liberty against arbitrary power was not so strong either in the Northwest Ordinance of 1787 or at the Constitutional Convention in Philadelphia. The Convention was meeting when the Ordinance was passed by the Congress of the Confederation in New York City. Its passage also coincided with the sale, by the Congress, of millions of acres of the Ohio Country to land speculators in exchange for depreciated government securities. At Philadelphia, Elbridge Gerry might have had this in mind when he noted the change between 1776 and 1787: "At the beginning of the war we possessed more than Roman virtue. It appears to me now the reverse. We have more land and stock jobbers than any place on earth." Roman and classical republican virtue demanded active citizens who understood liberty in political terms, and who were willing to

* I am grateful to Ira Strauber of Grinnell College and to Harry Scheiber of the University of California, Berkeley, for their comments on a first draft of this paper.

sacrifice private interests to the love of one's country and to the public good. Such virtue was present in 1776 in an Americanized republicanism that was oppositionist in style; it was especially marked by jealousy of power, suspicion of corruption, and fear of a British conspiracy to reduce Americans to slavery.[1]

The 1787 Northwest Ordinance was republican in its promise of future self-government and in its demand for liberty, instead of slavery, north of the Ohio River. Republicanism was tempered, however, by the Ordinance's linkage to land jobbers and by the private-interest implications of its declaration that no law should be passed that "shall in any manner interfere with . . . private contracts or engagements." Rufus King, a recent member of Congress who had been interested in western lands, proposed at Philadelphia that the Ordinance's declaration on contracts be added to the Constitution. With little debate, King's proposal emerged as part of Article I, Section 10 of the Constitution, the famous obligation of contracts clause. This clause, with John Marshall's 1819 *Dartmouth College* gloss (that corporate charters were contracts which state legislatures could not impair), would plague midwestern legislators and constitution makers, benefit the Burlington Railroad, and become the popular symbol of midwestern republican dismay with the U.S. Supreme Court. And the land-jobbing context of the Ordinance remained as a precedent for a public land policy that made the settlement of the Midwest a "Great Speculation" and gave land grants to railroads of over 223 million acres.[2]

The citizen-delegates at the Philadelphia Convention presented a model of republican constitution making, although their debates reveal constant ambivalence over classical concepts of republican virtue and the public good. Some of the delegates, particularly Rufus King and Gouverneur Morris, were skeptical of the Northwest Ordinance's republican commitment to the entry of new states on equal terms. King and Morris argued that property, not the public good, was "the great object of government"; fear of a licentious, democratic West led Morris to say that "we must take care that we don't establish a Rule which will enable the poor but numerous inhabitants of the Western country to destroy the Atlantic States." Westerners would not know the "public interest," said Morris, and he added in anti-Jeffersonian language that "the busy haunts of men, not the remote wilderness, was the proper school of political talents." Such comments anticipate a persistent sectional rivalry, a patronizing Eastern attitude toward Western republicans, and an anti-democratic view about who would know the public interest and the public good.[3]

At the Philadelphia Convention and in the *Federalist,* repeated attention was paid to the public good as a constitutional ideal. For Hamilton, passions of ambition and interest must be used to make representatives "subservient to the public good." Before the Convention, Madison questioned whether the republican principle of majority rule was a safe guardian of the "the Public Good and Private Rights." Madison was also skeptical of rulers who would "veil their selfish views under the principle of the public good." He worried in *Federalist* No. 10 that a majority faction "could sacrifice to its ruling passion of interest both the public good and the private rights of citizens." He agreed with Hamilton that "the people might intend the Public Good" but might not always reason right about the means of promoting it. Madison placed some hope in representatives who would possess the virtue to pursue the common good, but such rulers might not always be at the helm to render factions "subservient to the public good." His most explicit sense of the public good was in *Federalist* No. 45:

> It is too early for politicians to presume on our forgetting that the public good, the real welfare of the great body of our people, is the supreme object to be pursued; and that no form of government whatever has any other value than as it may be fitted for the attainment of this object.[4]

The discourse of Madison and Hamilton represents the republican ideal of the public good as a normative constitutional value. Neither saw the public good as the mere aggregate of private goods or private interests. Madison's 1791 break with Hamilton reflects his conviction that Hamilton's means of promoting the public good were anti-republican. Madison and Jefferson were dismayed at Hamilton's acceptance of the British model of 'influence', a funded debt, and a national bank. They objected also to his view of implied powers in the Constitution that, for Madison, perverted "the limited government of the Union into a government of unlimited discretion." Madison contrasted governments "operating by corrupt influence; substituting the motive of private interest in place of public duty with republican governments deriving energy from the will of society." In 1792, Madison moved with Jefferson toward organized citizen opposition to Hamilton's program—creating the First Party System and affirming a more democratic republicanism. This republican ideology, or Jeffersonian persuasion, with its fear of power, monopoly, and corruption, repeated the republicanism of 1776. Committed to the equal rights of individuals—including individual property rights—this ideology offered a normative vision of the public good as distinct from private interest that would remain as a latent ideal in the constitution making of the Old Northwest, an area already caught up in the politics of private interest and growth.[5]

I

The frontier republic of Ohio, the first great state of the Old Northwest, offered early evidence of the impulse to growth. By 1800, twelve years of arbitrary territorial administration by Governor St. Clair culminated in attacks on him as a British tyrant who governed corruptly. St. Clair's opponents posed as defenders of republican liberty against arbitrary power and organized the new state of Ohio. But republican ideology here was less a map of reality than a mask for conflicting personal and economic interests. Early settlers of Ohio were more preoccupied with security, economic growth, and land speculation than with republican values. A case has been made that, in the Northwest in the late eighteenth century, the fear that private interest was a threat to republican virtue and the public good gave way to a belief that private interest could serve the public good if properly channeled. Development of the Northwest, fueling growth that prevented western separatism and created commercial links between the West and the East, was a public good that depended on opportunities for private profit. This was an ambiguous twist to republican ideology, but the stakes were large in the 1780s, and there were those who sensed "that the fulfillment of America's destiny in world history depended on the Union and the Union depended on development."[6]

Development and growth certainly occurred in Ohio after 1800, especially between 1810 and 1820: the population increased 452 percent and Ohio surpassed Massachusetts as the fourth most populous state in the Union. Here, in the best of all possible worlds, public policy promoted growth, growth produced private profit, and private profit served the public good of the Union. The boom period after 1815 was marked by road building which was financed by speculative public land sales under the lax credit terms of the Land Act of 1800; credit was furnished in easy loans from branches of the Bank of the United States. By the fall of 1818, the boom was over. The Bank of the United States set itself up as the scapegoat for the ensuing panic by demanding that its loans be paid in specie. And the Panic of 1819 hit Ohio hard—the first in a cycle of booms, panics, and depressions in the West, a cycle (to use the language of Bruce Ackerman) that regularly disrupted the "normal politics" of private interest and growth and provoked periods of "constitutional politics" in which republican attention to the public good was revived. In Ohio, Jeffersonian republicans attacked speculation, corruption, and the Bank of the United States. In February of 1819, Ohio legislators aimed to punish the Bank by levying a tax of $50,000 on its two branches in the state. The state auditor, Ralph Osborn, collected the tax; the bank appealed to the courts and ultimately to the U.S. Supreme Court.[7]

In 1824, in *Osborn v. The Bank of the U.S.*, Chief Justice Marshall declared the Ohio bank tax unconstitutional, relying on the precedent of *McCulloch v. Maryland.* Marshall characterized the bank somewhat ambiguously as a public corporation engaging in private business, trading with individuals for its own profit, but serving a "public purpose." Another Marshall dictum in the decision can be viewed with skepticism: "Courts are the mere instruments of law and will nothing. . . . Judicial power is never exercised for the purpose of giving effect to the will of the judge; always for the purpose of giving effect . . . to the will of the law."[8]

Osborn was one of a number of decisions (including *Fletcher v. Peck* and *Dartmouth College*) in which Marshall wrote Hamiltonian *will* into the Constitution and transformed political questions into neutral principles of law that protected banks and corporation charters from legislative control. In the mid-1820s, factional differences based on rival presidential candidates and conflicting sectional interests were creating a supposedly nonideological Second Party System in the nation. In Ohio, controversy over *Osborn* helped maintain the ideological differences of the First Party System, with Andrew Jackson inheriting the tradition of Jefferson, and Henry Clay, the bank's lawyer in *Osborn,* appearing as a westernized Hamilton.[9]

Jackson, of course, in his 1832 bank veto message, would contrast older republican values with the collusion of corporate and governmental power manifested by the bank, an example of "the rich and powerful too often bend[ing] the acts of government to their selfish purposes." Radical Jacksonians would repeat republican fears of a conspiratorial "Money Power" in the 1830s, but in Ohio and the West such fears were tempered by a return to the "normal politics" of interest and growth, this time expressed in Henry Clay's "American System" of internal improvements. In the party realignment of the late 1820s and 1830s, politicians who had been moderate National Republicans drifted into Clay's Whig Party, a party committed to state as well as national improvements. Ohio governors had earlier observed the success of New York's Erie Canal; by the completion of the state-owned Erie in 1825, Ohio had surveyed routes for canals and appointed a Canal Commission which recommended that the state build two of them. The commission justified state enterprise with the language of republicanism: projects "crucial to the public interest should not be parceled out to monopolies." A canal law was passed, state bonds were issued, and by 1831 Lake Erie was linked to the Ohio River. Here, the public interest was defined as growth.[10]

There was little argument with the well-managed Ohio canal system by proponents of private enterprise. Canal building on the Ohio scale was beyond the means of private capital and could only be financed by state bonds (and debts), and the system spurred private speculation and growth. Ohio's population continued to increase—160 percent between 1820 and 1840. The only objection to the public–enterprise system came from localities without access to canals. Such localities demanded "equal benefits." An 1837 Loan Act, also known as the "Plunder Act," overcommitted the state to more canals, to loans to private railroads, and to stock purchases in "mixed-enterprise" canal, railroad, and turnpike companies. Preoccupation with growth, especially transportation improvements, diminished republican fears about the public interest, particularly when growth came about through public enterprise.[11]

Alexis de Tocqueville was both bothered and fascinated by Ohio when he stopped there in 1831: "In Ohio everyone has come to make money . . . there is not a *single,* absolutely not a *single* man of leisure, not a *single* speculative mind." Tocqueville soon had a kindred spirit in James Handasyd Perkins, cousin and father of later presidents of the Burlington. James left Boston, business, and the law and came to Cincinnati as a poet, essayist, and "Minister to the Poor." Perkins did not believe republicanism could be easily harmonized with growth and money-making; he wrote of "Dangers to the West" from the "prevalent spirit of money-making." As a "Christian Republican," he complained that the "the state of society in the country is opposed to republicanism . . . because property in the place of knowledge or goodness, is made too much the graduating scale of our democracy." He said that "the intense spirit of gain which fills our money making community is opposed to the highest good of the members of the community, for the essence of it is selfishness." For Perkins, the rich abundance of the West and its potential for growth corrupted republican ideals; growth promoted mere money-making and self-interest. His son Charles, later President of the Burlington, would repudiate the ideas of his father and would make self-interest his virtue and money-making his goal.[12]

James Perkins was out of place in the boom years of Ohio and the West in the mid-1830s. Between 1835 and 1837, thirty-eight million acres of public land were sold, and twenty-nine million of those were acquired for purposes of speculation. In 1836 and 1837 the "Great Speculation" occurred in Indiana, Illinois, and Michigan. These three states exceeded all other states in public land sales and in "Mammouth" programs of internal improvement. State laws provided for canals, railroads, and turnpikes—some state owned, some subsidized. Indiana's system was estimated to cost $13 million and the state immediately issued $10 million in bonds. Illinois, with half the population of Indiana, also borrowed $10 million. Michigan, which in 1830 had only 3 percent of the population of Ohio, authorized a $5 million loan—following the injunction of its 1835 Constitution to promote works of internal improvement. Banks were back in fashion (except among a few hard-money Jacksonians), and they fed the land speculation and bought state bonds, on the eve of the Panic of 1837.[13]

By the early 1840s, Indiana, Illinois, and Michigan were on the verge of state bankruptcy. Ohio barely escaped; New York had to "Stop and Tax" to avoid repudiation. Azariah Flagg, the state comptroller, wrote his brother in Illinois: "I sold two railroads at auction for $16,000; to which the State had loaned its credit to the amount of $515,000. . . . These are some of the results of that system of developing the resources of the state which has made such sad havoc in Illinois." Most railroad projects in the 1830s in the West met a similar fate. In Michigan, the state-owned Central Road was sold in 1846 for $2 million in depreciated state securities to a group of associates of John Murray Forbes of Boston, and Forbes (the cousin of James Perkins) accepted the presidency of the private Michigan Central and began his railroad empire in the West.[14]

II

Azariah Flagg was a New York "Barnburner." He and more radical Jack-sonians, some inspired by the egalitarian republican rhetoric of William Leg-gett of the *New York Evening Post,* initiated a new period of "constitutional politics." Leggett had been extreme in his attacks on special corporate char-ters, exclusive privileges, and internal improvements. He said: "We hope to see the day . . . when the maxim of 'Let Us Alone' will be acknowledged to be better, infinitely better than all this political quackery of ignorant legislators, insti-gated by the grasping monopolizing spirit of rapacious capitalists." Leggett's language matched the mental set of many midwestern and New York Jackson-ians who were fearful of the collusion of legislative and corporate power. He sought general incorporation laws and espoused an equal rights, laissez-faire individualism. Like Jefferson, who in 1788 had recommended "freedom of commerce against monopoly" as one of the articles in a Bill of Rights, Leggett opposed monopoly and special privilege. Individuals should have equal rights under general laws of incorporation. This was a laissez-faire individualism closer to Jeffersonian republicanism than to a Lockean "liberalism" which looked to legislatures and courts to promote growth, protect corporate prop-erty rights, and release entrepreneurial energy. New York's Constitution of 1846 reflected some of Leggett's ideas, but it compromised with the impulse to growth by allowing legislators discretion to grant special charters.[15]

The 1844 Draft Constitution of Iowa was more radical than New York's in its distrust of legislative and corporate power. The Iowa convention, domi-nated by Jacksonian farmers, was determined to avoid the fate of its neighbors to the East, where legislative abuse of power and enthusiasm over growth had led to speculation, special privilege, panic, and depression. The Iowa conven-tion anticipated New York's with limitations that prohibited the state from engaging in internal improvements, loaning the credit of the state to corpora-tions, purchasing stock in corporations, creating a state debt, or granting special charters. More radical were provisions for the unlimited liability of corporate officers or stockholders and the reservation of the right of the legislature to alter and repeal corporate charters. Accused by a Whig delegate of "making a war on corporations," a Jacksonian responded that "the bias of the legislature would be the other way around, in favor of rich monopolies." This remark would be echoed time and again in the series of constitutional conven-tions between 1846 and 1851 in all of the states of the Old Northwest. These conventions revived a period of "constitutional politics" in which activist republicans who feared corruption and collusion placed constitutional limita-tions on legislative power.[16]

Without great debate, convention delegates everywhere reached a con-sensus on prohibitions of state debts and of loans to, or stock purchase in, corporations. Participation in internal improvements was prohibited, and distrust of legislators was clear in provisions that commanded short biennial sessions at little pay. When conventions confronted the continuing desire for growth, however, the results were ambiguous. Each state made compromises. The Draft Constitution of 1844 in Iowa was turned down by voters (chiefly because of a boundary dispute), and the approved 1846 constitution dropped unlimited liability for corporate officers and stockholders and qualified the right to amend or repeal charters. In Wisconsin in 1846, Jacksonian delegates reasserted their fears of the "Money Power." However, they could barely sustain Edward Ryan's demand for a total prohibition of banking—a prohibition that helped defeat the 1846 Constitution and was removed in the approved constitution of 1848. Ryan had migrated from New York, where he was a disciple of William Leggett, and he deplored the "Soft" Democrats who combined with Whigs to oppose his "hard" money policy. He also complained about the weak clauses on corporations—clauses that reflected the desire for growth in the new state.[17]

The debate on banks in Wisconsin, as in other conventions, looked back on old controversies and obscured the emerging power of private railroad corporations. The railroad era of the Midwest was just beginning as the conventions met, and only in the conventions of Ohio, Indiana, and Michigan were railroads explicitly discussed. The issue of railroad development was implicit, however, in the Illinois Convention of 1847. "Soft" Democrats and Whigs interested in growth held a majority. This was evident in the Article on Corporations, which ordered the legislature to "encourage internal improvements by passing liberal laws of incorporation for that purpose." Like New York, the constitution also gave legislators discretion to pass special charters.[18]

Railroads sought special charters, and Illinois legislatures obliged. An example was the effort of the Forbes Group to obtain charters that would enable them to link the Michigan Central to consolidated local lines from Chicago to the Mississippi. After placing directors on the board of the local Central Military Tract road, the group in 1852 directed Chauncey Colton of Galesburg, a local director of the road, to seek a new charter which would allow the connections necessary for a through line. Colton wrote of this meeting with legislators, revealing the type of pressure that railroads could bring on politicians anxious for the growth created by railroads:

> I told the members and the committee that we could not raise money to build a railroad upon the uncertainties of future legislation on the subject of rates; I told them that under the old style of charter we could not build a road, but under the principle of *no future legislation* we could; and that it was a question of road or no road; upon this plain distinct understanding we secured the grant of a charter subject to no legislative control.

Colton got his charter free of legislative control of rates; the Forbes Group took over the CMT, and several years later the group received legislative approval to use the CMT charter to form the consolidated Chicago, Burlington, and Quincy Railroad (CB&Q).[19]

The constitutional and legislative promotion of railroads in Illinois in the 1850s rapidly increased railroad mileage from 111 miles in 1850 to 2,790 miles in 1860 (ranking second only to Ohio). Illinois was the great growth state of the nation in the 1850s, doubling its population from 851,000 to 1,711,000, an increase greater than that of New York's. This increase was principally a result of internal migration—a migration to the small towns and vast prairies of the state. The townspeople of Galesburg and boosters like Colton knew that railroads were economic necessities. As Forbes wrote in 1857:

> The Railway in the Western prairies is the most economical machine ever invented, for it doubles and trebles the value to the farmer of the coarser grains . . . . Since Railways have been made in Illinois, it is far easier to sell land in their neighborhood at $10.00 than it was to sell at $1.25 three years ago.

But local efforts could not get a railway without Eastern capital, and Forbes would furnish capital only if he could consolidate local roads and acquire control. This was Forbes's strategy of growth; he could write in 1857: "Our Western roads are earning tremendously."[20]

"Public good" in the Illinois Constitution of 1848 meant special charters, liberal charters, and economic growth. The Michigan Constitution of 1850 took a different approach, reserving the right to repeal charters and prohibiting special ones. The delegate who pressed for these provisions was John D. Pierce, who condemned the *Dartmouth College* decision: "Those vested rights created by charters must yield when they come into conflict with the supreme law— the public good." Or: "The fathers of Republicanism in this country asserted the right to repeal a charter whenever the public good required it." Pierce was another "Christian Republican," a Congregational minister and former state superintendent of public instruction who had laid the base for Michigan's noted educational system. As a legislator, he won recognition as the author of Michigan's homestead exemption law. His values transcended economic growth, and in the 1840s he had been radicalized by the activities of John Murray Forbes's Michigan Central. A "Railroad War" developed in south-central Michigan when the Central refused to assume the same liability for cattle killed by its trains that the old state-owned road had accepted. Farmers stopped trains, burned bridges, and finally set fire to the Detroit depot. The state government showed little sympathy for this action of "the people out of doors," and brought the alleged arsonists to trial. Pierce attacked the legislature for giving rights to corporations that brought "them into conflict with citizens." His support for the activist farmers continued as the war went on and the Michigan Convention met. There he expressed his animus against legislatures and corporations in Leggett's language: "The spirit of aggregated capital is aggressive. It has no limit, no bounds. Controlling the legislation of the world it has been remorseless in its sway."[21]

Pierce had a radical 1840s consciousness of the state as the ruling committee of the capitalist class, but few delegates were as outspoken as he was at the Michigan Convention. For example, he had to settle for the repeal of charters only when two-thirds of the legislature agreed. The convention did provide for general incorporation laws with no discretion for special charters, but that was not enough. When the legislature tried to pass a general railroad law in 1853, James Joy of the Forbes Groups successfully campaigned against it. This led the young editor and lawyer, Thomas M. Cooley, to lament that "we may as well consider the State for a long time to come as the property of the Central Railroad Company." Cooley, known as a "Progressive Democrat," was also from New York, where he had absorbed the equal rights ideas of William Leggett.[22]

The Ohio Convention of 1850-51 witnessed a clear expression of republican ideology. The Democratic majority contained just enough "Softs" to combine with Whigs to prevent a revolutionary convention, although Charles Reemelin, a radical Democrat from Cincinnati, defined the Convention as, indeed, a revolutionary body. Whigs saw Reemelin as a "red republican" when he sought legislative power to alter and repeal all corporate charters, retrospectively as well as prospectively. Debate on this question continued throughout the convention as Reemelin and others attacked the *Dartmouth College* view of charters as contracts. By very narrow votes, provisions for the retrospective repeal of charters were defeated, although the convention gave the legislature the power to alter and repeal all future charters.[23]

Reemelin's colleague in these battles was Rufus Ranney, a noted Democratic lawyer and later an Ohio supreme court justice. Ranney argued that the right to repeal charters was inherent in the legislature. *Dartmouth College* was an "utter and palpable perversion" of the Framers' intent. "The only true ground . . . is that the legislature shall have no power to grant what it may not resume." Ranney, Reemelin, and other Democrats constantly spoke of the "public good" as a constitutional ideal that should direct the convention's business. Reemelin said that delegates had not met to frame a Constitution "such as would suit men who desire to use the government for their private ends, instead of the public good." He warned of corporations "which under the pretence of the public good have obtained charters and then violated every public interest, only subserving private interest."[24]

The fifteen hundred or more pages of text in the Ohio debates are replete with the language and symbols of republican ideology. Delegates spoke of "the public good" in the rhetoric of republican constitutionalism, different from the legal usage of concepts of "public use" and "public purpose" by state courts that justified grants of the power of eminent domain to corporations for purposes of economic growth. This doctrinal development in state courts, as the legal historians Willard Hurst, Harry Scheiber, and Morton Horwitz have noted, denoted an instrumental use of the law to aid growth. Scheiber has written of the tension between growth and the public good, between entrepreneurial imperatives and public and private rights. Such tension was evident in the debates at the Ohio convention.[25]

The use of the power of eminent domain by railroads to take property or make a right-of-way was conditioned on compensation to the individual property owner whose land was taken. "But," as Ranney complained, "the judiciary have allowed him to be paid in a mere fanciful abstraction—the supposed benefits to the worth to the property he has left." Ranney echoed Leggett in claiming that this was another example of corporations "constantly feasting upon government partiality." When a railroad president opposed a motion that damages to private property should be paid in advance, Reemelin asked "why so carefully conceal under the pretence of fighting for the obtaining of private property from public good, the fact—that they really want it for private speculation."[26]

The convention adopted specific provisions securing compensation for private property taken by the power of eminent domain. But when Whigs tried to extend this compensation to corporations when their charters were repealed, Ranney demurred: *"Public good and public use are different terms."* Property was taken for public use; charters were taken for the public good. Ranney added: "If the exercise of corporate power promotes the public good, continue it; if it does not, take it away." He complained of the *Dartmouth College* rule: "When you come to touch the charter of a corporation, gentlemen would be down upon you with the cry of a contract." Ranney and Reemelin feared the power of corporations and believed that the "public good" as a republican value was more legitimate than a corporate charter. The convention agreed. A Whig motion that said the repeal of a charter should entail compensation failed by a vote of 22-75.[27]

This vote immediately followed a Whig delegate's remark that "the people of Ohio have no sympathy with socialist notions imported from Europe." He asserted that "the rights of property, whether it be that of a corporation or an individual, are sacred in their eyes and will continue to be so regarded. Liberty which did not protect property, would in their opinion become licentiousness and anarchy." But the Ohio Convention made a republican distinction between individual property rights and corporate charters, and did not believe American liberty depended upon the special protection of corporations. As for railroads and growth, the comment of an old Jacksonian delegate, Daniel Robertson, reflected the tone of the debates: "I tell you that it is of more importance in a republican country that the pure equal principles that your

Fathers have sent down to us should be maintained in every possible contingency than whether a Railroad shall connect this town to that town."[28]

The fierce debates at the Ohio Convention were the climax of mid-century midwestern republicanism. Indiana's 1850 Convention was more ambiguous. While republican in their distrust of legislative power and their prohibition of special charters, the delegates were principally interested in railroads that connected towns to towns. A proposal that would have given the legislature power to repeal charters after 1880 if the "public good" required it failed by a vote of 55-63; a railroad director protested that the provision would keep capital out of the state and prevent growth. Schuyler Colfax (a Whig leader in the convention who, as Grant's vice-president, would later acquire notoriety in the Credit Mobilier scandal) said in a debate on bank charters that he did not want to give the people a constitution that had written on it "Hostility to Banks and Corporations."[29]

There was, however, a long debate on taking property for public use under the power of eminent domain. Daniel Kilgore, a railroad director, opposed greater restrictions on the power: "I believe in the old maxim that it is right to take individual property for the public good. The public interest should always be considered as above private interest." A farmer delegate, Alexander Morrison, pointed out the hypocrisy of Kilgore's remarks: "But very few corporations are called into existence for the public good; they are generally formed for the advancement of private interests." And another delegate, Jacob Chapman, asked: "Shall corporate power override personal rights?" Chapman repudiated the idea of giving special privileges "upon the plea of the public good." Reflecting Madison's 1787 fear of rulers who would "veil their selfish views under the principle of the public good," Chapman concluded: "Mr. President, no abuse ever existed under the patronage of any government that was not defended by the same plea."[30]

III

Mid-century constitution making concluded with Ohio's radicalism and Indiana's compromises, including the latter's compromise on banking that allowed the legislature to pass free banking laws, a state banking law, or both. Banking questions diminished after 1850 in the Midwest, although not without a final flurry in Ohio in 1853 and 1854. This came as a reaction to a series of U.S. Supreme Court decisions that declared an 1851 Ohio bank tax law unconstitutional on grounds that it violated the "obligation of contracts." The Ohio supreme court had upheld the tax, Justice Ranney remarking in one case (in which he criticized the *Dartmouth College* decision) that he could not believe "that the great sovereign power of taxation was included in the well known and clearly defined term 'contract.'"[31]

The 1854 Kansas-Nebraska Act raised constitutional questions more basic than bank charters, questions central to republican values. Lincoln's 1854 Peoria address reflected those values when he condemned slavery as a system that forced good men into "criticizing the Declaration of Independence and insisting that there is no right principle of action but *self-interest*." As the sectional crisis deepened, older republican anxieties were revived in fear of a conspiratorial "Slave Power" dominating the national government and the Supreme Court. Lincoln restated the principle of equal rights when he defined liberty at Independence Hall on the way to his inaugural. "It was that which gave promise that in due time the weights should be lifted from the shoulders of all men, and that all should have an equal chance. This is the sentiment in that Declaration of Independence."[32]

More immediate to many midwesterners in the 1850s than the developing sectional crisis was the promise of railroads bringing all things to market. The Midwest in the 1850s was "the great theatre of railroading in the country." Speculative enthusiasm was mixed with economic realism: midwesterners knew that a railroad connection was necessary for survival. Three hundred ninety million dollars of private capital was invested in midwestern roads in the 1850s, as private corporations assumed the task of development. This was not laissez-faire development. The mid-century constitutions prohibited direct state aid to railroads, but roads still sought federal land grants, special charters, tax exemptions, and judicial recognition as "public purposes" deserving the power of eminent domain and subsidies from local governments. These governments levied taxes to issue bonds to railroads in exchange for stock. The railroads then sold the bonds in the East to raise capital. Legislatures and courts encouraged all this, sometimes corruptly—as in 1856, when almost the entire Wisconsin legislature was bribed to secure a federal land grant for the LaCrosse and Milwaukee Railroad. At the same time, the Wisconsin Supreme Court showed little sympathy toward thousands of farmers who had mortgaged their farms to buy bonds in exchange for stock in railroads that never were built or that went bankrupt in the Panic of 1857. The bonds had been sold to third parties in the east who demanded payment. Farmers organized, but legislative efforts to give them relief were nullified by the Wisconsin court's reliance on the *Dartmouth College* rule.[33]

The progress of the Burlington is more instructive as a model of serious railroad development—marked by planned incremental growth connecting local lines into a larger system. In 1852, forty-six leading cititizens of the Mississippi River town of Burlington, Iowa, organized the Burlington and Missouri River Railroad (B&M) and sent a memorial to Congress for a land grant. The B&M organizers looked east to connect with the Illinois road that the Forbes Group was consolidating. That group looked west to the B&M, promised it financial aid, and by July of 1853 had directors on its board. An 1856 federal land grant to Iowa of four million acres for four east-west roads increased the interest of the Forbes Group. They sought a share of the grant, gave more financial support to the B&M, and replaced local directors with eastern investors. The Panic of 1857 hit, and Iowa was in a depression, with southern counties growing skeptical of the B&M as a foreign corporation demanding county tax aid before building the road while holding back its land grant for speculative purposes. Especially resented were James Joy's tactics of demanding depots and right-of-ways, as well as his decision to take counties into court to force them to issue the bonds that voters had approved. Facing Iowa localism and discontent, Forbes sent his young cousin, Charles Elliott Perkins, to Burlington in 1859 to help oversee the B&M; the future of the B&M and the CB&Q would henceforth belong to Perkins.[34]

The Civil War and the closing of river traffic on the Mississippi brought prosperity to the CB&Q in Illinois, and it became one of the most prosperous roads in the country. The B&M did not fare so well, and local suspicion of eastern control continued, not helped by threats to withdraw all eastern money from Iowa if a proposed 1862 Iowa tax law allowing counties to tax railroad property were passed. The law failed, suspicion continued, and the B&M was unsuccessful in its suit to force Wapello County to issue its railroad bonds.[35]

The Iowa Constitution of 1846 prohibited the state from indirectly or directly holding stocks or bonds in a railroad, but a section of the 1851 Code allowed counties to tax for "roads or bridges." A casual Iowa Supreme Court decision in 1853 ruled that railroads were "roads" and that counties could tax themselves to aid railroads. In the 1862 *Wapello County* case, the Iowa Court reversed itself and said that local tax aid was unconstitutional. This was one of a series of complicated cases on local tax aid in Iowa litigated before both state and federal courts; the most notorious was *Gelpcke v. Dubuque.* The City of Dubuque had refused to honor railroad tax bonds, and Gelpcke, an out-of-state bondholder, sued in federal court. On appeal from a district court decision that ruled against Gelpcke on the basis of *Wapello,* Justice Swayne ruled for Gelpcke in an 1864 Supreme Court decision. Swayne disregarded the Court's recent rule that it would follow the latest decisions of a state supreme court on the interpretation of its state constitution. Swayne also implied that a state supreme court could impair the obligation of a contract (although he did not say so). His opinion appears to rest on the moral view that "we shall not immolate truth, justice, and the law, because a State tribunal has erected the altar and decreed the sacrifice." *Gelpcke* has been a mystery to those looking for its constitutional basis. Even Charles Fairman, in his erudite treatment of bondholding cases, could not understand it, although he appears to agree with Justice Miller's dissent, which accused the Court of usurping power. Fairman also appears to accept Miller's view of bond cases as "a farce whose result is invariably the same, namely to give more to those who have already, and to take from those who have little, the little they have."[36]

Iowa farmers and Iowa towns continued to protest tax aid to railroads, the protest approaching violence in southeast Iowa. The issue was similar to that of railroads taking private property for "public use" under the eminent domain power. But now the issue was the taxation of private property for the benefit of railroads under the doctrine of "public purpose." To defeat the state constitutional prohibition of purchasing stock in corporations, the railroad lobby pushed a bill through the legislature in 1868 allowing counties to tax themselves to present their bonds to railroads as a gift. Iowa's chief justice, John Dillon, declared the act unconstitutional, on the principle that taxation must serve a public purpose. Railroads, he said, were private corporations serving private purposes. Dillon's comment on the relation of growth, railroads, and money-making is relevant; railroads "were organized not for the purpose of developing the material prosperity of the state . . . but they are organized solely to make money for their stockholders."[37]

What occurred in Iowa during the 1860s was paralleled in all midwestern states—bond controversies, rate disputes, legislative corruption, and consolidation of local lines into larger systems. The growing regional discontent of farmers and townsmen should be understood as a new period of "constitutional politics" aimed at the concentrated power of railroad corporations. Farmers and merchants might differ in the grievances at issue—farmers protested high rates at noncompeting points, while merchants in once-proud Mississippi River towns like Burlington complained of the loss of trade through rate discrimination, which reduced their communities to local way stations. But farmers and townsmen both felt helpless in the face of arbitrary and monopolistic railroad power.

Wisconsin is a case in point. There, the wartime rise of rates led to a short-lived Anti-Monopoly Revolt in 1865. Like Justice Dillon, Chief Justice Dixon of the Wisconsin Supreme Court ruled in 1870 that tax bonds presented as gifts to railroads were unconstitutional. The U.S. Supreme Court overruled Dixon in 1873; on the same day, the Court upheld a Nebraska law allowing a county (without a popular vote) to issue $150,000 in railroad bonds. The beneficiary here was the Burlington, as it also was the recipient of a 2.5-million-acre federal land grant in Nebraska. Entry into Nebraska was the ambition of Charles Elliott Perkins, who was also instrumental both in consolidating the old B&M with the CB&Q and bringing the CB&Q into the Iowa Pool to avoid rate competition.[38]

In Wisconsin, as in Iowa, the railroad lobby defeated bills for rate regulation in every legislative session between 1864 and 1874. By 1874, Wisconsin's local roads of the 1850s were consolidated into two large systems—the Chicago, Milwaukee, and St. Paul and the Chicago and Northwestern—with interlocking directors. In an 1873 law school address the old Jacksonian, Edward Ryan, said: "Already here, at home, one great corporation has trifled with the sovereign power and insulted the State, and there is great fear that it and its great rival have secretly confederated, to make partition of the state and share its spoils." He warned that the "great enterprises of the country are aggregating vast corporate combinations of unexampled capital, not for economical conquests, but for political power."[39]

Two years earlier in Michigan, Thomas M. Cooley had anticipated Ryan's anxiety in a law school address on "Corporations": "They can make great combinations. Their monopolies are a third source of power. They are able to exercise more influence over the state than both political parties." On the favoritism received by railroads, Cooley said "the class legislation that has been turning over the public domain to railroads was corrupt. . . . The whole thing is illegitimate. . . the whole thing is necessarily corrupting." In other lectures, Cooley deplored unrestrained growth and the national longing to become "immediately rich and great." Cooley was a professor at the law department of the University of Michigan, a justice of that state's supreme court, and the author of the celebrated 1868 *Treatise on the Constitutional Limitations Which Rest Upon The Legislative Power of the States of the American Union*. In the second edition in 1871, Cooley added a footnote on the *Dartmouth College* case that expressed a republican concern over corporate power and corruption:

> It is under protection of the decision in the *Dartmouth College* that the most enormous and threatening powers in the country have been created; some of the great and wealthy corporations having greater influence in the country at large, and upon the legislation of the country, than the states to which they owe their corporate existence.[40]

Cooley had railroad power in mind; railroads exercised great influence in Michigan in the 1860s, particularly on questions of local tax aid. The legislature passed local aid acts only to have them vetoed. An 1867 Constitutional Convention framed clauses allowing local aid, but the constitution was defeated. In 1870, in the noted case of *People v. Salem,* Cooley declared local aid void on the grounds that taxation must be for a public purpose. Tax subsidy to private railroads was "illegitimate," a "violation of that equality of right which is a maxim of state governments." Cooley, like Dixon in Wisconsin, was overruled by that bondholder's friend, the United States Supreme Court. In Michigan, the *Salem* decision helped mobilize a reform movement, led by Democrats who deplored the class legislation that local aid represented. An 1870 constitutional amendment authorizing the payment of railroad bonds failed. However, an amendment authorizing the state to regulate railroad rates passed.[41]

In 1870, Charles Francis Adams Jr., fresh from his exposure of legislative and railroad corruption in *Chapters of Erie,* published a despairing article on "The Railway Problem in 1869." The problem was one of power, and Adams's fears were similar to those of Ryan and Cooley. He wrote of "corrupt systems of legislative manipulation and log-rolling," and argued that "our political system cannot much longer sustain the conflict with corporations. Modern civilization has created a class of powers which are too strong for the control of our governments." The next year Adams wrote a similar article; this time he saw some hope in the western states, Illinois in particular:

> In the remarkable Constitution just adopted there the great principle is for the first time recognized that the railroad system is exceptional among all industrial pursuits, and must be recognized and dealt with as such.[42]

IV

The real principle recognized in the Illinois Constitution of 1870 was that republican governments had to be powerful enough to control the power of railroad corporations. Detailed clauses defined railroads as public highways and specified how they should maintain books, file reports, issue stock, consolidate their lines, and exercise the power of eminent domain. Local tax aid to railroads was prohibited, and the legislature was ordered to pass laws regulating rates and prohibiting rate discrimination. The constitution also attacked legislative corruption. Illinois legislatures in the 1860s were notoriously corrupt and especially flagrant in granting special charters to railroads; the 1867 session was characterized as "the most disgraceful legislative body that ever convened in the state." The 1869 session was probably worse, reviled for a "Tax Grab Act" that allocated state taxes to pay railroad bond debts of local governments and for a "Land Grab Act" that turned over the Chicago lake front to railroads. The constitution demanded an oath from legislators to prevent bribery and corruption, and told them never to make an irrevocable grant of special privilege.[43]

In a convention debate on the repeal of corporate charters, Lorenzo Whiting, known as the "Farmer's Statesman," read from Adam's 1870 article and announced that "we are in the presence of the great question of the age." In the debate, Orville Browning, an old Whig and now a leading Burlington attorney, defended corporate charters and rejoiced that they were "beyond the reach of the states." Differences between Whiting and Browning represented the basic conflict of the convention, a conflict that revolved around the *Dartmouth College* rule, the West's symbol of collusive and corrupt legislative and corporate power. An article ordering the legislature to regulate warehouse storage charges was, for Browning, a "matter we should not touch." Browning was on the defensive throughout the convention; this is clear in his failure to command support against Reuben Benjamin's convincing argument to regulate railroad rates whenever such regulation was "essential to the public good."[44]

Discussing how railroads invoked "the public interest" to take the property of individuals but the "cry of a contract" kept legislatures from placing limitations upon railroad rates, Benjamin concluded that "the interest of the public has been declared to be subordinate to that of railroad corporations." Repeating the concept of "the public good" as a constitutional ideal and repudiating the *Dartmouth College* rule, Benjamin denied that "governmental powers to be used for the public good could be "the subject matter of contract, of mere bargain and sale." He argued, in the republican language of Reemelin and Ranney in the 1850 Ohio debates, that the sovereignty of the people placed limitations on the legislature that prevented it from abandoning the "governmental powers" intrusted to it. The power to regulate railroad charges was "a governmental power—one of the attributes of sovereignty confided to the legislature to be exercised for the public good." Benjamin's argument was a turning point in the Convention, as the convention was a turning point in the constitutional politics of the Midwest; it was a point when republicans, skeptical of legislative power and predisposed to a neutral state, accepted the supremacy of governmental power over corporate power. The shift of American republicanism here cannot be overestimated. There were overtones of the Philadelphia Convention of 1787, where republicans distrustful of power recognized the positive need of governmental power. In 1787, that power was accepted as necessary (among other reasons) for the protection of individual property rights; in 1870 that power was accepted as necessary in order to control a corporate power that threatened (among other things) individual property rights.[45]

In Illinois the demand for governmental power did not end with the constitutional convention. An imperfect 1871 law created a Railroad and Warehouse Commission, established maximum rates, and prohibited rate discrimination. Justice C.B. Lawrence found parts of the law constitutional. Angry and activist farmers met in conventions to hear Whiting and Benjamin denounce the *Dartmouth College* case, to form the Illinois Farmer's Association, to prepare a new railroad law, to plan the defeat of Justice Lawrence in the spring 1873 judicial elections, and to organize for the fall legislative elections. Willard Flagg was elected president of the association, which organized hundreds of clubs (Flagg estimated fifteen hundred by the fall of 1873, and the *Prairie Farmer* wrote of 200,000 organized farmers and 500 meetings). Flagg was the dominant figure in the Illinois farmers movement; he characterized himself this way in an 1874 speech:

> I have been and am a radical republican maintaining in its entirety and complete significance the doctrine of equality of rights laid down by Jefferson in the Declaration....My republicanism tells me that legislation in favor of corporate capital, to the detriment of labor, is hurtful and wrong. It is not the republicanism of Lincoln.

In an 1873 speech Flagg said that "self-interest" was the "railway rule of action," but that the experience of the last twelve months had proved that "the virtue inherent in the people" could control railroad corporations. His republican rhetoric stands out in all of his speeches; this example is from an address to an August 1873 convention of farmers:

> But if discussion does not convince, power must compel. This nation was not formed to be run by moneyed corporations. My liberties and yours are not to be bartered and sold away by venal legislators; and the government of this state and nation must be in the interests of liberty and the people. Our election of judges signified this, and the work when kept up must go on until legislatures, judges, and executive officers understand that there has been too much time and expense devoted to chartered capital and too little to promote the welfare of the people . . . And let no man be horrified when we propose to elect judges that stand by popular rights.[46]

E.L. Godkin of the New York *Nation* was horrified. In 1871 he worried about the Paris Commune and its impact on eastern cities. By 1873 and 1874 he saw confiscation and communism on the western prairies, prairies he thought of as full of "rude wild energy." Godkin criticized Flagg's lecture (delivered at an 1874 meeting of the genteel American Social Science Association) as "worthy of a Paris Communard." His opinion was similar to the *Railroad Gazette's* view of the lecture: "If this means anything it means Communism." The *Nation's* notorious campaign against western farmers was rivaled only by that of the *Railroad Gazette*.[47]

Railroads had more reason for concern than Godkin. The extra-judicial constitutional politics of activist agrarian republicans in Illinois conventions and clubs was emulated by farmers in Iowa in 1873 who spontaneously organized local Granges; the number of Iowa Granges increased that year from 718 to 1823. A.B. Smedley, the Master of the Iowa Grange, echoed Flagg when he said: "The time has come when we in our free republican country are cursed by a system of special rights, special privileges, special powers and monopolies of cliques and rings." Republican conspiracy theories are present in Smedley's view of railroads as "monster monied monopolies."[48]

In 1873, agrarian-based Anti-Monopoly parties had major success in Iowa, Minnesota, Wisconsin, and Illinois. In 1874 the first three of these states passed railroad rate laws roughly similar to the 1873 Illinois law. All this should be understood as the climax of a period of constitutional politics that was regional in scope and republican in ideology. Republicanism was evident in the mid-century constitutional conventions and pervasive in the 1870 Illinois debates; it is unmistakable in the language of Pierce, Reemelin, Ranney, Ryan, Cooley, Whiting, Benjamin, Flagg, and Smedley. And the language and symbols of that ideology were persuasive to thousands of activist citizens in the

protests of the Midwest in 1873 and 1874. The ideology reflected their experience with railroad corporations whose arbitrary power corrupted legislatures,
influenced courts, threatened individual property rights, and determined the
fate of communities.⁴⁹

Railroad corporations opposed the midwestern republicanism of the
1870s with threats to withdraw capital and limit growth. They also opposed
republicanism with an ideology of their own—the ideology of anti-communism,
a self-interested ideology sparked by the Paris Commune, advertised by Godkin, and utilized by profit-seeking railroad directors. As the most recent
historian of the Burlington has written: "when western tempers flared, eastern
capitalists attributed the anger to agrarian reaction or alien communism—
thereby concealing their own assault on local democracy and traditional
American values." The Red Scare of the 1870s particularly distressed Charles
Elliott Perkins of the Burlington. While other Burlington officials gathered to
prevent the passage of rate legislation and, failing that, to prepare legal
defenses, Perkins employed his friend, J. Sterling Morton (later a Senator from
Nebraska), to write articles and editorials for midwestern and eastern papers
attacking farmers and legislators as "communists." Morton took pride in a
Chicago Times article on "Legislative Communism" in which he discussed the
Wisconsin rate law and concluded that "Wisconsin is the first victim of
legislative Communism in America."⁵⁰

Perkins aimed to manipulate public opinion, not enlighten it. Betraying
his anti-republican views, Perkins wrote Morton that "commerce regards
public opinion only so far as it may result in profit or loss." Perkins did not
want to print copies of the C.B.&Q. report on the profits from its land grants;
such information only provided "Grangers and Communists" with ammuni-
tion. He accused Charles Francis Adams Jr. of doing just that in an 1875 speech
Adams had made in Oshkosh, Wisconsin. Distancing himself from the rhetoric
of railroad spokesmen, Adams had said he would not "inveigh against the
farmers and citizens of Wisconsin as Communists." He also remarked that
railroads were not subject to Adam Smith's laws of trade. He thought it a
mistake for railroads to shelter themselves behind the *Dartmouth College* case,
arguing that "the issue had much better be fought out on its merits in the great
arena of public discussion than wrangled over on technicalities in the courts of
law." All this aggravated Perkins, and he complained to Godkin of Adams's
"theory that railroads were not subject to the natural laws of trade." Perkins's
conception of the laws of trade differed markedly from Adams's, as the following remark indicates: "The law of trade, as I understand it, is the law of
self-interest."⁵¹

The anti-communist ideology with which Perkins and others (including
Orville Browning, who expressed an early Christian anti-communism) opposed
regulation masked the self-interested power of the nation's first great corporations and engines of growth. Those corporations and their lawyers were

shocked when midwestern judges upheld the rate laws with a close reading of railroad charters, which were subject to reserved rights of amendment in Iowa, Wisconsin, and Minnesota. In sustaining the Wisconsin law, Edward Ryan, now chief justice of the Wisconsin Supreme Court, lectured railroad lawyers on the unworthiness of their pleas of confiscation and communism. He acknowledged the role of railroads in the nation's growth, but added "such aggregations of capital and power, outside of public control are dangerous to public and private rights."[52]

Six railroad or "Granger Cases" were appealed to the U.S. Supreme Court. The rate laws were upheld by the Court as something of an afterthought to the more famous case of *Munn v. Illinois*. The firm of Munn and Scott was a Chicago grain elevator and warehouse business whose monopolistic and fraudulent practices, and excessive storage charges, had been regulated by an 1871 act of the Illinois legislature, an act commanded by the Constitution of 1870. Munn and Scott did not apply for the license required by the act; the state sued, and the Illinois Supreme Court upheld the act. On appeal, the United States Supreme Court also upheld it. Chief Justice Waite sounded like Reuben Benjamin when he defended warehouse regulation under the police power. He cited the *License Cases* definition of that power of Chief Justice Taney as "nothing more or less than the powers of government inherent in every sovereignty." Waite also sounded like Benjamin when he said that under the police power "the government regulates the conduct of its citizens towards one another . . . when such regulation becomes necessary to the public good." This was the language of republican constitutionalism. Republicanism was obscured, however, when Waite chose to rely primarily on a seventeenth-century legal treatise by Lord Hale that declared wharfs, cranes, and other activities in a busy port "affected with a publick interest" and subject to regulation. The chief justice applied Hale's concept to grain elevators in Chicago. A greater sense of midwestern republicanism might have prompted Waite to invoke the ideal of "the public good" as the basis for a constitutional doctrine of the police power. Hale's common law concept of "affected with a publick interest" was only an ambiguous approximation.[53]

When Waite turned to the *Granger Cases* and confronted railroads protected by charters (as Munn and Scott were not), there were ironical precedents for regulation in the many cases in which the Court has sustained local tax aid for railroads because the roads served a "public use" or a "public purpose." These doctrines had promoted railroad development, but Waite did not rely on any doctrine of "public use" or "public purpose" or "public good" to uphold railroad regulation. While he dealt with the roads on the principle of *Munn* as "affecting the public interest" and "subject to legislative control" when there was a reserved right to amend charters, this control was still limited by the *Dartmouth College* rule. Waite backed away from the republican argument of Benjamin that all railroad charters were subject to inherent "governmental power." In the Burlington case, Waite said it was "now too late to contend that the charter of a corporation is not a contract."[54]

Yet Westerners did know "the public interest," and *Munn* and the *Granger Cases* are the outcome of a continuous pattern of midwestern republican constitutionalism, present at mid-century and revived in the late 1860s and early 1870s by activist citizens, judges, and constitution makers. They asserted the primacy of the public good over the corporate power of railroads. For all the limitations in Waite's opinions, and for all the later legal wrangling over which businesses were "affected with a public interest" and whether the "due process of law" clause of the Fourteenth Amendment protected property from "unreasonable" regulation, *Munn* and the *Granger Cases* did maintain for the future the republican ideal of a "public interest" and a "public good" superior to mere property interests. The 1877 decisions did reflect Madison's comment of nearly a century earlier that "it is too early for politicians to presume on our forgetting that the public good, the real welfare of the great body of the people is the supreme object to be pursued."[55]

Many politicians and businessmen did forget this, of course, and tension continued between corporate power and the public good. In Iowa, the Burlington led the struggle in 1878 to repeal the Iowa rate law. Burlington lawyers largely drafted the bill that replaced it. Perhaps heeding the advice of Chief Justice Waite in *Munn*—"for protection against abuses by legislatures the people should look to the polls, not to the courts"—the Burlington increasingly entered into politics. In Iowa the "Burlington Ring" exercised great influence over the dominant Republican Party until the twentieth century, except for the governorship of William Larrabee; Perkins was no admirer of Larrabee, whom he characterized to Godkin in 1888 as a confiscator and a communist for his efforts at tightening up Iowa's railroad regulation. The same year, Perkins criticized Thomas M. Cooley (who was, appropriately, the chairman of the new Interstate Commerce Commission) for trying to intervene in a Burlington strike and for telling railroadmen to "stand before the community in some other light than lawbreakers." Perkins went on complaining to John Murray Forbes that "the spirit of the age is communistic" as he also continued to discuss the law of trade as "simply the law of self-interest."[56]

Thus the centennial of the Constitution in 1887 was marked by discordant ideologies. On the one hand, there was the republicanism of the Interstate Commerce Act, an act which continued on the national stage the Midwest's efforts to restrain the power of railroads and which marked the beginning of an administrative state that would try to regulate the economic growth of modern corporate America in the public interest. On the other hand, there was the ideology of anti-communism which, all too often in the future, would appeal to men like Charles Elliot Perkins who accepted "no right principle of action but *self-interest.* "At the bicentennial of 1987, the ideological discord continues.[57]

Notes

1. THE RECORDS OF THE FEDERAL CONVENTION 393 (M. Farrand ed. 1927); F. PHILBRICK, THE RISE OF THE WEST 121-32 (1965); Finckelman says "The final impetus for passage of the Ordinance. . . was the possibility of selling some five million acres of land to Cutler and his Associates." *See* Finckelman, *Slavery and the Northwest Ordinance: A Case Study in Ambiguity,* 6 JOURNAL OF THE EARLY REPUBLIC 343 at 351 (1986). The historiographical debate on early American republicanism has been influenced importantly by B. BAILYN, THE IDEOLOGICAL ORIGINS OF THE AMERICAN REVOLUTION (1967), G. WOOD, THE CREATION OF THE AMERICAN REPUBLIC (1969), and J. G. A. POCOCK, THE MACHIAVELLIAN MOMENT (1975). Historiographical concerns with language, discourse, and ideology mark the debate. I have given attention to 'discourse' but have emphasized ideology, using that concept in the manner of Geertz, *Ideology as a Cultural System* in IDEOLOGY AND ITS DISCONTENTS 47-76 (D. Apter ed. 1964). "Liberalism" as a countervailing ideology to "republicanism" has been especially emphasized by J. Appleby in numerous articles and in her CAPITALISM AND A NEW SOCIAL ORDER: THE REPUBLICAN VISION OF THE 1790s (1984). I find "liberalism" inappropriate to a discussion of nineteenth century transportation development, which moved from state mercantilism to monopoly, depended on legislative and legal promotion and protection, and seldom reflected the teachings of Adam Smith; *see* D. WINCH, ADAM SMITH'S POLITICS; AN ESSAY IN HISTORIOGRAPHIC REVISION (1978).

2. 2 Farrand, *supra* note 1 at 439-40, 619; Decker, *The Great Speculation: An Interpretation of Mid-Continent Pioneering,* in THE FRONTIER IN AMERICAN DEVELOPMENT: ESSAYS IN HONOR OF PAUL GATES 357-88 (D. Ellis ed. 1969); D. Ellis, *Comment,* in THE PUBLIC LANDS: STUDIES IN THE HISTORY OF THE PUBLIC DOMAIN 146 (V. Carstensen ed. 1963). The contract clause was appreciated by Sir Henry Maine when he looked at American growth in 1885: "It is this prohibition which has in reality secured full play to the economic forces by which the achievement of cultivating the soil of the North American Continent has been performed; it is the bulwark of American Individualism against democratic impatience and Socialistic fantasy." (Cited in Rappaport, *A Procedural Approach to the Contract Clause,* 93 YALE L.J. 918 at 919 (1984)).

3. 1 Farrand, *supra* note 1 at 533-34, 541, 583-84.

4. *Id.* at 376, 381; J. Madison, *The Vices of the Political System of the U.S.* in 9 THE PAPERS OF JAMES MADISON 354 (R. Rutland ed. 1975); FEDERALIST No. 10 at 57, No. 71 at 464, No. 45 at 299 (A. Hamilton, *et al.,* Modern Library ed. n.d.).

5. 14 Rutland, *supra* note 4, at 274-75, 233-34; *see* L. BANNING, THE JEFFERSONIAN PERSUASION: EVOLUTION OF A PARTY IDEOLOGY (1978); *see also* Ferguson, *Political Economy, Public Liberty, and the Formation of the Constitution,* 40 WM. & MARY Q. 389 at 410 (1980). On republicanism as a "semantic field for normative debate and constructive imagination," *see* Michelman, *Foreword: Traces of Self Government,* 100 HARV. L. REV. 4 at 17 (1986).

6. A. CAYTON, THE FRONTIER REPUBLIC: IDEOLOGY AND POLITICS IN THE OHIO COUNTRY, 1780-1825 68-79 (1986); Onuf, *Liberty, Development, and Union: Visions of the West in the 1780's,* 43 WM. & MARY Q. 179 at 213 (1986). Geertz, *supra* note 1, at 52 and 64,

distinguishes ideology as a mask of "interests" from ideologies as "maps of problematic social reality and matrices for the creation of collective conscience." Republicanism is of the latter type.

7. CAYTON, *supra* note 6, at 110-30; on 'normal politics' and 'constitutional politics' *see* Ackerman, *The Storrs Lectures: On Discovering the Constitution*, 93 YALE L.J. 1013 at 1022 (1984).

8. Osborn v. Bank of the U.S., 22 U.S. 279, 282 (1824).

9. *See* Nedelsky, *Confining Democratic Politics: Anti-Federalists, Federalists. and the Constitution*, 96 HARV. L. REV. 340-60 (1982) on Marshall's tendency to designate an issue as law and insulate it from politics; Ratcliffe, *The Role of Voters and Issues in Party Formation: Ohio, 1824*, 59 J. AM. HIST. 847-70 (1973).

10. H. SCHEIBER, OHIO CANAL ERA: A CASE STUDY OF GOVERNMENT AND THE ECONOMY, 1820-1861 26-27 (1969). Scheiber, *Enterprise and Development: The Case of Micajah Williams*, 37 BUS. HIST. REV. 345-68 (1963) charts the career of a Republican canal organizer who became a Whig speculator.

11. *Id.* at 128-33.

12. A. DE TOCQUEVILLE, JOURNEY TO AMERICA 262 (J.P. Mayer ed. 1960); Perkins, *Agrarianism* and *Dangers to the West* in THE MEMOIRS AND WRITINGS OF JAMES HANDASYD PERKINS 148-49, 139 (W.H. Channing ed. 1851); *infra* note 49 on Charles E. Perkins.

13. Gates, *The Role of the Land Speculator in the West*, in Carstensen, *supra* note 2, at 355; Cole, *Cyclical and Sectional Variations in the Sale of Public Lands, id.* at 234-35; R.C. BULEY, 2 THE OLD NORTHWEST: PIONEER PERIOD, 1815-1840 260-72 (1950).

14. Letter to G. Flagg, May 22, 1842, in Branz and Lawrence, *A Prairie Farmer and Loco-Focos, Speculators, Nullifiers, etc.*, 9 OLD NORTHWEST 345 at 352 (1983-84); J. L. LARSON, BONDS OF ENTERPRISE: JOHN MURRAY FORBES AND WESTERN DEVELOPMENT IN AMERICA'S RAILWAY AGE 36-41 (1984).

15. On Barnburners, *see* H. DONOVAN, THE BARNBURNERS (1925); 2 THE POLITICAL WRITINGS OF WILLIAM LEGGETT 233 (T. Sedgwick ed. 1840); also Trimble, *Diverging Trends in New York Democracy in the Period of the Loco-Focos*, 24 AMERICAN HISTORICAL REVIEW 398-421 (1919); Jefferson to A. Donald, Feb. 7, 1788 in 12 THE PAPERS OF THOMAS JEFFERSON 571 (J. Boyd ed. 1955). On law and the release of entrepreneurial energy *see* J.W. HURST, LAW AND THE CONDITIONS OF FREEDOM IN THE NINETEENTH CENTURY UNITED STATES (1956).

16. FRAGMENTS OF THE POLITICAL DEBATES OF THE IOWA CONSTITUTIONS OF 1844 and 1846 143-44 (B. Shambaugh ed. 1900).

17. THE STRUGGLE OVER RATIFICATION, 1846-1847 43, 62 (M. Quaife ed. 1920); on Ryan *see* A. BEITZINER: LION OF THE BAR (1960).

18. *Illinois Constitutions* 3 SOURCES AND DOCUMENTS OF U.S. CONSTITUTIONS, 250-72 (W. Swindler ed. 1974); also THE CONSTITUTIONAL DEBATES OF 1847 (A. Cole ed. 1919).

19. R. OVERTON, BURLINGTON ROUTE: A HISTORY OF THE BURLINGTON LINES 32-35 (1965); OVERTON, BURLINGTON WEST: A COLONIZATION HISTORY OF THE BURLINGTON RAILROAD 509 (1941).

20. J. STOVER, IRON ROAD TO THE WEST: AMERICAN RAILROADS IN THE 1850s 119 (1978); J. M. Forbes to Paul S. Forbes, Oct. 13, 1854, Nov. 26, 1854, in T. COCHRAN, RAILROAD LEADERS, 1845-1890: THE BUSINESS MIND IN ACTION 328 (1953).

21. MICHIGAN, REPORT OF THE PROCEEDINGS AND DEBATES OF THE CONVENTION TO REVISE THE CONSTITUTION OF THE STATE OF MICHIGAN 745, 659 (1850); *see* C. Hirshfield, *The Great Railroad Conspiracy*, 36 MICH. HIST. 92-219 (1952); on Pierce *see* London, *Homestead Exemption in the Michigan Constitution of 1850*, 37 MICH. HIST. 385-406 (1953).

22. Adrian Watchtower, Jan. 25, 1853; *see* A. JONES, THE CONSTITUTIONAL CONSERVATISM OF THOMAS M. COOLEY 58-59 (1987).

23. OHIO, REPORT OF THE DEBATES AND PROCEEDINGS OF THE CONVENTION FOR THE REVISION OF THE CONSTITUTION OF THE STATE OF OHIO, 1850-1851 852, 1252, 753, 293, 834, 865 (1851).

24. *Id.* at 826, 832, 378, 856.

25. *See* HURST, *supra* note 15; Scheiber, *The Road to Munn*, 5 PERSPECTIVES IN AMERICAN HISTORY 329-404 (D. Fleming & B. Bailyn eds. 1971); M. HORWITZ, THE TRANSFORMATION OF AMERICAN LAW: 1790-1860 (1977); Scheiber, *Public Rights and the Rule of Law in American Legal History*, 72 California L. Rev. 217 at 231 (1984). M. Tushnet in *Law and the Legal Process*, 1972 WIS. L. REV. 114 at 130 faults Hurst's legal history for its insensitivity to issues of power and ideology.

26. Ohio, *supra* note 23 at 871, 889.

27. *Id.* at 904 (my italics), 1253.

28. *Id.* at 1251, 405.

29. INDIANA, REPORT OF THE DEBATES AND PROCEEDINGS OF THE CONVENTION FOR THE REVISION OF THE CONSTITUTION 1956, 1954, 1957 (1850).

30. *Id.* at 364, 365, 399.

31. DeBolt v. The Ohio Life Insurance and Trust Co., 1 Ohio St. Rep. 563, 585 (1852).

32. A. LINCOLN, SELECTED SPEECHES, MESSAGES AND LETTERS 44, 157 (T.H. Williams ed. 1957); E. FONER, FREE SOIL, FREE LABOR, AND FREE MEN: THE IDEOLOGY OF THE REPUBLICAN PARTY BEFORE THE CIVIL WAR 97-102 (1976).

33. STOVER, *supra* note 20, at 115; R. HUNT, LAW AND LOCOMOTIVES: THE IMPACT OF THE RAILROAD ON WISCONSIN LAW IN THE NINETEENTH CENTURY 3-65 (1958).

34. LARSON, *supra* note 14, at 53-82.

35. *Id.* at 103-6; State of Iowa ex rel The B.& M.R.R. Co. v. The County of Wapello, 13 Iowa 380 (1862).

36. Gelpcke v. Dubuque, 1 Wall 175 (1864); C. FAIRMAN, 1 RECONSTRUCTION AND REUNION 1864-1888, 934-37 (1971). Justice Miller's republicanism is clear in an 1878 letter to his brother: "I have met with but few things of a character affecting the public good and the whole country that has shaken my faith in human nature as much as the united, vigorous, and selfish effort of the capitalists." (cited in Fairman, *Justice Miller and the Mortgaged Generation* 23 IOWA L. REV. 351, 352 (1938)).

37. FAIRMAN, *supra* note 36 at 971-86; Hanson v. Vernon, 27 Iowa 28, 52; *see* Beard, *Local Aid to Railroads in Iowa*, 50 IOWA J. HIST. 1-34 (1952).

38. F. MERK, THE ECONOMIC HISTORY OF WISCONSIN DURING THE CIVIL WAR DECADE 325-39 (1916); Whiting v. Sheboygan and Fond du Lac R.R., 25 Wis. 1 (1870), reversed in Olcott v. Supervisors 16 Wall 678 (1873); C.B.&Q.R.R. Co. v. County of Otoe, 16 Wall 667 (1873). Iowa and Nebraska land grants to the Burlington returned $17 million, more than the construction costs of the line from Burlington to Kearney Junction, Nebraska (OVERTON, BURLINGTON WEST 477-78). *See* J. GRODINSKY, THE IOWA POOL: A STUDY IN RAILROAD COMPETITION (1950).

39. MERK, *supra* note 38 at 298-303; Ryan, *Address to Graduates of the Law School*, Ryan Papers, Wisconsin State Historical Society.

40. JONES, *supra* note 22, at 127, 130-34, 215; *see* Cooley's opinions in Gale v. Kalamazoo, 23 Mich. 344 (1871) and East Saginaw Manufacturing Co. v. City of East Saginaw, 19 Mich. 259 (1871); COOLEY, TREATISE ON THE CONSTITUTIONAL LIMITATIONS WHICH REST UPON THE LEGISLATIVE POWER OF THE STATES OF THE AMERICAN UNION 353 (2nd ed. 1871).

41. People v. Salem, 20 Mich. 452, 487 (1870), overruled in Pine Grove Township v. Talcott, 19 Wall 666 (1874); H. DILLA, THE POLITICS OF MICHIGAN 108-21 (1912).

42. Adams, *Railway Problems in 1869*, 110 N. AM. REV. 116 at 126, 148 (1870); Adams, *The Government and the Railroad Corporations*, 112 N. AM. REV. 31 at 51 (1871).

43. Swindler, *supra* note 18, at 286-311; A. COLE, THE ERA OF THE CIVIL WAR, 1848-1873 406 (1919); 147 special charters were granted to railroads in Illinois between 1865 and 1870; *see* Eilert, *Illinois Business Corporations, 1816-1870*, 37 BUS. HIST. REV. 169 at 180 (1963).

44. ILLINOIS, DEBATES AND PROCEEDINGS OF THE CONVENTION TO REVISE THE CONSTITUTION, 1870 670, 1627, 1644, 1641.

45. *Id.* at 1641-43.

46. On the activities of Illinois farmers in 1873 *see* the 1873 issues of *The Prairie Farmer* and J. PERIAM, THE GROUNDSWELL: A HISTORY OF THE ORIGINS, AIMS, AND PROGRESS OF THE FARMER'S MOVEMENT (1874). PERIAM covers numerous conventions and the speeches of Benjamin, Flagg, and Whiting. On Flagg's 'republicanism' *see* his speeches in *The Prairie Farmer*, October 3, 1874, in PERIAM, 392-404, and his pamphlet, *The Aim and Scope of the Farmer's Movement* (1873) in the Illinois State Historical Library. Flagg was the son of Gershon Flagg (*supra* note 14). He was a Yale graduate, an active Lincoln Republican, a founder of Illinois Industrial College, later the University of Illinois, and a dominant figure in the Illinois farmer's movement. He has been neglected by historians.

47. Godkin, *Aristocratic Opinions of Democracy,* in PROBLEMS OF MODERN DEMO-CRACY (M. Keller ed. 1966); *Nation,* July 16, 1874; between 1873 and 1875, the *Nation* singled out Flagg in many issues during its continuous attack on Western farmers. *Railroad Gazette,* May 30, 1874.

48. Beard, *The Background of State Railroad Regulation in Iowa,* 51 IOWA J. HIST. 31 (1953).

49. *See,* G. MILLER, THE RAILROADS AND THE GRANGER LAWS (1971) for a careful account of the background to the Granger laws written from a non-ideological perspective that neglects issues of power. LARSON, BONDS OF ENTERPRISE emphasizes ideology and power more than Miller, as does A. Martin who gives importance to "the deep-seated mistrust, hatred and fear of large insulated aggregations of power" in the movement for railroad regulation; *see* A. Martin, *The Troubled Subject of Railroad Legislation in the Gilded Age* 61 J. AM. HIST. 339 at 370 (174).

50. LARSON, *supra* note 14, at 142; J. OLSON, J. STERLING MORTON 196 (1942); Morton to Perkins, Jan. 22, 1874, Feb. 2, 1874, Perkins In-Letters, Burlington Archives, Newberry Library.

51. Perkins to Morton, Aug. 16, 1877 CEP Transcripts, Burlington Archives; Perkins to J.W. Brooks, June 17, 1873, CEP Transcripts; clipping of Oshkosh speech in C.F. Adams Jr. Papers, Massachusetts Historical Society; Perkins to Godkin, Oct. 21, 1875, CEP Transcripts.

52. Browning, *Address* in PROCEEDINGS OF THE ILLINOIS STATE BAR ASSOCIATION, 1879 20 at 28; Attorney General v. The Railroad Companies, 35 Wis. 425, 579-80, 530 (1874).

53. Munn v. Illinois 94 U.S. 113, 125 (1877); *see* C.P. Magrath, *The Case of the Unscrupulous Warehousemen,* in QUARRELS THAT HAVE SHAPED THE CONSTITUTION 119-38 (J. Garraty rev.ed. 1987); on the limitations of Waite's use of the Lord Hale *see* Fairman, *The So-Called Granger Cases, Lord Hale, and Justice Bradley,* 5 STAN. L. REV. 587 (1953); also *see* Scheiber, *The Road to Munn, supra* note 25.

54. C.B.& Q.R.R. Co. v. Iowa 94 U.S. 158, 161 (1877). Waite did considerably narrow contract clause limitations on legislative rate regulation in Ruggles v. Illinois, 108 U.S. 526 (1882) where, ironically, the charter at issue was the one Chauncey Colton thought he had secured "subject to no legislative control whatsoever," *supra* note 19.

55. *See* C.P. MAGRATH, MORRISON R. WAITE: THE TRIUMPH OF CHARACTER 203 (1963).

56. Munn v. Illinois 94 U.S. at 134; Legal Papers, Box 33 in Burlington Archives; L. SAGE, A HISTORY OF IOWA 223-24 (1974); Perkins to W.B. Allison, Dec. 1, 1888, and September 1, 1889, and Perkins to H.L. Higginson, December 5, 1888, CEP Transcripts; JONES, *supra* note 22, at 318-26; Perkins to J.M. Forbes, Feb. 18, 1888, and Perkins to Godkin, Feb. 25, 1888, in COCHRAN, *supra* note 20, at 436-37.

57. *See* S. SKOWRONEK, BUILDING A NEW AMERICAN STATE; THE EXPANSION OF NATIONAL ADMINISTRATIVE CAPACITIES, 1877-1920 (1982) and J. ROHR, TO RUN A CONSTITUTION: THE LEGITIMACY OF THE ADMINISTRATIVE STATE (1986).

Up from Dred Scott; *Down to* Slaughterhouse: *Inventive Interim Judicial Protections for Property In Reconstruction America*

HAROLD M. HYMAN

I. The Argument

The Supreme Court's remarkable return to influence in "check-and-balance" governing in 1873's *Slaughterhouse* decision from 1857's *Dred Scott* depths deserves reevaluation, not only as measured by texts of High Court decisions, constitutions, or statutes, but also by contemporary standards. Reevaluation is warranted because in *Slaughterhouse* the majority justices embedded an imperfect and attenuated history of the Thirteenth and Fourteenth Amendments into tenaciously durable case law. The justices were responding to contextual concerns, especially about the stability of property rights. Stressing the primacy of economic liberties, the *Slaughterhouse* majority joined other conservative spokesmen in law and politics who saw some majoritarian interventions as threats to private property. And, tragically, the *Slaughterhouse* Court helped to erode concerns about equal justice under law for race and gender minorities.

Looking Backward—1873 to 1862

In May 1866, Salmon Portland Chase, chief justice of the United States, previewed a group portrait showing Lincoln announcing to the Cabinet in 1862 (Chase was then treasury secretary) his decision to issue the Emancipation Proclamation. Chase recalled that all the Cabinet officers had sat silent, stunned, "...thinking of what they had just heard, and the future it opens."[1]

How different that future from the constrained past for which standfast Union-as-it-was conservatives yearned! Preferring the dismemberment of the Union, outright reactionaries condemned commander-in-chief Lincoln's Emancipation order as a dictatorial usurpation of power aiming at interracial sex and as the death of federalism and all private property.

After the President and Cabinet sat for the 1862 portrait, they, the hundreds of thousands of Union soldiers (including over 100,000 black blue-coats), and their countrymen as a whole, had further defined that future in terms of soaring aspirations. As evidenced by the Emancipation Proclamation, in 1862 even Lincoln and Chase hoped primarily for a restored Union in which, as a punishment for stubborn rebels, slavery would end in the then-unsubmissive southern states. Nevertheless, Lincoln's Emancipation Proclamation raised goals mountainously higher than the perpetualized slavery that the *Dred Scott* decision implied.

By Appomattox in April 1865, Union war aims had escalated beyond a restored Union to one purified of that malignant, state-defined property, slavery, not only regionally but nationally, and cleansed also of unequal as well as unfree legal statuses. This dramatic elevation is reflected in the Thirteenth Amendment to the Constitution:

> Neither slavery nor involuntary servitude, except as a punishment for crime whereof the party shall have been duly convicted, shall exist within the United States, or any place subject to their jurisdiction.

In the spring of 1865, the Thirteenth Amendment proposal was out to the states for ratification, with enthusiastic endorsements from Republican congressmen and Lincoln. He heartily favored it as "a very fitting if not indispensable adjunct to the winding up of the great difficulty...[It is] a King's cure for all...evils." On April 11, 1865, Lincoln, further defining the Union consensus about the outreach of the Thirteenth Amendment, stated publicly that he wanted all the now-defeated southern states to allow blacks to vote who were literate and/or Union Army veterans, and to educate at public expense all citizens' children, white and black. To John Wilkes Booth as, apparently, to Lincoln, this meant "nigger citizenship," and so he killed Lincoln.[2]

Impressively many contemporaries assumed that the "Age of Lincoln" would continue after his death, and that the Thirteenth Amendment would eradicate racial inequities; perhaps also those of gender, and in all states, not only those of the South.[3] Subsequent amendments and implementing legislation necessitated by regional resistance against implementation were not on the horizon. The Thirteenth Amendment was seen as a finality because it embraced every official on all levels of government plus private relationships that by act or failure to act created conditions less than equal, and its implementation would be by self-help litigation. Concerning slavery, the core inequality, the Thirteenth Amendment would automatically cancel all its special protections in the 1787 Constitution (see below). Consensus was overwhelming in 1865 and later, however, that this society would remain a state-based federalism. Almost no national criminal law existed. Therefore the Thirteenth Amendment's "punishment for crime" and "duly convicted" phrases referred to state law. Equal criminal and civil justice under state law was the new federal minimum. Interstate, as before, diverse laws and customs would prevail, a far less troublesome prospect since slavery questions would no longer trouble slaveless jurisdictions.[4] But, intrastate, as a new and finer standard of national citizenship, each state resident would enjoy equal treatment under the state's civil and criminal laws and customs, with respect to both public policies and private rights.

So perceived, the meaning of the Thirteenth Amendment's prohibition against "involuntary servitude" emerges as a convenient label (not a definition) for what few white Americans had earlier needed systematically to ponder, i.e., their rights deriving from national as well as from state residence. Servitude had been long-defined; "freeitude" had not. Outlawing involuntary servitude everywhere in the reunited nation meant that its ennobling opposite would prevail.[5]

Looking ahead, we know that *Slaughterhouse* and like decisions reinterpreted the Thirteenth Amendment to mean "only" the end of formal slavery and the Fourteenth Amendment to affect formal "state action," not private relationships, and that females were legitimately unequal after all. Earlier visions of universal equality nurturing liberty and interstate diversity coexisting with intrastate uniformity would fade in the *Slaughterhouse* atmosphere. By century's turn lawyers steeped in an increasingly "positivist-formalist" legal culture that swiftly and deliberately divorced itself from realities of history and context would expand *Slaughterhouse's* progeny.[6] The racial viciousness and class hypocrisies of "economic due process," "separate but equal," and "liberty of contract" followed.[7] Why?

In some unquantifiable but significant part, because popular support for the Appomattox vision eroded under conservatives' eventually successful insistence in elections and litigations that the Republicans' liberal, liberating agenda was anti-property and anti-federalism. This was a powerful charge to a generation that had endured the wearying trials of the "Age of Jackson" and that yearned to stabilize the "Age of Lincoln." Many devout Republicans who detested slavery feared almost equally what they called "socialism" and revered state-based federalism. How without coercive centralization could the federal government enforce equality in thousands of communities whose residents preferred violence to acquiescence, and where state and local officials, alerted by *Slaughterhouse's* state-action stress, formally condemned but actually condoned racist tragedies?[8] In short, a causal element in what became the failure of Reconstruction was the priority of property rights that *Slaughterhouse* helped to reaffirm.

Property in Rights and Rights to Property

Back in 1862, veteran lawyers Lincoln and Chase knew that whatever else motivated opposition to emancipation both in the South and elsewhere in the country, a common justification for the opposition was the sacredness of all private property within the states as the organs of government that defined and protected property rights. The belief prevailed among their generation that Americans had fought the Revolution because "...they had inherited rights and that those rights were truly property."[9] Over decades spokesmen for many property interests, including slaveowners, opposed various federal interventions by reasserting this belief as formal legal and constitutional doctrine, labeled opportunistically as "natural rights," "property rights," "state rights," or "vested rights." Whatever the label, a consensus existed that acquiring, possessing, and protecting property through the procedures of litigation and politics was itself a substantive civil (i.e., property) right, as distinguished then from civil (i.e., political) liberty.[10]

Vested rights notions insulated property (defined as tangibles: chattels or real estate) from state intrusion, save in exceptional situations. Eminent domain court proceedings are one example of an exceptional situation. States could condemn (i.e., acquire title to) property needed for public purposes (roadways, utilities, etc.) upon payment of fair market value.[11]

Save in customs, postal, and slavery matters, federal impositions on private property were rare. States defined property and provided for its protection. True, under their 'police power' (the states' authority to safeguard the health, safety, welfare, and morals of their residents), northern states had prohibited property rights in humans, as had Congress concerning certain federal territories (the latter prohibition was condemned in *Dred Scott*). In slave states, authorities created complex suppression and surveillance networks around slaves, free blacks, and abolitionists. Generally speaking, however, the language of law writers about the imperial outreach of police power remained more expansive than the implementation. Yet state police power doctrines did lessen the sense of property's untouchability in a free society.[12]

Famous Supreme Court decisions of the John Marshall-Roger B. Taney chief justiceships, and influential law commentaries by James Kent and Joseph Story, extolled the contracts clause of the Federal Constitution and judge-made defenses of private property against diminutions by temporary majorities. These passionate defenses reflected the growth of intense fears, especially among many lawyers and their clients, that, exploiting the police power, demagogues might destabilize property, sometimes by championing humanitarian goals. Because state majorities decided public policies, property was vulnerable, their arguments ran, unless bench and bar protected owners' inviolable rights.

A few prewar social improvers did exploit state police constitutionalism, as in penitentiary systems and the curtailment of slavery in northern states. Otherwise, no prewar state successfully outlawed any allegedly evil private property, even alcohol. Antislavery advocates were spectacularly unsuccessful in analogous efforts to have Congress delegitimize slavery nationwide, until in the Civil War they linked patriotism with their cause,[13] finally, if temporarily, overpowering state rights arguments against federal destruction of a property interest.

One factor in the antislavery activists' success was the growth of cynicism among Lincoln's generation about the genuineness of state rights defenses for state wrongs. Roughly when Lincoln began lawyering, in 1829, Harvard law professor Nathan Dane noted that "States' rights and State sovereignty are expressions coined for party purposes, often by minorities, who happen to be dissatisfied with the measures of the General [i.e., the national] Government, and as they are...used, they produce only state delusion. In this business each large minority has had its turn."[14]

Slavery's Special Status

Cynicism rose, particularly as events, especially the dramatic arguments of 1819-60 about the extension of slavery into the federal territories and the spectacular recaptures of fugitive slaves in northern states, illustrated the fact that in 1787 the Constitution's framers had vested slave-owners with numerous special advantages for their state-defined property rights.[15] Slaveowners' spokesmen insisted that the abolition or inhibition by legislation of any class of property, even those that majorities might define as morally evil, threatened every property that allegedly manipulable voters might agree was immoral, as well as federalism and political democracy.[16]

In most non-slave states, doctrines protecting property coexisted with a growing body of police power laws and ordinances requiring, as examples, fire escapes for urban tenements, exclusions of diseased animals from commercial food channels, and state licensing for teachers, lawyers, and physicians. Lawmakers, lawyers, and judges developed ways to immunize entrepreneurs from liabilities from employees' job injuries or defective products.[17]

The police power proliferated less so in slave states. Despite its champions' claims that slavery was only another kind of property, southern lawmakers and lawyers themselves illuminated the fact that it was a "peculiar institution." Slavery raised particular questions in business and criminal law. Examples: A slave of one owner injured a "fellow-servant" belonging to another. What liabilities resulted? Should slaves (or free blacks) be permitted to testify adversely to white defendants in trials? Did the seller or lessor of a slave with a defect unknown to or hidden by the owner/lessor enjoy "caveat emptor" (i.e., let the buyer beware) immunities of sorts sellers were developing in non-slave states? Was a slave who committed murder, arson, or rape (of a white woman) responsible under law for his felonies? Or was his master? What of minor slave felons?[18]

But even while they adapted master-slave realities to varied local marketplace and judicial conditions, slave-state spokesmen insisted that federal law could evolve in only one way, i.e., by increasing implementations of the Constitution's several special protections for slavery. They focused particularly on slaveowners' access—with bondsmen, to the federal territories, and on the recapture of fugitive slaves—thereby escalating onto the national stage states' rights constitutional dogmas and legal concepts of vested rights and due process of law derived from state and community contexts. By the 1850s these mixed political pressures and legal-constitutional ideas made pacific emancipation politically impossible in the southern states and created crises about the extension of slavery into the imperially-enlarging federal territories.

Dred Scott and Substantive Due Process

In its 1857 *Dred Scott* decision the United States Supreme Court further magnified property rights as inhibitions on government, this time on the nation. Attempting to take out of politics the nation's single most tenacious problem, that of slavery in its territories, the Court majority held that the Fifth Amendment's due process clause—"No person shall be...deprived of life, liberty, or property without due process of law"—forbade the nation from depriving slaveowners of their vested property rights by a statute excluding this property from the territories. Congress had, in fact, already repealed the offending statute.[19]

Despite his claims to traditionalism, in *Dred Scott* Taney innovated spectacularly with the concept of due process of law. Its ancient roots were in Magna Charta's promise that even the king was bound to obey the "law of the land." Over centuries this root established branches. A major one was that due process meant the steps authority must follow in court proceedings, as expressed in constitutions, statutes, and rules. As an example, procedural due process limits the number of jurors and their manner of selection. Substantive due process transcends procedure: it is the requirement that a jury trial occur.

In 1856, only one year before *Dred Scott,* New York appeals court judges resorted (in *Wynehamer v. People*)[20] to one of the rare pre-Civil War substantive due process judgments.The state court prohibited legislative interference of any kind, beyond a judge-set degree, with the litigant's liquor business. *Wynehamer* suggested to alert opportunists that due process might insulate entrepreneurs against the feared effects of legislation as well as against abnormal or inadequate procedures.

In *Dred Scott,* Taney, having "proved" incorrectly that blacks had never enjoyed the protections deriving from the statuses of either national or state citizenship, employed incidentally *Wynehamer's* novel approaches and assumptions, stating:

> |An] Act of Congress which deprives a citizen of the United States of his liberty or property, merely because he came himself or brought his property into a particular Territory of the United States, and who had committed no

offense against the law, could hardly be dignified with the name of due process of law.

Were *Dred Scott* obeyed, slaveowners' special property rights specified in the Constitution and implied from legal doctrines of comity (i.e., reciprocal recognition by one state of another state's legal papers, including those on ownership of slaves) would redefine federalism. They would blanket future states developing from federal territories, plus existing slave states, and perhaps even non-slave states.

This was not a phantom fear. By late 1860, the New York Court of Appeals (its highest court) was deciding whether the Federal Constitution protected slaveowners' rights to sell their human property while sojourning in a non-slave state. The state judges decided against the claims of the Virginia slaveholders who announced their intention to appeal to the United States Supreme Court. Nationalized slavery seemed possible, even imminent.[21]

The Civil War would dissipate this threat. But the fact that the Civil War occurred measures the failure of the immediate purpose of the *Dred Scott* majority: i.e., to cut the slavery issue out of majoritarian politics. Instead, the decision reduced the prestige and authority of the Court as an institution of government.

Yet, within the short span of years embracing the Civil War and post-victory Reconstruction—the unlikeliest environments imaginable for judges to reclaim a leadership share in defining public law—the Court climbed very far from *Dred Scott's* depths. By 1873, in the *Slaughterhouse* decision, it functioned again as the equal of President and Congress. As noted earlier, the justices achieved this impressive recovery by exploiting popular fears about majoritarian threats to private property that many legal professionals shared and encouraged.

II. After Dred Scott

Dred Scott and the Civil War itself temporarily diminished the appeal of vested rights, except in the South.[22] Elsewhere, staunch defenders of property, including Lincoln and most Republicans of the late 1850s and early 1860s, increasingly redefined rights under the quickening lash of events. Their redefinitions advanced from negatives, as in the Bill of Rights (until then perceived as a bill of wrongs), to positive duties that Republicans perceived for government.

Wartime Test Oaths and Individual Rights

Paradoxically, wartime internal security policies raised concerns about individuals' positive rights, including those of personal liberty and property.

Wartime Congresses and state legislatures required increasing categories of civil and military officers, licensed professionals, and tradesmen to swear loyalty to the Union as prerequisites for commissions, positions, and/or privileges. A prewar consensus existed that property consisted of tangibles, including land or slaves. The loyalty tests inspired inventive antiwar spokesmen to argue that intangibles, including a qualified individual's right to practice his trade or profession, were also property, and that the exclusionary oaths could not deprive non-swearers, even disloyalists, of jobs, professional practices, or other benefits of labor and training. Proponents of loyalty tests insisted that a profession or trade was not property, and that the nation's war powers and the states' police powers permitted loyalty tests. Unless disloyalists were excluded from lawmaking, judging, teaching, voting, and influential vocations such as banking, neither adequate security nor equal justice would be possible.

As we will see, high jurists soon took sides in these arguments about loyalty tests in the dynamic context of a rising sentiment for abolitionism. Property rights became central to both passionate debates.

Test Oaths and Emancipation

Ironically, the abolitionists' success in raising consciousness about rights would work to the advantage of the persons most adversely affected by the test oaths, i.e., southern whites and their northern Democratic allies and defenders. Equalization of rights in the Thirteenth Amendment raised the question: should Congress and state lawmakers exclude non-swearers from rights to professions, trades, and other broadly-defined properties? The Thirteenth Amendment also spoke to the Union consensus that the nation, having extirpated slavery everywhere, should widen ways for individuals to participate in marketplace exchanges, politics, and litigation, which were basic ways that free men acquired and kept property.

Holders of escalating concepts envisaged a dual American citizenship. The Declaration of Independence and the Bill of Rights would minimally define individuals' rights deriving from both national and state citizenship, but state residence, where individuals lived and labored, would remain primary. Therefore, an individual's essential right from national citizenship would be a guarantee that his state equalize its own civil and criminal processes. Individuals could then contract labor, risk capital, and protect their labor's fruits. Equal justice under state law, allowing interstate diversity yet intrastate uniformity, would be itself perceived as a substantive right, one protecting all other property, although not itself a tangible like land or chattel.[23]

Of what did equal justice consist? On the criminal side, a right to testify, to enjoy trials before verdicts: on the civil side, a right to contract for labor, personal property, or land; to enjoy access to tax-supported schools; and to exercise legal remedies for all rights.[24] But if perjurious ex-Confederates controlled their states' courts, schools, government, and major businesses, could equal justice exist for disfavored persons or groups?

Dred Scott "Repealed" by Appomattox and the Thirteenth Amendment

In April 1865, at Appomattox, bluecoats made the proposed Thirteenth Amendment meaningful, nine months before voters ratified it in December. Where *Dred Scott* had denied the nation power even to bar slaveowners' property from federal territories, the Amendment prohibited anything like slavery not only in the territories but in all states, present and future. As noted, the Amendment applied to all officials, federal, state, and local, plus private persons: to private contracts[25] as well as public law. The Amendment's supporters from Lincoln down saw it as a finality, wholly capable of accommodating all social needs into the now-rosy future.[26] A consensus existed among the Amendment's creators and ratifiers that blacks, once freed, would, like whites, by ballots and/or lawsuits in their states, buffer their property earned through labor and thus avoid anything approximating "involuntary servitude." The defeated ex-Confederate states need only adopt color-blind civil and criminal law codes and two-party politics as had those self-reconstructing Union states even during the war. Office holders, as their oaths of office required, need only enforce the nation's amended Constitution and their own states' revised constitutions. But this halcyon vision proved far divergent from reality. Though now devoid of formal slavery, the ex-Confederate states' new constitutions and laws embraced less-than-equal "black codes."

The Test Oaths Again

Here the wartime test oaths intruded. Only rare Confederates could unperjuriously qualify for any federal or state office, the latter now all vacant, in thirteen states. An entirely new slate of Unionist and Negro (i.e., Republican) state officialdom, plus the political nuclei that historically formed around such officers, would be needed if the oath laws were to be obeyed.[27] If these officials enforced their states' revised constitutions and that of the nation, then all rights would stabilize. Except for individuals' self-protective litigation, federal government interventions would cease even in the crumpled Confederacy.[28]

True, once readmitted into the Union the southern states' representation in the House of Representatives would increase substantially, because the Thirteenth Amendment voided the Constitution's "three-fifths" clause. But this seemed a bearable price to pay for swift sectional reconciliation and decent race relationships.

Andrew Johnson

Through 1865-67, Chase and others argued fruitlessly with Lincoln's successor, Andrew Johnson, that the Thirteenth Amendment "incorporated a distinct recognition of the loyal colored men as citizens, entitled to the right of suffrage."[29] But unlike Lincoln, Johnson was ineducable on race matters. Johnson's immobility led to his famous misadventures of 1865-68 with Congress, to his unprecedented number of vetoes and to Congress's overriding of these vetoes, to his selective non-enforcement and impediments of laws he disfavored, and to his deserved impeachment and undeserved one-vote escape from conviction in 1868. Nevertheless, Johnson's obstructionism encouraged conservatives to exploit widespread concerns that property rights generally were in danger now that federal and state lawmakers had regulatory bits in their teeth. Inspired by Johnson's obduracy, by tenacious racism North and South, and by growing fears about popular demands for limitations on some property (the Knights of Labor had organized; early Grangers were rooting in midwestern states), southern whites resisted the racial equality provisions of the pioneering 1866 Civil Rights law, which had been enacted over Johnson's veto in order to enforce the Thirteenth Amendment. Congress responded with the proposed Fourteenth Amendment (ratified in 1868) and with Military Reconstruction statutes.[30]

The Fourteenth Amendment

In formulating the Fourteenth Amendment, Congress was supplementing—not replacing—the universal prohibition of the Thirteenth Amendment against "involuntary servitude." Reacting to unpunished state and private wrongs, including violated labor contracts and racially inequitable criminal law procedures that made a mockery of equal state justice, Congress incorporated "state action" and "due process" content into the Fourteenth Amendment:[31]

> All persons born or naturalized in the United States...are citizens of the United States and of the State wherein they reside. No State shall make or enforce any law which shall abridge the privileges or immunities of citizens of the United States; nor shall any State deprive any person of life, liberty, or property, without due process of law; nor deny to any person within its jurisdiction the equal protection of the laws.

Supporters of both Amendments understood that the Thirteenth retained relevance. For example, Texas's racially democratized 1869 constitution (revoked by white "redeemers" in 1876) specified (Art. I, Sec. 22) that "the adoption of any system of peonage, whereby the helpless and unfortunate may be reduced to practical peonage, shall never be authorized, or tolerated by the laws of this State; and neither slavery nor involuntary servitude, except as a punishment for crime whereof the party shall have been duly convicted, shall ever exist within this State."

III. The Supreme Court: On To *Slaughterhouse*

Since *Dred Scott,* the Supreme Court had been stressing whites' civil liberties and the sacredness of property. On circuit in 1861, Taney both accepted jurisdiction of a plea from an allegedly disloyal civilian arrested by soldiers under commander-in-chief Lincoln's authority, and directly condemned the President. But his fellow-Justices refused to follow his lead about condemning the security arrests.[32] In the *Prize Cases,* decided on a five to four vote, the Court sustained the Union blockade of trade with Confederate ports. Taney, in the minority, failed to enlist enough of the other justices in his injudicious antiwar crusade.[33] He died in 1864, Chase replacing him as Chief Justice.

Evil Cities and State Wrongs

The Court's performance on war issues restored a measure of popular confidence in the robed nobility, for despite Taney the justices had not, as feared, directly confronted President and Congress. Another litigation, this one a seemingly peripheral non-war topic, earned the Court the gratitude of important segments of the nation's commercial and financial communities.

In 1864 the Court decided *Gelpcke v. Dubuque,* which involved neither a suspect disloyalist nor a southern state. This litigation pleased Republicans by shifting attention away from military arrests of civilians, an uncomfortable topic. And Democrats liked this litigation because it had nothing to do with southern state wrongs, now identified with secession, treason, and bloody civil war, but rather focused on wrongs committed by northern cities. The case arose because corruption attended an issue of city bonds aimed at enticing a railroad to locate tracks and maintenance facilities in Dubuque. Reform-minded Iowa legislators repudiated the tainted bonds. Bondholders sued, and state supreme court judges sustained the lawmakers. Appeal followed to the United States Supreme Court.

The Court's tradition had been to respect the Constitution's Eleventh Amendment and to honor decisions of a state's highest court on state law. But in this instance the Court rejected the decision of the Iowa jurists. Instead, as the *Supreme Court Reporter* editorialized, in *Gelpcke* the justices imposed "high moral duties...upon a whole community seeking apparently to violate them."[34] Once a contract was valid under a state's law, even the state's highest court could not sanction its repudiation by the lawmakers, the jurists decided. Justifying this substantial jurisdictional bootstrapping, the Court majority stressed its members' concern—one shared widely by investors—about cities' notorious fiscal immorality and irresponsibility, especially in repudiations. Although the Framers of 1787 had ignored cities when sketching nation-state relationships, the Court, in *Gelpcke,* proclaimed that it would monitor the morality of cities' fiscal behavior if state legislators and judges failed to do so. Justice Noah Swayne asserted that the federal Supreme Court "shall never immolate truth, justice, and the law, because a state tribunal has erected the altar and decreed the sacrifice."[35]

Post-Appomattox Reconstruction

Then, a year after Appomattox, while Congress was crafting the pioneer 1866 Civil Rights Act to enforce the Thirteenth Amendment, the Court, despite its earlier self-denial of jurisdiction in such matters, now accepted jurisdiction of another appeal from a civilian of a wartime military trial. The justices decided that the arrest and military trial were unjustified. They occurred in Ohio, not an active combat area, though one where rebel guerrillas exploited resident Confederate sympathizers.

The Court insisted that rights emanating from the Constitution were diminishable only when actual combat justified the president in substituting martial justice for civilian processes. The justices, by implication, not the president or generals, would decide if combat conditions had prevailed.[36]

Negrophiles and equal rights-centered Republicans condemned the 1866 judgment as judicial usurpation. But conservatives, especially Democrats nationwide and southern whites, applauded the Court. Democratic party strategists perceived great advantages in the Court's stress on whites' civil liberties as against military authority, for first President Johnson's orders to the Army and then Congress's Military Reconstruction statute kept this military authority in the South.

Test Oaths: Defenses of Liberty or Infringement on Property?

In the same 1866-67 Court term, a bare majority of the justices also decided that wartime federal and state loyalty tests (for civil and military officers, for licensed professionals including lawyers, teachers, jurors, and peace officers, and some tradesmen) were unconstitutional. The Court held that they violated prohibitions in the federal and state constitutions on bills of attainder (i.e., legislative acts defining a crime, specifying a guilty class, and setting penalties, all without due process of law) and ex post facto laws (i.e., laws making criminal what was not a crime when committed).[37] Professionals and tradesmen had property rights in their practices and businesses. Even if procedurally correct, exclusion equalled a substantial deprivation of property without adequate legal process. True, Congress had created its contested loyalty oath law with all the usual legislative procedures: but that was not sufficient.

Similarly, concerning Missouri's oath test, which was simultaneously under fire in the Court, the state's 1864 constitutional conventioneers had included an oath in its reformed constitution. As the dissenting justices, including Chase, pointed out, virtually no precedent existed for the federal Supreme Court to take cognizance of a provision of a state constitution, that ultimate voice of the people with authority transcending police powers. But in *Cummings v. Missouri*, the state Test Oath case, the bare Court majority overpassed precedent in a manner reminiscent of its self-expansion in *Gelpcke*, accepted jurisdiction, and decided against the state constitution's provision.

The dissenters in *Cummings* argued that the loyalty requirements did not deal with tangible property interests and were qualifications, not punishments. No official or licensed person had vested rights in his office or position. The state and nation had legitimate interests in and authority over their officials.[38]

Though their views had the weight of precedent in their favor, the minority justices remained a minority. In realistic terms, the majority's decision against the loyalty tests opened the nation's courts and Congress, and southern states' and localities' offices, including those of justice, police, and taxation, plus classrooms and counting-houses, to control by recent rebels. And they poured in. All were white, of course. These functionaries overwhelmingly reinforced the most racially reactionary elements of the Democratic Party. This effect alone proved quickly to be tragic for millions of freedmen and white Unionists. Beyond this result, the Test Oath decisions expanded the definition of property from tangibles to intangibles, including the practice of professions and trades. By so doing, these decisions, building on ancient antipathies to bills of attainder and ex post facto laws, created an interim defense of property against nation and states that would serve until lawyers and judges found more generally usable tools in the Fourteenth Amendment's due process clause.[39]

Toward Slaughterhouse: 1866-71

Unimpressed by Congress' indignation at decisions such as *Cummings* and its ilk, the Court, in *Texas v. White* (1869), seized the opportunity afforded by Texas's efforts to regain title to prewar U.S. bonds that the Confederate government had sold for revenue to affirm Lincolnesque ideas on secession and military reconstruction.[40] In the same years (1866-1871), Supreme Court justices attended also to non-white males' and females' civil rights and liberties under the Thirteenth Amendment. Perhaps the jurists' sympathetic views of the Thirteenth Amendment in those years helped to blunt the irritations of Republicans at the military arrest and Test Oath decisions.

In 1866, on circuit in Kentucky in a criminal case, Justice Noah Swayne decided *U.S. v. Rhodes,* a case involving the state's new "black code," which still prohibited blacks from testifying against whites. The defendant (a white male) and other racist vigilantes had forced their way into a black woman's house intending to rob, perhaps to rape, and certainly to intimidate her and other Negroes. His counsel argued that in a criminal case the only parties with standing were the state and the defendant. Therefore, no federal question or jurisdiction existed.

Not so, decided Justice Swayne. Together, the Thirteenth Amendment and the enforcing Civil Rights law were "an act of grace" that revolutionized the federal system and extended federal protection to everyone. The Thirteenth Amendment "trenches directly under the power of the state and of the people of the state," Swayne declared. It made all Americans citizens of both nation and state, and federal citizenship included a color-blind right to testify. The exclusion of a black's testimony violated the Thirteenth Amendment. Swayne urged a liberal interpretation of the Civil Rights law "to carry out the wise and beneficent purposes of Congress in enacting it."[41]

The next year, while on (Taney's former) circuit, in *In re Turner,* Chief Justice Chase heard the petition of a black Maryland woman, a recent slave. She had contracted to continue serving her former master as a domestic exchange for instruction in his artisan skill, under a state apprenticeship statute. But the employer failed to offer the promised tutoring. His inaction in this private contract violated the 1866 Civil Rights Act which implemented the Thirteenth Amendment, Chase held.[42]

Impressed more by the Test Oath decisions than by *Rhodes* or *Turner,* Kentucky continued to exclude the testimony of blacks. In 1871 the Supreme Court further encouraged such holdouts. In *Blyew v. U.S.,*[43] the Court learned that Blyew had brutally murdered a black woman, according to Negro eyewitnesses whose testimony the state excluded. Federal attorney Benjamin Bristow argued that *Rhodes* controlled, that only state failure adequately to protect the dead woman permitted her injuries to occur. For the Court, Justice William Strong seemed to agree. The Thirteenth Amendment and the Civil Rights law protected "personal, relative or property rights, whenever they are denied in the State courts...." But, Strong continued, although among other goals Congress had clearly intended to end inequalities of race and other hierarchies in state justice, in this instance the fact that the murdered woman was "beyond" redress ended her federal civil rights. Yet, on circuit in 1873, Strong was to rule that the Thirteenth Amendment "made the right of personal liberty a Constitutional right," and that its "primary object" was to secure "to [all] persons certain rights which they had not previously possessed." It was "an exploded heresy that the national government cannot reach all individuals in the states."[44]

Meanwhile, in Alabama, federal district judge William Woods added to the weight of *Rhodes.* Woods held that whether combined with the Fourteenth Amendment or considered alone, the Thirteenth Amendment imposed a duty on the federal government to reach into states in order to sustain citizens' First Amendment rights against adverse private or state actions and inactions.[45] In sum, these initial judicial evaluations of the Thirteenth Amendment and the Civil Rights Act suggested that an absolute prohibition of substantial servitudes existed, affecting nation and states, private as well as official relationships, blacks as well as whites, and women as well as males.

But in the early 1870s, erosion, both from within the highest house of the law and from foreign sources, was already deepening. Externally, between 1865 and 1871 bloody race riots in long-emancipated, nearby British Caribbean islands, and bloodier Marxian-flavored class violence in France, dismayed even American Negrophiles and worker-focused reformers. In American locales where other minorities—Chinese, Hispanics, Indians—were numerous, fears grew of analogous equalization efforts. As we shall see, white women, encouraged by *Turner's* implications, were pushing for gender-free access to professions and juries under the Thirteenth and Fourteenth Amendments, thereby upsetting many males.

Sensing these shifting winds, and declaiming that federalism, family stability, race purity, and all property were in danger, Democrats rallied conservative and reactionary opinion nationwide against both Reconstruction in the South and efforts elsewhere to achieve equality. They highlighted every defect in federal efforts to achieve intrastate equality.

There were defects. Republicans, themselves dedicated to state-centered federalism, still insisted that the Thirteenth Amendment's universal outreach was enhanced, not diminished, by the Fourteenth Amendment's concentrations on state action. So believing, and reacting to repeated vigilantism in the South, in 1870 Republican majorities in Congress ratified the Fifteenth Amendment: "The right of citizens to vote shall not be denied or abridged by the United States or any State on account of race, color, or previous condition of servitude." Then, implementing the Fourteenth and the Fifteenth Amendments, Congress enacted "Enforcement" and "Ku Klux Klan" laws punishing both state actions and private conspiracies that contravened individuals' federal rights. These laws alerted lawyers to opportunities to exploit, on behalf of clients with seemingly irrelevant business interests, concerns about federal or state interventions in intrastate crimes and private relationships, especially property rights.[46]

In 1872 the Supreme Court in effect signaled attentive law practitioners about the justices' priority on property rights. The Thirteenth Amendment notwithstanding, the Court ruled that a prewar slave-purchase contract was still valid.[47] *Slaughterhouse* followed hard on this decision.

Slaughterhouse: Its Hour Come Round at Last

Originating in a badly-needed Louisiana public health, police-power reform law, the controversial *Slaughterhouse* statute created a licensed monopoly of New Orleans butchering. Persons excluded from the privilege sued unsuccessfully in state courts.[48] Their lawyer, John Campbell, an ex-U.S. Supreme Court justice and recent Confederate official readmitted to legal practice by *Garland's* ruling, contrived a Thirteenth and Fourteenth Amendment appeal to the federal high court. He argued that the excluded butchers' right to work was a property that the state had substantively destroyed, thus reducing them to involuntary servitude.

Again by a bare majority, the Court refused to read substantive due process into the Constitution. Butchering was historically subject to state police power. Did the Thirteenth and Fourteenth Amendments include monopolies as deprivations of nonparticipants' rights to due process, equal protection, and privileges and immunities? Not so, Justice Samuel Miller stated for the majority. All the Reconstruction Amendments and statutes had "one pervading purpose," to free slaves and to undergird their rights as citizens of nation and state, not to alter the federal system. Individuals' workaday rights remained for the states to protect and define; federal rights remained peripheral, pertaining to foreign travel and, less tangentially, to interstate mobility. To shift to the federal government the protection of such claimed rights as that to butchering would "fetter and degrade the State governments by subjecting them to the control of Congress" and would "constitute this court a perpetual censor upon all legislation of the States."[49]

Miller's famous opinion largely ignored or distorted the recent history, both external to and within the Court, surveyed in this paper. Significant majorities of the public had come to favor concurrent and/or dominant federal protections for individuals' rights.[50] Despite its lyrical expressions of concern for blacks, Miller's majority opinion in effect remanded their protection to the states, now already largely "redeemed" and under lily-white, recently rebel, leadership decidely unsympathetic to equal rights. The Miller view reduced the Fourteenth Amendment's privileges and immunities clause to inconsequentiality, and not even the "Second Reconstruction" a century later resuscitated it.

Dissents, especially by Justices Joseph Bradley and Stephen Field, anticipated later due-process arguments that, tragically, would find employment less in protecting civil rights and liberties than property rights alone. The dissenters, who included Chase, insisted that both under natural law predating the Constitution, and under the Thirteenth and Fourteenth Amendments, no state, even one exercising its police powers, could diminish an individual's right to labor as he chose and to garner the rewards of enterprise.

Erosions of Womens' and Blacks' Rights Hastened

Soon after the *Slaughterhouse* decision, the Supreme Court, having earlier validated a prewar slave sale contract, also redirected the Reconstruction Amendments away from women wishing to vote or practice a licensed profession. Alternative decisional roads back to *Gelpcke, In re Turner,* and the Test Oath cases dropped from most lawyers' collective memories.

In Missouri, for example, Virginia Minor tried to vote in 1872. The registrar denied her access to the polls because she was female. On her behalf, lawyers rang the changes on gender equality under the amended Constitution. But in both state courts and in the United States Supreme Court, jurists denied historical realities in favor of an increasingly formalist perception of those Amendments. Historical realities were prominently detailed in the *Minor* brief, which built on the Constitution, the Bill of Rights, and the Thirteenth to Fifteenth Amendments. Surveying pre-Civil War history, Minor's lawyer concluded that the exclusion of women from voting was a bill of attainder, a violation of the First Amendment, a kind of involuntary servitude, and a violation of due process. Reminding the jurists that the Fourteenth Amendment did not repeal the Thirteenth, her counsel interpreted the Fourteenth's denial to states of a right to exclude males from voting only for certain stated reasons (rebellion or crime) did not bar states from allowing females to vote. The Ninth Amendment, though dusty, still acknowledged that all undelegated rights were retained by people. And the Fifteenth merely confirmed the positive aspects of the Thirteenth and Fourteenth, he insisted. But the court unanimously rejected this brilliant and essentially correct argument, one that a scholar described recently as "a dazzling reconstitution of law as it ought to be, and a trenchant indictment of the way it was."[51]

But an attorney's brilliance combined with accurate history was no match for the *Slaughterhouse* Court's predisposition. Its members found ample reasons to reject Minor's appeal. The Court was soon to sustain New York's and Illinois's denials (to Susan B. Anthony and Myra Bradwell, respectively) of access to the vote and to the practice of law, claims based on the protections the Thirteenth to Fifteenth Amendments and statutes afforded the litigants. The very idea of women voters, lawyers, and physicians violated the "law of the Creator," according to leading male legalists of the time.[52]

Similarly with blacks' rights. Within a decade after *Slaughterhouse,* the Supreme Court, in the *Civil Rights Cases* (1883), declared the 1875 Civil Rights Act unconstitutional because it aimed at private discrimination, not state action.

Fated to be the last federal law on civil rights until 1957, the 1875 statute further implemented the Thirteenth Amendment and supplemented the 1866 Civil Rights law. The 1875 law sought to protect individuals' social equality as earlier implementations of the Thirteenth to Fifteenth Amendments had aimed at civil and political equality. Specifically guaranteeing to "all persons within the jurisdiction of the United States" equal access to all places of public accommodation, conveyance, or amusement except as regulations constrained access without regard to race, the law subjected violators to misdemeanor penalties including fines ($500-$1,000) or imprisonment (30 days-1 year). Further, the 1875 law gave federal lower courts exclusive jurisdiction in prosecutions of violators. Most plaintiffs were likely to be poor blacks. To relieve them from the financial burdens of lawsuits, the 1875 law required federal attorneys to initiate and conduct the suits, themselves risking penalties for nonperformance. Last, the statute forbade the exclusion of any person from federal jury service because of race or previous status as a slave. But in the 1883 *Civil Rights Cases* decision the Supreme Court declared the 1875 law to be unconstitutional because it aimed at private discrimination, not state action.[53]

Yet the 1866 Civil Rights Law remained on the books. Never declared to be unconstitutional, it spoke directly to the point of the 1875 statute, that private wrongs the states left unpunished or connived in were punishable in federal courts. Further, in its 1883 decision the Court admitted the possibility that the Fourteenth Amendment as well as the Thirteenth acted not only against wrongful state actions but also against inactions. Justice Joseph Bradley held that the Thirteenth Amendment gave Congress a duty to act to shield individuals' fundamental rights inherent in freedom, and to erase all persisting "badges and incidents" of slavery—a call to duty so merely rhetorical that the task remained largely unattended until the 1950s.

It remained basically unattended for so long because, as one author suggests, the *Slaughterhouse* legal culture was "bifurcated [artificially] between mutually exclusive public and private spheres. To late nineteenth-century conservatives, the primary threat to the private sphere was [government] intrusion on property rights through redistributive programs (such as bonding, regulation, or the income tax)."[54] Or, in another useful analysis, the Bradley admissions in the Civil Rights decisions that federal duties existed to call states to account for conditions less than fully free and equal, melted out of his "regard for federalism."[55]

By twenty years after Appomattox, then, individuals' federally defendable civil rights had become greatly attenuated from the large vision that inspired Lincoln, Chase, and so many others among their embattled countrymen in 1862, to risk emancipation of a race. Economic rights became the Court's cause, one that new generations of jurists and law writers ennobled in formalist imagery.

Notes

1. Quoted in 33 CIVIL WAR HISTORY 87 (1987).

2. 8 COLLECTED WORKS OF ABRAHAM LINCOLN 254-55 (R. P. Basler ed. 1953-54); W. HANCHETT, THE LINCOLN MURDER CONSPIRACIES 37, 155 (1983); cf. R. CURRENT, ARGUING WITH HISTORIANS: ESSAYS ON THE HISTORICAL AND THE UNHISTORICAL 64 (1987).

3. H. HYMAN, LINCOLN'S RECONSTRUCTION: NEITHER FAILURE OF VISION NOR VISION OF FAILURE *passim* (1980); Basch, *Reconstitutions: History, Gender, and the 14th Amendment* (paper, Conference on the American Constitution, Hebrew University of Jerusalem, May 1987). In press. Typescript used with permission.

4. P. FINKELMAN, AN IMPERFECT UNION: SLAVERY, FEDERALISM, AND COMITY (1981); M. TUSHNET, THE AMERICAN LAW OF SLAVERY, 1810-1860: CONSIDERATIONS OF HUMANITY AND INTEREST (1981), both *passim*.

5. P. LUCIE, FREEDOM AND FEDERALISM: CONGRESS AND COURTS, 1861-1866 127-47 and *passim* (1986), explains why Corfield v. Corywell, 4 C.C. Wash., 371 (1823) and Barron v. Baltimore, 7 Peters 243 (1833), the major relevant case law available in the 1860s, were of little help to Lincoln's generation. Lucie's *White Rights as a Model for Black: Or—Who's Afraid of the Privileges and Immunities Clause?*, 38 SYRACUSE L. REV. 859 (1987), requires attention. *See also*, Gerteis, *The Future of the Freedom in the United States: Antislavery Expectations for the Postemancipation South* (paper, American Historical Association meeting, 1986); Fields and Rowland, *Free Labor Ideology and Its Exponents in the South During the Civil War and Reconstruction* (paper, Organization of American Historians meeting, 1984).

6. Positivism "sought to identify law by total separation from [ethics and] moral justice." Positivists seek "objective meaning drawn from the [laws'] provisions themselves . . . [and] to be entirely formal, and free from all taint of history, ethics, politics, sociology, idealism, and other external influences." OXFORD COMPANION TO LAW 970 (D. Walker, comp., 1980).

7. Cf. B. SIEGAN, THE RISE AND FALL OF ECONOMIC DUE PROCESS—WHEN THE SUPREME COURT CHAMPIONED AND THEN CURTAILED ECONOMIC FREEDOMS (pamphlet, 1983).

8. McCrary, *The Party of Revolution: Republican Ideas about Politics and Social Change, 1862-1867*, 30 CIVIL WAR HISTORY 330 (1984). *See also*, Levy, *Property as a Human Right*, 5 CONSTITUTIONAL COMMENTARY 169 (1988); Reich, *The New Property*, 73 YALE L. J. 733 (1964).

9. J. REID, CONSTITUTIONAL HISTORY OF THE AMERICAN REVOLUTION: THE AUTHORITY OF RIGHTS 108, chs. 12-13, and *passim* (1986).

10. Contrary to *Dred Scott*, blacks in non-slave states did possess civil rights, so defined. Finkelman, *Prelude to the 14th Amendment: Black Legal Rights in the Antebellum North*, 17 RUTGERS. L. REV. 414 (1986).

11. *See* R. EPSTEIN, TAKINGS: PRIVATE PROPERTY AND THE POWER OF EMINENT DOMAIN (1985), for non-historical insights.

12. J. NELSON, JR., LIBERTY AND PROPERTY: POLITICAL ECONOMY AND POLICYMAKING IN THE NEW NATION, 1789-1812 *passim* (1987).

13. Finkelman, *States' Rights, North & South, in Antebellum America* (paper, Constitution Bicentennial Conference, Krefeld, Germany, May 1987). In press. Typescript used with permission. *See also*, Gerteis, *Slavery and Hard Times: Morality and Utility in American Antislavery Reform*, 29 CIVIL WAR HISTORY 316 (1983).

14. DANE, 9 GENERAL ABRIDGEMENT AND DIGEST OF AMERICAN LAW 32-33 (1829). Agreeing for our times, Mahoney, *States' Rights*, in 4 ENCYCLOPEDIA OF THE AMERICAN CONSTITUTION 1755 (L. Levy *et al.* eds. 1986), wrote that states' rights "is better understood not as a term of art denoting a constitutional principle but as a slogan with tactical value in political controversy."

15. Finkelman, *Slavery and the Constitutional Convention: Making a Covenant With Death*, in BEYOND CONFEDERATION: ORIGINS OF THE CONSTITUTION AND AMERICAN NATIONAL IDENTITY 188 (R. Beeman *et al.* eds. 1987), examines the three-fifths, fugitive slave, extradition, comity, capitation tax, and contracts clauses.

16. Bruchey, *The Impact of the Concern for the Security of Property Rights on the Legal System of the Early American Republic,* 1980 WIS. L. REV. 1135 (1980).

17. L. GERTEIS, MORALITY AND UTILITY IN ANTISLAVERY REFORM chs. 8-10 and *passim* (1987); H. HYMAN, A MORE PERFECT UNION: THE IMPACT OF THE CIVIL WAR AND RECONSTRUCTION ON THE CONSTITUTION chs. 17-20 (1973).

18. *See* Finkelman, *Slaves as Fellow-Servants: Ideology, Law and Industrialization;* Fede, *Legal Protection for Slave Buyers in the U. S. South: A Caveat Concerning Caveat Emptor;* and Cottroll, *'Liberalism and Paternalism' Ideology, Economic Interest, and the Business Law of Slavery,* all in 31 AM. J. LEGAL HIST. 269, 322, and 359 respectively (1987).

19. Dred Scott v. Sanford, 60 U.S. 393 (1857); D. FEHRENBACHER, THE DRED SCOTT CASE ch. 1 (1978).

20. 13 N.Y. 378 (1865). *See* A. MCLAUGHLIN, CONSTITUTIONAL HISTORY OF THE UNITED STATES 458-63 (1935).

21. Finkelman, *The Nationalization of Slavery: A Counter-Factual Approach to the 1860s,* 14 LOUISIANA STUDIES 213, 221-22 (1975); H. HYMAN & W. WIECEK, EQUAL JUSTICE UNDER LAW: CONSTITUTIONAL DEVELOPMENT, 1835-1875 192, 195-96 (1982).

22. Scheiber, *Federalism, the Southern Regional Economy, and Public Policy Since 1865,* in AMBIVALENT LEGACY: A LEGAL HISTORY OF THE SOUTH (D. Bodenhamer & J. Ely, Jr. eds. 1984); TUSHNET, *supra* note 4, at 23.

23. Haskell, *Capitalism and the Origins of Humanitarian Sensibility,* 90 AM. HIST. REV. 339 (1985); *Convention and Hegemonic Interest in the Debate Over Antislavery,* 92 *Id.* at 829 (1987); and Maltz, *Reconstruction Without Revolution: Republican Civil Rights Theory in the Era of the Fourteenth Amendment,* 24 HOUS. L. REV. 221 (1987).

24. M. CURTIS, NO STATE SHALL ABRIDGE: THE FOURTEENTH AMENDMENT AND THE BILL OF RIGHTS ch. 1 (1987); HYMAN & WIECEK, *supra* note 21, at chs. 8-10; HYMAN, AMERICAN SINGULARITY: THE 1787 NORTHWEST ORDINANCE, THE 1862 HOMESTEAD AND MORRILL ACTS, AND THE 1944 G.I. BILL ch. 2 (1986).

25. *See* Cl a s opini n in In re Turner, 24 Fed. Cas. 337, 247 (C.C. N.D. Md., Case No 14, 1867).

26. Aville, Property and R ht: he lem na of Sl e S le Re publican Con r ss-m n and the Or ins of Rec ns truc ion, 136 1867 2 HoI ERN TUDIES 1 5 (1 8 4).

27. H. HYMAN, ERA OF THE OATH: NORTHERN LOYALTY TESTS IN THE CIVIL WAR AND RECON-STRUCTION chs. 1-4 (1952).

28. Benedict, *Preserving the Constitution: The Conservative Bases of Radical Reconstruction,* 61 J. AM. HIST. 65 (1974).

29. INSIDE LINCOLN'S CABINET: THE CIVIL WAR DIARIES OF SALMON PORTLAND CHASE 271 (D. Donald ed. 1954); McCrary, *supra* note 8, at 345.

30. HYMAN & WIECEK, *supra* note 21, at chs. 8-13.

31. *Id.*

32. Ex parte Merryman, Fed. Cas. (C.C, Md., Case No. 9847, 1861).

33. Prize Cases, 2 Black 635 (1863).

34. Gelpcke v. Dubuque, 1 Wall. 175 (1864).

35. *Id.;* HYMAN & WIECEK, *supra* 21, at 348, 351-52, 356, 365-70.

36. Ex parte Milligan, 4 Wall. 2 (1866); H. HYMAN, QUIET PAST AND STORMY PRESENT? WAR POWERS IN AMERICAN HISTORY (1985).

37. Ex parte Garland, 4 Wall. 333 (1867); Cummings v. Missouri, 4 Wall. 277 (1867).

38. *Id.;* Cummings v. Missouri. Berger, *Bills of Attainder: A Study of Amendment by the Court,* 63 CORNELL L. REV. 355 (1978). Berger errs in his suggestion (p. 381ff.) about "The Inapplicability of the 'Contemporary Commentators.'"

39. Anderson, *The Formative Period of First Amendment Theory, 1870-1915,* 24 AM. J. LEGAL HIST. 56 (1980); Johnson, *Creativity and Adaptation: A Reassessment of American Jurisprudence, 1801-1857 and 1908-1940,* 7 RUT.-CAM. L. J. 625, 636 (1976).

40. 7 Wall. 700 (1869).

41. U.S. v. Rhodes, 27 Fed. Cas. 785, 788, 794, 151 (C.C.D. Ky., Case No. 16, 1866).

42. In re Turner, 24 Fed. Cas. 337, 339 (C.C.N.D. Md., 1867).

43. 80 U.S. (13 Wall.) 581, 593, 601 (1871).

44. U.S. v. Given, 25 Fed. Cas. 1324, 1325; 210 (C.C.S.D. Del., Case No. 15, 1873).

45. U.S. v. Hall, 26 Fed. Cas. 79, 81-82; 282 (C.C.S.D. Ala., Case No. 15, 1871).

46. M. BELKNAP, FEDERAL LAW AND SOUTHERN ORDER: RACIAL VIOLENCE AND CONSTITU-TIONAL CONFLICT IN THE POST-BROWN SOUTH 13-14 and chs. 1-2 (1987).

47. Osborne v. Nicholson, 13 Wall. 654 (1872). *See also,* White v. Hart, 80 U.S. 646 (1871).

48. Labbe, *New Light on the Slaughterhouse Monopoly Act of 1869,* in LOUISIANA'S LEGAL HERITAGE 143 (E. Hass ed. 1983).

49. 16 Wall. 36 (1873).

50. R. KACZOROWSKI, THE NATIONALIZATION OF CIVIL RIGHTS: CONSTITUTIONAL THEORY AND PRACTICE IN A RACIST SOCIETY, 1866-1883 (1987), and Kaczorowski, *To Begin the Nation Anew: Congress, Citizenship, and Civil Rights after the Civil War,* 92 AM. HIST. REV. 45 (1987), summarize recent reevaluations. *See also,* Fourteenth Amendment, §2, on federal prohibition against states denying suffrage to qualified male residents. Exclusion of females was a price of ratification, which suggests that pressure existed favoring female voting. Further, state and congressional debates on this point encouraged women to seek other Thirteenth and Fourteenth Amendment rights; *see* Basch, *supra* note 3, at 15 and *passim.*

51. Basch, *id.* at 15; Minor v. Happersett, 21 Wall. 163 (1875).

52. Bradwell v. Illinois, 16 Wall. 130 (1873); 2 E. STANTON *et al.,* HISTORY OF WOMAN SUFFRAGE 249 (1882); Weisberg, *Barred from the Bar: Women and Legal Education in the United States, 1870-1890,* 28 J. LEGAL EDUC. 499 (1977).

53. U.S. Statutes at Large, XVIII, 335 (1875); Civil Rights Cases, 109 U.S. 3 (1883).

54. Williams, *The Constitutional Vulnerability of American Local Government: The Politics of City Status in American Law,* 1986 WIS. L. REV. 83, 103 (1986).

55. A. KELLY, et al., THE AMERICAN CONSTITUTION: ITS ORIGIN AND DEVELOPMENT 367 (6th ed., 1983).

Contributors

ELLEN FRANKEL PAUL is Deputy Director of the Social Philosophy and Policy Center and professor of political science. She received her doctorate from the Government Department at Harvard University in 1976. She is the author of numerous scholarly articles and is, also, the author or editor of fourteen books. She has written three books: MORAL REVOLUTION AND ECONOMIC SCIENCE (1979), PROPERTY RIGHTS AND EMINENT DOMAIN (1987), and EQUITY AND GENDER: THE COMPARABLE WORTH DEBATE (1988). She is the editor, with Philip Russo, of PUBLIC POLICY: ISSUES, ANALYSIS, AND IDEOLOGY (1981); and editor, with Dan Jacobs, of STUDIES OF THE THIRD WAVE: RECENT MIGRATION OF SOVIET JEWS TO THE UNITED STATES. She has also coedited nine other books.

HOWARD DICKMAN is a Research Associate at the Social Philosophy and Policy Center. He received his Ph.D. in history from the University of Michigan in 1977. He was Research Director of the Manhattan Institute for Policy Research, and Senior Editor of *Harper's* magazine. He has written scholarly articles and is the author of the book INDUSTRIAL DEMOCRACY IN AMERICA: IDEOLOGICAL ORIGINS OF NATIONAL LABOR RELATIONS POLICY (1987).

MARY CORNELIA PORTER received her B.A. from Sarah Lawrence College and her M.A. and Ph.D. from the University of Chicago. She is Professor Emerita of Political Science, Barat College, Lake Forest, Illinois, and has been a Visiting Professor of Political Science at Knox College, Elmhurst College, Northwestern University and Northern Illinois University. Her publications include articles on constitutional history; women, law, and politics; civil rights; state constitutional law; and state judiciaries. She is coeditor of STATE SUPREME COURTS: POLICYMAKERS IN THE FEDERAL SYSTEM (1982) and coauthor of STATE SUPREME COURTS IN STATE AND NATION (1988).

PAUL L. MURPHY is Professor of History and American Studies at the University of Minnesota, and a lecturer in American legal history at the Hamline University Law School. He is the author of THE CONSTITUTION IN CRISIS TIMES, 1918-1969 (1972); THE MEANING OF FREEDOM OF SPEECH (1972), which won the American Bar Association Gavel Award for an "outstanding contribution to public understanding of the American system of law and justice"; and WORLD WAR I AND THE ORIGIN OF CIVIL LIBERTIES IN THE UNITED STATES (1979). Active in the constitutional bicentennial, his most recent study, THE CONSTITUTION IN THE TWENTIETH CENTURY, was published by the American Historical Association in 1986. He is currently at work on a history of the First Amendment, to be published by Oxford University Press.

GLEN O. ROBINSON is John C. Stennis Professor of Law at the University of Virginia, where he teaches administrative law, antitrust, property, and torts. He is a graduate of Stanford (J.D., 1961) and Harvard (A.B., 1958). After several years of private law practice in Washington, D.C., he taught at the University of Minnesota from 1967 to 1974, when he left to accept an appointment as Commissioner of the Federal Communications Commission. In 1976 he joined the law faculty at the University of Virginia. He returned briefly to government in 1978 and 1979 as U.S. representative to the World Administrative Radio Conference. Professor Robinson is coauthor of a textbook, THE ADMINISTRATIVE PROCESS, as well as author of books on the U.S. Forest Service and on communications policy. He has contributed articles and essays to legal journals and books on a range of legal topics in both public and private law. His most recent articles include *Public Choice Speculations on the Item Veto* (VIRGINIA LAW REVIEW, 1988), and *Structure and Process as Instruments of Political Control of Agencies* (VIRGINIA LAW REVIEW, 1989). Scholarly work in progress includes completion of a book, ADMINISTRATIVE GOVERNMENT: PUBLIC CHOICE AND PUBLIC LAW, and articles on *The Right to Die* and *Risk, Causation and Harm*.

RICHARD A. EPSTEIN is the James Parker Hall Distinguished Service Professor of Law at the University of Chicago, where he has taught since 1972. He has been the editor of the JOURNAL OF LEGAL STUDIES since 1981, and a member of the American Academy of Arts and Sciences since 1985. His books include TAKINGS: PRIVATE PROPERTY AND THE POWER OF EMINENT DOMAIN (1985), CASES AND MATERIALS ON TORTS (4th ed., with C. Gregory and H. Kalven, Jr., 1984); and MODERN PRODUCTS LIABILITY LAW (1980). He has taught courses in civil procedure, contract, land development, property, torts (including defamation and privacy), jurisprudence, legal history, Roman law, and workers' compensation. He has written extensively in these areas, as well as in constitutional and labor law. Before joining the University of Chicago faculty, he taught at the University of Southern California Law School from 1968 to 1972. He is a graduate of Columbia College, Oxford University (Juris.), and the Yale Law School.

TONY FREYER, Professor of History and Law, University of Alabama, has taught in the fields of constitutional, legal, and economic history at the London School of Economics, University of California, Los Angeles, and Indiana University School of Law, Bloomington. During 1986 he was a Senior Fulbright Scholar in the United Kingdom, and has also held postdoctoral fellowships at the Harvard Business School and the Charles Warren Center, Harvard University. His publications include FORUMS OF ORDER (1979), HARMONY AND DISSONANCE: THE SWIFT AND ERIE CASES IN AMERICAN FEDERALISM (1981), THE LITTLE ROCK CRISIS (1984), HUGO L. BLACK AND THE DILEMMA OF AMERICAN LIBERALISM (1989), JUSTICE HUGO L. BLACK AND MODERN AMERICA (ed.) (1989).

HARRY N. SCHEIBER is professor of law at the School of Law (Boalt Hall), University of California, Berkeley, where he has taught since 1980. Prior to this appointment, he taught history at Dartmouth College and the University of California, San Diego. A graduate of Columbia College (1955), he holds a doctorate in American History from Cornell University (1961). In support of his research, Scheiber has held numerous fellowships, including support from the National Endowment for the Humanities, the Rockefeller Foundation, the National Science Foundation, the Guggenheim Fellowship, and the American Council of Learned Societies. His published works include THE WILSON ADMINISTRATION AND CIVIL LIBERTIES (1960), OHIO CANAL ERA: A CASE STUDY OF GOVERNMENT AND THE ECONOMY (1969), AMERICAN LAW AND THE CONSTITUTIONAL ORDER (1978), and numerous journal articles and contributions to collections. He is also Director of the Berkeley Seminar on Federalism.

ALAN JONES is Parker Professor of History at Grinnell College. He received his B.A. from Grinnell and his Ph.D. from the University of Michigan. His dissertation on the noted nineteenth-century constitutional commentator and judge, Thomas M. Cooley, has recently been published by Garland, and his articles on Cooley have appeared in *The Journal of American History, The American Journal of Legal History,* and *The Political Science Quarterly.* He has also written on the New Deal. Jones has taught at Grinnell since 1955.

HAROLD M. HYMAN is William P. Hobby Professor of History at Rice University where he has taught since 1968. He received his doctorate in 1952 from

Columbia University, and has previously taught at Earlham College, the University of California, Los Angeles, and the University of Illinois. Several of his books have received prestigious awards: ERA OF THE OATH: NORTHERN LOYALTY TESTS DURING THE CIVIL WAR AND RECONSTRUCTION (1954: Albert O. Beveridge Award, American Historical Association); TO TRY MEN'S SOULS: LOYALTY TESTS IN AMERICAN HISTORY (1959: Sidney Hillman Prize Award). More recently, he has published A MORE PERFECT UNION (1973) and EQUAL JUSTICE UNDER LAW (1973). His scholarly contributions range widely over the discipline.

Index